# SHAKESPEARE
## *Pattern of Excelling Nature*

# SHAKESPEARE
## *Pattern of Excelling Nature*

Shakespeare Criticism
in Honor of America's Bicentennial
from
The International Shakespeare Association Congress
Washington, D.C., April 1976

*Edited by* David Bevington *and* Jay L. Halio

*Newark*
*University of Delaware Press*
London: Associated University Presses

©1978 by Associated University Presses, Inc.


Associated University Presses, Inc.
Cranbury, New Jersey 08512


Associated University Presses
Magdalen House
136-148 Tooley Street
London SE1 2TT, England


Second Printing 1979

Library of Congress Cataloging in Publication Data

World Shakespeare Congress, Washington, D.C., 1976.
Shakespeare, pattern of excelling nature.

"Presented at the World Shakespeare Congress held in Washington, D.C.
on April 19 through 25, 1976."
1. Shakespeare, William, 1564-1616—Congresses.
I. Bevington, David M.  II. Halio, Jay L.  III. Title.
PR2890.W66 1976                822.3'3                77-82878
ISBN 0-87413-129-4

PRINTED IN THE UNITED STATES OF AMERICA

# Contents

# *Foreword by the Editors*

This collection of essays represents, in our view, some of the best critical work presented at the World Shakespeare Congress held in Washington, D.C. on April 19 throught 25, 1976. Although we gave thought to criteria of distribution by nationality, sex, scholarly discipline, and the like, we held above all to the standards of excellence and orginality. As can be seen by comparing the contents of this volume with those of the Congress itself, some parts of that Congress are inadequately represented; this is not a cross-section or an official Proceedings merely, even though we do include reports on the seminars and a few other matters of official business. The organization of this volume arises from the essays chosen for inclusion, and should not be interpreted as a chronological series of excerpts from the Congress.

We have been assisted in our deliberations by an advisory board consisting of the following persons: Ann Jennalie Cook, Executive Secretary of the Shakespeare Association of America; Levi Fox, Vice-Chairman and Secretary of the International Shakespeare Association; David Hoeniger, Professor of English at the University of Toronto; Maynard Mack, Professor of English at Yale University, President of the Shakespeare Association of America (1975-76), and Vice-President of the International Shakespeare Association; and Kenneth Muir, Professor of English at the University of Liverpool and Chairman of the International Shakespeare Association. The most important task of this board was to make recommendations concerning the selection of essays. We owe thanks to these members not only for their unstinting efforts on this board, but also for being in most cases the architects of the Congress itself. This volume represents their work much more than our own.

One of our tasks as editors has been to provide some consistency of format. We have adopted American spelling and punctuation throughout, since this book results from a Congress held in celebration of America's bicentennial and since the book itself is published by an American university press. On the other hand, we have adopted the Arden Shakespeare as our standard text (except for those few plays not yet available in the Arden series), in recognition of the excellence of that edition and of the fact that Shakespeare was, after all, English.

Inevitably, we have been obliged to omit some deserving material from this volume, and we extend a particular apology to those not included. We would especially have liked to include some of the fine papers read and discussed in the seminars, but decided finally against doing so in the interest of fairness. Adequate representation of the seminars lay beyond our scope, and the choice of one or two papers as samples might well seem arbitary. Reports prepared by seminar leaders or recorders are included instead, along with a list of participants. We hope, despite these limitations, that the volume will help to recapture the achievement of the Congress for those who attended, and will help define that achievement for those who could not attend.

David Bevington

Jay L. Halio

# Introduction

by KENNETH MUIR

(Chairman, International Shakespeare Association)

The present volume contains a selection of the papers delivered at the first Congress of the International Shakespeare Association held at Washington, D.C., in April 1976, together with a summary of the proceedings. At the end of the World Shakespeare Congress held in Vancouver in August 1971 (under the direction of "the enthusiastic and indefatigable" Rudolph E. Habernicht) it was unanimously decided to establish an International Shakespeare Association with individual and corporate membership, one of whose functions would be to plan a further Congress. Subsequently the Shakespeare Birthplace Trust undertook the considerable task of enrolling members and in due course, at the Shakespeare Conference at Stratford-upon-Avon in 1974, representatives of different national associations met to agree to a constitution, to elect officers, and to appoint an executive committee. It was decided to accept with gratitude the offer of the Shakespeare Birthplace Trust to use the Shakespeare Centre at Stratford-upon-Avon as headquarters of the Association, and to allow Dr. Levi Fox to be our Vice-Chairman and Secretary.

From the various suggestions made for the venue of the 1976 Congress, it was decided to accept the invitation of the Shakespeare Association of America and of the Folger Shakespeare Library to hold the meeting in Washington as part of the bicentennial celebrations, under the title of "Shakespeare in America." That the Congress proved to be so representative was due very largely to the generosity of the National Endowment for the Humanities, whose funding was materially assisted by the Rockefeller Foundation, the British Council, the Copernicus Society of America, the Shakespeare Birthplace Trust, and three publishers: The Houghton Mifflin Company, Penguin Books, and Scott, Foresman and Company. There was, moreover, cooperation of a practical kind from the English-Speaking Union, St. Albans School, the Washington area colleges and universities, and Washington Cathedral, in which was held a special service to celebrate the republication of the 1559 Prayer Book, the one Shakespeare used.

At the request of the sponsors a number of sessions were open to the general public. These included the plenary sessions at which Alistair Cooke, Anthony Burgess, Joel Hurstfield, Lord Hailsham, Kenneth Muir, and Jorge Luis Borges spoke. There were more than forty closed sessions, a number of filmed versions of Shakespeare, and a recital by the veteran interpreter, G. Wilson Knight, not to mention numerous receptions, lunches, dinners, working breakfasts, and parties.

It will be apparent from the contents of the present volume that the standard of contributions was remarkably high, and for this the committee of the Shakespeare Association of America, including its president, Maynard Mack, its executive secretary, Ann Jennalie Cook, and J. Leeds Barroll deserve congratulations. The International Shakespeare Association for its part is indebted to Levi Fox, who took an active part in the planning and represented the views of the Association both by correspondence and in person.

It has proved impossible to include more than a fraction of the papers delivered at the Congress, but the editors hope and believe that many of the others will appear elsewhere. Some of the shorter papers have had their cuts restored.

At a meeting of the International Shakespeare Association during the Congress, it was unanimously decided to invite Professor Maynard Mack to be vice-president of the Association. It was also agreed to invite an eminent Shakespearean actor to be president, thus ensuring that we should not forget that Shakespeare was a theater poet. Sir John Gielgud has since consented to be the first president of the Association. As a great actor, whose roles have included Hamlet, Richard II, Cassius, Benedick, Leontes, and Lear, and as a director who was never tempted to imagine that he knew better than the dramatist, Sir John was the obvious and fitting choice.

We are grateful to Professor Jay Halio for arranging with the University of Delaware Press the publication of this volume. It will serve as a record of an enjoyable, an instructive, and a historic occasion.

# Introduction

## by MAYNARD MACK
### (President, Shakespeare Association of America, 1975-76)

To members of the International Shakespeare Association and the Shakespeare Association of America, together with other readers of this book — greetings.

It was a happy occasion, I like to think. Shakespeare in Washington, America's most beautiful city after San Francisco, and far and away its most human, having no high-rises to dwarf us. Shakespeare in the springtime too, in the very week of his birthday, though to be sure the temperatures proved to be those of a midsummer night and took effect on some of our more dignified visitors (saith Rumor) with the potency of Oberon's flower. Even more appropriate: Shakespeare in the United States' bicentennial year, celebrating roots.

A good moment, it seemed, for Americans and others to remember that they used to speak English. For Britons to thank their eighteenth-century forebears for jettisoning what could only have become an administrative headache to baffle even Edmund Burke. And for all whose mother tongue is not Shakespeare's to reflect that the treasures we share, Shakespeare paramount among them, do as much to knit us together as the territories we atomistically defend before the (alas) not very United Nations do to divide us. So it had the makings of a symbolic occasion too.

At the center, properly, stood the studies we profess and the communications we had prepared, of which this book is a partial record. To read it through is to be gratefully reminded of the traditions of scholarship, editorial, historical, critical, and theatrical, of which we are the current lucky heirs. One is gratified too by the extraordinary range of ideologies, interests, personalities, and points of view that can light up and be lit by a body of poetry and drama nearly four centuries old. And one recalls ever more vividly, in reading, the pleasure those of us who could attend the meeting took not simply in the substance of the best offerings, but, as Wallace Stevens might have put it, in the "complacencies" of the conference itself.

11

To be able, for example, to look round a room or down a corridor and discover what a man or woman whose work one had always admired looked like, talked like, ate like. Or to join a luncheon or coffee-hour conversation and learn of an essay in Ukrainian or Swahili that anticipated all or most of what one had just published in *Shakespeare Survey, Shakespeare Studies,* or *Shakespeare Quarterly.* Or to view from twenty paces figures as multifarious in design as those of Lord Hailsham, Sir Peter Ramsbotham, the Honorable Elliot Richardson, Jorge Luis Borges, Anthony Burgess, Alistair Cooke, Joel Hurstfield, and Kenneth Muir, not to mention the theater notables who attended and the scholars from six of the seven continents. Or—yet more exhilarating—to consume food and drink in the reading room of the Folger Library surrounded by Quartos and First Folios, gape at the gardens at the British Embassy and the food-sculptures at the Argentine, assist at a special service celebrating the 1559 prayerbook in the Washington Cathedral, where the voices of the boys' choir circled in the dome like doves descending—these, these were the joys; and all of them, however incidental to the main purpose, helped for a week to bring scholars and scholarship close to some of the other civilized concerns from which too often they are, and sometimes even mindlessly choose to be, exiled.

We owe the idea of the Washington conference to Leeds Barroll; its success to Ann Cook and Levi Fox with a devoted assist from O. B. Hardison; and its financing to a variety of benefactors: the Houghton Mifflin Company, the American branch of Penguin Books, Scott, Foresman and Company, the Rockefeller Foundation, and, most generous of all, the National Endowment for the Humanities, whose funds derive from the Congress and therefore from the American people. I believe it was a legitimate investment on their behalf. For under the notion of holding an International Shakespeare Congress in Washington in the bicentennial year, and of bringing together artists and scholars from all over the world to share and renew their commitment to an understanding that can never be of Shakespeare or literature alone but is always of ourselves as well as of our common humanity as reflected in the images of a great poet, lies the oldest of American dreams, which a nation of immigrants must particularly strive to honor: a dream of the good community, the Peaceable Kingdom.

At our gathering during Shakespeare's birthday week in 1976, certain moments of cosmopolitan courtesy, unanimity, and delighted fellowship gave evidence beyond doubt that a vision of some such kingdom holds its own among us and, as Falstaff says of that deliciously raffish Jane Nightwork evoked so touchingly in *2 Henry IV,* "lives."

# Contributors

Janet Adelman, University of California, Berkeley
James Black, University of Calgary
Nicholas Brooke, University of East Anglia, Norwich
Stephen J. Brown, George Mason University
Anthony Burgess
Alistair Cooke
Inga-Stina Ewbank, University of London
Helen Gardner, Oxford University
Michael Goldman, Princeton University
John Dixon Hunt, University of London
G. K. Hunter, Yale University
R. G. Hunter, Vanderbilt University
Joel Hurstfield, University of London
Alvin B. Kernan, Princeton University
L. C. Knights, Cambridge University
Richard Levin, State University of New York, Stony Brook
Kenneth Muir, University of Liverpool
Robert Speaight
T. J. B. Spencer, University of Birmingham
J. L. Styan, Northwestern University
Michael J. Warren, University of California, Santa Cruz

# I

# PLENARY LECTURES

# Shakespeare in America

## by ALISTAIR COOKE

Thirty-three years ago, when it began to seem that Hitler's armies would never be dislodged from the soil of France, the Allied statesmen felt obliged to brace the endurance of the peoples of Britain and America by telling them again what they were fighting for. Like most of the other combatants, they were, of course, fighting for survival. And that is what sustained the morale of the people — of Britain certainly — far more than the rousing propaganda promised that we were out to maintain "civilization as we know it," even though "civilization" as many of the best fighting men knew it was not so rewarding; even though the record of history can show that no great war ever leaves civilization in the state that we knew it.

During that weary spring of 1943, an American Cabinet officer had declared his faith that once Hitler was disposed of, this would become "the Century of the Common Man." The thought was admiringly echoed by Mr. Churchill. And just then, in Cambridge, England, Max Beerbohm was standing up in the Senate House to deliver the annual Rede Lecture. Mr. Beerbohm had been for more than thirty years an exile in Italy, and he may now be safely forgiven for not being in touch with the egalitarian trend of our time. "We are told on high authority," he said, "that this is to be the Century of the Common Man. . . . I am not a learned theologian, but I think I am right in saying that this religion has at least the hallmark of novelty. . . .It does not stir my soul. I take some comfort in the fact that its propagators do not seek to bind us to it for ever. . . . I like to think that on the morning of January the first, in the year 2000, mankind will be free to unclasp its hands and rise from its knees and look about it for some other . . . form of faith."

Well, there are some of us here who hope — and it is a daring thought to utter, in Washington of all places, in this year 1976 — that on the morning of January 1, 1977, the American people will be allowed to rise from their knees and cease the worship of the past two hundred American years, and get on with the business that preoccupied the Founding Fathers: the business of meeting the issues of the day and improving the government of their society: the business of making history instead of embalming it.

It would be easy, and it would seem to be no more than a courtesy, in addressing a conference that has chosen the title Shakespeare in America, to follow those works of American scholarship which ardently examine Shakespeare's view of the relations between the individual and the state and end in the discovery that he would have been either a Republican or a Democrat. If this sounds naive, it is not more naive than the continuing scholarly efforts to prove that on the contrary he was a lawyer, an atheist, a doctor, a spiritualist, a Christian Scientist, or a Marxist. The noblest of these attempts to show that Shakespeare was spiritually itching to be an American is that of the late Charles Mills Gayley. Alas, Professor Gayley was writing in 1917 during the First War, and he came to the triumphant conclusion that Shakespeare would have been solidly on the Allied side.

In a Bicentennial year, it is a natural folly to see all our heroes in retrospect as inevitable supporters of the American Revolution. However, I remember John Adams's remark that in the upheaval we are now celebrating, no more than a third of the population was on the revolutionary side; one third was openly or covertly Loyalist; and the other third was that dependable minority to which the Gallup poll pays regular tribute: the people who "don't know" anything, don't feel anything, and don't stand for anything.

I hope then that some of you will be enormously relieved to hear that I am not going to shuffle through those monographs — about what Shakespeare meant, say, to the English settlers of America — which also tend to come to the thoughtful conclusion that if Shakespeare had been born a hundred and fifty years later, he would certainly have emigrated to America and probably have beaten Thomas Jefferson to the writing of the Declaration of Independence. On the contrary, I imagine that if Shakespeare had been in America, and in his prime in 1783 or thereabouts, we might have had from him a play of such amused contempt for the sunshine patriots, such compassion for the persecution of the Loyalists, and such eloquent but mixed admiration for the Founding Fathers themselves that — in the first hot flashes of their change of life — they might well have forced him to seek a haven in Canada or the West Indies, or even back in that England in which, as one sad soldier wrote, "there will scarcely be a village without some American dust in it by the time we are all at rest."

But if we are to take a brief retrospective look at Shakespeare in America, you will be happy to hear that we hardly need to begin much before the 1830's. There is no need at all to wonder what the Founders of New England thought about Shakespeare. They didn't. In all the Colonial literature of the seventeenth century there is not, I believe, a single allusion to him. Harvard College showed its usual enlightenment by acquiring its first copy of Shakespeare in 1723, 87 years after its founding. And even forty or fifty years later, while the Founding Fathers of the Republic were thoroughly at home with Rousseau and Montesquieu and Voltaire, it is safe to guess that few if any of them were acquainted with Shakespeare. In the voluminous works of Benjamin Franklin, there is no single quotation or even a mention of him. Jefferson, who was known as a prodigy for the amazing eclecticism of his reading, mentions Shakespeare three times.

In such learned company as this, I had better throw it out as a suggestion rather than a thesis that New England as a Shakespearean desert may well be explained by the Puritans' intense obsession with theological literature, by their moral authoritarianism, which banished plays and players as summarily as Cromwell had done. As late as 1686, Cotton Mather was alarmed by what he called "much discourse of beginning stage plays," at a time when playhouses were scattered through the colonies from New York to Charleston — but not playing Shakespeare. And the dearth of Shakespearean productions after the Revolution may be charitably put down to the prevailing chauvinism, the determination of the new Americans to write their own plays and music and abjure, in particular, the works of the defeated enemy.

It took, indeed, about sixty years for the Republic to welcome Shakespearean productions, and not until the mid-nineteenth century did it spawn its first native Shakespearean actor (the son of an immigrant London actor) in Edwin Booth. Even then, Mrs. Trollope was shocked to find that in the more civilized cities, Shakespeare was thought to be obscene; which is not surprising now when you consider that for the thirty years or so before the Civil War, literate Americans were brought up on Noah Webster's authorized version of the Bible, in which "to go a whoring" was replaced by "go astray," "breast" was substituted for "teat," and "cone" for "nipple."

It comes, then, as a surprise — to me, at any rate — to find that the first *popularization* of Shakespeare happened far from the Eastern cities or seats of learning. It came from strolling players who followed the flatboats floating down the Allegheny and rode into the rowdier pioneer towns springing up around and across the Appalachians. Actors, then as now, were generally regarded as vagabonds, chronic debtors, and sexual fly-by-nights. And the expanding frontier was a wonderful wide place to perform in, pick up the box-office receipts, and get lost, before descending on another settlement that could be counted on to be gullible — for one night.

But where did these vagabonds get their knowledge of Shakespeare, and how could the frontier settlements know a little about him and want to know more? Well, it is a pleasure for me, among such a frightening body of *savants,* to point to a name that I doubt has ever been mentioned in scholarly circles. It is that of William Holmes McGuffey, the son of Scotch-Irish parents who moved into western Pennsylvania in the immediate wake of the defeated Indians. The family went on into what the noted encyclopedia published in Chicago calls "the primeval forests of Ohio." There McGuffey became a teacher in the rural schools at the age of thirteen, picked up private tuition here and there, and at twenty-five was an instructor in ancient languages. But his passion was for grounding the frontier children in the best models of their own language. In 1835 he put out two school readers, and they were bought in job lots and used as basic English textbooks in the very elementary schools of the empire of the Mississippi and the South. In the sixth edition there were 138 selections from over a hundred authors, and Shakespeare was the preferred author of choice with nine extracts. Time and again the memoirs of pioneers across three thousand miles are studded with saws and instances from the Bible, *Pilgrim's Progress,* and Shakespeare. Children in log huts who could only imagine New York or London and who, unlike the divines of New England, had never heard of Rousseau or Goethe, could—unlike the divines of New England—yet quote Hamlet and recite the Fall of Wolsey. For the distribution of the McGuffey readers stopped short of New England. Everywhere else, the readers sold, at last count, something like 200 million copies.

It is too much to believe that while Boston and Philadelphia were honoring Shakespeare in the breach, the Republic's literate reputation was redeemed by such genteel, florid scoundrels as the type of W. C. Fields, always one step ahead of the bailiffs. But these early roving actor-managers discovered two things: that their audiences on the rivers and the prairie wanted to know where Wolsey had fallen from, and why Henry V got so excited at Agincourt. They also found that once Shakespeare had been dinned into simple folk as the grandest figure of the literary Establishment, he was—like other grandees of the Establishment—fair game for burlesque.

I hope it does not pain any patriot present to know that within fifty years of the founding of the Republic, the revolutionary heroes too were quickly stripped of their haloes and became, on the frontier, comic characters. And so with Shakespeare's magnificoes. The frontier appetite for blood and thunder matched that of the Elizabethans themselves. After all, stabbings and gunfights in the audience were fairly common. And what these tough audiences wanted were murders and ghosts and sleepwalkings, and a noisy suffocation of Desdemona. The comedies were very rarely played, because the playing of the tragedies was comedy enough. In a performance of *Hamlet* in Pittsburgh, a city said at the time to be "sunk in sin and coal," the actor playing the gravedigger saw the bailiffs in the wings and hopped into the grave, beat it through the trap door, and was never seen again. A popular performance of *Othello* ended with the Moor rolling in agony over the stage apron so that he could pick up a fiddle and play his own funeral march. For a couple of decades such theater as could be called legitimate came to a stop and was overtaken by burlesque. Byron's *Manfred* was played in blackface, and a moving chorus of "Nearer My God to Thee" was interpolated in the third act of *Faust.*

Oddly enough, the only serious plays to which the frontier audiences came to pay an almost ritual respect were ones glorifying the American Indian. In Florida in the 1830's a company took the risk of putting on a Shakespearean performance during the second Seminole War. The entire company was butchered by the Indians, who looted the costume trunks and galloped off dressed as Orlando, Macbeth, and Othello. But once the Indian had been pushed out of the Mississippi Valley and driven west, he — who was not acceptable as a neighbor — became admirable as a tragic hero. Far more than any Shakespearean character, he was applauded and wept over, by the people who had hounded him, as a noble and cheated figure.

But in the great age of burlesque, the Indian was represented as a character equally as comic as the conquering white. In the parodies of the sentimental Indian melodrama, the vehicle of parody is Shakespearean. There is one that contrives a witty switch on a mixed marriage. It is about the hoariest of American legends, that about Captain Smith confronting the Indian chief Powhatan to be saved by his beautiful daughter, though Smith makes pretty clear that that was not his prime purpose in crossing the Atlantic. He begins:

> Most potent, grave and reverend fellow —
> To use the words of that black Othello —
> My very noble and approved good savage,
> That we came out here your lands to ravage
> Is most true; for this you see us banded.

Powhatan says:

> Pray, sir, how do you mean to set about it?

*Smith:*

> Easy enough; we have full powers to treat.

*Powhatan:*

> If that's the case, I'll take some whiskey neat.

Together they then burst into a duet of "The Widow Machree."

Throughout the nineteenth century this theatrical impudence never flagged. In the mining towns of Colorado and California, Macbeth disposed of Duncan with a six-shooter, and the celebrated Emma Abbott soliloquized as Juliet on the trapeze. If this spirit is a wounding thing to academics, it is what made life bearable among the peoples who tried to knot a social lifeline across the wilderness. It is that saving sort of American humor which reaches from these river-men and players through Mark Twain to the Marx Brothers and Woody Allen: the humor of the sceptical or soured immigrant. When the frontier was officially pronounced closed in 1890, an anonymous poet wrote its epitaph:

> Across the plains where once there roamed the Indian and the scout,
> The Swede with alcoholic breath sets rows of cabbage out.

By then there were enough established cities ready for the real thing: for the full-fledged Shakespearean performance.

But if we now look back with condescending tolerance on the audacities of these frontier folk, I don't think we should deceive ourselves that modern audiences, either in America or Britain, are that much more sensitive to the depth and subtlety of Shakespeare's language. It is why we need to study it all the time, with all the resources of rational scholarship and responsive feeling. For I suspect that for most of the audiences today as yesterday, his language is a kind of rich Muzak against which— as Fritz Kreisler said about his violin music—the audience sits back and indulges its fantasies. Certainly, I have sat through many performances in this country in which, for instance, Mercutio's raw vulgarity at the expense of the Nurse provoked not a wince in the audience. I have yet to hear a ripple of recognition for the definitive account of the three most potent effects of alcohol on man as given by that veteran alcoholic, the Porter in *Macbeth*. And when it comes to such dense and brilliant syntax as that in Hamlet's lesser known soliloquies, or in the special pleading of Iachimo, one is bound to feel that a modern audience has only the faintest idea what even the argument is all about.

The stock answer to this rather haughty complaint, which implies that whoever else Shakespeare is for he is not for children, is that even barely understood music is good for the soul, that children are like the French beans in Charles Darwin's famous experiment: if you play a trombone at them, something is bound to happen.

I have said enough, I hope, to show that Shakespeare has had, for more than a century at any rate, a lively and peculiar life in America, apart from his industrial usefulness in the manufacturing of graduate theses. This conference is an international one, and even in this festival political year it is surely not our business to vindicate the ways of Shakespeare to the Constitution of the United States, or to any other ideology. For if Shakespeare had not transcended all ideologies, he would not be the universal man we meet here to honor. Sooner or later, students, theatergoers, scholars, all of us have to say why he is unique and why—through all the tidal waves of fashion down four centuries—he still rides the crest.

I shall end, then, by trying to distinguish two types of genius.

I don't know if it is an act of legitimate criticism or a wistful exercise in wishful thinking to see in the most universal artists a temperament of great sweetness allied to an unflinching perception of the human condition. The men I have in mind are Chaucer, Michelangelo, Mozart, and Shakespeare.

Below them is a small flock of more positive, and possibly braver, characters whose genius lies in the honesty of their striving for the sublime tolerance that the greater ones appear to have at birth. I am thinking now of Goethe, Wagner, Tolstoy, Mark Twain.

Well below them are all the rest of us, who oscillate between acceptance and protest and fall short of wisdom precisely to the extent that we see only part of the nature of men and women or rail at it.

I doubt that there has been in our time a wiser distinction made between artists of the first rank than that which Sir Isaiah Berlin picked up and elaborated from a line of the Greek poet Archilochus: "The fox knows many things, but the hedgehog knows one big thing." Taken figuratively, says Berlin, "these words can be made to yield a sense in which they mark one of the deepest differences which divide writers and thinkers, and it may be, human beings in general. For there exists a great chasm between those, on the one side, who relate everything to a single central vision . . . and, on the other side, those who pursue many ends, often unrelated and even contradictory . . . seizing upon a vast variety of experiences and objects for what they are in themselves without, consciously or unconsciously, seeking to fit them into . . . a unitary vision."

Berlin gives as supreme examples of the hedgehog: Plato, Dante, and Dostoevski. And of the fox: Aristotle, Shakespeare, and Pushkin. This thesis has the advantage, over my rather more desperate one, of making no judgment of value. It does not praise Molière at the expense of Ibsen, or Shakespeare at the expense of Dostoevski. It says: here are two types of genius, two fundamentally distinct, if not opposed, views of life. Bearing in mind the remarkable researches in our time into molecular biology, I should prefer to say that it distinguishes not so much between two views of life (since it is possible to *adopt* a view of life that may not fit one's character): it distinguishes between two temperaments radically differentiated at birth—perhaps by no more than an inherited disposition of chromosomes. However it comes about, the distinction is true and blinding. It is not possible to mistake *Don Giovanni* for a work of the *Ring* cycle. No one has ever thought that *Le Bourgeois Gentilhomme* was written by Ibsen. Or that Bernard Shaw wrote *The Tempest*.

Artists apart, I do believe that all of us fall into one or the other category. Rarely in social life does the difference appear sharper than between two people of not necessarily different political views but different political temperaments. There is the idealist—the hedgehog—who, often nobly, wants to set things right. He is always in danger of corruption from the Peer Gynt syndrome, the impulse to break everybody in sight on the wheel of his precious integrity. There is the realist, so called—the fox—who sees, or pretends to see, more clearly the complexities and contradictions of the political situation. Shakespeare registers the force of both impulses, and records what the life of the politician so often reflects—the natural tragedy of their failure to reconcile themselves in useful action.

Nowhere does he illumine this sense of political realism better than in *Coriolanus*. And nothing could be more Shakespearean than the fact that the best critics—from Coleridge to Dowden—have argued whether *Coriolanus* is a political play at all. Stopford Brooke was convinced that Shakespeare sided with the people, Hazlitt that he was prejudiced in favor of the patricians.

This conflict between the two types has, so far as I know, never been more consciously or confidently provoked than in the armed assault of Bernard Shaw, alive, on Shakespeare, dead. For much of the fire that fueled Shaw's famous campaign sprang from his exasperated envy of a playwright who successfully plumbed the depths of human goodness and evil, reason and instinct, common sense and idiosyncrasy, without once wishing to enlist his insight in the service of a cause, a crusade, a religion, or a nonreligion. Shaw could not bear the thought that Shakespeare knew better than Shaw the damaging power of sexual passion and yet gave no hint that Cleopatra ought to be taken out and scrubbed and compelled to become a lieutenant in the army of General Christabel Pankhurst.

This is the anger of the crusader against the man of the world. It is the contempt of the evangelist for the reporter. And that brings us to what I hope is the relevance of Shakespeare to us, considered as involuntary victims of the media, in the twilight of the twentieth century. Simply, if you can bear the humble word, that Shakespeare is the greatest reporter we have had in English.

I speak feelingly about this, because most of my life I have been a reporter, embracing in public no political party, supporting no faction, on the principle that a reporter must try to represent, as fairly yet as vividly as possible, the flux of argument and emotion mobilized to defeat the complexity of the facts of life around him. It is the stance of the fox. (He is, by the way, not to be confused with the dedicated "investigative" reporter, who is a hedgehog in fox's clothing.)

Definition makes the reporter sound very high-minded indeed. But no ordinarily honest man can escape the suspicion that it is, in some societies, a very tactful position to adopt. Looking on from above the battle, and reporting it as disinterestedly as one can, very easily coincides with the safe position of sitting on the fence and with the daily practice of that "craven scruple/Of thinking too precisely on th' event,/A thought which, quarter'd, hath but one part wisdom/And ever three parts coward." And all reporters should be warned by that remark which Lloyd George made about a Cabinet Minister who prided himself on his sense of fairness and balance: "He sat on the fence so long that the iron entered into his soul."

As a citizen, one must commit oneself. One must vote. As a reporter, one must strive to recognize that, in a clash of political factions on even the weightiest issues, the antagonists are equally endowed — if not with wisdom — with the follies and frailties of human nature.

It is inevitable that the hedgehogs should despise this stance as one of prudence at best, and Shakespeare's serenity as nothing better than surrender. Hence the blazing Shavian sentence (all the more pointed, in that it was not written by him but by his most brilliant parodist): "Shakespeare had glimpses of the havoc of displacement wrought by Elizabethan romanticism in the social machine . . . (but in the end) he consoled himself by offering the world a soothing doctrine of despair." I hope we are all here to say — as incurable foxes — not so.

So I end on hailing him as the king of the foxes. It may be said that he remains the supreme expression, in the English language, of the human spirit — but only if we are prepared to define that resonant platitude. I can define crudely its most elementary exercise as the inextinguishable urge of one human being *to say freely* what has happened to him, what he feels, and what is on his mind, and by so doing strike a spark of grateful recognition in another human being. The essential condition is "to say freely." And it is an instinct more and more liable to suppression since the most frightening political phenomenon of our time is the general contraction or abolition of free societies.

I don't know if there are nations that ban Shakespeare on ideological grounds. I am told that among what we sheepishly call closed societies — that is to say, among tyrannies — it is thought better simply to ignore him. If so, an ideologue of our day may say that it was only Shakespeare's cunning talent as a fox that saved him from the Tower of London. For there is always something in Shakespeare that can be used, or manipulated, to bolster any political position, any religious or skeptical view of life. I would rather say that it is the universality of his sympathy for all the expressions of the human spirit, benevolent or malign, committed or neutral, that makes him, three hundred and sixty years after his death, the archetype of the literary genius as a free man, and makes even tyrants pay him the skulking tribute of neglect.

# The Search for the Good Society in Shakespeare's Day and Our Own

## by JOEL HURSTFIELD

I was last in Washington some two and a half years ago, having passed the spring and summer of 1973 here, to my great instruction and delight. During those months I would spend the days working on the sixteenth-century documents at the Folger Shakespeare Library and my evenings watching the television recordings of the Watergate enquiry. I was, in a sense, living in two periods and felt that the drama that unfolded in the evening was indeed worthy of a Shakespearean setting. I remember that when I left America in August 1973, I wrote that I felt like a man who has watched the first two acts of a great piece of theater but has had to leave early to catch his plane to London: flying through the night he wonders what the final act will bring.

We all know now what the final act brought. But, because during those five months I was living in two different societies, the Shakespearean and our own, both troubled by profound moral questions, I find that a good deal of what I have since published reflects my own heightened awareness of these great historic issues. When, therefore, the International Shakespeare Association Congress did me the honor of asking me to return to Washington to reflect on these questions, I at once accepted, partly for the reason I have already given but also because of the prospect of returning here. For, though I was born in one capital city across the ocean that I love deeply, I also fell in love with another capital city on this side of the Atlantic.

But all the time that I was here I had a strong sense that Americans were asking themselves: what has happened to the good society that our Founding Fathers believed they were establishing? To an English historian the problem appears in a different perspective. For, though the founders of this republic

26

two centuries ago were rejecting the name and form of British rule, they were also affirming and preserving some of the ideals of British self-government and human rights of which they believed themselves to be unjustly deprived. For example, in 1576, exactly two centuries before the American Revolution, Peter Wentworth, a contemporary of Shakespeare, stood up in the House of Commons and addressed these memorable words to the Speaker in what was, in essence, a rebuke to the great Queen Elizabeth herself:

> Mr. Speaker, I find written in a little volume these words in effect: "Sweet indeed is the name of liberty and the thing itself a value beyond all inestimable treasure." So much the more it behoveth us to take heed lest we, contenting ourselves with the sweetness of the name only, do not lose and forgo the value of the thing.[1]

He died, a prisoner of conscience, in the Tower of London.

What was said by Peter Wentworth in 1576 and what is enshrined in the Declaration of Independence of 1776 are surely part of our common heritage of liberty and the quest for the good society. These ideals and rights were beginning to emerge in the time of Shakespeare and it is within this framework of the good society that my contribution is concerned.

The search for the good society is, of course, not peculiar to the age of Shakespeare. If we look at the early literature of the Greeks or the Hebrews or other races we find notions of a better order to be enjoyed in this world or the next with men ready to change the existing society for the sake of justice or liberty or sometimes just for the sake of a pretty face.

> Ah love! could thou and I with fate conspire
> To grasp this sorry scheme of things entire
> Would not we shatter it to bits—and then
> Remould it nearer to the heart's desire.[2]

But we are especially fortunate in that in the early sixteenth century one of the greatest minds of his generation, finding himself with some enforced leisure abroad, drew up a plan for a society based on justice, equality, and peace. It was stimulated in part by the recent discovery of the New World and is the description of a visit to an imaginary island. I am referring of course to Thomas More's *Utopia*. Now I am aware that thirty years before Shakespeare was born Thomas More was judicially murdered by his master, Henry VIII. And for a time *Utopia* was in any case treated in England with a measure of scorn. But to Shakespeare as well as to others—whatever they thought of *Utopia*—More was a great statesman; and to the link between Shakespeare and More I shall return at the appropriate time.

*Utopia*, because it described a perfect republic, has given us the adjective *utopian*, which has come to mean so perfect as to be unreal, so idealistic as to be unattainable. Yet More was not searching for the unattainable but using an imaginary commonwealth as others have done before him and since to comment on the failure of his own society. He says: here is a pagan republic to which the spirit of Christ has not been revealed yet *these* people are trying to apply the Christian principles while we who are Christians are betraying those same principles. About this interpretation most scholars who have worked on the subject would agree, from R. W. Chambers writing forty years ago to J. H. Hexter in his recent studies, though they would differ as to More's conception of the good society.[3] Whatever these divergences in outlook, it is not open to dispute that More's ideas were rejected by Shakespeare's contemporaries and that More himself was a failure in politics, as saints usually are. As we know from our own experience, it is only in times of great danger that nations call upon brilliant men to lead the government. In all other circumstances we have a preference for mediocrities.

In 1515 More was in the Netherlands as one of the representatives of his government. And, like some modern diplomats, he found that he had nothing to do because decisions, as they say nowadays, were being taken at the highest level. He therefore sat down and wrote a masterpiece, a practice that few of his successors have tried to emulate. The work was published in Latin in 1516 in Louvain, in 1517 in Paris, and in 1518 in Basle. By the very nature of the work the use of Latin was obvious. For More was addressing himself to scholars; and in the company of scholars a man may speak as he pleases. It was not until 1551 that it was translated into English.

More uses of fictitious character, Raphael Hythlodaye, recently returned from his travels in the New World, to describe Utopian society, and More himself poses as no more than the reporter of his extraordinary story. But he is in fact doing two things. He is setting forth the imaginary features of Utopia and, from the historian's point of view at least as important, he is commenting critically on the conditions of early Tudor England. Like most, but not all, writers about ideal commonwealths, his principal aim is not to establish that commonwealth but to criticize and reform his own. In Utopia itself, as More describes it, there is no inequality of wealth or property; in fact private wealth does not exist at all. Gold is despised and is used to make fetters for those few criminals who exist in Utopia. Educational opportunity is free and equal, not only to all men but to both sexes, and all inhabitants employ their appropriate talents working a six-hour day. Their leisure they spend with literature, music, athletics or other ways of improving their minds and bodies. They have no territorial ambitions and never engage in the expansionist wars of their predatory neighbors; and they will only take up arms in a defensive war, in which case both men and women will engage in battle. There is no established faith and various religions exist side by side. All are tolerated provided that they are not hostile to the common good.

Such in brief is the Utopian state described by Hythlodaye to a sometimes skeptical More, though the conception, of course, is More's own. This cannot, by the way, be taken to mean that either More thought it the best form of society, or wished to bring it about. Modern writers have attempted to show that Utopia has to some extent at least been established in our world. Some have claimed that it is to be found in those monasteries which have adhered faithfully to the ideals of their founders; some have seen it in Calvin's Geneva. Others have seen it established in a commune of the kind to be found in the eastern parts of the Soviet Union or in the western parts of the United States. Others have found its heroic qualities best affirmed in an Israeli Kibbutz. *Chacun à son goût.* For my part I have no contribution to make to these efforts at identification save to add that wherever More's Utopia is, or may one day be established, it cannot fail to be one of the dullest places on earth: a uniform, regimented, humorless, self-righteous community of bores. Yet it continues to haunt us to this very day, as it has done the generations that have preceded us.

It might appear from what I have just said that I am a hostile critic of More and his work. I am in fact the reverse. For the creator of Utopia was not himself a Utopian. His purpose was to provide what sociologists call a model, a scale of values, against which men could measure their own way of life. He expresses in unforgettable terms the corruption of the good society that he sees not only in England but throughout Christian Europe. The moral debasement of international relations is no worse than what is to be found in the internal relations of England itself. Greed dominates the men who have access to economic and political power, even the greatest in the country. Land hunger is causing selfish men to enlarge their possessions by force or fraud. Poor men are being forced off the land to make way for sheep because the price of wool is rising above the price of grain. Their few miserable possessions they sell to get food, and when that is finished they beg, for which they are prosecuted, or steal, for which they are hanged.

So the work continues, a humanist and humanitarian critique of the entire fabric of contemporary society. Nothing is missed: extravagance in clothes and style of living at the expense of the poor; failure in the educational system; religion corrupted; private interest sought at the expense of the public good. The attack driven home with great skill and detail occupies the first of the two books of *Utopia.* The second is a full account of the government, administration, and life of Utopia itself, which I have briefly summarized. And as he brings his account to a close he reverts to his original theme: that private property lies at the root of all suffering and evil while in Utopia, as he puts it, "Though no man have any thing; yet every man is rich!"[4]

And then, as we come toward the end of the book we meet that astonishing outburst which, when I first read it as a student, profoundly shocked me and still after all these years produces the same impact whenever I read the passage. It is Hythlodaye's parting comment on the political morality of western Europe:

> when I consider and weigh in my mind all these commonwealths which nowadays anywhere do flourish, so God help me I can perceive nothing but a certain conspiracy of rich men procuring their own commodities under the name and title of the commonwealth.[5]

I know of no passage anywhere in the Marxist scriptures that is so effective or devastating as this famous sentence where More excoriates the governing classes of his time, men who have subverted the Christian order for their own selfish ends, who have sanctified and legitimized expropriation, who have turned society, in More's contemptuous words, into "a certain conspiracy of rich men."

The question, of course, arises: was More the protocommunist, the revolutionary who, in the formative years of modern capitalism, sought to overthrow it in favor of a universal socialist system? I cannot enter into this prolonged, and in a sense unrewarding, controversy. I will do no more than say that I am entirely satisfied that he was neither a revolutionary nor a communist. He had an essentially conservative cast of mind; he had a deep hatred of excess which, he held, perverted the Christian framework of society. If we read his text closely we see that he was using his ideal, imaginary world, Utopia, not to show how far Europe had drifted from the Utopian ideals, which after all it had never known, but from its own Christian ideals on which it had been nurtured. It is these ideals that he feels Europe must recover; it must show that it could renew its search for, and establish, the good society by reducing to their proper proportions the material temptations of the modern world. It is this that may offer a consistency to his own career, which otherwise it is so difficult to find.

I will put it another way. More always wore a hair shirt, even when he was Lord Chancellor of England, the highest officer in the state. It was a shirt that caused him discomfort, pain, bleeding. To him the hair shirt was the symbol of Christian rejection of the materialist standards of the world in which he lived and worked.

More, then, transmitted to Shakespeare's contemporaries and to succeeding generations including our own two contributions toward the good society. The one was negative, which appears in Book I and warns us how a civilized society can come to behave corruptly, ruthlessly, devoid of compassion and justice to those without power or wealth in the community. The other concept of the good society, which is in Book II, dealing with the commonwealth of Utopia, is an abstraction, useful in any discussion of the nature of legitimate authority, justice, and individual rights. Did More ever hope that Tudor England would move toward such a system of government? I know of nothing in his other writings or actions that encourages for a moment any such notion. More, of course, in the book speaks with two voices: that of Hythlodaye, who has spent five years there, and in his own voice as skeptic. For example, when he says that no society could survive that abolished private property, Hythlodaye retorts: I spent five years in Utopia and I saw it work. Is there a characteristic piece of More's irony in all this, for Utopia means nowhere? Is he saying that there is no organized society in which private property has been abolished — that is still true today — but the important thing is to tame its exercise, restrain its abuse, and prevent its becoming an intolerable source of power?

I pause here for one moment to strike a contrast between what More is writing and the work, for example, of a distinguished contemporary, Sir Thomas Elyot, whose book *The Governor* was meant to be a political guide to members of the ruling classes. For him a system under which "everything should be to all men in common without discrepancy of any estate or condition," that is, common ownership and equality in government, was a monstrosity. To him the state was made up of "sundry estates and degrees of men, which is disposed by the order of equity and governed by the rule and moderation of reason." In short, each man had his place, and this was good Tudor doctrine.[6]

It is well known that Thomas More did not conceive of Utopia wholly out of his imagination. It has been possible to trace the influence of Plato's *Republic* and his *Laws,* of St. Augustine's *City of God,* and of other works. But it was also a response to a rapidly changing society, to the emergence and strengthening of the nation state, to the rise of political sovereignty, to the endowment of the monarchies with almost divine attributes, to the submission of the individual spirit to secular, centralized authority and its agents. A century and a half was to pass before Thomas Hobbes was to give a name, *Leviathan,* and a description to this developing order under which all of us work and live; but Thomas More saw it coming. Hence he tormented himself with the question: should he serve the new order, or should he choose the quieter ways of the scholar, the philosopher, the inquirer into the fundamental aspects of society? He chose the former, government service, and found no peace until, divested of all office, he sat a prisoner in the Tower, awaiting execution and reflecting on the nature of this world and the next.

We may find many echoes of *Utopia* in the writings and speeches of the later decades on into Shakespeare's day and beyond. But they are not necessarily derived from More. There emerged in the middle years of the sixteenth century a group of reformers, some of whom were called "Commonwealth's Men," a mixture of laymen and churchmen, like Robert Crowley, Henry Brinklow, John Hales, Thomas Lever, Hugh Latimer, perhaps even Archbishop Thomas Cranmer himself. The young William Cecil was sympathetic; the Protector Somerset, in his foolhardy, clumsy way, tried to be their patron. But though some of them were starry-eyed, they were not Utopians. They held radical views in religious matters and some of them vigorously opposed a Protestant Reformation that halted at a compromise. But socially they were not revolutionaries. They looked to an English past where the peasants were secure and prosperous on their holdings, where lords were just, where the Church was full of charity and care for men's souls and bodies. Such a past was almost as unreal as Utopia. The Commonwealth's men lamented as conservatives the world they had lost. They offered no new, imaginative world order that they wanted their contemporaries to adopt.

We possess also a remarkable example of what one Englishman, a member of the governing class, considered the good society, in a work *De Republica Anglorum* — The State of England. (Only the title is in Latin: the work itself is in English.) It is by Sir Thomas Smith, an early contemporary of Shakespeare. Since it is the only account we possess by an Elizabethan of government *from the inside*, ranging right through from monarchy to parliament, to the law courts, to local institutions, it has often puzzled me that it has been so much neglected by Shakespearean scholars.

It may not surprise an American audience to learn that Smith considered that the good society already existed — in England. Smith was in government for most of his adult life as Secretary of State (twice), privy councillor, a member of important government missions, and ambassador. He was also an economist, a classical scholar, Provost of Eton, and Vice-Chancellor of Cambridge University. But when he came to write *De Republica Anglorum,* he wrote it in the precise language of the public servant. Indeed, he goes out of his way to say that his is a factual statement based on things as they are:

> not as Plato made his commonwealth, or Zenophon his kingdom of Persia, nor as Sir Thomas More his Utopia, being feigned commonwealths such as never was nor never shall be, vain imaginations, fantasies of philosophers to occupy the time and to exercise their wits, but so as England standeth and is governed at this day the 28th of March, anno 1565, in the seventh year of the reign and administration thereof by the most virtuous and noble Queen Elizabeth, daughter to King Henry VIII, and in the one and fiftieth year of mine age, when I was ambassador for Her Majesty in the Court of France.[7]

How exact! And how misleading! If More idealized his Utopia, Smith idealized his England. Smith was living at the Court of France and among a nation deeply divided on religion and politics, already experienced in the bloody skirmishes of civil strife and soon to be engulfed in bitter internal struggles — the so-called Wars of Religion, which were to last until the end of the century. By contrast, as Smith looked across the Channel to England he saw a nation living at peace, in freedom and under good government, with just and representative institutions, a paternalistic nobility and gentry committed to the welfare of their dependents, and a contented artisan and peasant class of men who knew their place.

Was this the England that Shakespeare knew during the twenty years of his dramatic greatness, that is, the last decade of the sixteenth century and the first decade of the seventeenth? The men who now governed England, and the

England they governed, were vastly different from the men and society of their grandparents, More's contemporaries. Too much had happened in between, not only in England but more significantly and memorably on the continent of Europe. By the time that Shakespeare was working in London in the 1590s some horrific events were half a century old, but their trauma remained and others were too recent—indeed contemporary—to be far from the consciousness of the men who held responsibility and power.

I am not referring to riots and local outbursts of violence. These were endemic in Western society and could arise from genuine discontent over unemployment or famine, or from the sudden combustion of a local conflict. Such disorders continued as they had done for centuries: historians have been inclined to forget that at most times in England somebody was rioting somewhere over some issue, or simply because a few people had got drunk on a Saturday night. (Similarly there is a widespread fallacy that student unrest was a phenomenon peculiar to the 1960s. Students have been rioting since the thirteenth century, although it is true that in those days heads of universities did not apologize to the rioters for having provoked the riot.)

If, then, disorder was common enough in the sixteenth century and could usually be coped with, there was a new and dangerous element that greatly troubled the men in power: it was ideological. I said earlier that Utopia was nowhere, a figment of More's imagination, as he himself says in his correspondence. But men in various places were setting up Utopias. They had almost certainly never read the book or even heard of Thomas More. But they believed that they could establish a new and more just social order. If there was a literary source for this it was not *Utopia* but an equally revolutionary document, the Bible in the vernacular.

There is a long and obscure history going well back into the Middle Ages of various movements that saw both in the Old Testament and the New doctrines of freedom and equality which set good men free from the authority of church and state. To them, and to some of their charismatic leaders—about whom Norman Cohn has taught us so much—the Bible pointed the way to forms of society based on the liberated commune in which private property had ceased to exist.[8] To these vague and confused aspirations the Reformation gave its own impetus, though Martin Luther was astonished and appalled when the peasantry seized on his doctrine of equality, which he meant to be understood wholly and solely in spiritual terms, and turned it into a revolutionary claim for political, economic, and social equality. The Peasants' Revolt in Germany coming in 1525, only eight years after Luther's 95 theses that in fact inaugurated the Reformation, threatened to discredit Luther and his works and he turned against the revolutionaries with the savagery of a prophet betrayed. He called upon the princes and nobility to put down the revolt with a bloody sword. To Thomas More and his fellow humanists, the events of 1525 and related developments seemed once for all to close the door on peaceful change. It seemed better, surely, to preserve as much as was good in the existing order rather than to encourage or yield to the pressures of religious and social change and let loose the forces of violence. More and Erasmus did not break faith with the cause of reform; that, they believed, had already been done by the Reformers.

Worse was to follow. There had emerged in various places in Europe groups of people calling themselves Anabaptists, as well as going by other names, who owed their title to their opposition to infant baptism, believing that it should not take place until one was old enough to appreciate the responsibilities of a Christian. But elements of the movement extended their scope to fundamental social objectives that they believed the Bible enjoined. In its most extreme form it took shape in the city of Münster where, in the years 1533-34, it led to a violent seizure of power and the establishment of a communist state with the universal ownership of all property, the abolition of the marriage laws, and a leadership cult of John of Leyden, recognized as king and prophet. The town administration was destroyed and a free republic was established, but without effective rule or the capacity for defense. They resisted siege for months until, in the summer of 1535, their defenses collapsed, the city was overrun, and 30,000 Anabaptists were massacred. The good society, as they saw it, was drowned in blood. Thereafter the movement itself changed. It became pacifist, quietist, separatist, and it continued under various names like Mennonites, Huttites, the Family of Love; and overseas it took root in Pennsylvania where, as the Amish sect, it still survives. But the memory of a republic of equality established in violence endured, and late in the sixteenth century English statesmen could still be deeply disturbed by stray references to scattered fragments of the Family of Love that made brief appearances in their territory.

There was less ideology about the English popular movements of the mid-Tudor period, but there were several outbreaks that for a time seemed serious threats to the central government. The most dangerous was Ket's Rebellion of 1549, coming as it did at the height of an economic crisis reflected in inflation, a trade slump, unemployment, food shortage, and some eviction of the peasantry from the land. The rebels demanded no fundamental reconstruction of their society: some of them believed indeed that they were guided by the worthy aims of the head of the government, the Protector Somerset who, in his curious, muddled way had identified himself with a policy of economic and social reform. So in demanding the end of villeinage, the rebels believed that the Protector and God were on their side. "We pray," they declared, "that all bond men may be free, for God made all free with his precious blood shedding." If to our ears there are echoes of the Peasants' War in Germany of a quarter of a century earlier, the sources for these demands were in fact nearer home: the economic instability in East Anglia as well as local, personal, and religious discontents. But as in all other rebellions in England in the sixteenth century, their leaders claimed that they had no intention of overthrowing the existing order though the effect was to topple Somerset and bring to power the forces of reaction under the Earl of Warwick.

There were other risings in these years, of mixed origins and aims, but none of them carried any basic threat to the established system. The most dangerous one in the whole century was the Rising of the North of 1569, which was a major regional upheaval and committed itself, as did the Pilgrimage of Grace, its prototype of 1536, to restore the old faith and remove the evil counsellors of the crown, men who possessed none of the inherited authority of the traditional advisers of the feudal monarchy. Had the Rising succeeded—which is unlikely—it would have changed the personnel of government, and perhaps some of its aims and organization, but it could hardly have established a new society or restored an old.

Yet, having said this, I must at once acknowledge that things were happening at the grass roots of these movements about which historians know all too little. I will give one example. The 1569 Rising was put down ruthlessly; many of those who surrendered were put on trial and publicly hanged as examples to their communities. But many were pardoned and their cases were entered on the Pardon Rolls, which still survive. Fortunately for us the clerk entered not only the name of the man pardoned but the things he said and did when he committed the crime; and here, buried and unused in the Pardon Rolls, we have not only some marvelous examples of the spoken English of Shakespeare's day but also insights into the opinions of some of the country folk whose anger had broken all restraint. We may listen for a moment to James Fuller, sawyer, of Lanham, not himself involved in the Northern Rebellion but in a lesser disorder further south in Suffolk:

> If there were but forty good fellows that would be ruled by me and be true one to another I would devise that the world should go better with them, for I do know half an hundred that I am assured of will take my part. And I have agreed with the sexton of Lanham Church that he shall deliver unto me the keys of the said church door upon Sunday next. And then about ten of the clock in the night I and others shall meet at a place called the Gravel Pits near to Lanham and from thence we will go to the town of Brent Illeigh and raise up the people in that town, and from thence to Lanham and there to ring the bells awake . . . And then to proceed and bring down the prices of all things at our pleasure. And we will not be deceived as we were at the last rising, for then we were promised enough and more than enough. But the more was an halter. But now we will appoint them that shall take the rich churls and set them on their horsebacks under a tree, whereupon we will hang a withe and put it about their necks and then drive their horses from under them and so let them hang, but such as be gentlemen of old continuance they shall not be hurt but such as be new come up and be herdmen those we will kill.[9]

These are violent words, but we notice again that the threats are uttered against the new rich, the upstarts who for private gain are destroying the traditional ways. The speaker has no moral program for a better world. What he wants is to get back to the good old days, real as he thought they were, imaginary as we believe them to have been.

Shakespeare was five years old at the time of the Northern Rebellion, but he would have heard talk of it throughout his youth and early manhood. In 1596 he was over thirty and living in London. It was the worst economic crisis of the sixteenth century and laborers' real wages were lower than they have ever been before or since. In that year starvation drove the Oxfordshire peasantry to rebellion after the third disastrous failure of the harvest, a failure so vividly described for us in *A Midsummer Night's Dream*. In that year, for example, two Cardiff laborers were hanged for stealing ten loaves of bread.[10] Clearly, starvation had driven their families to the breaking point. England was at war, as she had been for a decade, and it was leading nowhere; Ireland was in revolt, an appalling drain on England's resources; and in government, the queen and her minister, Burghley, bankrupt of ideas as their last years ebbed away, were aware of an imminent struggle for power within the younger generation of politicians that could bring the country to destruction.

I have dwelt upon the preceding decades and the contemporary conditions of Shakespeare's working life in order to pose the question: Was this the time to plan for the good society, or was it wiser to preserve the best that was left of the old? What kind of advocacy of the good society do we find in Shakespeare?

I have become increasingly skeptical from my reading of the plays and attendance at their performance as to whether they carry any message at all. Instead we have explorations, shrewd and deep, involved yet detached, of every moral issue that confronted his contemporaries as they confront us today. But I would emphasize their detachment, *not* their commitment. To use Shakespeare, as some scholars have done, to condemn national wars, to expound the class struggle or, less exaltedly — as I once heard the plays used — to express an obscure and unaccountable hostility to middle-aged ladies, is to diminish Shakespeare's stature and smother his diversity under a one-dimensional moral code of selected truths.

But what does seem clear is that the social upheavals — more especially in the middle fifty years of the sixteenth century between the Peasants' Revolt of 1525 in Germany and the Massacre of St. Bartholomew's Day of 1572 in France — took the heart out of any drive for the good society to be obtained by a recasting of its structure on new concepts of self-government. To Shakespeare's contemporaries who wielded power the good society was just, paternalistic, hierarchical, orderly, and sufficiently strong to maintain internal peace. In that system the artisan in the city or the peasant in the field had no choice. Government, it was held, acted on his behalf but not on his authority. Self-government meant not the Gettysburg concept of popular involvement in the personnel and practice of government, but the exercise of authority on behalf of the people by the gentry and the urban patriciate. Government by consent, as the expression *consent* is used in the parliamentary statutes, meant the consent of the governing class: crown, lords, and gentry. Those forces which oppose this concept, whatever the cause they are pursuing, are inimical to the good society and open the prospects of mob rule.

It is often said that Shakespeare's history plays reflect the fear and hostility that survive from the memories of the Wars of the Roses. But the last battle in the Wars of the Roses had taken place more than a hundred years before Shakespeare came to London. Rather, one notices that the power of the mob in *Coriolanus* and *Julius Caesar* is of the kind exercised, for example, at intervals in the Rising of the North or more strikingly in France by the Paris mob when they slaughtered 6,000 Huguenots during the Massacre of St. Bartholomew's Day of 1572.

I do not need to quote the too-much-cited speech about order and degree by Ulysses in *Troilus and Cressida*. For the last thirty years the point has been made that these expressions were commonplace. Everybody who held power and office believed, or affected to believe, that each man or group had his place in the hierarchical Tudor society and it was good for all concerned that this established order and degree should be maintained. But the point that does need to be stressed is that this description of Tudor society was simply not true. It was a notion favored by men like Burghley, who was an *arriviste,* the first of his line to be ennobled; and so too, of course, was Shakespeare an *arriviste,* the first of his line to buy a coat of arms from the College of Heralds, which he then gave to his father. John Shakespeare could now call himself a gentleman, and so, therefore, could William.

"Order and degree" was not a securely established framework; it was a goal, a dream of security and obedience in a society that had been unstable for more than a hundred years. Of course, medieval England had known a great deal of instability, including sporadic peasant movements, but the main conflicts had been within the governing order, feudal, aristocratic, factious. Now the threats coming all too often from *outside* the governing order were the principal menace. This was most striking in France, Germany, and the Low Countries, but the English Channel is narrow and infection could spread. Apart from this, there were sufficient elements in the English Puritan movement that could threaten the fundamentals of Tudor-Stuart rule, as the mid-seventeenth century was to show beyond doubt. To Shakespeare's contemporaries the good society was conservative and traditional, one that preserved stability against disorder, division, experiment, and popular government.

But this is not to imply that their good society was hostile to any notion of political improvement or social welfare. Quite the contrary. If time served I would show how the Elizabethans first evolved the concepts of a welfare state that now form the characteristic features of Britain and have done so much to preserve its stability in spite of economic crisis and rapid social change and enabled us, slowly and painfully, to move toward a more humane society. It may seem a strange word to use but what I find in the Elizabethans, in spite of plenty of instances of cruelty, is their compassion, and that feature I find dominant in Shakespeare's work. And here is my link between Thomas More and Shakespeare.

In 1517, a year after the publication of *Utopia,* when More was back in London fulfilling his duties as under-sheriff, a riot broke out in the capital against foreign workers, in which the mob plundered their possessions and came near to bloodshed. The whole episode became known as Evil May Day. More addressed the mob and—a remarkable achievement in the circum- stances—pacified them. No foreigner lost his life and, though the ringleaders of the riot were themselves hanged, the rest were spared, again it is said through the eloquent appeal of More to the king and Wolsey. The event is reenacted in a play called *Sir Thomas More,* to which Shakespeare is con- sidered to have contributed a small section, which includes More's speech to the London mob, adapted from the chronicler who first reported it. In it More passionately reminds his listeners of the pain and suffering they would have inflicted on these strangers and their innocent families and then, in Shakespeare's words, goes on:

> What had you got? I'll tell you. You had taught
> How insolence and strong hand should prevail,
> How order should be quelled; and by this pattern
> Not one of you should live an aged man;
> For other ruffians, as their fancies wrought
> With self same hand, self reasons and self right
> Would shark on you; and men like ravenous fishes
> Would feed on one another.[11]

We notice that the speech is based on two principles of social conduct. The first is a plea for toleration and compassion for the minority, the stranger in our midst. The second is the plea for order: if you act by violence to achieve your ends (he tells the Londoners), then order will break down and you will find yourselves living in a violent society.

At about the time when Shakespeare was putting More's speech into dramatic form, Robert Cecil, Secretary of State to Queen Elizabeth, was ad- dressing the House of Commons with a comparable plea for minorities. This involves, he told them, the whole question of "charity to relieve strangers, and especially such as do not grieve our eyes." And at this point he spoke eloquent- ly of England's historic role of providing a haven for the persecuted. "This," he declared, "hath brought great honour to our kingdom, for it is accounted the refuge of distressed nations, for our arms have been open unto them to cast themselves into our bosoms."[12]

What we find in the fragment of the More play we find explicitly and in detail in at least two of Shakespeare's own plays, *The Merchant of Venice* and *Othello.* In both cases the pattern is the same. Here are members of minority communities, in one case the Jews, in the other the Negroes, who, treated with injustice and contempt, withdraw behind their own defenses.

> You call me misbeliever, cut-throat dog,
> And spet upon my Jewish gaberdine.
> (1.3.106-7)

To Brabantio, father of Desdemona in *Othello,* the marriage of his daughter to a Moor could have been accomplished only by witchcraft:

> She is abus'd, stol'n from me, and corrupted,
> By spells and medicines, bought of mountebanks,
> For nature so preposterously to err. . . .
> (1.3.60-62).

But the explanation is given by Othello himself. Desdemona, pressing him to tell the story of his life and his people, was moved to compassion:

> She lov'd me for the dangers I had pass'd,
> And I lov'd her that she did pity them.
> This only is the witchcraft I have us'd.
> (1.3.167-69).

The hope of a symbolic union between the two races is converted into tragedy by Iago, who plays upon the implanted sense of racial inferiority in the Moor, once his suspicions are aroused. *The Merchant of Venice* ends more hopefully, with a union between Jessica, the Jew's daughter, and Lorenzo, though it has been brought about by deceit. But there remain also in the mind the words of Portia, who has always seemed to me one of the most preposterous and repulsive characters in Shakespeare: she reads Shylock a sententious lecture on mercy and shows him none.

But in both plays we see alike the detachment and compassion of the playwright, for he sees both the Jew and the Moor not only as victims of the dominant race but as prisoners of their own past. They must conform to their inherited pattern though it divides them from the rest of the community:

> I will buy with you [says Shylock], sell with you, talk with you, walk with you, and so following: but I will not eat with you, drink with you, nor pray with you. (1.3.30-33)

Shylock's daughter breaks the barrier and, as far as we can tell, succeeds. Othello breaks the barrier and fails.

In the three instances I have cited, the More fragment, the *Merchant of Venice*, and *Othello*, Shakespeare seems to be saying that the good society has a tolerant place for its minority. There is another large minority that figures far more prominently in his plays. I refer, of course, to women. Having referred to the subject I shall say little about it for several good reasons. In the first place, until the several thousand Ph.D theses now being written on women in Tudor England have been completed, digested, and computerized, it would be premature to draw any conclusions. Second, I am a man of peace and, although I am one hundred percent behind "women's lib," they might indeed feel I was too far behind.

And yet what stands out to the historian, familiar with the legal and economic status of women in the period, which is one of subservience, is that Shakespeare's women often have a strength of character and personality, a wit and wisdom greater than their male counterparts. Beatrice is always wittier than Benedick; Katherina is a more impressive person than Petruchio, and her submission at the end of *The Taming of the Shrew* is a superb and manifest piece of make-believe; Katherine of France can twist that great warrior Henry V round her little finger when she wants to; Cleopatra has a strength of will that Antony does not possess; Volumnia carries reserves of power that are not given to her son Coriolanus; Lady Macbeth's influence and ambition, though baleful, are vastly stronger than her lord's, though in the end her nerve breaks. If one judged Tudor women by what many of the pamphleteers and preachers were saying, still living in the world of Adam's rib, one would get a very different picture from that of the full-blooded, independent, experienced, and politically mature people Shakespeare places on the stage. My own impression as a historian is that in this respect the playwright comes closer to reality than the pamphleteer.

T.S. Eliot tells us, in his Introduction to Wilson Knight's *The Wheel of Fire*, "I once affirmed that Dante made great poetry out of a great philosophy of life; and that Shakespeare made equally great poetry out of an inferior and muddled philosophy of life."[13] Far be it from me to contest the assertion of a great and confident critic. For I have throughout this paper been careful to leave the discussion of philosophies and influences upon Shakespeare to the literary critics who possess an expertise that I do not enjoy. My primary concern throughout has been with the political and social crisis of rapid change, instability, and violence in Europe prevalent throughout the sixteenth century and reaching its climax in Shakespeare's lifetime. If, as T. S. Eliot said, Shakespeare's philosophy was muddled, then I would, again only as a historian, say that the times themselves were also muddled and adrift and that Shakespeare not only reflected these conditions but responded to them also. He was showing us how politicians, and kings, and ordinary men faced these unparalleled issues, became hostile to popular and radical movements, and moved away from any desire for experiment and change toward conditions of order and containment. I am not suggesting that Shakespeare was a mirror reflecting the changing pattern of his age. But he *was* a man of his age. The literary critic quite rightly draws attention to the intellectual influences playing upon his mind. The historian speaks of the physical and political developments of which so sensitive a writer could not fail to be aware. But, of course, no writer of genius can be alone explained in terms of the exterior forces playing upon his mind.

I will conclude with a contrast. When Shakespeare wrote *The Tempest*, almost exactly a century had passed since the appearance of More's *Utopia*. Both deal with an island: the one is civilized, ordered, full of optimism. Hythlodaye is its spokesman to point the way to his fellow Europeans for establishing a new and better order. The other, in *The Tempest*, is an uninhabited, stormy, windswept island with nothing more civilized than the monstrous Caliban. When rescue comes, the island will be abandoned and forgotten: it has nothing to offer the Western world. Yet Hythlodaye has his counterpart not in Prospero but in Gonzalo. For Gonzalo also has an ideal commonwealth to propagate. We listen for a moment to what he has to say and to the manner in which he is received.

> I' th' commonwealth I would by contraries
> Execute all things; for no kind of traffic
> Would I admit; no name of magistrate;
> Letters should not be known; riches, poverty,
> And use of service, none; contract, succession,
> Bourn, bound of land, tilth, vineyard, none;
> No use of metal, corn, or wine, or oil;
> No occupation; all men idle, all;
> And women too, but innocent and pure:
> No sovereignty; —
>
> (2.1.143-52)

Sebastian and Antonio receive his plans with derision. "The latter end of his commonwealth," says Antonio, "forgets the beginning." But still Gonzalo persists:

> All things in common Nature should produce
> Without sweat or endeavour: treason, felony,
> Sword, pike, knife, gun, or need or any engine,
> Would I not have; but Nature should bring forth,
> Of it own kind, all foison, all abundance,
> To feed my innocent people.
>
> (2.1.155-60)

Again he is received with merriment. Sebastian cries out, "No marrying 'mong his subjects?"; and Antonio answers: "None, man; all idle; whores and knaves." Once more Gonzalo presses on, ignoring the interruptions:

> I would with such perfection govern, sir,
> T' excel the Golden Age.
>                 (163-64)

Again more ribaldry. "Save his Majesty!" says Sebastian. "Long live Gonzalo!" echoes Antonio. Gonzalo tries to continue, "And, do you mark me, sir?" But he gets no further. Alonso intervenes: "Prithee, no more: thou dost talk nothing to me." The joke is over. No one wants to hear any more about ideal commonwealths, least of all from some windy old courtier long out of touch with the realities of power politics.

I am not suggesting that, in creating Gonzalo, Shakespeare was caricaturing More's Hythlodaye and his Utopia. It was time that had made the caricature.

When Sir Thomas Smith warned his fellow countrymen against being seduced by "feigned commonwealths such as never was nor never shall be, vain imaginations, fantasies of philosophers," it was the voice of the experienced politician — and of fear.[14] "And have not our countrymen, think you," wrote William Lambarde, "by their continual travel abroad transported unto us the evils of those nations with whom they have been conversant?"[15] "Let conformity and unity in religion be provided for," said Bishop Sandys, "and it shall be as a wall of defence unto this realm."[16] Where in the writings of Ralegh or Bacon or Donne shall we find in these years any advocacy of experiments in politics? Bacon was, of course, a powerful exponent of experiment in science and we can still learn from his New Atlantis about the role of the scientist in society. But this Lord Chancellor, unlike his illustrious predecessor at the beginning of the century, wasted no time constructing political Utopias. There would before long be a struggle for power in England, but both sides would appeal to the past: Charles I to the ancient prerogative of kingship, the parliamentarians to Magna Carta and the early forms of government. Both were citing bad history, as is common enough among politicians. But the fact is that they were looking to the past, not to some speculative republic of virtue, some fantasy of the philosophers. When such people did arise during the Civil War they were promptly suppressed by their own side. And before long Thomas Hobbes would be writing that these troubles had begun at the universities, where young men had been taught to read all the wrong books and had come to believe that all power should be transferred to the people.

The last hundred years had seen ideal commonwealths and popular movements come crashing down in violence and disorder. Even the more traditional forms of self-government, the estates and the cortes, were lapsing into desuetude. And no one could be sure in the 1630s whether the English parliament would survive. Power was passing to the monarchs, their officials, their propagandists, and their armies. The idealists and the theorists were getting short shrift: "Prithee, no more: thou dost talk nothing to me." The initiative in government had returned to the princes of Europe and would long stay with them. Centuries would pass before an American statesman could hail the opening era as the century of the common man, though the ambiguity of this expression was only to emerge with the passage of time. Meanwhile, among Shakespeare's countrymen the search for the good society had lost the vigor and drive of the early sixteenth century when their grandfathers had believed that new education, changes in religion, responsible government would bring better and fuller lives to the whole community. Now men were war-weary, tired, afraid, uncertain of what new troubles or wars would engulf their country when the old queen died. A good society was one that could preserve and sustain order and internal peace before the coming storm.

As this address draws to a close it occurs to me that some of my listeners may say that I have not dealt with the last three words of my title which, in full, is "The Search for the Good Society in Shakespeare's Day and Our Own." But it may be that others of you will say that my whole lecture has been in fact concerned with the crisis of our own day. Perhaps indeed this is a recurrent crisis of Western society and it is best to consider it in the Shakespearean setting for we have the advantage of the larger perspective of time. What is this crisis? Is it not the result of a mixture of idealism with violence and illusion betrayed into despair? We may take Erasmus as our guide. The greatest intellectual of his generation, he admired and was proud of the work of his close friend Thomas More on *Utopia*. Erasmus believed that they and men of like mind would bring to pass an age of reform in religion and society by the sheer force of reason. Instead they witnessed one movement after another of blood, disorder, and violent change. Erasmus turned away from the revolutionaries. The role of the intellectual, he had always argued, was to stay clear of the battle, detach himself from the disputing factions, and preserve freedom of enquiry in the search for truth. The role of the intellectual, in short, was to stay out of politics. More who, after much heart-searching, decided to enter politics, identified himself in part with the forces of reaction. By the time of Shakespeare the forces of reaction were sweeping into power; those of reform were in full retreat.

Is there not something familiar in all this? I am not arguing that history repeats itself. It is probably more true to say of historians what Francis Bacon once said of doctors, that they tend to repeat each other. But does there not come in every historical period a parting of the ways between those who seek reform by the slow processes of consent and those who believe it can only be gained by the dramatic processes of violence?

I was a schoolboy and an undergraduate in the period between the wars and, in spite of much that was socially unjust and evil, we were still conscious of the long afterglow of Victorian optimism. Yet before this first, early, exciting phase of our lives was over the skies had darkened. The expression about the extension of the boundaries of civilization and liberty had become no more than an exploded cliché. In Europe barbarians were moving into positions of power, in Italy, Germany, Spain. The war extended these prospects. In the first quarter of a century after the Second World War other tyrants, white and black, moved into positions of power in Africa and in Latin America and elsewhere, all in the name of self-government, when self-government was the one thing denied to their subject peoples. And the greatest barbarian of them all presided over a Russian Empire that was larger than the most ambitious of the Czars had ever dreamed of. In the vast majority of countries freedom of speech and the press are denied. The use of torture became an established and sophisticated instrument of government. Even in countries like the United States, Great Britain, and France it looked as though the whole liberal consensus was at risk. For whereas the liberal intellectual had felt that his first task was to protect the minority against suppression by society, he now found himself needing to protect society against the minority armed with self-righteousness, threats, and such weapons as they could lay their hands upon. Once again violence was sanctified in the name of justice.

What is the intellectual to do in these circumstances? Should he be Hythlodaye, boldly outlining his Utopia though it can exist nowhere under the sun; or should he be his creator, Thomas More, turned servant of a repressive state, believing he may yet help to conserve the best that the past has to offer; or should he serve John of Leyden and help establish a revolutionary commune in faith and blood; or Sir Thomas Smith congratulating himself and his fellow countrymen on the good society they have established in Elizabethan England; or Gonzalo prattling on about an ideal commonwealth to a vanished audience; or should he be Erasmus, the servant of no state or social order, pursuing his independent inquiry into the nature of the good society? It is Thomas More's dilemma. Can we, as intellectuals, stay out of the conflict, or should we enter the service of the state, accepting its appointments, rewards, titles, but wearing closest to our spirit the hair shirt of a troubled conscience? "For what sin, in the name of Christ," wrote Sir Henry Wotton, "was I sent hither among soldiers, being by my profession academical and by my charge pacifical."[17] It would be presumptuous on my part to offer any advice to my colleagues on this subject, even if I were sure of the answer. But there is one suggestion I need hardly offer to an audience such as this. If we return to Shakespeare, not only for the continuous delight his plays bring us but for the issues which, without comment, he constantly presents to us, then it is true that we do not find answers to our questions, but we do find, brilliantly formulated, the questions that cry aloud for answers.

## Notes

1. As cited in J. E. Neale, *Elizabeth I and Her Parliaments, 1559-1581* (London, 1953), pp. 318-19.

2. *The Rubaiyat of Omar Khayyam,* trans. Edward Fitzgerald, 4th ed., Stanza 99.

3. R. W. Chambers, *Thomas More* (London, 1935); J. H. Hexter, *More's Utopia: the Biography of an Idea* (Princeton and London, 1952). See also Professor Hexter's valuable introduction to *The Complete Works of Thomas More,* vol. 4, ed. E. Surtz and J. H. Hexter, Yale ed. (New Haven and London, 1965).

4. T. More, *Utopia,* ed. J. R. Lumby (Cambridge, 1885), p. 160. I am not quoting from the best modern translation, which is by G. C. Richards (Oxford, 1923), and which is the basis for the Yale edition, but from the translation made by Ralph Robinson in 1551, which would have been the one familiar to Shakespeare's contemporaries.

5. Ibid, p. 162.

6. As cited in W. R. D. Jones, *The Tudor Commonwealth, 1529-1559* (London, 1970), p. 14. For a full discussion of Elyot's work and the relations between More and Elyot, see S. E. Lehmberg, *Sir Thomas Elyot, Tudor Humanist* (Austin, Tex., 1960); J. M. Major, *Sir Thomas Elyot and Renaissance Humanism* (Lincoln, Neb., 1964); P. Hogrefe, *The Life and Times of Sir Thomas Elyot, Englishman* (Ames, Iowa, 1967).

7. Sir Thomas Smith, *De Republica Anglorum* (London, 1583), p. 118.

8. Norman Cohn, *The Pursuit of the Millennium,* rev. ed. (London, 1970).

9. *Calendar of Patent Rolls,* Eliz. I, vol. 5, 1569-72 (1966), p. 210.

10. G. Williams, "Glamorgan Society, 1536-1642," in *Glamorgan County History,* vol. 4, Early Modern Glamorgan (Cardiff, 1974), p. 88.

11. *The Book of Sir Thomas More,* ed. W. W. Greg, The Malone Society (London, 1911), p. 76.

12. Simonds D'Ewes, *Journal of the House of Commons* (London, 1693), p. 509a.

13. G. Wilson Knight, *The Wheel of Fire* (London, 1949), p. xv.

14. Sir Thomas Smith, *De Republica Anglorum, p. 118.*

15. *William Lambarde and Local Government,* ed. C. Read, Folger Shakespeare Library (Ithaca, N. Y., 1962), p. 95.

16. Cited in Neale, *Elizabeth I and her Parliaments,* p. 186.

17. L. Pearsall Smith, *The Life and Letters of Sir Henry Wotton* (Oxford, 1907), 1: 142.

# Will and Testament

## by ANTHONY BURGESS

When Ben Jonson was let out of jail he went straight to William Shakespeare's lodgings in Silver Street and said:

"Let us drink."

"Ben," Will cried. "Your ears are untrimmed and your nose whole. The shearers were held off, then, I'm glad to see you well."

"But thirsty. Let us go and drink."

"We can drink here and shall. Malmsey? Sherrisack? Or shall I send out for ale? Ben, Ben, have a care. Next time the shearer may be the ultimate trimmer, the sconce-chopper as they call him."

"I've a mind to drink in a tavern. Let us go."

"As you will, this being a sort of great day for you. How was it in jail? Are Marston and Chapman there yet?"

"There still and like to stay. After all, the offending line was of their making. As for the jail—stink, maggots, rats, lepers, pocky chankers. But there was a man I will tell you of while we drink."

"You swore to me the line was your line, the best line in the whole of *Westward Ho* as you would have it. How does it go now? 'The Scotch— 'It begins with 'The Scotch—' "

"*Eastward Ho* is the title. You look as ever the wrong way. Back when the rest of us look forward. It is this: 'The Scotch are good friends to England, but only when they are out of it.' Well, indeed I wrote it, but it seemed politic to father it on the other two. Under oath, aye, but a poet could not live did he not perjure." They went down the stairs and past the workshop of the tiremaker Mountjoy, Will's landlord. Mountjoy was scolding, in Frenchified English, the apprentice Belott.

"Immortal," Will said. "He can never say I did not make him immortal. But no gratitude there."

"How immortal?"

"I have him in *Harry Five* as the herald."

"He taught you the dirty French for the same?"

"He put right the grammar. I knew the dirt already." Out in Silver Street, which the sun had promoted to gold, they saw beggars, legless soldiers, drunken sailors, whores, dead cats, ordinary decent citizens in stuff-gowns, a kilted Highlander with a flask of usquebaugh in place of a sporran. A ballad-singer with few teeth sang:

> For bonny sweet Robin was all my joy,
>     And Robin came oft to my bed.
> But Robin did wrong, so to end his song
>     The headsman did chop off his head.

"An old one," Ben said. "And still I cannot hear it without a shudder."

"It seems older than it is. Four years. A great deal has happened in four years. Poor Robin."

"That was your name for him? You called him Robin to his face?"

"He was Robin to my lord of Southampton, and my lord of Southampton was Harry to me. So it was always out-on-titles. But, he was ever saying, when he was become King Robert the First of England there would be no familiarity then. Would it had been so, so sometimes I think, though bloodless, bloodless."

"Treason, man, careful."

"What will you do, report me to Gobbo Cecil? 'An't please you, good my lord, there is this low playmaker that doth say how that the Essex rebellion should have succeeded.' He'll say, 'Aye aye, and maybe he's in the right of it.' He's no love for slobbering Jamie with his bishops and buggery and smoking is an unco foul sin to the body, laddie, and doth inflame the lung; if thou lovest tobacco then lovest thou not thy king."

Ben sighed. "I know how it is. I say too many Scotchmen about and I go to jail. You could tell the king to his face that he's a — I say no more, you see that sour man in black there? Following us, is he? Nay, he turned off. You could skite in his majesty's mouth and he'd say, 'Aye, I do dearly love a guid witty jest, laddie, will ye be made a Knicht of the Garrrterrr?' Some men are born jailmeat. Others — Here, round here. At the bottom of this lane. Go tipatoe, 'tis all slime underfoot. Careful, careful."

"The Swan with Two Nicks." Will read the warped sign with a great nose-wrinkle. "This is not a tavern I mind to have ever visited before."

"It is quiet," Ben said, leading the way into noise, stench, striding over a vomit-pool, between knots of swarthy men with daggers. "We can talk quietly." They sat on a settle before a rickety much-punished table whereon flies fed amply from greasy orts and a sauce-smear unwiped. A girl with warty bosom well on show showed black teeth and took an order for wine. "Red wine," Ben said. "Of your best. Blood-red, red as the blood of our blessed

Saviour." Some villains turned to look with surly interest. A man with an eye-patch nodded as in friendly threat at Ben. *"Buenos dias, señor,"* Ben said.

"For God's sake, Ben, what manner of place is this?"

"A good place, though something filthy. Good fellows all, though but rogues to look on. Now let me speak. A great change is come into my life."

The wine arrived. Will poured. "Change? You have fallen in love with some pocked tib of the Clink and think her to be a disguised angel?"

"Ah, no. Ah, good wine, red, red as the blood that is decanted daily on the blessed holy altars of the one true faith."

"For Christ's sake, Ben."

"Aye, for Christ's sake, you say truly. What I do I do for Christ's dear sake. Let me tell you, my dear friend. In this noisome stinking rathole behold the word of the Lord came to me."

"Oh Jesus the word of the—"

"Aye, a good old priest of the true faith, aye, though earning his bread as a dancing-master, thrown into jail for debt, aye, spoke to me loving words and told where the truth lies. It was by way of being in the manner somewhat of a revelation." Ben drank fiercely and then said: "Good wine. *Enim calix sanguinis.* Drink a salute to my holy happiness."

"Keep your voice well down," Will said, his voice well down. "See how they all listen."

"They may listen and be glad. I have friends, have I not? Have I not friends here?" he called to the drinkers. *"Amigos?"* There was no response save for a man hawking, though all looked still.

"I am getting out of here," Will said.

"Aye, ever the prudent. Well, there is another word for prudence, and you know it well. A plague on all cowards. Why should I not speak aloud my joy in being restored to the one true holy bosom? Is not the Queen's self of the blessed company? I tell you, the day is at hand when we may take to the holy body in sunlight before the eyes of all men, not skulking in a dark hold. Hallelujah."

"You know the danger, fool," Will said, sweating. "There was an expectation of tolerance, but it is not fulfilled. The bishops will see it is not. Let us be out of here."

"With this blessed red wine unfinished? With this blood of the grape crimson as the blood of."

"I am going." Will drained the sour stuff and turned down his cup with a clank.

"Well, well, very well. I have told my story. Now, thanks be to God, my true story doth begin." Ben drank from the jug, beastlily, emerging spluttering. He wiped his mouth with the dirty back of his hand and nodded in a friendly manner at the company. "Give you good day, all. And God's blessing be ever on your comings and goings and eke your staying still."

"Come, idiot."

They left. Ben said, "Aye, aye, we will see how the spirit works. Is anyone following?"

"None. None yet. Do you wish someone to follow?"

"I say no more of it now, my conversion. Except that you may speak of it to your friends and colleagues and all you will. I care not. I dare all for the lord Jesus. I owe him a death."

"That is mine. I wrote that."

"You did? It is all one. There is a tale they tell of you, do you know that?"

"What tale? Where?"

"Marston told me. It is of Master Shakespeare going to heaven's gate and demanding admittance. St. Peter says we have too many landlords here, we need poets to sweeten long eternity. 'Well,' says Master Shakespeare, 'I am well known to be a poet.' 'Prove it,' says St. Peter. 'I am of poor memory,' says Master S, 'and can remember no line I wrote.' 'Well then,' says heaven's warder, 'extemporize somewhat.' At that moment little bowlegged Tom Kyd goes by, a poetic martyr, with his fingers all broke by the late Queen's Commissioners. 'A bow-legged man,' says the saint. 'Extemporize on him.' Whereupon, fire-quick, Master S comes out with:

> How now, what manner of man is this
> That carries his ballocks in parenthesis?

Whereupon St. Peter sighs and says we have no room for landlords."

"Not funny," Will said. And then: "So they talk of me as already dead, do they?"

"Not dead. Shall we say retired? Your sun sets. Westward Ho is your cry." Ben looked behind him to see two daggered ruffians following. He said in some small excitement: "Leave me here. Take your leave, aye. I think there are two coming who will show me where I may hear mass Sundays and saint-days. The blessing of Mother Church on you, Will."

"No, no, I want no such blessing."

It was some week or so later that Ben Jonson sat at dinner with new friends. There was Bob Catesby at the head of the table, very fierce and sober, and a swarthy one that had been in that low tavern that time they called Guy—though his true name was Guido—somewhat drunk on Spanish wine, and there were Rob Winter, little big-eyed Bates, Kit Wright, Tom Winter—brother of Rob—and also Frank Tresham, who kept wetting a dry lip and looking shifty. Catesby said to Ben:

"You are wide open, Master Jonson. Your days are numbered."

"By whom?" Ben said. "If you mean that I talk of the brotherhood, by God you are mistaken."

"You have not done that, no, you have been prudent enough there. If you had not been so, Guy here—a soldier, remember, who will cut off ten heads before breakfast—Guy, I say, would have had you, by God. No, I mean imprudent in that you talk too much of the Godless King and the runagate Queen, who will show her bosom and legs to all and go to mass hiccuping with the drink. I mean treason. I believe you are destined for a martyr's crown."

"No," Ben said. "I want not that. I will not force heaven's opening to me. Heaven may open in its own good time with none of my prompting. There is wine for the drinking yet and wenches for the fondling. No, no martyrdom."

"Speak out the scheme, Rob," Catesby said to Tom Winter's brother. "You are the one that must hold it in his memory. You are our living parchment."

"Well, then," Rob Winter said, looking at Ben, "it is this. It is to do with the new session of the parliament. All will be there—King, Queen, Prince Henry, bishops, nobles, judges, knights, esquires and all, all for the forming of new acts and laws to put down the true faith. They will be blown up."

"They will be—?" Ben asked carefully.

"Blown up. We are to place twenty barrels of gunpowder in the cellar beneath with faggots on top. Set but light to the faggots and there will be a greater blowing up than has ever been seen before in the long story of human oppression."

"Blown up," Catesby said after a pause, as to make sure Ben properly understood.

"The Queen," said Ben, "is of the true faith. Is it right she too should be blown up?"

"You are always ready to talk of her Godlessness," Catesby said. "Well, she will be punished. Alternatively, she will be a martyr. Destiny puts forth a choice."

"However you gloss it," Ben said, "she will be blown up."

"Everybody will be blown up," Tom Winter said, pausing in the picking of his teeth. "Everybody."

"And then there will be a new era of love for the true faith?" Ben asked.

"We will think of that after the blowing up," said Catesby. "Certainly there will be a many problems, but sufficient to the day as the Gospel saith. First the blowing up."

"And the choice of the one to whom shall be given the glory of setting flame to the faggots for the blowing up," Kit Wright said. They all now looked at Ben.

"He too will be blown up?" Ben asked.

"There is every likelihood that he will be blown up," Catesby said. "But he will at once be endued with a crown of martyrdom. You, Master Jonson, are wide open." They all continued to look at Ben. Ben said:

"How first are you to convey the barrels to the cellar?"

"It is a wine cellar," Rob Winter said. "The barrels will be brought on a vintner's dray. 'What have you there,' the guards will ask. 'Wine,' will come the answer. 'Wine, as ordered.' It is all very simple."

"And the faggots?"

"The faggots will be in another barrel, dry and ready for the laying on. And he that is to do the brave deed will go as a guard in a borrowed livery. Carrying a torch."

"In broad daylight?" Ben asked.

"He will say he has orders to search the cellar for possible treasonable men lurking. It is all very simple."

Francis Tresham now spoke. "I am against it," he said. "It is a plot of some cruelty. Also of some injustice. The Queen, true, is a foreigner and does not matter. But there are enow Catholics in hiding among those of the parliament. We are blowing up our own."

"Martyrs' crowns," Ben said. "Think not of it."

"You will do the deed?" Catesby said, leaning closer to Ben and, indeed discharging a hogo of garlic on him.

"I will think on it," Ben said. "Your reasons are of a fairly persuasive order. I will go home now and start to think on it."

"Guy here will go home with you," Catesby said, "and help you think on it."

"No, he will not," Ben said. "I want none breathing on me while I think. I go into this freely. I cannot be made to do it."

"That is true," Catesby said. "Except by the promptings of your own destiny, Master Jonson. I see the martyr's crown hovering above you." He looked somewhat fiercely at Tresham. "Frank," he said, "you waver. It is strange you waver when you were fiercest once in saying perdition to the betrayer of the faith of his own mother. There are measures may be taken to discourage waverers." He looked at dark Guido then back at Tresham.

"I am no waverer. I ask only that we right our souls on this matter of the killing of Catholics along with Protestants. It is a matter of theology."

"Theology," little Bates now said. "There is enow of theology at the Godless court, holy Jamie and his atheistical bishops. Out on theology. Let us have the true faith back and God's enemies blown up. I drink to you," he said, "Master Jonson," and drank.

"I too drink to me," Ben said, and drank. He wiped his loose lips and wrung his beard and said, looking at the company severally, "Now I go home. To pray. For guidance and blessing."

"Guido will go with you for guidance through the perilous streets," Catesby said.

"I go alone. I am in no peril."

Ben, with Guido Fawkes at his side, was some way advanced through the warren of stinks and drunkenness and stinking drunken bravoes that led to his lodgings when Fawkes said:

"Spy."

"I cry your mercy, what was that?"

"Spy, I said. I think you to be a manner of spy."

Ben ceased walking or rolling and looked at him under the moon. "You are drunk, man. You know not what you say."

"Spy. I asked myself long who it was you put me in mind of, and he too was a poet and a spy. He cried his sodomitical atheism to the streets, and none did him harm. I conclude he was under protection. His name was Kit Marlowe."

"Marlowe." Ben said soberly. "He was all our fathers, though he died young, God help him. You flatter me more than you can know. But I am no spy." And then with incredulous relief he heard drunken singing:

> Sit we amid the ewes and tegs
> Where pastors custodise their gregs
> And cantant avians do vie
> With fluminous sonority.

"O Jesus," Ben prayed. "Jack Marston."

It was Marston, true, drunk, true, but able to see, mainly from the bulk, who stood in his path. "Jonson, cheat, rogue, liar, ingrate, thief too. Graaaargh." The sound was of blood rising in his throat.

"You speak too plain to be true Marston. Where be your inkhorn nonsensicalities? Thief, you say. No man says thief to Jonson. Any more," he added to Fawkes, "then he says spy."

"Thief I say again. You said that you would pay me when Henslowe paid you, that Henslowe had not paid you, therefore you could not pay me. But Henslowe has paid you, has, thief. I was with him this night, I saw his account book. Draw, thief." He himself drew, though staggering.

"If it is but six shilling and threepence you want, let us have no talk of drawing. Come to my lodgings and you shall have a little on account. I will not have that *thief*, Jack. I am a man of probity and of religion."

"Of that we hear too," Marston cried. "The lactifluous nipples of the Christine genetrix and the viniform sanguinosity of the eucharistic abomination. Draw."

"Very well." Ben sighed and unsheathed his short dagger. "I have killed, Jack," he said, "and my adversary was sober. I killed Gab Spencer, remember, and he too said *thief*." Ben now saw the reflection of flames in a bottle-window. Torches coming round the corner. Four men with swords and cudgels, the watch. With relief he lunged toward Marston. Lunging, he saw Fawkes flee. Wanted no trouble, right too, right for his filthy cause. Marston lunged and fell. Ben sheathed his dagger and leapt on Marston's back, took his ears like ewer-handles and began to crack his nose into the dirt. Then the watch was on him.

It was four in the morning when Will received the message to go to the Marshalsea. A boy hammered at the door below and Will went to his window,

Mountjoy in his nightshirt also appearing, a minute later, at his.

"Master Shakespaw?"

"Shakespeare, boy. What?"

"Master Jonson in the jail and wants you there, now, this minute."

"He wants money?"

"I think not so. He gave me money, a whole groat and a penny."

"Go away, boy," Mountjoy cried harshly, "disturbing the neighborhood so. We want no talk of prisons in this quarter. This is a respectable quarter."

"I'll come," Will sighed. "I'll come now."

Few were sleeping in the Marshalsea. There was a kind of growling merriness, with drink, cursing, fumbling at plackets, a richer though darker version of the day-world of the free. There was even a man selling hot possets. Will listened, sipping. "The names," Ben said, "take down the names."

"I can remember the names."

"You cannot. You are poor at remembering. You cannot remember your own lines. Take your tablet, take down the names. And then to Cecil."

"Now?"

"Now, yes. Easy enough for you. You're a groom of the bedchamber, a sort of royal officer."

"This is no jape?"

"This is by no manner of means a jape, God help us. Go. I am, thank God, safe enough here. Cecil will understand all that, why I wish to be shut away. I am safe enough here till he has them."

"I will write them down, then."

"Do, quick. Then go."

"So," Will said. "Kit is really your master. Though look where his spying got him. A reckoning in a little room. Keep off it, Ben. Playwork is duller and pays less well. But it is safer."

"Go now. He will be up now. He does a day's work before breakfast."

Will sat, in groom's livery, too long in the anteroom. He had spoken of his business to secretaries of progressively ascending status, and none would come alive to the urgency of it. One had even said: "If you would speak of plots for new plays, then you must go to the Lord Chamberlain. Here there is grave work to be done."

"You will do none today of greater gravity than scotching this that I tell of." Weary, three hours gone by, Will took to sketching of a drinking song he had been asked for by Beaumont, something for a comedy to be called *Have At You Now Pretty Rogue:*

> Red wine it is the soldier's blood
> And if it but be old and good
> So take a rouse
> And let's carouse
> And

Strange, he had been infected by Ben's feigned unreformed eucharisticism. No, it was the other way about. Blood turned to wine, not wine to. His head was spinning with lack of sleep, he needed much sleep these days, past his best, looking westward. He began to calculate his fortune in real estate, but that led him to things needed to be done in Stratford. The load of stone still encumbering the grounds of New Place and neither paid for yet by the Council nor taken away. His brother Gilbert had written of some odd useful acres he might — He was shaken to here and now by the top secretary, who said:

"You are to come in now. And quickly. My lord speaks of urgency."

"He was not very urgent in speaking of it."

"Come your ways."

Robert Cecil, Earl of Salisbury, big-headed and dwarf-bodied, stood with his hunchback to the great fire. Papers, papers everywhere. He said,

"I am glad to be acquainted with the man. The plays I know. What is this story?"

Will told him. "And Master Jonson fears for his life now. He deserves, if I may say this, my lord, very well of you."

Cecil picked up a letter from his desk. "This has but now come to me. You know of a certain Francis Tresham Esquire?"

"His name is, I think, on the list I gave."

"He has a brother-in-law, Lord Monteagle. Lord Monteagle has sent me a letter from this Tresham, and it says nought but this: 'They shall receive a terrible blow this parliament, and yet they shall not see who hurts them. The danger is past as soon as you have burned this letter.' As you see, it was not burned, nor will it be. I am conveying it at once to His Majesty. So what you bring from Master Jonson conjoined with this does but confirm what the King will say he knew all along, that he hath enemies." Cecil smiled very thinly. "Moreover, it would seem that his dreams are often charged with what may be termed a *memoria familialis*. Blowing up comes much into them, Master Shakespeare. His father, the Lord Darnley, was, as you well know, blown sky-high at Kirk-of-Fields in Scotland, while his royal mother was dancing at some rout or other. So, I thank you for this loyal work —"

"It was nothing, my lord."

" — And will have Master Jonson out of the jail where he languisheth as soon as the conspirators be apprehended." Cecil gave his hand, very crusty with rings, to Will. Will was not sure whether he was meant to kiss it. But he shook it sturdily and left.


When Ben Jonson was let out of jail he went straight to William Shakespeare's lodgings in Silver Street and said:

"Let us drink."

"Ben," Will said, "if you mean we are to go to this low papist tavern full of vomit—"

"Nay, show sense, man, that was but show. That was part of the part I played and played well. I am as good a son of the English Church as any that was fried under Bloody Mary and will prove it Sunday by drinking the chalice off before all the world. I say let us drink. I say also let us eat, it being near noon. I have gold, King's gold." He made dangle the little purse at his waist or no-waist. Clink clank. "We will eat fish pie and flawns at the Mermaid."

Ben told it all over the fishbones and pasty fragments. "Of course," he said, "the King will have it that he foreknew all. Let them, he says, get in theirrr godless butts of gunpowderrr and I myself laddies will marrrch thither with guard and witness to prove it was no tale. So he did, and so he says that he has single-handed saved the realm. Will you come with me to the hanging?"

"I will not," said Will.

"Squeamish as ever. Twelve men swinging aloft in the sun and enow guts and blood and hearts ripped out to feed the King's kennels a whole day. There is a little book to come," he coughed modestly.

"I thought you were waiting to print all your plays, such as they be, in one great work called Ben Jonson's *Works,* mad notion. Or is it epigrams and corky expatiations all in Greco-Latin?"

"I will let pass your pleasantries. This little book will have no name beneath the title, though all shall know from the mastery whose it is. The title is to be *A Discourse of the Manner of the Discovery of the Late Intended Treason.*"

"That is too long."

"Have a care, man. It is the King's own title. And it is to be spread abroad that the King's self had the writing of it but was too royally modest to set his name thereto. It is a terrible false world."

Will now quoted from something he was writing. " 'We have seen the best of our time. Machinations, hollowness, treachery, and all ruinous disorders follow us disquietly to our graves.' "

"You sound as though you quote from some new kennel of misery you are hammering together unhandily."

"A tragedy, aye. About a king that insists on divine right and kneekilling deference and fulsome flattery and will not have the plain truth. He is cast out into the cold and goes mad and dies."

"Have a care, Will, a care."

"It is for the court."

"O Jesus, O blood of Christ not really present on the altar. You will be hanged like any Guy Fawkes."

"I care not. We have seen the best of our time."

When Christmas came to court, Lear, done by Burbage, ranted and tore his beard, and Queen Anne slept or woke and pouted at what seemed most unseasonable for Yule, a time of drunken showing of one's legs in some pretty wanton masque, while James drank steadily and chewed kickshawses offered by a lord on his bended knee. After the play he ranted. The Grooms of the Royal Bedchamber were there, in livery after their acting, yawning, Will among them hound-weary, half-listening.

"There ye see, my lorrrds and ladies and guid laddies a', what befalleth a king that trusts too much in human naturrre. It is the trrragedy of ane that insisteth not enough on his divine rrricht. He lets gang the rrule o's realm tae ithers. Weel, thank God, though I hae drunken sons I hae nae ambitious dochters. Aye aye aye." Then he suddenly shouted: "Kingship, kingship, kingship," so that many of the drowsy started full awake. "I was but rrreading in the Geneva Bible this day, aye, and find there mickle to offend, aye. Much flouting I find of the divinity of kingship in the saucy margins thereof. Aye, I was in the rrricht of it, the divine richt I may say, to hae thrown oot of the realm a buik nae matter how holy that hath been defiled by the pens of Godless republicans, aye. It is very partial in its notes and glosses, very untrue, seditious, and savoring too much of dangerous and traitorous conceits. When, my lorrrd arrrchbiship, shall we see our ither, our new, our Godly?"

"They are hard at work, your grace," said the Archbishop of Canterbury, huge archepiscopal rings of weariness under his eyes. "All fifty-four translators, all six companies. Andrewes and Harding and Lively report well of the progress of the holy work and say but four years more will see it sail safely into port."

"So Harrrding looks lively and Lively labourrrs harrrd, eh eh?" There was loud and immediate laughter that went on long while the King beamed round and said: "Aye aye aye." Will could see he was looking in vain for a pun that should bring Lancelot Andrewes, head of the Westminster translating groups, into his fancy. Without thinking Will came out, in a firm actor's voice, all too audible, with:

> Each Bible scholar, so the ungodly say,
> Works lively hard Englishing for no pay
> The royal Bible, aye, and rewes the day
> When such an unholy labor came his way.

There was a terrible silence into which the King waded rather than leapt. He said:

"And wha micht ye be, laddie? Wait noo, I ken, I ken, ye are he that writ the play of this nicht, are ye not?"

"Aye, William Shakespearrre, your majesty," Will said, hearing with horror an effortless parody of the royal accent.

"Ye maun write it doon, yon saucy blasphemous irreverrrent and impairrr-tinent lump o' clarty doggerel, aye, that all may see, laddie."

"I have forgot it already, your royal majesty."

"Aye." It was clear than James did not know well what to do. Will had often met this situation when pert to the great. He now willed the King out of the problem. *Be sick, great greatness.* "Aye, ye and your saucy rhymes." He looked green and began to heave. It was, indeed, the usual end of a court soirée—the King's vomiting. Some writer of music for the virginals, Tomkins or somebody, had spoken of producing a tiny suite consisting of the King's Carousing, the King's Vomiting, the King's Rest. "I maun gang," the King said, very green. "I mind ye, laddie, I'll mind your sauciness." Then, on the arms of two simpering earls, he was led away to the Harington water closet.

"By Christ," Burbage said, "you get away with murder."

"What Ben Jonson says," Will said evenly. "Thank God the revels are ended."

When Ben Jonson was let out of jail he went straight to William Shakespeare's lodgings in Silver Street and said:

"Let us drink."

"Ben," Will cried. "Your ears are untrimmed and your nose whole. I'm glad to see you well."

"But thirsty."

"Drink water then. It seems to me that less and less of wine makes in you more and more oppugnancy. If this watch-beating continues it will be a matter of one day's holiday between longer and longer lingerings in the Clink."

"The Marshalsea. Listen, it was a strange time. I worked on the Bible."

"What?" They went down the stairs, past Mountjoy scolding his daughter Marie about loving the apprentice Belott, into the street, demoted to lead by the dull day. There were more drunk about than usual, because belike of the dull day. "The Bible has already been worked on, nay worked out. They are at the great final stage of the galleys. And it is Harding and Lively and Andrewes, not you, that had the making of it. You are a man of some reasonable small talent, Ben, but you are no man of God. It is work for men of God that gratuitously or necessarily know Greek and Hebrew and Latin."

"I know those tongues," Ben said. "I can Hebrew you as well as any atheistical rabbi. It is, indeed, the work that comes before the final launching that has made lively my days in the stinking rathole of the Marshalsea. For, since I am a poet, they brought to me the poesy of the Bible. Meaning Job and the Psalms and the like. 'You are a poet,' they said. 'Tickle our sober accuracy into poetic life.' So I dip quill in horn and correct the galleys to a diviner beauty."

"Who brought the galleys and said all this to you?" Will said with some jealousy.

"Some man of the Westminster company—Bodkin or Pipkin or some such name. No whit abashed at the prospect of seeing God's work buffed and polished in a foul and pestilential prison. The apostles, he said, were in prison before being variously crucified."

"That will not be your fate. Whatever your fate is, it will not be that. That is the fate of the godly." And then, before they entered the Dog Tavern, "Is it you only of all our secular poets that are asked to trim the sails of the galleys?"

"Oh, there is Chapman, also Jack Donne—not properly secular, there is talk of his taking holy orders this year. Marston's name was mentioned but I was quick there. If, I said, you want a Bible that beginneth with *In the initialities of the mondial entities the Omnicompetent fabricated the celestial and terrene quiddities,* then have Jack Marston by all means. There were others mentioned, smaller men."

"Was I," Will asked, "mentioned?"

They sat down not far from Beaumont and Fletcher with their one doxy who, being born under the signs of Libra, was fain to bestow kisses and clips equally on both. When the Canary came, Ben was able to have his laugh out.

"Why do you laugh? What is there risible in me or others or elsewhere?"

"There were special orders that you should not be brought in. No Latin nor Greek nor Hebrew—that was brushed aside as of small moment. But the King himself had said he would not hae that quick laddie that was so pert with his impertinencies."

"How do you know this?"

"There is some silly rhyme fathered on you about the King sticking his lively hard andrew up the translators to make them come quicker and threatening to cut off their old and new testicles if they did not. It could not be you, it is too corky and bad even for you. But I will be kind. You shall not be in the cold and dark like the foolish virgins. I, Ben-oni, the Benjamin that Jacobus loveth, though he cannot keep me out of jail, I am ready to deliver sundry psalms into your palms."

"Is there money in it?"

"Honor, glory, perhaps an eternal crown."

"I am done with all writing," Will said, "even for money. I grow old. I am forty-six years this year. I will return to Stratford and hunt hares and foxes."

"You would rather be hunted with them. And you have said this too often before of being done with writing. You will go and stay a week and then be back here thirsting to scribble some new nonsense. I know you."

"You *poets,*" Will said, "may keep your Bible. You may stuff your old and new testes up your apocrypha."

"There speaketh sour envy. Well, we will keep it and be glad. For the day may come, some thousand years hence, when even the Works of Ben Jonson will be read little, but the bright eyes of Ben Jonson will flash out here and there in a breathtaking felicity of phrase in God's own book that may never die."

"You may stick your holofernes up your methuselah."

"Master Shakespeare," said Jack Fletcher timidly, "there is a matter we would talk of, to wit a collaboration betwixt you and us here."

"She has enough to do fumbling two let alone three."

"I mean with Frank and myself. A comedy called *Out On You Mistress Minx* which must be ready for rehearsing some two days from now and not yet started though the money taken. You are quick, sir, as is known. A night of work with Frank and me as amanuenses and it can be done."

"I have done with writing," said Will proudly. "I go to tend my country estates. All you *poets* may stick your zimris up your cozbis."

"Nay, Jack and I," said Beaumont, "were bidden work on the Song of Songs that is Solomon's. Kitty here, to be true, gave us a good phrase: love, she said, is better than wine. Is not that a good phrase?"

"She carries two fairsized flagons on her, I see. If by love she means comfort more than intoxication, then she is not right."

"*Comfort me with flagons,*" Beaumont said to Fletcher. "*Flagons* is better than *apples*. Make a note."

"You may all," Will said, getting up, "comfort your deuteronomies with your right index leviticus. I go now."

"It is jealousy," Ben Jonson said when he was gone. "He has no part in the holy work."


Will rode to Stratford nevertheless with three or four psalms in galley proof rolled into his saddlebag, a gift from Ben Jonson. He was to see what he could do with them; to Ben they seemed not to offer matter for further poeticization. But for Will there would be much nonwriting work in Stratford, save for the engrossing of signatures. The hundred and twenty acres bought from the Coombes, which brother Gilbert was managing ill: these must be worked well. Gardeners needed for gardens and orchards. The tithes in Old Stratford and Welcombe and Bishopston. He, Will, was now a lay rector, a front-pew gentleman. Thomas Greene, the town clerk, together with his bitch of a wife and two beefy squallers, should be out of New Place by now, the lease up on Lady Day 1610, this year. Forty-six years of age. Four and six make ten. One of the psalms in his saddlebag was number forty-six.

New Place, when he got there, was bright as a rubbed angel, Anne his wife and Judith his daughter yet unmarried having nought much to do save buff and sweep and pick up hairs from the floor. The mulberry tree was doing well. Anne was fifty-four now and looked it. Ben was right: his home was a place for dreaming of going back to; he would be in London before the month was over, nothing more certain. On his second day home a flock of black-suited Puritans infested his living-room. Anne gave them ale and seedcake. They had a session of discussing a knotty dull point of Scripture, something to do with Elijah or some other hairy unwiped prophet. When they came out of the living-room to find Will poking for woodworm at a timber in the hall, they sourly nodded at him as if to begrudge his being in his own house. The following day they came again for a prayer-meeting. He spoke mildly enough to Anne about his Brownist, or black, intrusion.

"While I am here," he said, "I will not have it. Tell them that, tell them I will not have it."

"They are godly," she said, "and are a blessing on the house."

"I can do without their blessing. Besides, their aliger faces show no warmth of blessing."

"They know what you are."

"I am a gentleman with an escutcheon. I am, moreover, one of the King's servants. I am, if you will, a player and a playmaker, but that was but the step to being gentleman. Will they begrudge me my ambition?"

"Plays are ungodly, they say. They will have no plays in this town. Nor will it be of use to flaunt your king's livery in their faces. They know that kings are mortal men and subject to the will of the Lord."

"Genevan saints, are they? Holy republicans? What did they say of Gunpowder Plot?"

"They said that it showed at least a king might be punished for his sins by an action of the people, though to put down the Scarlet Woman of Rome is no sin and the voice of papists is no part of the voice of the people."

"God help us, Christ give us all patience."

"You blaspheme, you see, you are in need of the power of prayer."

"I am in need of nothing, woman, save a quiet life after a feverish one. I would have some seedcake with my ale."

"There is none left and there has been no time for baking."

"If you must give up your hussif's duties in the name of dubious godliness, at least there is an idle daughter who could set to and bake."

"Judith has a green melancholy on her. It is a sad life for the girl. None asks for her hand."

"Ah, they cannot stomach to have a player as a father-in-law. Well, at least Jack Hall takes me as I am. Jack is a poor physician but a good son-in-law and husband and father. Susannah, thank God, has done well."

Susannah came next afternoon, with her husband Dr. Hall and little two-year-old Elizabeth. Will played happily with the child and sang, in a cracked baritone, *Where the bee sucks*. Anne said:

"Is that from a play?"

"Not yet. The play that it is to be in is not yet writ, but it will be, fear not."

"I fear not anything," Anne said, "save the Lord's displeasure." She called to Judith to bring in ale and seedcake. Seeing married Susannah and the child now drowsy on her lap, Judith let out a howl of frustration and left. Anne said:

"It is the father's office to seek a husband for a daughter. Judith is ripe and over-ripe."

"So ripeness is not all," sighed Will. "I will go seeking in the taverns and hedgerows, crying *Who will wed a player's daughter?*" He turned to Jack, whose lips were pursed, and said, "Will you come stroll a little in the garden?"

Jack said, after a strolling silence, "Your book has been read here, you may know that."

"What book?"

"The book that is called *Sonnets.*"

"But God, man, that is old stuff, it came out all of a year ago, and I have disclaimed the book, I did not publish it. What do they say that read it, not that I care, does it confirm them in their conviction of Black Will Shakespeare's damnation?"

"It is a book of things that a man might do in London," Jack Hall said gloomily. "It is a pity that Dick Field brought a copy home."

"Ah, poor corrupted Stratford. So you too join the head-waggers?"

"There is such a thing as propriety. Dick Field has been long a London man like yourself, father-in-law, but he has ever shown propriety. If you will forgive the observation of one who is, besides your son-in-law, a professional man and your physical adviser."

"Dick Field is a printer, a man tied to a cold craft, not one like me who has had to make himself a motley to the view and unload his soul to the world." Then he said: "What has being my physical adviser to do with the *Sonnets*?"

"I have wondered somewhat about your cough, your premature baldness. Now I read records of licentiousness in that book."

"You mean," groaned Will, then gasped, then growled, then cried aloud, "I have the French pox, the disease of that pretty shepherd Syphilis of Fracastorious of Verona his poem? Oh, this drinks deep, this drinks the cup and all. And what thinks Anne?"

"Mother-in-law? She knows nought of it. The book has been kept from her and from her friends the brethen. The bridge of the nose," said Dr. Hall, looking, "seems soft in the cartilege. That is an infallible sign. Do keep your voice low. It will crack if you shout out so and not easily be mended."

Will howled like a hound and strode into the house to his study, passing his womenfolk on the way. He growled at them, even at gooing little Elizabeth. In his study he took from a drawer the galleys of the psalms Ben had given him. He took them, weaving in the draught of his passage, to shake like banners at his family, crying: "These, you see these? The King's new Bible that is not to appear till next year, given to me in part, along with my brethren the other poets of London, that the language be strengthened and enriched. You think me Godless and a libertine but it is to me, me, me, not the black crows of Puritans that infest this house and shall not infest it more, that the task of improving the word of the Lord is given. You see," he said to Anne, "you see, see?"

"A new Bible," she said. "It is all too like what one may expect of unreligious London, where the Geneva Bible is not good enough for them. That it is the King's Bible renders it no whit more holy. Nay, less, from what we hear. Even kings should be subject to the law."

"The King," cried Will, "is my master and bathed in the chrism of the Lord God. Generous and good and holy." Then he stopped, seeing he had gone too far. "The King has his faults," he now said. Yes, indeed; ingratitude to Ben and himself; pederasty; immoderate appetite; cowardice; but half the man the old Queen had been. "But still," he said, and then: "All men have their faults, myself included. But I deserve better of the world and of this little world, and, by God, I will have my eternal reward."

"That," said Anne, "is the sin of presumption." John Hall was now back with them, listening to his father-in-law rave, grow quiet, rave again: infallible symptoms.

"My name, I mean, my name. My son, poor little Hamnet, dead. And the name Shakespeare dishonored in its town and soon to die out along with the poor parchments that put words in actors' mouths." John Hall shook his head slightly: self-pity too perhaps a symptom. "Wait," cried Will. "Do not leave. I, your king, lord of this little commonweal, do order you to wait. Wait." And he sailed back to the study, galley-pennants flying, and took the forty-sixth psalm out of the bundle. He sat to it, calling "Wait wait" as he dipped quill in ink and counted. Forty-six words from the beginning, then. It would do, the change improved, not marred. He crossed out the noun and put another large in the margin. He then, ignoring the cry or cadence *Selah* at the bottom, counted forty-six words from the end, felt awe at the miracle that this forty-sixth word too could be changed for the better, or certainly not for the worse, by the neat deletion mark and the new word writ clear and large in the margin. "Wait," he cried. Then he was there to show them.

Anne's jaw dropped as in death. Susannah, whose sight was dim, squinted at the thing he had done. Jack said: "This also is a," and then kept his peace. Will said:

"You see, you see? To do this I have the right. I am not without right, do you see? Now another thing. On Sunday I will read this out in the church, aye, in Trinity Church during matins will I, and eke at even song too if I am minded to do it. For I am a lay rector. Not without right. And I have a voice that will fill the church to the rafters, not the piping nose-song of your scrawny unlay rector, do you hear me? *Non sanz droict*, which is the Shakespeare motto, and the name too shall prevail as long as the word of the Lord. Now, mistress," he said to Anne, "I would have supper served, and quickly." Then he strode to stand beneath his mulberry tree in the garden, granting her no time to rail.

On Sunday morning he stood, every inch a Christian gentleman in his neat London finery, on the altar steps of Trinity Church. Family, neighbors, the scowling brethren, shopkeepers, nose-picking children filled the pews. His voice rose clear and strong, an actor's voice:

"This Sunday you are to hear from me not the Lesson appointed for the day but the word of the Lord God in a form you do not know. Next year you will know it, for it is His Majesty King James's new Bible. But now you have this for the first time on any stage, I would say any altar. The word of the Lord. The forty-sixth Psalm of King David." He read from the galley expressively, an actor, clear, loud, without strain, so that all attended as they were in a theater and not in the house of God:

```
God is our refuge and strength, a very present helpe
    in trouble.
Therefore will not we feare, though the earth be remoued;
    and though the mountaines be caried into the midst
    of the sea.
Though the waters thereof roare and be troubled, though
    the mountaines tremble with the swelling thereof.  Selah.
There is a riuer, the streames wherof shall make glad the
    citie of God:  the holy place of the Tabernacles of
    the most High.
God is in the midst of her:  she shal not be moued;
    God shall helpe her, and that right early.
The heathen raged, the kingdomes were moued:  he vttered
    his voyce, the earth melted.
The Lord of hosts is with vs; the God of Jacob is our
    refuge.  Selah.
Come, behold the workes of the Lord, what desolations hee
    hath made in the earth.
He maketh warres to cease vnto the end of the earth: hee
    breaketh the bow, and cutteth the sword in sunder, he
    burneth the chariot in the fire.
Be stil, and know that I am God:  I will be exalted
    among the heathen, I will be exalted in the earth.
The Lord of Hosts is with vs; the God of Jacob is our
    refuge.  Selah.
```

*Shake/*

*speare/*

He ceased, looked fearlessly on them all, then stepped down, with an actor's grace, to return to his pew. One man at the back, forgetting where he was, began to applaud but was quickly hushed. Before Will arrived at his seat, Judith said to her mother:

"I wonder that God has not struck him down."

"Wait," said Anne grimly. "The Lord does things in his own good time. Fear not, the Lord God will repay." Will sat down next to her. Then, having looked on her and Judith and Susannah and Jack Hall and Mrs. Hart his sister with a peculiar lingering hardness, he knelt and prayed. He prayed long and with evident sincerity, so that his wife grew tight-mouthed with suspicion. Then he got up, looking much refreshed, sat down, and waited till the sermon was finished. Then he said very clearly to Anne and, indeed, to any on the pew that would hear:

"I am minded to turn papist."

"God forgive you. Keep your voice down. This is no place nor time for japes."

"I will turn papist." He tasted the term then gently spat it out: *tpt.* "I will not say that. It is a word of contempt. More, it puts overmuch emphasis on the Pope of Rome. It is the faith that matters."

"Be quiet," she said in quiet fury. The service was continuing and eyes were on Will, ears striving to pick up his words.

"Catholic," he said. Then he said no more. She remained tight-lipped. He did not speak of the matter again in the two days more he remained in Stratford.


When Ben Jonson was let out of jail he went straight to William Shakespeare's lodgings in Silver Street. Before he could say aught of going out to drink, Will said:

"I have writ this new play. It is based on Gunpowder Plot."

Ben sat down carefully on a delicate French chair. "It is based on — ?"

"Gunpowder Plot. There is a king that is a fool and an ingrate. He believes that God exists but to confirm the holiness of his kingship. Conspirators led by a poet seek to destroy him for his blasphemy."

"A *poet?*"

"I had you much in my mind there. Not a very good poet and most apt for meddling in state matters. His name is Vitellius. Here is one of his speeches. Listen."

"No," said Ben. "Let me read instead." He looked at the fair copy that was also the first draft and read to himself:

> Conserve agst ye putrifying feende
> The fathe yt fedde oure fathers, quite put doune
> His incarnacioun in thes worst of tymes,
> Casting hys hedde discoronate to ye dogges.

Then he said: "They will not let you. This will be construed as present treason."

"I am sick of it all," Will said. "The black bastards of Puritans in Stratford that will have nothing but grimness, and a church that is the lapdog of a slobbering king and no king. My father died quietly in the old faith, I will die more noisily in it."

"Have you spoke of this yet to any?"

"To my lord Cecil, aye, and he said he needed no more spies aping to be papists to dig out papist plots. I have said it to many, but none will take it that I mean what I say. It is part of the peril of being a player, that all one says is thought to be but acting."

Ben said: "The great work now is in page proof. They expect it to be out in the new year."

"What is all this to do with what I said?"

"The forty-sixth psalm has *shake* and *speare* in it."

"That is not possible. None would have it, this I knew. It would be seen as bombastic and overweening."

"Tillitson, one of those charged with the overseeing of our emendations, said that the two words came nearer to the original than what they formerly had."

"That is not possible."

"He had never, I could see," and Ben smiled sweetly, "heard of the name Shakespeare."

"Let us," said Will, "go and drink."

# The Singularity of Shakespeare

## by KENNETH MUIR

The theme for today is Shakespeare as an International Presence. But I think
you will agree that the holding of this Congress, with delegates from the four
imagined corners of the world, makes it a work of supererogation to enlarge
on this theme; and I may add that the editor of a Shakespeare journal earns
an adventitious popularity with his philatelist colleagues. But I want nevertheless to call attention to one curious fact about Shakespeare's international
presence. I have seen performances of Shakespeare's plays in Moscow,
Prague, and Dubrovnik as well as Kozintsev's great films and the Japanese
*Throne of Blood.* The curious thing is that the *Hamlet* that ran for a dozen
years in Moscow, the performances in the state theaters of Germany, the
wonderful *Othello* in Dubrovnik were, of course, not Shakespeare precisely,
but Boris Pasternak's *Hamlet,* or Schlegel-Tieck's *Macbeth,* or a Serbo-Croat
version of *Othello.* It is curious, because those who share Shakespeare's
language, and those who are truly bilingual, must regard the plays thus
robbed of their authentic poetry as *Hamlet* without the Prince of Denmark.
One is not surprised that readers of Shakespeare's poetry should lose
themselves in superlatives — that A. C. Bradley, for example, should say in a
letter that the appreciation of Shakespeare was "the whole duty of man,"
although the elders of the Kirk in Glasgow would have been startled to hear
this piece of heresy. One expects Emily Dickinson to say that while
"Shakespeare remains, literature is firm." It is a little more surprising to read
an inscription by Bernard Shaw, the scourge of the bardolators, in his facsimile of the First Folio, "one of the great books of the world"; and most surprising to find Flaubert saying "What a man Shakespeare was! How small all
the other poets are beside him . . . I think that if I were to see Shakespeare in
the flesh, I should perish with fear." Another great novelist, Turgenev, wrote
to Flaubert about Zola: "I believe that he hasn't read Shakespeare: that is an
indelible stain in him, which can never be washed away." Yet another great
novelist, Stendhal, thought that Shakespeare was far and away the greatest of

66

poets; and even declared that he was the Unknown God. It is significant, however, that after calling him divine, he added, "and yet to me he is almost in prose."

I am far from undervaluing the translators, even though none can hope to provide an adequate substitute for the original. Yet, it is odd that in the 1950s and 1960s there were more professional productions of Shakespeare in Germany and the Soviet Union than in the United States or England. Indeed, some years ago it was suggested by a nameless Philistine that since the language of the translators was more accessible to modern audiences than Elizabethan language could be a modern poet—Sir Osbert Sitwell was incredibly suggested—should be persuaded to translate the plays into a modern idiom. We can guess from some modern versions of the Bible what disasters would ensue. (Although there is no truth in Kipling's intriguing story "Proofs of Holy Writ," that Shakespeare put the finishing touches to the King James version, it may be argued that on strictly literary grounds we could deduce that that version alone was dictated by the Holy Ghost!)

What, therefore, I wish to share with you today are some thoughts on this question—if we strip Shakespeare of his poetry, does enough remain to justify his position as the greatest of dramatists? It is not an easy question to answer, for two main reasons. First, because a good translator can convey *some* of the poetic effect of the original. Although Pasternak oddly supposed that the repetition of sickness imagery in *Hamlet* was a stylistic fault caused by haste in composition and lack of revision, a translator can faithfully reproduce Shakespeare's iterative imagery. He can likewise, as Flatter tried to do, copy the metrical irregularities of the Folio texts, and differentiate between the style of the Dido speeches in *Hamlet* and that of the soliloquy that follows—"O! What a rogue and peasant slave am I!"—where the brutal realism contrasts with the inflation of the epic style. He can differentiate, too, between Hamlet's colloquial exchanges with Ophelia and the rhymed couplets of *The Murder of Gonzago*. Nevertheless, however devoted and cunning the translator, much will inevitably be lost: and, of course, the greater the poet the greater the loss. We get a much better idea of *Le Misanthrope* in Wilbur's translation than we do of *Phèdre* in Lowell's, although, I suppose, Lowell would generally be regarded as a more important poet than Wilbur.

The second of the difficulties to which I have referred is of much greater importance: the inseparability of Shakespeare's gifts of poet and dramatist. Let me try to sharpen this point by supposing that the young Shakespeare received, by some mistake of the Post Office or some shift in the space-time continuum, the letter Rilke wrote to a young poet:

> Time doesn't enter into it. A year doesn't count; ten years are nothing. To be an artist is not to count and calculate; it is to grow like the tree which does not hurry its sap, which confidently resists the great winds

of Spring, without doubting that Summer will come. Summer does come: but it comes only for those who know how to wait, as patient, confident and receptive as if they had eternity before them . . . Patience is all.

Shakespeare would have smiled to receive such advice; but, being notoriously polite, he would perhaps have replied:

> I thank you from my heart for your advice, free and honest as it is, for the betterment of my poetry. But I fear that you are ignorant of the hard conditions under which I work. I am not, alas, a full-time poet. I am by profession a Player, and most of my time is taken up with the learning of lines, sometimes inferior to my own, with interminable rehearsals and time-consuming performances. I am much in demand for kingly and ducal roles. It is true that my fellows accept the two plays I provide each year as my main contribution to the affairs of the company; but even in this I enjoy only a limited freedom. I have to provide long and impressive parts for the leading actors, and smaller parts within the capacities of the others. I spend many precious hours in a desperate search for stories to turn into plays and, although I try and map out the plots of the next two plays during my annual visit to my family in the country, the dialogue is hardly finished before the first rehearsals. Indeed, I have often been persuaded, against my better judgement, to make alterations during rehearsals. You will appreciate that in these circumstances I smile at your statement that ten years are nothing.
>
> > At my back I always hear
> > Time's winged chariot hurrying near.
>
> I cannot wait for ten years, for during that period I must endeavor to write another twenty plays — poor things, but my own. So, my honored sir, I cannot pretend to be an artist. You rightly compare poetry to the sap of the tree; but the process is less protracted than you describe. Our poesy is as a gum, which oozes from whence 'tis nourished. The fire in the flint
>
> > Shows not till it be struck; our gentle flame
> > Provokes itself, and like the current flies
> > Each bound it chafes. It does not take ten years.
> > Perhaps it takes less in this my workaday world
> > Because I have not, unlike you, a bevy
> > Of wealthy flattering ladies to coddle me
> > While I am lying fallow.

In some such way Shakespeare might have replied — though I confess he would not have anticipated Andrew Marvell — but if he sometimes regretted that he was dyed in the colors of his trade, and did not always appreciate the advantages of the hurly-burly in which he had to write, these at least preserved him from the damaging detachment that separates some dramatists from their audiences, and some poets from their fellow men. He was, he was compelled to be, a man speaking to men.

Consider, for example, the effect on Shakespeare of his profession. An actor, first of all, spends much of his time in observing other people, so that when the appropriate part comes along, he can incorporate in his performance characteristics he has observed. (As Laurence Olivier watched the behavior of West Indian immigrants and introduced their mannerisms, brilliantly if disastrously, into his portrayal of Othello.) An actor who is also a dramatist does not merely utilize gestures and facial expressions, he picks up tricks of speech: the malapropisms of Dogberry, the anecdotage of Justice Shallow and Juliet's Nurse, the Old Testament flavor of Shylock's speech. Even more important, the actor-playwright comes to know instinctively what an audience will take, and the qualities and limitations of his fellow actors. Most important of all, he knows that *Hamlet* and *King Lear* are merely scripts, which come to life fully only when they are performed. By which, of course, I don't mean that they are scripts that should be hacked about to suit the whims of a director, but rather, as Bernard Shaw was always insisting, musical scores, spoken by actors who bring to life the characters they represent. Each time this happens, the dramatist rewitnesses Pygmalion's miracle. Richard Burbage deserved the legacy in Shakespeare's will with which to purchase a memorial ring.

Everyone realizes how much a dramatist owes to the response of his audience, whether positive or negative. Although *Troilus and Cressida* is a particularly subtle and fascinating play, one should perhaps be glad that its comparative failure on the boards made Shakespeare devote himself to other sensations: to the writing of *Othello* and *King Lear.*

Keats's phrase recalls another, more famous one: that the poet has as much delight in depicting an Iago as an Imogen. It is equally true that the actor has as much delight in playing Iago as today an actress has in playing Imogen. I am not sure whether anyone has pointed out that what Keats described as Negative Capability—"when a man is capable of being in uncertainties, mysteries, doubts, without any irritable reaching after fact and reason"—is a quality that is demanded equally of an actor. It is obvious that an actor playing the role of a villain must (for the time being) play it from that character's point of view. There is a case to be made for Edmund, and Goneril, even for Regan, but woe betide the director who allows that evil trio to quench our sympathy for Lear. Even Rosencrantz and Guildenstern, as Tom Stoppard neatly demonstrated, are not quite what Hamlet makes us think they are.

You will recall that Una Ellis-Fermor in her British Academy lecture (which was afterwards incorporated in *Shakespeare the Dramatist)* argued that the quintessential dramatic gift, which Shakespeare possessed more abundantly than any other dramatist, was the power of giving life to all his characters, not merely to his protagonists. Of course there is a difference between the characterization in depth of Angelo and Isabella on the one hand, and that of Barnardine and Froth on the other; but within the limits of Barnardines's 112 words and Froth's 57 we are given extraordinarily vivid portraits, very much more alive than the minor characters of other dramatists. There are, of course, many minor characters in the early plays who are not fully individualized, and I think perhaps that Una Ellis-Fermor considered too curiously when she took as one of her examples an anonymous sentry in *Antony and Cleopatra*. But her main argument seems to me to be sound. It is, indeed, fairly common for a dramatist to make a character memorable by tricks of speech or by the repetition of catch-phrases: the oaths of Bob Acres, the malapropisms of Mrs. Malaprop, the clichés of Boniface, the nautical imagery of Ben Sampson in *Love for Love*; the similitudes of Witwoud, or the fashionable twittering of Belinda in Congreve's first comedy, *The Old Bachelor,* when she encounters Araminta:

> Lard, my Dear! I'm glad I have met you — I have been at the Exchange since, and am so tir'd . . . Oh, the most inhumane, barbarous Hackney-Coach! I am jolted to a Jelly. Am I not horridly touzed?
> ARAM. Your Head's a little out of order.
> BEL. A little! O frightful! What a furious Fiz I have! O most rueful! Ha, ha, ha, O Gad, I hope nobody will come this way, till I have put myself a little in Repair! . . . Good Dear, pin this . . . very well — So, thank you my Dear — But as I was telling you — Pish, this is the untoward'st Lock — So, as I was telling you — How d'ye like me now? Hideous, ha? Frightful still? Or how?

It would be wrong to undervalue such a passage. It illustrates Congreve's wonderful ear — not, as used to be said, for vowel music, but for capturing the different speech cadences of a wide variety of people. But such ventriloquism, superb as it is, is surpassed in dramatic effectiveness by sudden strokes that seem at first to be absurdly out of character but that *by that very fact* convince us of its truth to life. It is unnecessary before such an audience to give examples of this from Shakespeare, but I hope you will allow me to refer to a single example, the recruiting scene in *2 Henry IV*. We have been laughing with Falstaff at the senility of Shallow, at the passing of bribes, and at Falstaff's cruelly funny comments on the countrymen lined up for his inspection. Feeble, the woman's tailor, is apparently the most unsuitable of all the recruits. His trade and his name are both against him. He is the butt of Falstaff's jokes and obscenities. But after he has been enlisted, he has the following speech:

> By my troth I care not, a man can die but once, we owe God a death. I'll ne'er bear a base mind — and't be my destiny, so; and't be not, so. No man's too good to serve's prince, and let it go which way it will, he that dies this year is quit for the next.

Feeble's dignified acceptance of the situation, his religious resignation, makes us see him (and the whole scene) with different eyes; and some members of the audience will remember Falstaff's reply in Part I when he is reminded by Hal that he owes God a death: " 'Tis not due yet."

The point I am making about Shakespeare's method of characterization may be made clearer if I describe briefly the very different method of three great dramatists — Molière, Racine, and Ibsen — whose characters are, compared with Shakespeare's, remarkably unambiguous. It is almost as though the poets had based them on lucid, well-considered character sketches in which every stroke was entirely consistent.

There can hardly be any disagreement about Molière's major characters. Although Tartuffe does not actually appear until the beginning of Act 3, he is the focus of attention throughout the earlier scenes, and there is no ambiguity in his portrayal. He is shown in all his *hypocritic turpitude* (to use Blake's phrase), and every member of every audience agrees about him, including even the devout who wanted the play banned. We watch him from the outside — we are never allowed inside his mind — and he is given no redeeming characteristics. A greedy, avaricious, sensual conman, he deliberately uses the cloak of piety to further his criminal schemes — and we rejoice in his downfall. Alceste, in *Le Misanthrope,* is a more complex character and audiences and readers are divided into those who regard him as a self-righteous and humorless prig, and those who regard him as a nearly tragic hero, greatly superior to the society in which he lives. Notice, however, that the different reactions to the character are not due to any real ambiguity: they merely reflect the views and temperaments of different members of the audience — whether they agree with the compromiser Philinte or not. In the same way some people find Milton repellent and Shelley a cad, using the same evidence as those who think that Milton was noble and Shelley a secular saint.

If we turn now to Jean Racine, we find the same refusal to blur the outlines of his characters. We could describe the characters and motivation of Andromache, Agrippine, Bérénice, Phèdre, or Athalie in a few sentences, as school texts do, and no one would disagree with the summaries. No one, I think, could write a good book about Racine's tragedies that concentrated attention on the characters as Bradley did in *Shakespearean Tragedy.*

The greatest of the moderns, Ibsen, is also careful to guide the responses of his audience; though in *The Master Builder* and *John Gabriel Borkman* he moved into a more ambiguous realm. In nearly all his plays we gradually learn more and more about the past lives of the characters at the same time as we watch them developing in the present. We learn, for example, how Mrs. Alving in *Ghosts* was driven into a loveless marriage, how she left her husband and was driven back to him by the clergyman she loved; how this led to freethinking and (at the same time) to a hypocritical pretense that her late husband was a paragon of virtue. In the course of the play, she is compelled not merely to tell Oswald that his father was a diseased debauchee, but also to recognize that Captain Alving's debauchery was partly due to her own sin in marrying him when she was in love with someone else. There are, of course, many subtleties that I have had to omit in this brief summary, but Ibsen leaves us with no excuse for misunderstanding his meaning.

The revelation of the past concurrently with the development of the present is also apparent in *Rosmersholm;* the mystery of Mrs. Rosmer's suicide, hinted at first by Rosmer's refusal to cross by the bridge from which she plunged to her death, the revelation that the suicide was caused by Rebecca West's false confession that she was pregnant; the indication that the murder was politically motivated, so that Rosmer would be free to join the progressive party; Rebecca's later confession that she acted under the influence of a wild, uncontrollable passion; and her last confession in which she describes how under the influence of Rosmer and the Rosmersholm view of life, which kills joy, even though it ennobles, her passion was changed to an unselfish love. Ibsen adds to the portrait of Rebecca several further details: that she was illegitimate and that she had unwittingly committed incest. It is a complex portrait, but one that is not open to diverse interpretations—I say this despite the fact that faced with this story of murder and redemption some members of a youth movement asked Ibsen if the message of the play was not the call to work for mankind.

If we turn now from these admittedly great characters from some of the greatest plays since Shakespeare said farewell to his art, to any of *his* major characters, the differences will be apparent—differences that caused Edgar Elmer Stoll such a lot of needless anxiety. Iago may be taken as an example. A recent book by Stanley Edgar Hyman, published posthumously, has the subtitle "Some approaches to the illusion of his motivation." Hyman had no difficulty in showing that Iago could be treated simply as a stage villain; but, equally obviously, there is plenty in the text of the play to show that he is a devil, hating goodness and plotting the damnation of Othello; that he is an image of the playwright in his criminal aspect; that he is a Machiavel; and, less convincingly to me, that he is in love with Othello and Cassio, a love that is turned into hatred "by the defense mechanism called reaction formation." Oddly enough, Hyman did not discuss a number of other motivations that are suggested in the course of the play—that Iago is in love with Desdemona (as in Shakespeare's source); that he suspects Othello and Cassio of seducing Emilia; that he is a racist; and that he wants Cassio's job—all of which are at least as significant as those suggested by Hyman.

The case of Hamlet is even more notorious. There are more than a thousand rival interpretations of his character and of the reasons for his delay. To Coleridge he suffered from over-reflective intellectualism; to Madariaga and Rebecca West he was an egotist; to Roy Walker, borrowing Niebuhr's terminology, he was moral man in immoral society; to Goethe he was an oak tree planted in a costly vase; to Schoepenhauer he suffered from world-weary cynicism; Bradley thought he was unable to act because of the shock of his father's death and his mother's remarriage; Freud, not unnaturally, diagnosed an Oedipus complex; and Wertham, until he was branded as a heretic by his fellow analysts, diagnosed an Orestes complex. Confronted with these, and many other, contradictory theories, C. S. Lewis suggested first that all critics saw themselves as Hamlet and attached to him their own prepossessions. Coleridge gave the game away when he said "I have a smack of Hamlet myself, if I may say so." Second, C. S. Lewis argued that Hamlet has no character: he was Everyman, guilty of original sin. This point would be more convincing if we did not know that C. S. Lewis had written several books of popular theology and that, like the critics he complained of, he had read into Hamlet his own prepossessions. I find it difficult to accept the idea of a Hamlet without a character: but it is true that many of the rival theories are supported by selective quotations from the text of the play. This extraordinary state of affairs has been attributed to the fact that Shakespeare was grafting on a play ten or a dozen years old the ideas and motivations of his maturity and that this pouring of new wine into old bottles made the play (in Eliot's words) "most certainly an artistic failure." Eliot later retracted, but Waldock clung to this theory. Yet the varied responses of the critics to the play may properly reflect its complexity and ambivalence. As Norman Rabkin showed in his admirable lecture at the Vancouver Conference, the tendency of critics to find a single, incontrovertible meaning in a play is reductive in its effect:

> Yet by the end [he said] we have been through a constantly turbulent experience which demands an incessant giving and taking back of allegiance, a counterpoint of ever-shifting response to phrase, speech, character, scene, action, a welter of emotions and ideas and perceptions and surprises and intuitions of underlying unity and coherence rivalled only by our experience in the real world so perplexingly suggested by the artifact to which we yield ourselves.

I do not know whether Professor Rabkin would agree that this account of our experience of a Shakespearean play would not really fit any of the great plays by other dramatists that I have been discussing. It seems to me that in this respect — and particularly in the matter of characterization — we come close to the singularity of Shakespeare.

I have given two examples of complex characterization — Iago and Hamlet — and if there were time I could give a score of others. I need remind you only of the contrast between the views of Bradley and Leavis on Othello, of Stoll's conviction that the jealous maniac of Acts 3 and 4 is incompatible with the portrait we have of the Moor in Act 1 and again at the end of the play. Then again, there is the well-known contrast between the prudential motives Macbeth offers in his soliloquy in Act 1 for not murdering Duncan, and the impression we get from the same soliloquy that he is overcome with horror at the thought of the murder. The overt meaning is "I won't murder Duncan because of what people will say and do." The inner meaning, conveyed by the imagery of naked babe and angelic trumpets, is quite different. The imagery is used to reveal the unconscious mind of the protagonist, as it is also with Coriolanus.

The singularity of Shakespeare was pointed out by Strindberg, when he used Shakespeare as a stick to beat Ibsen with, as Professor Ewbank reminds me. In one of his *Open Letters* he discusses Hamlet, Ophelia, Polonius, and Claudius and argues that

> Shakespeare describes people, in all their facets, as inconsistent, as contradictory, as torn — and tearing themselves to pieces — as aggressive and as incomprehensible as the sons of men really are.

Strindberg goes on to admit that Shakespeare "does not always do it, and not completely and exhaustively, for no one could do that!"

Many of you, whether you have read this particular essay or not, will be reminded of a famous eighteenth-century piece of criticism, Maurice Morgann's essay on the Dramatic Character of Sir John Falstaff. It is particularly appropriate that we should celebrate Morgann's genius in the year 1976, although it is only 199 years since it first appeared, for if Morgann's advice had been followed the American colonies would probably not have signed the Declaration of Independence. Morgann was Lord Shelburne's secretary in charge of what was called the "American desk." He urged on Shelburne and the British government a conciliatory policy, the repeal of Rockingham's Act, which affirmed parliament's right to tax the colonies whenever they wished, and the rescinding of the Mutiny Act. It may be added that Morgann advocated the abolition of slavery in the West Indies years before anyone else. (I owe these facts to Daniel A. Fineman's introduction to his edition.)

It is commonly thought that Morgann's main purpose was to prove that Falstaff was not a coward and that in so doing he ignored the distinction between art and life, thus opening the door to a great deal of bad criticism of Shakespeare — such as *The Girlhood of Shakespeare's Heroines*. But this is totally to misunderstand Morgann's aim. Whether Falstaff was a coward or not is largely a matter of definition; but Morgann was fully aware that the characters in a play are not real people. His real distinction lies in his realization of the method of Shakespearean characterization. He points out that characters "which are seen only in part, are yet capable of being unfolded and understood in the whole"; that a "felt propriety and truth from causes unseen" is the "highest point of poetic composition"; and that, by means of "secret impressions," Shakespeare contrives to introduce "an apparent incongruity of character and action" so as to suggest the complexity of people in real life.

Morgann's *Essay* contains on page after page passages of astonishing insight into Shakespeare's method, some of them added after publication. Shakespeare's characters are original, "while those of almost all other writers are mere imitation." We can account for their conduct "from latent motives, and from policies not avowed." There is one splendid paragraph, clarifying the 1777 text, in which Morgann explains that when our impressions and understanding of a scene may be at variance, the effect may be calculated by the poet. This may seem to foreshadow Stoll's idea of Shakespeare as the great illusionist who tricks us into accepting impossibilities, but Morgann insists not merely that delight may be derived from the apparent opposition between impression and understanding, but that the "Principles of this Disagreement are really in human Nature."

This, then, is the grand justification for the conflicting impressions Shakespeare gives us of his main characters: life is like that. In most plays and most novels we are presented with neat, rational, well-organized, and consistent characters. Our friends are not like that, as we can tell from the varying impressions different people have of them, and indeed, our own differing views from year to year, and even from day to day. Shakespeare's characters have the same Protean quality.

I come back to the point from which I started. If Shakespeare is enjoyed in dozens of different languages, despite the overriding importance of his poetry, what quality or qualities does he possess that enable him to be regarded as the greatest of dramatists, a quality that survives the perils and betrayals of translation? It can hardly be the structural brilliance of the plays, since directors usually make considerable changes in adapting the plays for a modern theater. It certainly cannot be the profound interpretation of life that can be extracted from the plays, a blend of medieval morality, pious platitudes, and stoical consolation, for the plays are admired by many who reject the whole of the Shakespearean ideology, as I do not. Nor can it be his psychological realism, since the psychology that formed the basis of Elizabethan characterization is now regarded as obsolete. But, as you will have deduced from the line of my argument, Shakespeare's characters appear to be real — not real people, of course, but convincing on the stage, and even on the page. This is due partly, as Morgann believed, to the conflicting views of a character that we are asked to assimilate. There is nothing more likely to convert a flat character into a round one as when two pictures seen through a stereoscope merge into one that appears to be solid. It is due also, as Morgann hinted, to the way Shakespeare was able to project himself and his experience into a wide range of characters and, conversely, to the way he himself learned from his characters. Can we doubt that Shakespeare emerged from the writing of *Hamlet or King Lear* like a man who had undergone a baptism of fire?

Nor is this all. The reality of the characters depends on a quadruple interaction. First, the conflicting impressions that avoid entanglement with obsolete psychological theories. Second, the identification of the poet with his characters, imagining himself in the position of Hamlet or Caliban. Third, the pressures of the actual plot, the deeds that somehow have to be harmonized with the doer of them — and the greater the gap between deed and doer, the greater the intensity of the action. Fourth, there is the actor who embodies the poet's creations, adding to them, subtracting from them, never quite coinciding with them, and by that very fact lending a penumbra to them, and providing yet another conflicting impression to give the illusion of life.

Critics brought up on a tidier, more rational kind of drama — such as William Archer who greatly preferred Pinero, Jones, and Galsworthy to the great Jacobean dramatists, not to mention Wycherley and Congreve — such critics protested that Hamlet was not the sort of man who would murder Rosencrantz and Guildenstern, that Othello, as depicted by Shakespeare, would never have smothered Desdemona, that the puritanical Angelo is the last person to be guilty of the sin into which he falls. We can see how wrong-headed such critics were, not merely because Shakespeare convinces us that these characters did behave in these ways, but because every discovery of modern psychology has vindicated the truth of Shakespeare's portraits.

This, then, I suggest, is the secret of Shakespeare's continued popularity in languages other than his own. His poetry may be seen through a glass darkly, but the subtlety of his characterization survives the process of translation, the transplanting into alien cultures, and the erosion of time. Not altogether undamaged, however. As Bernard Shaw was always insisting,

> The individualization which produces that old-established British speciality, the Shakespearean "delineation of character," owes all its magic to the turn of the line, which lets you into the secret of its utterer's mood and temperament, not by its commonplace meaning, but by some subtle exaltation, or stultification, or slyness, or delicacy, or what not in the sound of it. In short, it is the score and not the libretto that keeps the work alive and fresh.

And who, Shaw might have added, would bother to read the libretto of *Don Giovanni* or of *The Magic Flute,* if it were not for the music of Mozart?

We often speak of the universality of great poetry, accessible, we like to think, to people of different civilizations, with different beliefs and prejudices. Everyone will recall Wordsworth's splendid claim:

> In spite of difference of soil and climate, of language and manners, of laws and customs; in spite of things silently gone out of mind and things violently destroyed: the Poet binds together by passion and knowledge the vast empire of human society, as it is spread over the whole earth, and over all time.

Perhaps one may be permitted to add in a Shakespeare conference, if with the prejudice due to such an occasion, that the only poet who really satisfies Wordsworth's claim is Shakespeare.

Let me conclude with an eloquent prophecy by Maurice Morgann, appropriate at a congress of Shakespearan scholars, and doubly appropriate in a congress held in Washington at this particular time.

Yet whatever may be the neglect of some, or the censure of others, there are those who firmly believe that this wild, this uncultivated Barbarian has not yet obtained one half of his fame; and who trust some new Stagyrite will arise, who instead of pecking at the surface of things will enter into the inward soul of his composition. . . . When the hand of time shall have brushed off his present Editors and Commentators, and when the very name of Voltaire . . . shall be no more, the *Appalachian* mountains, the banks of the *Ohio,* and the plains of *Scioto* shall resound with the accents of this Barbarian: In his native tongue he shall roll the genuine passions of nature; nor shall the griefs of *Lear* be alleviated, or the charms and wit of *Rosalind* be abated by time.

# II

# SELECTED PAPERS FROM TOPICS SECTIONS

# Shakespeare's Tragic Sense As It Strikes Us Today

## by G. K. HUNTER

*Shakespeare's tragic sense* is a phrase that, tragically no doubt, I can make little sense of. I propose therefore to talk about Shakespeare's tragedies, the actual objects within which Shakespeare's tragic sensibilia will have to be found if they are to avoid being merely a subject of speculation or conjecture. I further propose that asking how the thing that happened *then* strikes us *now* involves us in a study in misunderstanding. The only thing one can be sure of in this field is that the present cannot recapture the past. The most that can be hoped for is that some dimensions of the gap between them can be described. This therefore, perforce, is what I shall try to do.

The first point that seems possible to make turns out to be a rather painful one, for it is both basic (and therefore unavoidable) and obvious (and therefore unspeakable): Shakespeare's tragedies were performed and accepted then but are read and talked about now. This is basic and obvious, as I say; but I do not think its implications are always followed through. Shakespeare's plays were performed then: that is, they were known by being experienced in the theater — and they seem to have provoked little or no desire to talk about them. The relationship between experience and discourse in respect of Shakespeare's tragedies *then* has some similarity to the relationship between experience and discourse in terms of pornography *now*. As today in this field of human endeavor, so then in that field there seems to have been no very useful vocabulary for talking about the experience, though this does not inhibit the press to experience pornography now and I suppose did not much halt the rush to the theater then. The lack of a relevant critical vocabulary only measures, I take it, the lack of desire to use one: it seems pointless, I suppose one might say, to spend time talking about something so simple, so obvious, so basic. But if this was the attitude of Shakespeare's auditors in 1600 or so, what a change has occurred! Today the experience of Shakespeare's tragedies is almost completely swamped in the vocabulary for talking about it. I wonder how many of us today can even conceive of the plays apart from the critical theories and attitudes that attach to them. Even to ask such a question, of course, implies the answer to it; to formulate the idea of the play-in-itself is to pass beyond the stage where the thing is possible.

It might seem that this is rather a long way round a rather simple point — that the tragedies are so remote from our natural experience now that we need the critics (and their vocabularies) to help us get close to the plays again. I am certainly happy to agree with one part of this formulation and to endorse the view that the critics, like the poor, are here to stay. That they are useful because they help us recover the plays seems more doubtful. We seem to expect too much if we expect the critics to take us back into precritical attention. What the critics seem able to bring us close to is not the play itself but a contemporary critical construct made out of the demolished or "deconstructed" remains of the actual play. It is probably inevitable that this should be so; in order to talk about the plays we have to organize our perceptions of them so that they can be talked about. This may well be true of all literature and all criticism; but the truth has a particular sharpness in the case of dramatic criticism, where the conditions of the original experience (the theater) are so sharply demarcated from those of the reconstruction (the study, the classroom). Indeed this might seem to allow us to apply certain authenticating standards to the criticism of Shakespeare's plays. If we are not to assume that the critic is free to present whatever critical ingenuity can devise for the play, then we must prefer the criticism that can draw on the authenticating experience of the theater. In saying this I am not making any large claim for positive knowledge, either of the past or of theatrical conditions; I am only suggesting that certain hallowed critical procedures ignore the basic conditions of theatrical experience, and that this raises a question mark against them.

Time is short (even if art is not long) and I will confine myself to talking around one critical concept — though an important one — the concept of unity. Unity is not a new idea, of course; it can be found in Aristotle and Horace, though befogged by time. Let me quote Northrop Frye, an unbefogged Aristotle of our own critical scene: Frye, writing a general account of "Literary Criticism," tells us that the first duty of the literary critic is to "see the whole design of the work as a unity . . . a simultaneous pattern radiating out from a center, not a narrative moving in time" (*Aims and Methods of Scholarship in Modern Languages and Literatures*, ed. J. E. Thorpe [New York, 1963], p. 65). I ought to add perhaps that this statement comes to us nimbused with the glory of the MLA. My humble submission is that this advice cannot be matched against the actual experience of a play in the theater. Shakespeare's tragedies are, like other plays, processes through time whose power over us as spectators (and to a lesser but still perceptible extent as readers) depends on their capacity to force us into sharing their forward movement from known into unknown. A play differs from a novel characteristically in that time present on the stage is also time present in the auditorium, so that the individual character's projection into his future is at the same time a projection into our future. As we sit through the play we pursue a sequence of present moments, picking up clues, hints, and signals about the meaning of what we are seeing—meaning defined in terms of what we have seen already and what we expect to see later. When the experience is of the richness of Shakespearean tragedy, we are faced from moment to moment with a bewildering complexity of such information. But we are not simply bewildered. We also feel free, as we suppose the characters before us are free, to choose the sequence of relationships that has most significance for us at that moment and gives us what is properly called understanding. It is difficult to deny that such freedom is present in the situaton for all who deal with it. It is inherent in the nature of performance that it changes from night to night, not only in the larger and cruder sense that particular producers, conductors, performers impose individual and varying interpretations, but also in the narrower sense that halls, audiences, imponderable accidents and changes of environment produce relevant variables in a text responsive to such variation and probably defined in its excellence (certainly in its powers of survival) by this responsiveness. Our experience of the play in the theater is not constant and cannot be so.

It is sometimes argued by scholars that this is the case only because theater people are so unscholarly, never still, always chasing the latest fashion. If only they would get down to the actual text (and that must mean the text as read) they would find, the implication runs, a simple, unchanging, solid truth that they could then embody in a definitive "classic" performance, to which the audience could then respond in a normative way. Alas for simplicity, this seems not to be so. Even in reading, the inescapable variations that arise from complex movement through time are a part of our experience. A text is a text is a text (more or less) only if by *text* we mean a physical object, words on a page, pages in a book. As soon as these words are taken up into a human mind they reenter the world of contingency and variation. I have spoken about theatrical performance as focusing the original experienced nature of the play; but in fact a sensitive reading also reflects many of these characteristics. Every such reading is a new reading, a different reconstitution of the text, a divergent route through the rich variety of alternatives that the play offers. Take only one example. In the first scene of *Hamlet* we hear of young Fortinbras and old Fortinbras. At the time we are given this information we do not know what to do with it. And this characteristic uncertainty in the text does not relate only to a single point but to a complex sequence of points that offers the possibility of multiple connections (and so meanings) in relation to a series of contexts throughout the play. Under which heading should we sort the original information so that we can pick it up usefully when the next reference comes along? Under the antitheses of public versus private, old v. young, Norway v. Denmark, military v. civil, flamboyant v. reticent, order v. disorder, instinct v. law, individual v. national . . . or what else? The human mind is not well adapted to carry forward every possibility from every moment and match it against every other possibility from every other moment, not at least while sustaining that positive enjoyment in and commitment to the action which is the point of the whole exercise. A computer might be able to make the astronomical number of relationships required, but then a computer is not designed to enjoy anything (I am authoritatively informed). And this is in many ways the crux of the matter. The enjoying mind is the choosing mind, which exercises the individuality of its freedom by creating a new pathway through the labyrinth of alternatives. We make sense of what we read by reading it, by willing a route through material which, looked at from a distance or with detachment, seems pathless. And it is this will and commitment that keeps an audience or reader from falling into the dilemma of Buridan's ass, forever poised between two equally attractive alternatives. The choices may differ from occasion to occasion, but on each separate occasion our sense of ourselves and our experience will drive us in one direction and determine the particular understanding of the play we derive.

The critic searching for unity is required by the nature of his profession to abstract the play from particular occasions and seek for a description that will apply to all occasions. In so doing he may be thought to be offering *a* description as if it were *the* description. Certainly some such substitution could be invoked to explain the phenomenon — well known to all of us, I imagine — of critical essays that convince us till we read the next ones. Moreover, Shakespeare's plays seem designed to please us in terms of specific events and excitements and to demand only enough unity to keep these particulars from flying apart. This would seem to be a common condition of performed art. Mozart, writing to his father from Paris in 1778, tells him that his new symphony (K.278) has been written specially to appeal to what he regards as the absurd Parisian tastes: "I still hope, however, that even asses will find something in it to admire — and, moreover, I have been careful not to neglect *le premier coup d'archet* — and that is quite sufficient. What a fuss the oxen here make of this trick" (letter 309A). In a later letter (311) he reports on the actual performance of the symphony: " . . . just in the middle of the first Allegro was a passage which I felt sure must please. The audience were quite carried away — and there was a tremendous burst of applause. But as I knew, when I wrote it, what effect it would surely produce, I had introduced the passage again at the close — when there were shouts of 'Da capo.' . . . having observed that all last as well as first Allegros begin here with all the instruments playing together and generally unisono, I began mine with two violins only, piano for the first eight bars — followed instantly by a forte; the audience, as I expected, said 'hush' at the soft beginning, and when they heard the forte, began at once to clap their hands. I was so happy that as soon as the symphony was over, I went off to the Palais Royal, where I had a large ice, said the rosary as I had vowed to do—and went home." What made Mozart happy, we must note, was not the abstract achievement represented by his symphony, but its success, the occasion. This clearly was what Mozart was writing for; and it is hard to think of Shakespeare and other Elizabethan working dramatists in very different terms.

Mozart designed his "Paris" symphony to produce particular effects and was elated when its progress was interrupted by applause and cries for a repeat. He did not complain that the unity of the work had been violated, and indeed seems only to have been aware of such unity at the level of staying inside a reasonable limit of key-relationships and fulfilling the structural assumptions that the word *symphony* implies. Within the boundary walls of such expectation the artist is free to give excitement and pleasure by accumulating all the details that he knows his audience will be responsive to. Even as archromantic an artist as Beethoven, contemptuous of what might be thought of as servility to the audience and strongly assertive of the artist's power to impose his conceptions on the public, seems to have remained happily acquiescent when the audience insisted on his playing the Allegretto of his A-major symphony three times. The conception of unity in a performance seems in fact to be simply a matter of social convention. The current convention is that we do not applaud after movements, but only after "works"; but it is hard to see any necessity why this should be so. If a day at the Athenian theater offered three tragedies and a satyr play, what was the appropriate limit of unity—four plays, or three, or one?

The title pages of Elizabethan plays often spell out their similar concern for the details rather than the totality of the material, presenting the work rather as if it were the occasion for its parts. Take the bad quarto of *2 Henry VI:*

> The first part of the contention betwixt the two famous houses of York and Lancaster, with the death of the good Duke Humphrey: and the banishment and death of the Duke of Suffolk, and the tragical end of the proud Cardinal of Winchester, with the notable rebellion of Jack Cade: and the Duke of York's first claim unto the crown.

One may compare with this the comparatively pithy form of the same thing found in Shakespeare's *Richard III:*

> The tragedy of King Richard the third. Containing his treacherous plots against his brother Clarence: the pitiful murder of his innocent nephews: his tyrannical usurpation: with the whole course of his detested life, and most deserved death.

Compare again the interestingly different extended title of *Arden of Faversham:*

> The lamentable and true tragedy of Master Arden of Faversham in Kent. Who was most wickedly murdered, by the means of his disloyal and wanton wife, who for the love she bare to one Mosbie, hired two desperate ruffians Blackwill and Shakebag, to kill him. Wherein is shewed the great malice and dissimulation of a wicked woman, the unsatiable desire of filthy lust and the shameful end of all murderers.

Two quick points may be made about such title pages, one about their syntax and one about their epithets. The form of the two Shakespearean titles is one that avoids hypotaxis: the strong events are strung along a very weak thread—and this is what the Restoration adapters (for example Tate and Ravenscroft) were to find characteristic of Shakespeare's plots. Any transformation of the structure into hypotactic form ("a simultaneous pattern radiating out from a center") or even the designation of a "center" is the critic's business and not the play's requirement. The answer put forward to the question "What is the play about?" is the commonsense answer that the play is about the things it contains (deaths, banishments, murders, usurpations, etc.); and this corresponds to the view advanced above that the basic theatrical experience of the play, which critics abandon at their peril, is a chronological experience of exciting events.

But it would be less than honest to take this confirmation as total, which brings me to the epithets in these title pages. The *Arden* title page in particular offers a different kind of answer to the question "What is the play about?", and the answer may seem to be one that reinstates the idea of "center" and the importance of "unity." The final sentence obviously refers to that moment in the experience of a play when, at the end, we look back into the action and see the meaning of what has happened. There is a sense in which we can say that this glance back unifies the play; but (as represented here) it is a unity markedly different from that of the modern critic. The epithets that qualify virtually every action in these title pages, "treacherous . . . pitiful . . . tyrannical . . . detested . . . deserved . . . wickedly . . . disloyal and wanton . . . desperate . . . unsatiable . . . filthy . . . shameful," imply a unifying moral perspective on the various activities of the plays. But the morality that is depended on seems to come from outside rather than inside the play. When the *Arden* title page says *Wherein is shewed . . .* it invites us to find confirmation of the attitudes we brought to the play with us rather than anything that emerges organically from the action itself. The unity within which the action can be seen to cohere at the end of the play derives (like the unity of Mozart's "Paris" symphony) from the unity of the audience's expectations.

This difference between then and now may be thought to relate to that noted above, between the absence of critical interest in Shakespeare in his own day and the critical overkill today. If *Richard III* is held together by the a priori assumptions about good and bad that the audience brings with it to the theater, then the critic must be parasitic on received opinion. He may sophisticate and refine the relationship between the particular fictions and the moralistic framework, but he cannot cut any great figure. Today, however, the situation is rather inverted. Instead of requiring the play to confirm truths validated elsewhere, we look to art to present the truths we cannot find elsewhere. And in this situation the critic comes into his own. He occupies the important role of an ethical broker who sells us moral truths and underwrites them from his organic experience of the unified fictional life of the book. When he is able to convince us of the unity of his aesthetic experience, we trust his collateral. But as so often with enterprising middlemen, even the best collateral of this kind is ambiguous. The unity of the experience of Shakespeare's tragedies that the modern critic sells us as objective, really out there, is in large part subjective. A touch of ambiguity or corner-cutting here or there — need I say it — does not, however, undercut the value of entrepreneurial initiative. The rhetoric by which the critic persuades us to share his perceptions is not, and cannot be, that of the scientist. It is rather that of the lawyer, imposing the appearance of logic on material inherently resistant to such patterning, though not so totally free that he can rearrange the facts in any way that suits his wit and the convenience of his client. The unity of Shakespearean tragedy is, it seems appropriate to say on a bicentennial occasion, like other unities *e pluribus unum,* a unity that has to be continually reinvented by those who wish to assert it. It is a tribute to the power of the human mind that we are sustained by the belief that we can do it.

# Tragic Mysteries

## by HELEN GARDNER

Not being an alchemist, and indeed having no confidence in the feasibility of the alchemical quest, I am making no attempt to distil in the limbeck of my poor brain a "quintessence" from Shakespeare's tragedies that might be called his "tragic sense." Nor do I feel it possible to attempt to establish a "meaning" or "meanings" from his tragedies that would be valid for "us" today. Seeing or reading a Shakespearean tragedy is an experience that is profoundly meaningful; but the experience cannot be conceptualized into some "meaning," and certainly not into a universally valid meaning. I have always shown, I hope, polite skepticism when told that this or that was what "the Elizabethans" thought or believed. I feel an even deeper skepticism over the idea that, even if I were to attempt to project a meaning for myself, it would be a meaning for "us today." I therefore propose to speak on Tragic Mysteries.

"It seems probable," wrote Henry James, in his preface to *The Princess Casamassima,* "that if we were never bewildered there never would be a story to tell about us," and he adds that the "wary reader warns the novelist against making his characters too *interpretative* of the muddle of fate." It is not a warning that any spectator or reader of Shakespeare's tragedies could feel that Shakespeare stood much in need of. In their exploration of their own natures and their exploration of the nature of the universe, as both are progressively revealed to them in the dangers, bewilderment, and perplexity into which they are thrust, the characters of Shakespeare's tragedies do not ultimately arrive at interpretations of themselves or of their fate. Indeed, those to whom Shakespeare is most generous in providing opportunities for self-revelation in soliloquy are precisely those who leave us at the close with the greatest sense of the mysteries of man's nature and of the universe in which he acts and suffers: Hamlet, Macbeth, and Iago.

Shakespeare often seems to evade presenting—or to feel the impossibility of presenting—the actual movements of the mind when a man sways between two possibilities to find himself committed to one. The most striking example, which has often been commented upon, is Brutus's soliloquy "It must be by his death," in which he is concerned to find reasons for doing what he has already decided he *must* do: "It *must* be by his death." What, we may well ask, is "It"? In a marvelous passage, a little later, Brutus describes the state of a man between the acting of a "dreadful thing" and the "first motion"; but Shakespeare does not show us the state of indecision and inner warfare when the mind sways between two courses, or what finally tips the balance of decision and directs the will. Years ago Wilson Knight drew a parallel between Brutus and Macbeth, who presents with such thrilling force all the arguments against the murder of Duncan, holds out against his wife's taunts with the splendid

> I dare do all that may become a man;
> Who dares do more, is none

only to capitulate with the feeble "If we should fail?" Reassured on this point, which is totally irrelevant to the profound moral repugnance at the deed that he had finally arrived at, he declares "I am settled." We see him go toward the murder like a man irresistibly impelled. But, by what? Or to turn to a character who is not the hero: Let me refer to the silence of Claudius on his knees, after he, like Macbeth, has seen so clearly the course he must take if he is to gain release from the burden of guilt and its inevitable consequences in further guilt if he does not now turn back. The tame couplet with which he rises merely announces the result of the battle between his *words* and his *thoughts*. I am reminded of a famous passage in a sermon of John Donne, where he speaks of falling on his knees and calling God and the angels to listen and then neglecting God and his angels for the noise of a fly or a coach in the street, saying that he prays on but the last time he thought on what he was saying he cannot remember. The "thoughts" of Claudius, like Macbeth's "black and deep desires," are only to be guessed at by us from their actualization. Perhaps the most extraordinary silence is that of Coriolanus, when, having listened in silence to Volumnia's first long speech and risen to turn away, he turns back and once more listens until she, in turn, turns to go, when, as the stage direction has it, "He holds her by the hand, silent." Is there any parallel in drama for the hero at the crisis of his fate being silent for so long? The conflict in Coriolanus's inmost being is not verbalized. What is the moment of decision? Is it when he weeps, a "broken Coriolanus"? Are his tears only for his family, tears of natural love for those he has, with Rome, abandoned? Are they perhaps also tears for himself, his broken vow, his lost integrity, and for the price he knows he must pay if he returns to the Volscians, having betrayed them and robbed them of their victory?

I have begun with some silences, where Shakespeare leaves unrevealed what perhaps can never be wholly understood—and certainly not by means of weighing the rational arguments for and against a course—what finally impels a human being at a crossroad. We can, of course, and do, and indeed we must, debate motives, recognize pressures, acknowledge vulnerabilities, and attempt to be more interpretative of the persons and their fate than they themselves are. But one reason for their illusory reality in our imaginations is this residue of mystery. Any criticism that is too certain of the finality and completeness of its own analysis of the characters and their fate destroys the essence of the Shakespearean tragic experience: that it shows us a world of dangers within and without, of bewilderment and perplexity in the extreme, in which men voyage into themselves to discover what they did not know of themselves, capacities for good and evil, and encounter a world in which certainties crumble and profound questions are raised to which at the close neither they nor the spectators can provide adequate answers.

In the great play in which Shakespeare launched out into the deep, the longest play he ever wrote, in which the hero has the longest part of any hero in any play, that hero's last word is "silence." The most famous line he utters ends with the word "question." As Professor Levin pointed out, the word *question* and its derivative *questionable* are key words in *Hamlet*, as reference to the Concordance will show. At the close, as Hamlet lies dying, it seems that the anonymous bystanders—for all the main actors except Hamlet and Horatio are dead—and *we*, the audience, who have with them watched the action of the play, are to receive *some* revelation:

> You that look pale and tremble at this chance,
> That are but mutes or audience to this act,
> Had I but time, as this fell sergeant Death
> Is strict in his arrest, O, I could tell you—
> But let it be.

The revelation—if there ever could have been one—is withheld. Hamlet in his last few moments instead takes up his public burden as Prince of Denmark. He turns to Horatio. As a Renaissance Prince he thinks of his reputation. Horatio is to "tell his story," and the summary Horatio gives of the action of the play is a just one. He gives his voice to Fortinbras. And then "The rest is silence."

It is Hamlet himself who, late in the play, tells us he does not know the answer to the question that most critics of the last century thought the main question in the play:

> I do not know
> Why yet I live to say "This thing's to do,"
> Sith I have cause and means and strength to do't.

And, in rebuking Rosencrantz and Guildenstern, Hamlet seems to speak to us also, when he protests at their attempts to make an unworthy thing of him, to "pluck out the heart" of his mystery.

If *Hamlet* is all questions, a play in which uniquely the audience is in the dark with the hero, by contrast, and perhaps by an artist's deliberate reaction, *Othello* is all clarity. The audience is in no doubt of what is true and what is not. We are no longer groping for our way in doubts and uncertainties with the hero, but watching from our seats around the stage. In the great central action Shakespeare for once, masterfully, traces the movement of a mind, showing us, stage by stage, Othello's progress from curiosity, to uneasiness, to tormented acceptance of what we know to be false. We never doubt Desdemona's truth or Cassio's loyalty, and we know exactly what was the course of the fatal handkerchief from Desdemona's hand to Bianca's. The mystery here is concentrated in Othello's single unanswered question at the close:

> Will you, I pray, demand that demi-devil
> Why he hath thus ensnar'd my soul and body?

> Demand me nothing, what you know, you know,
> From this time forth I never will speak word.

*Othello,* for all its clarity, for all our certainties about the facts, is the tragedy that has most baffled the interpreters searching for a meaning. (And in passing I would like to say that critics discussing why Othello yielded to Iago's insinuations perhaps do not make enough allowance for the difficulty we have in believing that anyone really hates us. Of course, we are aware that some people dislike us or do not value us at our true worth, and that we annoy some people; but that anyone with a cold hate could actually want to destroy us is an idea almost impossible to entertain.) With *Hamlet,* most write as if they were sure there was or could be some final interpretation of the play, even if they are not certain they have arrived at it. With *Othello* many have given up, either declaring the tragedy "meaningless," or falling back on the notion that Shakespeare wrote this most moving and beautiful play to expose the weakness of the hero he created out of Cinthio's erring barbarian.

In the play that we may regard as Shakespeare's induction to great tragedy, Brutus, hard pressed by Cassius, exclaims

> Into what dangers would you lead me, Cassius,
> That you would have me seek into myself
> For that which is not in me?

The dangers into which Cassius leads Brutus, the misty region of doubt and metaphysical and moral uncertainty to which the Ghost beckons Hamlet, the extremity of perplexity to which Iago brings Othello, the wilderness that Lear chooses when he "abjures all roofs" and accepts "necessity's hard pinch," the nightmare world into which the promises of the weird sisters lure Macbeth — all are regions in which the hero discovers what he had not known was in him and is driven to extremes that seem beyond the possibilities of the personality displayed to us at the beginning. Their conduct shocks and bewilders those who thought they knew them:

> Is this the noble Moor, whom our full senate
> Call all in all sufficient? This the noble nature,
> Whom passion could not shake? whose solid virtue
> The shot of accident, nor dart of chance,
> Could neither graze, nor pierce?

In Shakespeare's earliest attempt at tragic writing, *Titus Andronicus,* Titus, confronted with his mutilated daughter and the heads of his murdered sons, and with the hand he had cut off in vain to save them cynically returned to him, exclaims

> When will this fearful slumber have an end?

In this nightmare of intolerable horror he breaks down into madness, expressing his grief and rage in wild gestures of extravagant fury, and in words in which "matter and impertinency" are mixed. In the four great central tragedies, the journey into the interior, the self-discovery to which the hero is driven, either involves, or borders on, the world of madness, in which the single state of man is shaken and "nothing is, but what is not." When Hamlet declares that he will put on "an antic disposition," he ventures onto the tricky borderline that lies between sanity and madness. Role-playing is dangerous. He who plays the madman may play it too well, and by throwing off restraint and taking the madman's license to "unpack his heart with words," to insult and mock and baffle, may risk loss of control: feigning may cease to be feigning. Or perhaps it is only those who fear the loss of control who act such loss in order not to break down in reality. Johnson saw no purpose in Hamlet's pretended madness and was distressed that he, "a brave and good man," sheltered himself in his apology to Laertes by a lie. As for the purpose, the assumption of an antic disposition allows Hamlet to speak truths, and discover truths, and to dominate a world in which he is powerless. But I cannot take Hamlet's behavior to Ophelia, or to his mother in the closet scene, or in his fight with Laertes in the grave as simply an act he puts on: that he is here merely "mad in craft." When Hamlet follows the ghost on the battlements he risks his "sovereignty of reason," and I believe that we are meant to take his apology to Laertes as heartfelt. At the latest moment, with the

premonition that his end is upon him, he looks back, like somone who has
awaked from a nightmare, and feels he is now himself again, feeling "It was
not I." In the central action of *Othello,* Othello becomes the victim of an
obsession in which all acts, gestures, and words, however innocent and tri-
fling, only serve to confirm the monstrous and intolerable idea that
Desdemona is false. *Othello* is exceptional in that the hero's ordeal is so long
delayed and Shakespeare expends so much time and genius in establishing
him as a heroic figure. It is not until the third act that Iago begins to under-
mine what had seemed an invulnerable confidence. But in the darkest and
most mysterious of the tragedies, *Macbeth,* the hero is no sooner before us
than he is "rapt," obsessed with "horrible imaginings," and through the whole
action more and more he makes his companions of "sorriest fancies," is
shaken "in the affliction" of "terrible dreams," forced to know his deed and
know himself until

> all that is within him does condemn
> Itself, for being there.

Macbeth, though we cannot call him insane, shares with the insane the "awful
privacy of the insane mind." If *question* is a dominant word in *Hamlet, mad*
and *madness* are dominant words in *King Lear,* occurring in the first act in
Kent's outburst:

> Be Kent unmannerly,
> When Lear is mad.

But in this play madness and sanity, like vision and blindness, invert their
usual values, so that the sane seem mad and the mad sane. Lear, who struggles for control and patience, and prays the heavens that he may not be mad,
discovers in his madness a prophetic voice, and the Fool is here the wise man.
In his journey of discovery, unlike the other heroes, Lear finds unexpected
virtues within himself, such reserves of patience, and such fellow-feeling for
suffering humanity that when he wakes from his madness to meet again his
"child Cordelia" he seems utterly different from the willful autocrat of the
first scene. Many critics have seen in *King Lear* a tragedy of redemption
through suffering, and indeed, if the play had ended with the reunion of Lear
and Cordelia, it would be hard to reject such an interpretation. But it does
not. The Lear who enters at the close, with Cordelia dead in his arms, is not
"a pattern of all patience." Granville-Barker noted years ago how closely the
end parallels the beginning. The bodies of Goneril and Regan are brought
onto the stage, so that at the end as at the beginning we have before us Lear
and his three daughters and by his side his good counsellor and faithful servant, Kent. Here, as then, Lear's whole being is concentrated on Cordelia's
lips. He can no more accept the silence of death than he could accept her

reply — "Nothing" — to his loving and eager — if foolish — demand, "What can you say . . . ? Speak."


In *King Lear,* above all the other tragedies, Shakespeare seems on the very verge of justifying the harsh world of tragic experience and of giving us, the audience, the privilege of being "God's spies." But at the close the philosophic Edgar and the moralist Albany have nothing to offer us, and it is left to Kent, the faithful companion of Lear's journey through the wilderness, to make the only fitting comment:

> The wonder is he hath endur'd so long:
> He but usurp'd his life.

It recalls Lear's own cry in the storm: "Pour on; I will endure," rather than Edgar's moralization to Gloucester: "Ripeness is all."

In Shakespeare's tragic art the image of the hero as he was is in some way reaffirmed at the close, most spendidly in *Othello,* to match the splendid opening, most briefly in Macbeth, who, at the very end, "whole in the present," with no future to torment him with vain hopes and fears, is last seen, as he was first reported to us, as a fighting man and a brave one. At the close of the tragedies also, the bystanders, passing no judgment on their acts, pay tribute to the essential qualities of the heroes. In the Roman plays the tributes are paid by those who have destroyed them and have a kind of public formality. In the other tragedies it may be only a phrase, such as "He was great of heart," or a word of rich connotation but imprecise denotation such as "noble." But tribute is always paid, with one exception. No tribute is paid to Macbeth. He is dismissed as "this dead butcher." It is only we, the audience, who can pay a tribute of silent awe to his endurance in the most terrible of all the journeys into the interior that Shakespeare shows us.

*Macbeth* ends the phase of Shakespeare's tragic art that begins with *Julius Caesar.* He turned from these tragedies of discovery to tragedies of another kind. It is particularly with these plays that we, who try to interpret them, need, I think, to remember Lafeu's warning to "philosophical persons" who "make modern and familiar, things supernatural and causeless," lest we "make trifles of terrors, ensconcing ourselves into seeming knowledge when we should submit ourselves to an unknown fear." Of all great writers Shakespeare has the greatest power to show us how men act and suffer and to convince us of the truth of what we hear and see, but to the question, "why" his tragedies return no clear answer.

# Quarto and Folio King Lear and the Interpretation of Albany and Edgar

by MICHAEL J. WARREN

I

The two texts of *King Lear* present obvious editorial and critical problems. The Quarto of 1608 prints about 283 lines that are not printed in the 1623 Folio; the Folio prints about 100 that are not printed in the Quarto.[1] A variation of nearly 400 lines in a text of around 3,300 lines is significant;[2] in addition, there are also a very large number of variant substantive readings. However, far from alarming editors and critics to the delicate problems involved in printing and discussing a single play called *King Lear,* this wealth of material has been treated as an ample blessing from which a "best text" of Shakespeare's *King Lear* may be evolved. Indeed, the standard methods of bibliography and editing — the application of critical principles "to the textual raw material of the authoritative preserved documents in order to approach as nearly as may be to the ideal of the authorial fair copy by whatever necessary process of recovery, independent emendation, or conflation of authorities"[3] — such methods and the accepted assumptions of the origins of each text have led to the editorial habit of establishing and publishing a *King Lear* text that is produced by a process of conflation, by the exercise of a moderate and quasi-scientific eclecticism, and by a studied disregard for the perils of intentionalism.[4]/In a recent article Kenneth Muir writes:

This paper is an enlarged version of that delivered at the International Shakespeare Association Congress in Washington, D.C. in April 1976. As a consequence of delivering the paper I have become aware that three scholars are currently writing dissertations arguing for the distinctness of the Quarto and Folio texts of *King Lear*: Steven Urkowitz of University of Chicago, Georgia Peters Burton of Bryn Mawr College, and Peter W. M. Blayney of Cambridge University; each of us has arrived at the same major conclusion independently of the others. I would like to thank my colleague Professor John M. Ellis for his helpful advice and criticism with respect to the argument of the first part of this paper.

Until the work of bibliographers and textual critics in the present century, editors chose readings from either text, according to taste. It is now generally agreed that, whatever the basis of the Quarto text, the Folio text of *King Lear* is nearer to what Shakespeare wrote; but, even so, editors are still bound to accept a number of readings from the inferior text and, since there were cuts in the prompt-book from which the Folio text was derived, a number of long passages.[5]

This statement reveals certain clear attitudes of editors to their task. It is assumed that there is one primal lost text, an "ideal *King Lear*" that Shakespeare wrote, and that we have two corrupted copies of it. It is hypothesized that F is a less corrupt version of the ideal text than Q, though both preserve features of the ideal original; and that while there is more corruption in Q, some uncorrupted elements remain that can mitigate the admittedly lesser corruption of F. The concept of the "ideal *King Lear*" is problematic here, first, because its existence cannot be known, and second, because in the absence of such knowledge it is nevertheless further assumed that all alterations of any nature from that imaginary text are by hands other than Shakespeare's. Such an assumption is based on no evidence, and is counter to our experience of authors and their habits—for example, the modification of texts after first publication by Jonson, Pope, Yeats, James, and Pinter. Of course, it is conceivable that this standard hypothesis may indeed be true, but the confidence with which it is assumed is unwarranted, and the lack of a constant awareness that it is an assumption leads to poorly founded judgments. For instance, a statement such as "editors are still bound to accept a number of readings from the inferior text" is merely an editor's justification of the right to be eclectic; although editors may well be advised at times to adopt readings where comparison of texts indicates simple misprints or nonsensical readings, circumspection and wariness are always necessary, for nonsense may merely be sense we do not yet understand, and further we cannot know that alterations between Q and F are not authorial in origin. Most editors admit that the examination of the two texts leads to the conclusion that editing has taken place, and yet they are generally reluctant to take that editing seriously.

Having asserted the necessity of a decent skepticism in relation to the concept of the "ideal" text, I wish to argue that in a situation where statements about textual status are never more than hypotheses based upon the current models of thought about textual recension, it is not demonstrably erroneous to work with the possibility (a) that there may be no single "ideal play" of *King Lear* (all of "what Shakespeare wrote"), that there may never have been one, and that what we create by conflating both texts is merely an invention of editors and scholars; (b) that for all its problems Q is an authoritative version of the play of *King Lear*; and (c) that F may indeed be a revised version of the play, that its additions and omissions may constitute Shakespeare's considered modification of the earlier text, and that we certainly cannot know that they are not.[6]

Of course, I am once more introducing, after over fifty years of relative quiescence, the specter of "continuous copy": not, I would hope, in the confident, fantastic, and disintegrationist mode of Robertson and Dover Wilson, but in a skeptical and conservative way. In his famous lecture *The Disintegration of Shakespeare*, E. K. Chambers dismissed the excesses of his contemporaries as much by the force of ironic rhetoric and an attractive appeal to common sense as by any real proof; but he nowhere succeeded in denying the possibility of authorial reworking. He instanced the few cases of recorded extensive revision as indicative that revision of any kind was rare; and he asserted as follows: "That any substantial revision, as distinct perhaps from a mere abridgement, would entail a fresh application for the Master's allowance must, I think, be taken for granted. The rule was that his hand must be 'at the latter end of the booke they doe play'; and in London, at least, any company seriously departing from the allowed book would run a considerable risk."[7] Which is an interesting hypothesis; but what in this connection would constitute "substantial revision" or "serious departure"? Chambers to the contrary, that same common sense which leads me to praise him in his rejection of disintegrationist excesses leads me nevertheless to believe that a play like *King Lear* may have undergone revision beyond "mere abridgement" — what Chambers, following Henslowe, might classify as "altering" — without the necessity of resubmission to the Master of the Revels.

In putting forward this argument I have ignored many of the complexities of relation that have been the stuff of textual debate for many years. I have done so because they are merely the current working hypotheses of the editing world, and because they are not immediately relevant to my contention. I would maintain that Q and F *King Lear* are sufficiently dissimilar that they should not be conflated, but should be treated as two versions of a single play, both having authority. To substantiate my argument I wish to present three brief studies. In the first I will deal with a short exchange of dialogue to illustrate the impact of conflation on the text as script for the theater; in the second and third I will discuss the varying presentations of Albany and Edgar in Q and F.

## II

In Act 2 Lear discovers Kent in the stocks; the two texts present the following dialogue (2.4.12-23):[8] first Q:

*Lear.* Whats he, that hath so much thy place mistooke to set thee here?
*Kent.* It is both he and shee, your sonne & daugter.

    *Lear.* No.                           *Kent.* Yes.
    *Lear.* No I say,                   *Kent.* I say yea.
    *Lear.* No no, they would not.      *Kent.* Yes they haue.
    *Lear.* By *Iupiter* I sweare no, they durst not do't,
    They would not, could not do't, . . .

then F:

    *Lear.* What's he,
    That hath so much thy place mistooke
    To set thee heere?
    *Kent.* It is both he and she,
    Your Son, and Daughter.
    *Lear.* No.
    *Kent.* Yes.
    *Lear.* No I say.
    *Kent.* I say yea.
    *Lear.* By *Iupiter* I sweare no.
    *Kent.* By *Iuuo*, I sweare I.
    *Lear.* They durst not do't:
    They could not, would not do't: . . .

Editors here customarily conflate these texts so that both "No no, they would not / Yes they haue," and Kent's "By *Iuuo*, I sweare I" are retained; in consequence four exchanges are produced where three exist in each of the original texts. Muir's note in the Arden text (p. 83) is concerned with the integrity of the Q lines and critics' opinions of their quality. But the more important issue is that his text (like most others) presents us with a reading that has *no* authority. If F was printed from a copy of Q, as is widely and reasonably accepted, then one ought to assume that any omission may have had a purpose: but that assumption is doubly imperative when new material is included in F that appears to make up for the omission. However, even if one ignores the standard theory concerning the recension, there is still no case for four exchanges. In each text the climax on the third exchange is powerful, and sufficient; neither can be proved to be un-Shakespearean — they are both probably "what Shakespeare wrote"; and so respect for the theatrical proportions of the play dictates that conflation cannot be other than textual tinkering, distortion. Either Q or F; *not* both together.

### III

    As the above passage indicates, the editor, like any other reader of Shakespeare, must always be conscious that play texts are scripts for performance; when they are realized on the stage, presence, absence, action, inaction, speech, and silence have far more impact than when they are noted on the printed page. With this observation in mind I wish to argue that Q and F reveal significant differences in the roles of Albany and Edgar, differences sufficiently great that one is obliged to interpret their characters differently in each, and, especially in relation to the alterations in the last scene, to appreciate a notable contrast in the tone and meaning of the close of each text. These differences go beyond those which may be expected when two texts descend in corrupted form from a common original; they indicate that a substantial and consistent recasting of certain aspects of the play has taken place. In brief, the part of Albany is more developed in Q than in F, and in Q he closes the play a mature and victorious duke assuming responsibility for the kingdom; in F he is a weaker character, avoiding responsibility. The part of Edgar is shorter in F than in Q; however, whereas in Q he ends the play a young man overwhelmed by his experience, in F he is a young man who has learned a great deal, and who is emerging as the new leader of the ravaged society.

In both texts Albany speaks little in the first act. Neither Albany nor Cornwall speaks in the first scene in Q; their joint exclamation "Deare Sir forbeare" (1.1.162) appears in F only. In the fourth scene, which Goneril dominates in both texts, Q lacks two of the eight brief speeches that F assigns to Albany, and a phrase that completes a third. Missing are "Pray Sir be patient" (1.4.270) and "Well, you may feare too farre" (1.4.338), and the phrase "Of what hath moued you" (1.4.283), which in F succeeds "My Lord, I am guiltlesse, as I am ignorant." Albany, who is bewildered and ineffectual in either text, is more patently so in Q, where he is given no opportunity to urge patience in response to Lear's question — "is it your will that wee prepare any horses" (F "Is it your will, speake Sir? Prepare my Horses") (1.4.267) — and no opportunity to warn Goneril of the unwisdom of her acts. Goneril's part also is smaller in Q than in F — she lacks 1.4.322-43 — but she dominates the scene nevertheless.

However, when Albany enters in the fourth act after a period in which he does not ride to Gloucester's house with Goneril and is mentioned only in the context of the always incipient conflict between himself and Cornwall, his reappearance is different in quality in each text. In both texts the scene begins with Oswald reporting Albany's disaffection (4.2.3-11) while Goneril scorns "the Cowish terror of his spirit" (4.2.12). In F Albany's speech on entering is very brief:

> Oh *Gonerill,*
> You are not worth the dust which the rude winde
> Blowes in your face.
> (4.2.29-31)

However, Q continues:

> I feare your disposition
> That nature which contemnes ith origin
> Cannot be bordered certaine in it selfe,
> She that her selfe will sliuer and disbranch
> From her materiall sap, perforce must wither,
> And come to deadly vse.
>
> (4.2.31-36)

And Goneril's prompt dismissal "No more, the text is foolish" leads to a
longer speech of powerful moral reproach, likening the sisters to tigers, and
reaching its climax in the pious pronouncement that

> If that the heauens doe not their visible spirits
> Send quickly downe to tame this vild offences, it will come
> Humanity must perforce pray on it self like monsters of the deepe.
>
> (4.2.46-50)

The speeches that follow in Q are much reduced in F, and both Albany and
Goneril lose lines. The cuts in Goneril's part are largely references to Albany
as a "morall foole," statements critical of his mild response to the invasion of
France; her stature is not notably diminished by the loss. The reduction of
Albany's part, by contrast, severely reduces his theatrical impact. In F he is
left with barely six lines between his entrance and that of the messenger, and
there is no sense of the new strong position that lines such as the following,
even allowing for Goneril's belittling rejection, establish in Q:

> *Alb.* Thou changed, and selfe-couerd thing for shame
> Be-monster not thy feature, wer't my fitnes
> To let these hands obay my bloud,
> They are apt enough to dislecate and teare
> Thy flesh and bones, how ere thou art a fiend,
> A womans shape doth shield thee.
> *Gon.* Marry your manhood mew . . .
>
> (4.2.62-68)

In Q the succeeding lines of moral outrage at the news of the blinding of
Gloucester present Albany as a man of righteous wrath, outraged by injustice;
the same sequence in F presents Albany as equally outraged, but because of
the brevity of his previous rebukes he appears more futile in context, less obviously a man capable of action. The cutting diminishes his stature.

Although Albany does assert himself in the fifth act in both texts, he is
much stronger in Q by virtue of the presence of three passages that are not his
in F. At his entrance he asserts control over the situation in both texts with his
first speech; Q reads:

> Our very louing sister well be-met
> For this I heare the King is come to his daughter
> With others, whome the rigour of our state
> Forst to crie out, . . .
>
> (5.1.20-23)[9]

The speech continues in Q, but not in F:

> where I could not be honest
> I neuer yet was valiant, for this busines
> It touches vs. as *France* inuades our land
> Not bolds the King, with others whome I feare,
> Most iust and heauy causes make oppose.
>
> (5.1.23-27)

The inclusion of this passage in Q gives immediate prominence to the complexity and scrupulousness of Albany's understanding of the political and moral issues. More important, however, are the two alterations in the closing moments of the play: at 5.3.251 Q assigns to Albany the order "Hast thee for thy life," which F gives to Edgar; and Q assigns the final four lines to Albany, which again F gives to Edgar. I shall discuss these changes more fully as I deal with Edgar, but it is sufficient to point out at this stage that Albany is in command throughout the last scene in Q, while in F he is considerably effaced at the close.

## IV

In both Q and F Edgar presents far more complex problems than Albany, not least because he is intrinsically a more complex and difficult character even before textual variations are considered. Edgar's part, which in conflated texts is second only to that of Lear in length,[10] is reduced in size in F, but unlike Albany, Edgar receives some new material which, however it is interpreted, tends to focus attention more precisely upon him.

The differences in Edgar's role between Q and F in the first act are not of major significance: at 1.2.98-100 Q includes and F omits an exchange between Edmund and Gloucester about Edgar that reveals more about Gloucester's character than Edgar's; F omits Edmund's imitative discourse upon the current crisis and Edgar's ironic reply "How long haue you been a sectary Astronomicall?" (1.2.151-57); and F includes a passage not in Q in which Edmund proposes concealing Edgar in his lodging, and recommends going armed, to the surprise of his brother (1.2.172-79). More important variations appear in the third act. At 3.4.37-38 in F (after a stage direction *"Enter Edgar, and Foole,"* which contradicts Kent's speech a few lines later

"What art thou that dost grumble there i'th' straw? Come forth"), Edgar utters a line that Q lacks: "Fathom, and halfe, Fathom and halfe; poore *Tom*";
this offstage cry makes a chilling theatrical introduction to Edgar-as-Tom,
and it is moreover the event that, coupled with his entrance, appears to pro-
pel Lear finally into madness. Later in the third act F omits material that Q
includes. F lacks the trial of Goneril that Lear conducts with the support of
Edgar and the Fool (3.6.17-56). While F provides the Fool with a new last line
in the play "And Ile go to bed at noone" (3.6.88), it omits Kent's tender
speech over Lear in Q, which begins "Oppressed nature sleepes" (3.6.100-
104). However, very important alterations in this middle section of the play
follow immediately; they are F's omission of the soliloquy with which Edgar
closes 3.6 in Q and F's minor amplification of Edgar's first speech in the
fourth act, two speeches that provide the transitions to and from the climactic
scene of the blinding of Gloucester. These alterations need to be discussed in
the larger context of the character and function of Edgar in the play.

In recent years serious challenges have been made to the traditional conception of Edgar as the good, devoted, abused but patient, loving son. Some
of this examination has led to the formulation of extreme positions in which
Edgar has appeared as almost as culpable and vicious as Edmund, dedication
to an ideal of selfless virtuous support being interpreted as an unconscious
psychic violence, a dangerous self-righteousness that must exercise itself on
others.[11] It is unnecessary, however, to censure Edgar so strongly to accommodate some of the distance that one frequently feels from him; one may
allow him his virtue while still seeing its weakness. Speaking much in aside
and soliloquy, Edgar is distanced theatrically from many of the events of the
play. However, despite his involvement with Lear in the mad scenes, he also
appears at times to be distanced emotionally from the events around him; his
moral commentary reflects his response to the events, his assessment of his
philosophical position in their light. The problem is that his response is frequently inadequate. As the play proceeds Edgar is obliged to confront the
shallowness of his rationalizations, and yet much of the time he nevertheless
appears impervious to the new knowledge that is being forced upon him. He
possesses a naively pious and optimistic faith in the goodness of the world and
the justice of the gods, and in his own youthful, romantic vision of his role in
this world of conflict. In his mind his father's despair will be conquered by his
endless encouragement; the triumphant climax will be the restoration to
Gloucester of the knowledge of his son's existence and readiness to go off to
recover his dukedom for him. The mode of Edgar's thought is Christian
romantic-heroic, in which virtue usually triumphs spendidly. That it bears little relation to the realities of the universe in which the play takes place is evident; but it does save Gloucester from abject misery, and provides incidentally a happy, well-deceived death for him. We can appreciate Edgar's love and
concern for his father, while doubting the maturity of many of his judgments.

It is in the context of this conception of Edgar, which is appropriate to either text, that I wish to demonstrate the major alterations in the role. When the soliloquy beginning "When we our betters see bearing our woes" is spoken at the close of 3.6. in Q (3.6.105-18), we are aware of Edgar's ability to comment upon the king's suffering, the power of fellowship, and his capacity to endure; in F, which lacks these meditations, Edgar has played a very small part in a rather brief scene, and the play rushes to the blinding of Gloucester. But F compensates for these cuts by expanding the speech with which Edgar opens the fourth act in both texts by adding an extra sentence. The speech reads:

> Yet better thus, and knowne to be contemn'd,
> Then still contemn'd and flatter'd, to be worst:
> The lowest, and most deiected thing of Fortune,
> Stands still in esperance, liues not in feare:
> The lamentable change is from the best,
> The worst returnes to laughter.
>
> (4.1.1-6)[12]

But F continues:

> Welcome then,
> Thou vnsubstantiall ayre that I embrace:
> The Wretch that thou hast blowne vnto the worst,
> Owes nothing to thy blasts.
>
> (4.1.6-9)

And then Gloucester enters. In both texts Edgar expresses the philosophic confidence of the man who has reached the bottom, but in F Edgar speaks still more facilely courageous lines of resolution against fortune just prior to having the inadequacy of his vision exposed by the terrible entrance of his father. What the revision in F achieves is this. The play is shortened and speeded by the loss from 3.6 and the opening of 4.1 of about 54 lines (three minutes of playing time at least). The absence of Edgar's moral meditation from the end of 3.6 brings the speech at 4.1.1 into sharp focus, isolating it more obviously between the blinding and the entrance of Gloucester; in F the two servants do not remain onstage after Cornwall's exit. The additional lines at this point emphasize the hollowness of Edgar's assertions; while the quantity of sententiousness is reduced, its nature is made more emphatically evident. Edgar gains in prominence, ironically enough, by the loss of a speech, and the audience becomes more sharply aware of his character.

The last act reveals major alterations that surpass those briefly described in the discussion of Albany. In both texts Edgar describes the death of his father with rhetorical fullness and elaborate emotional dramatization (5.3.181-99). In Q, however, he is given an additional speech of seventeen lines (5.3.204-21) only briefly interrupted by Albany, in which he reports his meeting with Kent. The removal of this speech not only speeds the last act by the elimination of material of no immediate importance to the plot, but also reduces the length of the delay between Edmund's "This speech of yours hath mou'd me, / And shall perchance do good" (5.3.199-200) and the sending of an officer to Lear. It also diminishes the sense of Edgar as the immature, indulgent man displaying his heroic tale of woe, for in F Albany's command "If there be more, more wofull, hold it in" (5.3.202) is obeyed; in Q by contrast Edgar nevertheless continues:

> This would haue seemd a periode to such
> As loue not sorow, but another to amplifie too much,
> Would make much more, and top extreamitie . . .
>                          (5.3.204-7)

and the speech reveals Edgar's regard for his own dramatic role in the recent history:

> Whil'st I was big in clamor, came there in a man,
> Who hauing seene me in my worst estate,
> Shund my abhord society, but then finding
> Who twas that so indur'd . . .
>                          (5.3.208-11)

F, then, maintains the fundamental nature of Edgar as philosophical agent through the play, but in the last act reduces somewhat his callowness, his easy indulgence of his sensibility in viewing the events through which he is living. In so doing F develops Edgar into a man worthy to stand with the dukes at the close of the play, capable of assuming power.

The elevation of Edgar at the close and relative reduction of Albany that distinguish F from Q can be documented from three other places. At 5.3.229[13] in Q Edgar says to Albany "Here comes Kent sir," but "Here comes Kent" in F. The transfer of the command "Hast thee for thy life" (5.3.251) from Albany in Q to Edgar in F gives Edgar a more active role in the urgent events; indeed, Q may indicate that it is Edgar who is to run. All Edgar's lines after "Hast thee for thy life" are shared by Q and F apart from the last four, which Q assigns to Albany. Though they are partial lines at most, they are susceptible of quite different interpretations according to whether Edgar speaks the last lines or not. If one considers Edgar's behavior in Q in the light of his lachrymose speech about Kent and his apparently subordinate role to Albany, he appears to be silenced by Lear's death: initially in Q he cries out "He faints my Lord, my Lord" (5.3.311), then appeals to Lear "Look vp my Lord" (312), only to say after Kent has assured him of the death "O he is gone indeed" (315), and to fall silent for the rest of the play. By contrast, F omits the "O" in this last statement, and then gives Edgar the last lines. In Q, then,

Edgar concludes the play stunned to silence by the reality of Lear's death, a very young man who does not even answer Albany's appeal "Friends of my soule, you twaine, / Rule in this Realme" (5.3.319-20), so that Albany reluctantly but resolutely accepts the obligation to rule: "The waight of this sad time we must obey" (323). This characterization of Edgar is a far cry from the Edgar of F who comes forward as a future ruler when he enables Albany to achieve his objective of not ruling; F's Edgar is a young man of limited perceptions concerning the truth of the world's harsh realities, but one who has borne some of the burdens and appears capable of handling (better than anybody else) the responsibilities that face the survivors.[14]

In summary, Q and F embody two different artistic visions. In Q, Edgar remains an immature young man and ends the play devastated by his experience, while Albany stands as the modest, diffident, but strong and morally upright man. In F Edgar grows into a potential ruler, a well-intentioned, resolute man in a harsh world, while Albany, a weaker man, abdicates his responsibilities. In neither text is the prospect for the country a matter of great optimism, but the vision seems bleaker and darker in F, where the young Edgar, inexperienced in rule, faces the future with little support.

## V

In discussing these two texts I have focused on what seem to me to be the two major issues of the revision; I have not attended to the absence of 4.3 from F, nor to the relatively minor but nevertheless significant differences in the speeches of Lear, the Fool, and Kent. However, I submit that this examination of the texts and the implications of their differences for interpretation and for performance make it clear that they must be treated as separate versions of *King Lear*, and that eclecticism cannot be a valid principle in deciding readings. Conflated texts such as are commonly printed are invalid, and should not be used either for production or for interpretation. Though they may give their readers all of "what Shakespeare wrote," they do not give them Shakespeare's play of *King Lear*, but a play created by the craft and imagination of learned scholars, a work that has no justification for its existence. The principle that more is better, that all is good, has no foundation. What we as scholars, editors, interpreters, and servants of the theatrical craft have to accept and learn to live by is the knowledge that we have two plays of *King Lear* sufficiently different to require that all further work on the play be based on either Q or F, but not the conflation of both.

## Notes

1. I am using the figures cited by Alfred Harbage on p. 1104 of his appendix to his text of *King Lear* published in *The Pelican Shakespeare* (Baltimore, 1969), pp. 1104-6.

2. *The Pelican Shakespeare* states that *King Lear* is 3,195 lines long; *The Norton Facsimile: The First Folio of Shakespeare*, ed. Charlton Hinman (New York, 1968), gives *King Lear* 3,301 lines.

3. Fredson Bowers, *Textual and Literary Criticism* (Cambridge, 1966), p. 120.

4. Harbage, "Note on the Text": "In 1608 a version of *King Lear* appeared in a Quarto volume sold by Nathaniel Butter at his shop at the Pied Bull. Its text was reproduced in 1619 in a quarto falsely dated 1608. Various theories have been offered to explain the nature of the Pied Bull text, the most recent being that it represents Shakespeare's rough draft carelessly copied, and corrupted by the faulty memories of actors who were party to the copying. In 1623 a greatly improved though 'cut' version of the play appeared in the first folio, evidently printed from the quarto after it had been carefully collated with the official playhouse manuscript. The present edition follows the folio text, and although it adds in square brackets the passages appearing only in the quarto, and accepts fifty-three quarto readings, it follows the chosen text more closely than do most recent editions. However, deference to the quarto is paid in an appendix, where its alternative readings, both those accepted and those rejected, are listed. Few editorial emendations have been retained, but see. . . ." (p. 1064). See also G. Blakemore Evans, "Note on the Text" of *King Lear*, in *The Riverside Shakespeare* (Boston, 1974), pp. 1295-96, and Kenneth Muir, "Introduction" to *King Lear* (Arden Shakespeare) (Cambridge, Mass., 1959), pp. xix-xx.

5. Kenneth Muir, "King Lear," in Stanley Wells, ed., *Shakespeare: Select Bibliographical Guides* (Oxford, 1973), p. 171.

6. Nor, of course, can we know with absolute confidence that they are, though that is my suspicion. The views of four other scholars are notable on this subject of revision. Dr. Johnson remarked that "I believe the Folio is printed from Shakespeare's last revision, carelessly and hastily performed, with more thought of shortening the scenes than of continuing the action," quoted by H. H. Furness, ed., *King Lear* (New Variorum Edition), 9th ed. (London, 1880), p. 215. In *The Pictorial Edition of the Works of Shakespeare*, ed. Charles Knight, 8 vols., (London, [1839]-1843), Knight argued vigorously that the Folio represents an authorial revision of the play (VI,391-93); but he nevertheless included the passages that derive from Q alone in brackets in his published text. In *The Stability of Shakespeare's Texts* (Lincoln, Neb., 1965), E. A. J. Honigmann regards the differences in the texts of *King Lear* as authorial in origin (pp. 121-28), but conceives of them as cases of "authorial 'second thoughts' *before* its [the play's] delivery to the actors. I envisage, in short, two copies of a play, each in the author's hand, disagreeing in both substantive and indifferent readings: the play being regarded as 'finished' by Shakespeare in each version though not therefore beyond the reach of afterthoughts" (p. 2). By contrast, Peter W. M. Blayney (see unnumbered footnote on first page of this essay) informs me in a letter that he believes that Shakespeare's was not the only hand involved in the revision that led to F.

7. E. K. Chambers, *The Disintegration of Shakespeare* ([London], 1924), p. 17.

8. For convenience I shall cite line numberings based on Muir's Arden edition throughout this essay; apparent inconsistencies occasionally result from the Arden relineation. All quotations from Q are from *King Lear, 1608 (Pied Bull Quarto):* Shakespeare Quarto Facsimiles No. 1, ed. W. W. Greg (Oxford, 1939); all quotations from F are from *The Norton Facsimile: The First Folio of Shakespeare*, ed. Charlton B. Hinman (New York, 1968). The text will normally make clear whether Q or F is being quoted; on occasions when the text is not specified and the lines under discussion appear in both Q and F with only insignificant differences in spelling and punctuation, I quote from F alone.

9. At 5.1.21 F reads "Sir, this I heard," for "For this I heare."

10. See *Pelican Shakespeare*, p. 31.

11. For sympathetic readings of Edgar, see (among others), R. B. Heilman, *This Great Stage* (Baton Rouge, La., 1948), and William R. Elton, *King Lear and the Gods* (San Marino, 1966). For more unsympathetic interpretations, see William Empson, "Fool in Lear," in *The Structure of Complex Words* (London, 1951); Nicholas Brooke, *Shakespeare: King Lear* (London, 1963); Stanley Cavell, "The Avoidance of Love," in *Must We Mean What We Say?* (New York, 1969); Marvin Rosenberg, *The Masks of King Lear* (Berkeley, Calif., 1972); S. L. Goldberg, *An Essay on King Lear* (Cambridge, 1974). However, there are signs of a restoration of honor and respect to Edgar; see, for instance, F. T. Flahiff, "Edgar: Once and Future King," in Rosalie L. Colie and F. T. Flahiff, eds., *Some Facets of King Lear: Essays in Prismatic Criticism* (Toronto, 1974), pp. 221-37, and Barbara A. Kathe, rsm, "The Development of the Myth of the Birth of the Hero in the Role of Edgar," a paper delivered at the International Shakespeare Association Congress in Washington, D.C., in April 1976.

12. At 4.1.4 Q reads "experience" for "esperance."

13. This is the Arden placing that follows F; Q places this line in the middle of Albany's next speech at 5.3.232.

14. If this distinction between the presentations of Edgar in the two texts is made, the subtitle of Q makes more than merely conventional sense in its place: *"With the vnfortunate life of* Edgar, *sonne* and heire to the Earle of Gloster, and his sullen and assumed humor of TOM of Bedlam."

# "Anger's My Meat": Feeding, Dependency, and Aggression in Coriolanus

## by JANET ADELMAN

*Coriolanus* was written during a period of rising corn prices and the accompanying fear of famine: rising prices reached a climax in 1608. In May 1607, "a great number of common persons"—up to five thousand, Stow tells us in his *Annals*—assembled in various Midlands counties, including Shakespeare's own county of Warwickshire, to protest against the acceleration of enclosures and the resulting food shortages.[1] It must have been disturbing to property owners to hear that the rioters were well received by local inhabitants, who brought them food and shovels;[2] doubly disturbing if they were aware that this was one of England's first purely popular riots, unlike the riots of the preceding century in that the anger of the common people was not being manipulated by rebellious aristocrats or religious factions.[3] The poor rioters were quickly dispersed, but—if *Coriolanus* is any indication—the fears that they aroused were not. In fact, Shakespeare shapes his material from the start in order to exacerbate these fears in his audience. In Plutarch the people riot because the Senate refuses to control usury; in Shakespeare they riot because they are hungry. Furthermore, the relentlessly vertical imagery of the play reflects the specific threat posed by this contemporary uprising: in a society so hierarchical—that is, so vertical—as theirs, the rioters' threat to level enclosures implied more than the casting down of particular hedges; it seemed to promise a flattening of the whole society.[4] Nor is Shakespeare's exacerbation of these fears merely a dramatist's trick to catch the attention of his audience from the start, or a seventeenth-century nod toward political relevance: for the dominant issues of the uprising—the threat of starvation and the consequent attempt to level enclosures—are reflected not only in the political but also in the intrapsychic world of *Coriolanus*; taken together, they suggest the concerns that shape the play and particularly the progress of its hero.

The uprising of the people at the start of the play points us toward an underlying fantasy in which political and psychological fears come together in a way that can only make each more intense and hence more threatening. For the political leveling promised by the contemporary uprising takes on overtones of sexual threat early in Shakespeare's play:[5] the rising of the people becomes suggestively phallic; and the fear of leveling becomes ultimately a fear of losing one's potency in all spheres. In Menenius's belly fable, the people are "th' discontented members, the mutinous parts," and "the mutinous members" (1.1.110,148): an audience for whom the mutiny of the specifically sexual member was traditionally one of the signs of the Fall, and for whom the crowd was traditionally associated with dangerous passion, would be prone to hear in Menenius's characterization of the crowd a reference to a part other than the great toe (1.1.154). In this fantasy the hitherto docile sons suddenly threaten to rise up against their fathers, the Senators (1.1.76); and it is characteristic of *Coriolanus* that the contested issue in this Oedipal rebellion is food.[6] The uprising of the crowd is in fact presented in terms that suggest the transformation of hunger into phallic aggression, a transformation that is, as I shall later argue, central to the character of Coriolanus himself: when the first citizen tells Menenius "They say poor suitors have strong breaths: they shall know we have strong arms too" (1.1.58-60), his image of importunate mouths suddenly armed in rebellion suggests the source of Coriolanus's rebellion no less than his own.

If the specter of a multitude of hungry mouths, ready to rise and demand their own, is the exciting cause of *Coriolanus*, the image of the mother who has not fed her children enough is at its center. One does not need the help of a psychoanalytic approach to notice that Volumnia is not a nourishing mother. Her attitude toward food is nicely summed up when she rejects Menenius's invitation to a consolatory dinner after Coriolanus's banishment: "Anger's my meat: I sup upon myself / And so shall starve with feeding" (4.2.50-51). We might suspect her of having been as niggardly in providing food for her son as she is for herself, or rather suspect her of insisting that he too be self-sufficient, that he feed only on his own anger; and indeed, she has apparently fed him only valiantness ("Thy valiantness was mine, thou suck'st it from me" [3.2.129]). He certainly has not been fed the milk of human kindness: when Menenius later tells us that "there is no more mercy in him than there is milk in a male tiger" (5.4.28-29), he seems to associate Coriolanus's lack of humanity not only with the absence of any nurturing female element in him but also with the absence of mother's milk itself.[7] Volumnia takes some pride in the creation of her son, and when we first meet her, she tells us exactly how she's done it: by sending him to a cruel war at an age when a mother should not be willing to allow a son out of the protective maternal circle for an hour (1.3.5-15). She elaborates her creation as she imagines herself mother to twelve sons and then kills all but one of them off: "I had rather had eleven die nobly for their country, than one voluptuously surfeit out of action" (1.3.24—25). To be noble is to die; to live is to be ignoble and to eat too much.[8] If you are Volumnia's son, the choice is clear.

But the most telling—certainly the most disturbing—revelation of Volumnia's attitude toward feeding comes some twenty lines later, when she is encouraging Virgilia to share her own glee in the thought of Coriolanus's wounds: "The breasts of Hecuba / When she did suckle Hector, look'd not lovelier / Than Hector's forehead when it spit forth blood / At Grecian sword contemning" (1.3.40-43). Blood is more beautiful than milk, the wound than the breast, warfare than peaceful feeding. But this image is more disturbing than these easy comparatives suggest. It does not bode well for Coriolanus that the heroic Hector doesn't stand a chance in Volumnia's imagination: he is transformed immediately from infantile feeding mouth to bleeding wound. For the unspoken mediator between breast and wound is the infant's mouth: in this imagistic transformation, to feed is to be wounded; the mouth becomes the wound, the breast the sword. The metaphoric process suggests the psychological fact that is, I think, at the center of the play: the taking in of food is the primary acknowledgment of one's dependence on the world, and as such, it is the primary token of one's vulnerability.[9] But at the same time as Volumnia's image suggests the vulnerability inherent in feeding, it also suggests a way to fend off that vulnerability. In her image, feeding, incorporating, is transformed into spitting out, an aggressive expelling; the wound in turn becomes the mouth that spits "forth blood / At Grecian sword contemning." The wound spitting blood thus becomes not a sign of vulnerability but an instrument of attack.

Volumnia's attitudes toward feeding and dependence are echoed perfectly in her son. Coriolanus persistently regards food as poisonous (1.1.177-78, 3.1.155-56); the only thing he can imagine nourishing is rebellion (3.1.68-69,116). Only Menenius among the patricians is associated with the ordinary consumption of food and wine without an allaying drop of Tiber in it; and his distance from Coriolanus can be measured partly by his pathetic conviction that Coriolanus will be malleable—that he will have a "suppler" soul (5.1.55)—after he has had a full meal. But for Coriolanus, as for his mother, nobility consists precisely in *not* eating: he twice imagines himself starving himself honorably to death before asking for food, or anything else, from the plebeians (2.3.112-13; 3.3.89-91).[10] And the transformations in mode implicit in Volumnia's image—from feeding to warfare, from vulnerability to aggressive attack, from incorporation to spitting out—are at the center of Coriolanus's character and of our responses to him: for the whole of his masculine identity depends on his transformation of his vulnerability into an instrument of attack, as Menenius suggests when he tells us that each of Coriolanus's wounds "was an enemy's grave" (2.1.154-55). Cominius reports that Coriolanus entered his first battle a sexually indefinite thing, a boy or Amazon (2.2.91), and found his manhood there: "When he might act the woman in the scene, / He prov'd best man i'th' field" (2.2.96-97). The rigid masculinity that Coriolanus finds in war becomes a defense against acknowledgment of his neediness; he attempts to tranform himself from a vulnerable human creature into a grotesquely invulnerable and isolated thing. His body becomes his armor (1.3.35, 1.4.24); he himself becomes a weapon "who sensibly outdares his senseless sword, / And when it bows, stand'st up" (1.4.53-54), or he becomes the sword itself: "O me alone! Make you a sword of me!" (1.6.76). And his whole life becomes a kind of phallic exhibitionism, devoted to disproving the possibility that he is vulnerable.[11] Anger becomes his meat as well as his mother's: Volumnia's phrase suggests his mode of defending himself against vulnerability, and at the same time reveals the source of his anger in the deprivation imposed by his mother. We see the quality of his hunger and its transformation when, after his expulsion from Rome, he reminds Aufidius that he has "drawn tuns of blood out of thy country's breast" (4.5.100). Fighting here, as elsewhere in the play, is a poorly concealed substitute for feeding (see, for example, 1.9.10-11; 4.5.191-94, 222-24); and the unsatisfied ravenous attack of the infant on the breast provides the motive force for warfare. The image allows us to understand the ease with which Coriolanus turns his rage toward his own feeding mother, Rome.[12]

Thrust prematurely from dependence on his mother, forced to feed himself on his own anger, Coriolanus refuses to acknowledge any neediness or dependency: for his entire sense of himself depends on his being able to see himself as a self-sufficient creature. The desperation behind his claim to self-sufficiency is revealed by his horror of praise, even the praise of his general:[13] the dependence of his masculinity on warfare in fact makes praise (or flattery, as he calls it) particularly threatening to him on the battlefield; susceptibility to flattery there, in the place of the triumph of his independence, would imply that the soldier's steel has grown "soft as the parasite's silk" (1.9.45). The juxtaposition of soldier's steel and parasite's soft silk suggests both Coriolanus's dilemma and his solution to it: in order to avoid being the soft, dependent, feeding parasite, he has to maintain his rigidity as soldier's steel. And the same complex of ideas determines the rigidity that makes him so disastrous as a political figure. The language in which he imagines his alternatives as he contemptuously asks the people for their voices and later as he gives up his attempt to pacify them reveals the extent to which his unwillingness to ask for the people's approval, like his abhorrence of praise, depends on his attitude toward food: "Better it is to die, better to starve, / Than crave the hire which first we do deserve" (2.3.112-13); "Pent to linger / But with a grain a day, I would not buy / Their mercy at the price of one fair word"

(3.3.89-91). Asking, craving, flattering with fair words are here not only preconditions but also equivalents of eating: to refuse to ask is to starve, but starvation is preferable to asking because asking, like eating, is an acknowledgment of one's weakness, one's dependence on the outside world. "The price is, to ask it kindly" (2.3.75): but that is the one price Coriolanus cannot pay. When he must face the prospect of revealing his dependence on the populace by asking for their favor, his whole delicately constructed masculine identity threatens to crumble: in order to ask, a harlot's spirit must possess him; his voice must become as small as the eunuch's or the virgin's minding babies; a beggar's tongue must make motion through his lips (3.2.111-18). Asking, then, would undo the process by which he was transformed from boy or woman to man on the battlefield. That he imagines this undoing as a kind of reverse voice change, from man to boy, suggests the extent to which his phallic aggressive pose is a defense against collapse into a dependent oral mode, when he had the voice of a small boy. And in fact, Coriolanus's own use of language constantly reiterates this defense. Flattery and asking are the linguistic equivalents of feeding (1.9.51-52): they are incorporative modes that acknowledge one's dependence. But Coriolanus spits out words, using them as weapons. His invective is in the mode of Hector's wound, aggressively spitting forth blood: it is an attempt to deny vulnerability by making the very area of vulnerability into the means of attack.[14]

Coriolanus's abhorrence of praise and flattery, his horror lest the people think that he got his wounds to please them (2.2.147-50), his insistence that he be given the consulship in sign of what he is, not as a reward (1.9.26), his refusal to ask — all are attempts to claim that he is *sui generis*. His attitude finds its logical conclusion in his desperate cry as he sees his mother approaching him at the end:

> I'll never
> Be such a gosling to obey instinct, but stand
> As if a man were author of himself
> And knew no other kin.
> (5.3.34-37)

The gosling obeys instinct and acknowledges his kinship with mankind; but Coriolanus will attempt to stand alone. (Since Coriolanus's manhood depends exactly on this phallic standing alone, he is particularly susceptible to Aufidius's taunt of "boy" when he has been such a gosling as to obey instinct.) The relationship between Coriolanus's aggressive pose and his attempts to claim that he is *sui generis* are most dramatically realized in the conquest of Corioli; it is here that Coriolanus most nearly realizes his fantasy of standing as if a man were author of himself. For the scene at Corioli represents a glorious transformation of oral nightmare ("to th' pot" [1.4.47] one of his soldiers says as he is swallowed up by the gates) into a phallic adventure that both assures and demonstrates his independence. The dramatic action itself presents the conquest of Corioli as an image of triumphant rebirth: after Coriolanus enters the gates of the city, he is proclaimed dead; one of his comrades delivers a eulogy firmly in the past tense ("Thou wast a soldier / Even to Cato's wish" [1.4.55-56]); then Coriolanus miraculously reemerges, covered with blood (1.6.22), and is given a new name. Furthermore, Coriolanus's own battlecry as he storms the gates sexualizes the scene: "Come on; / If you'll stand fast, we'll beat them to their wives" (1.4.40-41). For the assault on Corioli is both a rape and a rebirth: the underlying fantasy is that intercourse is a literal return to the womb, from which one is reborn, one's own author.[15] The fantasy of self-authorship is complete when Coriolanus is given his new name, earned by his own actions.[16]

But despite the boast implicit in his conquest of Corioli, Coriolanus has not in fact succeeded in separating himself from his mother;[17] even the very role through which he claims independence was designed by her — as she never tires of pointing out ("My praises made thee first a soldier" [3.2.108]; "Thou art my warrior: / I holp to frame thee" [5.3.62-63]). In fact, Shakespeare underlines Volumnia's point by the placing of two central scenes. In 1.3, before we have seen Coriolanus himself as a soldier, we see Volumnia first *describe* her image of her son on the battlefield and then *enact* his role: "Methinks I see him stamp thus, and call thus: / 'Come on you cowards, you were got in fear / Though you were born in Rome' " (1.3.32-34). This marvelous moment not only suggests the ways in which Volumnia herself lives through her son; it also suggests the extent to which his role is her creation. For when we see him in the next scene, acting exactly as his mother had predicted, we are left with the impression that he is merely enacting her enactment of his role. That he is acting under her direction even in the role designed to insure his independence of her helps to explain both his bafflement when she suddenly starts to disapprove of the role that she has created ("I muse my mother / Does not approve me further" [3.2.7-8]), and his eventual capitulation to her demand that he shift roles, here and at the end of the play. When he finally agrees to take on the role of humble supplicant, he is sure that he will act badly (3.2.105-6) and that he will lose his manhood in the process (3.2.111-23). For his manhood is secure only when he can play the role that she has designed, and play it with her approval.[18] He asks her, "Why did you wish me milder? Would you have me / False to my nature? Rather say I play / The man I am" (3.2.14-16). But "I play the man I am" cuts both ways: in his bafflement, Coriolanus would like to suggest that there is no distance between role and self, but in fact suggests that he plays at being himself. Given that Volumnia has created this dilemma, her answer is unnecessarily cruel — but telling: "You might have been enough the man you are, / With striving less to be so" (3.2.19-20). Volumnia is right: it is the intensity and rigidity of Coriolanus's commitment to his masculine role that makes us suspect the intensity of the fears that this role is designed to hide, especially from himself.

The fragility of the entire structure by which Coriolanus maintains his claim to self-sufficient manhood helps to account for the violence of his hatred of the plebeians. Coriolanus uses the crowd to bolster his own identity: he accuses them of being exactly what he wishes not to be.[19] He does his best to distinguish himself from them by emphasizing his aloneness and their multitudinousness as the very grounds of their being.[20] Throughout, he associates his manhood with his isolation, so that "Alone I did it" becomes a sufficient answer to Aufidius's charge that he is a boy; hence the very status of the plebeians as *crowd* reassures him that they are not men but dependent and unmanly things, merely children—a point of view that Menenius seems to confirm when he tells the tribunes, "Your abilities are too infant-like for doing much alone" (2.1.36-37). His most potent image of the crowd is as a common mouth (3.1.22,155) disgustingly willing to exhibit its neediness. He enters the play identified by the plebeians as the person who is keeping them from eating (1.1.9-10); and indeed, one of his main complaints about the plebeians is that they say they are hungry (1.1.204-7).[21] Coriolanus himself has been deprived of food, and he seems to find it outrageous that others should not be. His position here is like that of the older brother who has fought his way into manhood and who is now confronted by an apparently endless group of siblings—"my sworn brother the people" (2.3.95), he calls them—who still insist on being fed by mother Rome,[22] and whose insistence on their dependency threatens the pose of self-sufficiency by which his equilibrium is perilously maintained. Indeed, the intensity of his portrayal of the crowd as a multitudinous mouth suggests not only the neediness that underlies his pose, but also the tenuousness of the pose itself: his insistent portrayal of the plebeians as an unmanly mouth, as feminine where they should be masculine, in effect as castrated, suggests that his hatred of the crowd conceals not only his own hunger but also his fears for his own masculinity.[23] It is characteristic of Coriolanus's transformation of hunger into phallic aggression that the feared castration is imagined predominantly in oral terms: to be castrated here *is* to be a mouth, naked in one's dependency, perpetually hungry, perpetually demanding.[24]

Coriolanus's absolute horror at the prospect of showing his wounds to win the consulship depends partly, I think, on the complex of ideas that stands behind his characterization of the crowd. In Plutarch, Coriolanus shows his wounds; in Shakespeare, the thought is intolerable to him and, despite many promises that he will, he never does. For his wounds would then become begging mouths (as they do in *Julius Caesar* [3.2.225-26]), and their display would reveal his kinship with the plebeians in several ways: by revealing that he has worked for hire as they have (that is, that he and his deeds are not *sui generis* after all); by revealing that he is vulnerable, as they are; and by revealing, through the persistent identification of wound and mouth, that he too has a mouth, that he is a feminized and dependent creature. Moreover, the exhibition of his wounds to the crowd is impossible for him partly because his identity is sustained by exhibitionism of another sort. The phallic exhibitionism of his life as a soldier has been designed to deny the possibility of just this kinship with the crowd; it has served to reassure him of his potency and his aggressive independence, and therefore to sustain him against fears of the collapse into the dependent mode of infancy. To exhibit the fruits of his soldiership not as the emblems of his self-sufficiency but as the emblems of his vulnerability and dependence, and to exhibit them precisely to those whose kinship with him he would most like to deny, would transform his chief means of defense into a proclamation of his weakness: it would threaten to undo the very structure by which he lives.[25]

Behind Coriolanus's rage at the plebeians, then, stands the specter of his own hunger and his own fear of dependence. But this rage is properly directed toward his mother: and though it is deflected from her and toward the plebeians and Volscians for much of the play, it finally returns to its source after he has been exiled from Rome. For Rome and his mother are finally one:[26] although in his loving farewell his family and friends are wholly distinguished from the beast with many heads, by the time he has returned to Rome they are no more than a poor grain or two that must be consumed in the general fire (5.1.27). (Even in his loving farewell we hear a note of resentment when he consoles his mother by telling her, "My hazards still have been your solace" [4.1.28].) And as he approaches Rome, we know that the destruction of his mother will not be merely incidental to the destruction of his city. For in exiling him, Rome reenacts the role of the mother who cast him out; the exile is a reliving of the crisis of dependency that Coriolanus has already undergone. Coriolanus initially meets this crisis with the claim that he himself is in control of the independence thrust upon him, a claim akin to the infant's fantasy of omnipotent control over the forces that in fact control him: "I banish you!" (3.3.123). He then attempts to insure himself of the reality of his omnipotence by wishing on his enemies exactly what he already knows to be true of them ("Let every feeble rumour shake your hearts! / . . . Have the power still / To banish your defenders" [3.3.125-28]): few curses have ever been so sure of instantaneous fulfillment. Having thus exercised his rage and assured himself of the magical power of his invective, Coriolanus finally makes his claim to true independence: "There is a world elsewhere!" (3.3.135). But he cannot sustain this independence, cannot simply separate himself from the world of Rome; the intensity of his identification with Rome and with his mother forces him to come back to destroy both, to make his claim to omnipotent independence a reality by destroying the home to which he is still attached, so that he can truly stand as if a man were author of himself. The return to Rome is an act of retaliation against the mother on whom he has been dependent, the mother who has cast him out; but it is at the same time an acting out of the child's fantasy of reversing the roles of parent and child, so that the life of the parent is in the hands of the omnipotent child. For Coriolanus can become author of himself only by first becoming author of his mother, as he attempts to do here: by becoming in effect a god, dispensing life and death (5.4.24-25), so that he can finally stand alone.

But Coriolanus can sustain neither his fantasy of self-authorship nor his attempt to realize a godlike omnipotent power. And the failure of both leaves him so unprotected, so utterly devoid of a sense of self that, for the first time in the play, he feels himself surrounded by dangers: for the capitulation of his independent selfhood before his mother's onslaught seems to him to require his death. Indeed, as he cries out to his mother, he embraces his intuition of his own death with a passivity thoroughly uncharacteristic of him:

> O my mother, mother! O!
> You have won a happy victory to Rome;
> But for your son, believe it, O, believe it,
> Most dangerously you have with him prevail'd,
> If not most mortal to him. But let it come.
>                                 (5.3.185-89)

His attempt to ward off danger by pleading with Aufidius is strikingly half-hearted; and when he says, "Though I cannot make true wars, / I'll frame convenient peace" (5.3.190-91), we hear the tragic collapse of his personality. We of course know by this time that the self-sufficient and aggressive pose by which Coriolanus maintains his selfhood is as dangerous to him as its collapse, that Aufidius plans to kill him no matter what he does (4.7.24-26, 56-57). It is a mark of the extent to which external dangers are for Coriolanus merely a reflection of internal ones that he feels himself in no danger until the collapse of his defensive system. But Volumnia achieves this collapse partly because she makes the dangers inherent in his defensive system as terrifying as those which it is designed to keep at bay: her last confrontation with her son is so appallingly effective because she invalidates his defenses by threatening to enact his most central defensive fantasies, thereby making their consequences inescapable to him.

The very appearance of his mother, coming to beg him for the life of her city and hence for her own life, is an enactment of his attempt to become the author of his mother, his desire to have power over her. He has before found her begging intolerable (3.2.124-34); when she kneels to him here, making the role reversal of mother and child explicit (5.3.56), he reacts with an hysteria that suggests that the acting out of this forbidden wish threatens to dissolve the very structures by which he orders his life:

> What's this?
> Your knees to me? to your corrected son?
> Then let the pebbles on the hungry beach
> Fillip the stars. Then let the mutinous winds
> Strike the proud cedars 'gainst the fiery sun,
> Murd'ring impossibility, to make
> What cannot be, slight work!
>                               (5.3.56-62)

At first sight, this speech seems simply to register Coriolanus's horror at the threat to hierarchy implied by the kneeling of parent to child. But if Coriolanus were responding only — or even mainly — to this threat, we would expect the threatened chaos to be imaged as high bowing to low; and this is in fact the image that we are given when Volumnia first bows to her son as if — as Coriolanus says — "Olympus to a molehill should / In supplication nod" (5.3.30-31). But Coriolanus does not respond to his mother's kneeling with an image of high bowing to low; instead, he responds with two images of low mutinously striking at high. The chaos imaged here is not so much a derivative of his mother's kneeling as of the potential mutiny that her kneeling seems to imply: for her kneeling releases the possibility of his mutiny against her, a mutiny that he has been suppressing all along by his exaggerated deference to her. His response here reveals another of the bases for his hatred of the mutinous and leveling populace: the violence of his images suggests that his mother's kneeling has forced him to acknowledge his return to Rome as a rising up of the hungry and mutinous forces in himself. With her usual acumen, Volumnia recognizes the disarming of potential mutiny in Coriolanus's response and chooses exactly this moment to assert, once again, his dependence on her: "Thou art my warrior" (5.3.62).

The living out of Coriolanus's forbidden wish to have power over his mother had seemed to Coriolanus impossible; but now that protective impossibility itself seems murdered, and he is forced to confront the fact that his wish has become a reality. Nor are the hungry and mutinous forces within himself content to murder only an abstract "impossibility": the murderousness of the image is directed ultimately at his mother. And once again, Volumnia makes Coriolanus uncomfortably clear to himself: after she has enacted his terrifying fantasy by kneeling, she makes it impossible for him to believe that her death would be merely an incidental consequence of his plan to burn Rome.[27] For she reveals exactly the extent to which he has identified mother and Rome, the extent to which his assault is on both. Her long speech builds to its revelation with magnificent force and logic. She first forces him to see his attack on his country as an attack on a living body by accusing him of coming to tear "his country's bowels out" (5.3.103). Next, she identifies that body as their common mother ("the country, our dear nurse" [5.3.110]). Finally, as she announces her intention to commit suicide, she makes absolute the identification of the country with herself; after she has imagined him treading on his country's ruin (5.3.116), she warns him:

> thou shalt no sooner
> March to assault thy country than to tread —
> Trust to't, thou shalt not — on thy mother's womb
> That brought thee to this world.
> (5.3.122-25)

The ruin on which Coriolanus will tread will be his mother's womb — a warning accompanied by yet another assertion of his dependence on her as she recalls to him the image of himself as a fetus within that womb.

If Coriolanus's mutinous fantasies are no longer an impossibility, if his mother will indeed die as a result of his actions, then Coriolanus will have realized his fantasy of living omnipotently without kin, without dependency. In fact this fantasy, his defense throughout, is articulated only here, as he catches sight of his mother (5.3.34-37); and its expression is the last stand of his claim to independence. Throughout this scene, Volumnia has simultaneously asserted his dependence on her and made the dangers inherent in his defense against that dependence horrifyingly clear; and in the end it is the combination of her insistence on his dependency and her threat to disown him, to literalize his fantasy of standing alone, that causes him to capitulate. Finally, he cannot "stand / As if a man were author of himself / And knew no other kin"; he must become a child again, a gosling, and admit his neediness. The presence of his own child, holding Volumnia's hand, strengthens her power over him: for Coriolanus seems to think of his child less as his son than as the embodiment of his own childhood and the child that remains within him; even when we are first told about the son, he seems more of a comment on Coriolanus's childhood than on his fatherhood. The identification of father and child is suggested by Coriolanus's response as he sees wife, mother, and child approaching: "My wife comes foremost; then the honour'd mould / Wherein this trunk was fram'd, and in her hand / The grandchild to her blood" (5.3.22-24). Here Coriolanus does not acknowledge the child as his and his wife's: he first imagines himself in his mother's womb, and then imagines his child as an extension of his mother. Even Coriolanus's language to Menenius as he earlier denies his family reveals the same fusion of father and son: "Wife, mother, child, I know not" (5.2.80) he says, in a phrase that suggests that his own mother is the mother of the child, and the child he attempts to deny is himself. Volumnia had once before brought Coriolanus to submission by reminding him of himself as a suckling child (3.2.129); now virtually her last words enforce his identification with the child that she holds by the hand: "This fellow had a Volscian to his mother; / His wife is in Corioles, and his child / Like him by chance" (5.3.178-80). But at the same time as she

reminds him of his dependency, she disowns him by disclaiming her parent-
hood; she exacerbates his sense of himself as a child, and then threatens to
leave him—as he thought he wished—alone. And as his fantasy of self-
sufficiency threatens to become a reality, it becomes too frightening to sustain; just as his child entered the scene holding Volumnia's hand, so Coriolanus again becomes a child, holding his mother's hand.

The ending of this play leaves us with a sense of pain and anxiety; we are
not even allowed the feelings of unremitting grief and satiation that console us
in most of the other tragedies. The very nature of its hero insists that we keep
our distance. Coriolanus is as isolated from us as he is from everyone else; we
almost never know what he is thinking, and—even more intolerably—he does
not seem to care what we are thinking. Unlike an Othello or an Antony,
whose last moments are spent endearingly trying to insure our good opinion,
Coriolanus makes virtually no attempt to affect our judgment of him: he dies
as he has tried to live, heroically mantled in his self-sufficiency, alone. Nor is
it only our democratic sympathies that put us uncomfortably in the position
of the common people throughout much of the play: Coriolanus seems to find
our love as irrelevant, as positively demeaning, as theirs; and in refusing to
show the people his wounds, he is at the same time refusing to show them to
us. In refusing to show himself to us, in considering us a many-headed
multitude to whose applause he is wholly indifferent, Coriolanus denies us our
proper role as spectators to his tragedy. The only spectators that Coriolanus
allows himself to notice are the gods who look down on this unnatural scene
and laugh, who are so far removed from men that they find this human
tragedy a comedy. And as spectators we are in danger of becoming as distant
from human concerns as the gods: for Coriolanus's isolation infects the whole
play and ultimately infects us. There are very few moments of relaxation;
there is no one here to love. We are made as rigid and cold as the hero by the
lack of anything that absolutely commands our human sympathies, that
demonstrates to us that *we* are dependent creatures, part of a community.
Even the language does not open out toward us, nor does it create the sense of
the merging of meanings, the melting together, that gives us a measure of
release in *King Lear* or *Antony and Cleopatra*, where a world of linguistic fusion suggests the dependence of all parts. Instead, the language works to
define and separate, to limit possibilities, almost as rigidly as Coriolanus
himself does.[28] And finally, the nature of our involvement in the fantasies embodied in this distant and rigid hero does not permit any resolution: it also
separates and limits. For Coriolanus has throughout given free expression to
*our* desire to be independent, and we delight in his claim. But when he turns
on his mother in Rome, the consequences of his claim to self-sufficiency suddenly become intolerably threatening to us. We want him to acknowledge
dependence, to become one of us; but at the same time we do not want to see

him give in, because to do so is to force us to give up our own fantasy of omnipotence and independence. Hence at the final confrontation we are divided against ourselves and no solution is tolerable: neither the burning of Rome nor the capitulation and death of our claims to independence. Nor is the vision of human dependency that the play allows any compensation for the brutal failure of our desire to be self-sustaining. In *Lear* and *Antony and Cleopatra,* dependency is finally shown to be what makes us fully human: however much the characters have tried to deny it, it finally becomes their salvation, and ours, as we reach out to them. But dependency here brings no rewards, no love, no sharing with the audience; it brings only the total collapse of the self, the awful triumph of Volumnia, and Coriolanus's terribly painful cry: "O mother, mother! / What have you done?"

## Notes

1. John Stow, *Annales* (London, 1631), p. 890. See Sidney Shanker, "Some Clues for *Coriolanus,*" *Shakespeare Association Bulletin* 24 (1949): 209-13); E. C. Pettet, "*Coriolanus* and the Midlands Insurrection of 1607," *Shakespeare Survey* 3 (1950): 34-42; and Brents Stirling, *The Populace in Shakespeare* (New York, 1965), pp. 126-28, for discussions of the uprising and its political consequences in the play.

2. Stow, *Annales*, p. 890.

3. See Edwin F. Gay, "The Midland Revolt and The Inquisitions of Depopulation of 1607," *Transactions of the Royal Historical Society*, n.s., 18 (1904); 195-244, for valuable contemporary commentary on the uprising and an analysis of it in comparison with earlier riots of the sixteenth century. See also Pettet, "*Coriolanus* and the Midlands Insurrection," p. 35.

4. The participants in the uprising were commonly called "levelers" and their activity "leveling," in startling anticipation of the 1640s. The common use of this term suggests the extent to which their fight against enclosures seemed to threaten hierarchy itself. (See, for example, Stow, *Annales*, p. 890, and Gay, "The Midland Revolt," pp. 213 n. 2, 214 n. 1, and 216 n. 3, and 242.) The vertical imagery is so prominent in the play that it scarcely needs to be pointed out; at its center is Cominius's warning that the stirring up of the people is "the way to lay the city flat, / To bring the roof to the foundation, / And bury all which yet distinctly ranges / In heaps and piles of ruin" (3.1.201-5). The threat of the people to rise and cast Coriolanus down from the Tarpeian rock, Coriolanus's horror of kneeling to the people or of his mother's kneeling to him, and ultimately the image of the prone Coriolanus with Aufidius standing on him — all take their force partly from the repetition and intensity of the vertical imagery throughout.

5. Shakespeare had in fact just used the word *level* to suggest a sexual leveling at the end of *Antony and Cleopatra*, when Cleopatra laments: "The soldier's pole is fall'n: young boys and girls / Are level now with men" (4.15.65-66).

6. Coriolanus himself occupies an odd position in the psychological myth at the start of the play: though he is a father, we almost always think of him as a son; though the populace considers him prime among the forbidding fathers, he himself seems to regard the patricians as his fathers. His position midway between father and sons suggests the position of an older sibling who has made a protective alliance with the father and now fears the unruliness of his younger brothers. Instead of fighting to take possession of the undernourishing mother, he will deny that he has any need for food.

7. Menenius's words point to the rigid and ferocious maleness so prized by Rome. The ideal Roman woman is in fact one who denies her womanhood, as we see not only in Volumnia but in Coriolanus's chilling and beautiful description of Valeria (5.3.65-67). (Indeed, Valeria seems to have little place in the intimate family gathering of 5.3; she seems to exist there largely to give Coriolanus an excuse for speaking these lines.) The extent to which womanhood is shrunken in Roman values is apparent in the relative unimportance of Coriolanus's wife, Virgilia; in her the female values of kindly nurturing have become little more than a penchant for staying at home, keeping silent, and weeping. (Given the extreme restrictions of Virgilia's role, one may begin to understand some of the pressures that force a woman to become a Volumnia and live through the creation of her exaggeratedly masculine son. Gordon Ross Smith ["Authoritarian Patterns in Shakespeare's *Coriolanus,*" *Literature and Psychology* 9 (1959): 49] comments perceptively that, in an authoritarian society, women will either be passive and subservient or will attempt to live out their thwarted ambition via their men.) At the end, Rome sees the consequences of its denial of female values as Coriolanus prepares to deny nature in himself and destroy his homeland. When Volumnia triumphs over his rigid maleness, there is a hint of restitution in the Roman celebration of her as "our patroness, the life of Rome" (5.5.1). But like nearly everything else at the end of this play, the promise of restitution is deeply ironic: for Volumnia herself has shown no touch of nature as she willingly sacrifices her son; and the cries of "welcome, ladies, welcome!" (5.5.6) suggest an acknowledgment of female values at the moment in which the appearance of these values not in Volumnia but in her son can only mean his death. Phyllis Rackin, in an unpublished paper entitled *"Coriolanus*: Shakespeare's Anatomy of *Virtus"* and delivered to the special session on feminist criticism of Shakespeare at the 1976 meeting of the Modern Language Association, discusses the denial of female values as a consequence of the Roman overvaluation of valor as the chiefest virtue. Her analysis of the ways in which the traditionally female images of food, harvesting, and love are turned to destructive purposes throughout the play is particularly revealing.

8. The association of nobility with abstinence from food, and of the ignoble lower classes with excessive appetite for food in connection with their traditional role as embodiments of appetite, was first demonstrated to me by Maurice Charney's impressive catalogue of the food images in the play ("The Imagery of Food and Eating in *Coriolanus,*" *Essays in Literary History*, ed. Rudolf Kirk and C. F. Main [New Brunswick, N.J., 1960], pp. 37-54).

9. Hence the persistent identification of mouth and wound throughout the play (most striking in the passage discussed here, and in 2.3.7); hence also the regularity with which images of feeding are transposed into images of cannibalism and reveal a talion fear of being eaten (1.1.187, 257; 2.1.9; 4.5.194). At the center of these images of vulnerability in feeding is Menenius's comparison of Rome to an "unnatural dam" who threatens to eat up her own children (3.1.290-91).

10. In fact, Coriolanus frequently imagines his death with a kind of glee, as the final triumph of his noble self-sufficiency; see, for example, 3.2.1-5, 103-4; 5.6.111-12.

11. The extent to which Coriolanus becomes identified with his phallus is suggested by the language in which both Menenius and Aufidius portray his death; for both, it represents a kind of castration ("He's a limb that has but a disease: / Mortal, to cut it off; to cure it, easy" [3.1.293-94]; "You'll rejoice / That he is thus cut off" [5.6.137-38]. For discussions of Coriolanus's phallic identification and its consequences, see Robert J. Stoller, "Shakespearean Tragedy: Coriolanus," *Psychoanalytic Quarterly* 35 (1966): 263-74, and Emmett Wilson, Jr., "Coriolanus: The Anxious Bridegroom," *American Imago* 25 (1968): 224-41. Charles K. Hofling ("An Interpretation of Shakespeare's Coriolanus," *American Imago* 14 (1957): 407-35) sees Coriolanus as a virtual embodiment of Reich's phallic-narcissistic character. Each of these analysts finds Coriolanus's phallic stance to some extent a defense against passivity (Stoller, pp. 267, 269-70; Wilson, passim; Hofling, pp. 421, 424).

12. David B. Barron sees Coriolanus's oral frustration and his consequent rage as central to his

character ("*Coriolanus:* Portrait of the Artist As Infant," *American Imago* 19 (1962): 171-93); his essay anticipates mine in some of its conclusions and many of its details of interpretation.

13. Most critics find Coriolanus's abhorrence of praise a symptom of his pride and his desire to consider himself as self-defined and self-sufficient, hence free from the definitions that society would confer on him. See, for example, A. C. Bradley, "Coriolanus," reprinted in *Studies in Shakespeare*, ed. Peter Alexander (London, 1964), p. 229; G. Wilson Knight, *The Imperial Theme* (London, 1965), p. 169; Irving Ribner, *Patterns in Shakespearean Tragedy* (London, 1960), p. 190; Norman Rabkin, *Shakespeare and the Common Understanding* (New York, 1967), p. 131; and James L. Calderwood, "*Coriolanus:* Wordless Meanings and Meaningless Words," *Studies in English Literature* 6 (1966): 218-19. There are dissenters, however. Brian Vickers, for example, finds a concern with political image-making at the center of the play: in his view, the patricians' praise of Coriolanus as a war machine serves their own propagandistic class interests and should be rejected by the audience as a false image of him; Coriolanus's rejection of this praise is therefore perfectly justified, not an indication of his pride (*Shakespeare: "Coriolanus"* [London, 1976], pp. 23-25).

14. In his discussion of Coriolanus's cathartic vituperation, Kenneth Burke suggests that invective is rooted in the helpless rage of the infant ("*Coriolanus*—and the Delights of Faction," *Hudson Review* 19 [1966]: 200).

15. To see Corioli as the mother's womb here may seem grotesque; the idea becomes less grotesque if we remember Volumnia's own identification of country with mother's womb just as Coriolanus is about to attack another city (see above, pp. 117-18). Wilson ("Coriolanus: The Anxious Bridegroom," pp. 228-29) suggests that Corioli represents defloration; specifically, that it expresses the equation of coitus with damaging assault and the resultant dread of a retaliatory castration.

16. The force of this new name is partly corroborated by Volumnia, who delights in reminding her son of his dependence on her: she has trouble learning his new name from the start (2.1.173), and eventually associates it with the pride that keeps him from pity for his family (5.3.170-71). But several critics have argued convincingly that the self-sufficiency implicit in Coriolanus's acquisition of his new name is ironically undercut from the beginning by the fact that naming of any kind is a social act, so that Coriolanus's acceptance of the name conferred on him by Cominius reveals his dependence on external definition just at the moment when he seems most independent. See, for example, Rabkin, *Shakespeare and the Common Understanding*, pp. 130-32; Lawrence Danson, *Tragic Alphabet: Shakespeare's Drama of Language* (New Haven, Conn., 1974), pp. 150-51; Calderwood, "*Coriolanus:* Wordless Meanings and Meaningless Words," pp. 219-23.

17. The father's role in the process of individuation and the consequent significance of Coriolanus's fatherlessness have been pointed out to me by Dr. Malcolm Pines: the father must exist from the start in the potential space between child and mother in order for separation from the mother and hence individuation to take place; the absence of Coriolanus's father thus becomes an essential factor in his failure to separate from his mother.

18. Volumnia's place in the creation of her son's role, and the catastrophic results of her disavowal of it here, have been nearly universally recognized. For a particularly perceptive discussion of the consequences for Coriolanus of his mother's shift in attitude, see Derek Traversi, *Shakespeare: The Roman Plays* (Stanford, Calif., 1963), pp. 247-54. In an interesting essay, D. W. Harding suggests Shakespeare's preoccupation during this period with the disastrous effects on men of their living out of women's fantasies of manhood ("Women's Fantasy of Manhood: A Shakespearean Theme," *Shakespeare Quarterly* 20 [1969]: 252-53). Psychoanalytically oriented critics see Coriolanus as the embodiment of his mother's masculine strivings, or, more specifically, as her longed-for penis: see, for example, Ralph Berry, "Sexual Imagery in *Coriolanus*," *Studies in English Literature* 13 (1973): 302; Hofling, "An Interpretation of Shakespeare's Coriolanus," pp. 415-16; Stoller, "Shakespearean Tragedy: Coriolanus," pp. 266-67, 271; and

Wilson, "Coriolanus: The Anxious Bridegroom," p. 239. Several critics have noticed the importance of acting and the theatrical metaphor in the play: see, for example, William Rosen, *Shakespeare and the Craft of Tragedy* (Cambridge, Mass., 1960), pp. 171-73, and Kenneth Muir, *Shakespeare's Tragic Sequence* (London, 1972), pp. 184-85. Harold C. Goddard in *The Meaning of Shakespeare*, Vol. 2 (Chicago, 1951) discusses acting specifically in relation to the role that Volumnia has cast for her son (pp. 216-17); Berry ("Sexual Imagery in *Coriolanus,"* pp. 303-6) points to the acting metaphors as a measure of Coriolanus's inner uncertainty and his fear of losing his manhood if he shifts roles. In an interesting psychoanalytic essay, Otto Fenichel discusses the derivation of acting from exhibitionism; like all such derivatives, it is ultimately designed to protect against the fear of castration. This argument and his discussion of the actor's relationship to his audience and of shame as the characteristic emotion of an actor at the failure of his role seem to me to have important implications for *Coriolanus,* especially given both Coriolanus's fear that a change of role here would make him womanish and the shame that he feels later when his role begins to fail (5.3.40-42); see Fenichel, "On Acting," *Psychoanalytic Quarterly* 15 (1946): 144-60.

19. It is telling that Coriolanus tries unsuccessfully to assert that the people are not in fact Roman, hence are no kin to him ("I would they were barbarians—as they are, / . . . not Romans—as they are not" [3.1.236-37]): he insists on their non-Romanness as simultaneously a condition contrary to fact and a fact; and his unusual incoherence suggests the tension between his fear that he and the crowd may be alike and his claim that there is no resemblance between them. Goddard (*The Meaning of Shakespeare,* p. 238), Hofling ("An Interpretation of Shakespeare's Coriolanus," p. 420), and Smith ("Authoritarian Patterns in Shakespeare's *Coriolanus,"* p. 46), among others, discuss Coriolanus's characterization of the crowd as a projection of elements in himself that he wishes to deny, though they do not agree on the precise nature of these elements.

20. And so does Shakespeare. In Plutarch, Coriolanus is accompanied by a few men both when he enters the gates of Corioli and when he is exiled from Rome; Shakespeare emphasizes his isolation by giving him no companions on either occasion. Eugene Waith, in *The Herculean Hero* (New York, 1962), p. 124, and Danson, *Tragic Alphabet,* p. 146, emphasize Coriolanus's position as a whole man among fragments.

21. Barron (*"Coriolanus:* Portrait of the Artist As Infant," pp. 174, 180) associates Coriolanus's hatred of the people's undisciplined hunger with his need to subdue his own impulses; here as elsewhere, his argument is very close to my own.

22. See n. 6 above. The likeness of the crowd to younger siblings who threaten Coriolanus's food supply was first suggested to me by David Sundelson in conversation.

23. Given the importance of Coriolanus's phallic self-sufficiency as a defensive measure, it is not surprising that he should show signs of a fear of castration. This fear may help to account for the enthusiasm with which he characterizes Valeria, in strikingly phallic terms, as the icicle on Dian's temple (5.3.65-67): the phallic woman may ultimately be less frightening to him than the woman who demonstrates the possibility of castration by her lack of a penis. The same repudiation of the female and hence of the possibility of castration may also lie behind his turning away from Rome and his mother and toward a relationship with Aufidius presented in decidedly homosexual terms (4.5.107-19, 199-202). Shakespeare takes pains to emphasize the distance between the Aufidius we see and the Aufidius of Coriolanus's imagination: the Aufidius invented by Coriolanus seems designed to reassure Coriolanus of the reality of his own male grandeur by giving him the image of himself; his need to create a man who is his equal is in fact one of the most poignant elements in the play and helps to account for his tragic blindness to his rival's true nature as opportunist and schemer.

24. The fusion of oral and phallic issues in the portrayal of the crowd, and throughout the play, is confirmed by the image of the Hydra. The beast with many heads was of course a conventional analogue for the populace, but the extent to which Shakespeare intensifies and sexualizes

this conventional image can be suggested by the grotesqueness of the context in which it first appears overtly in the play, a context of monstrous members and tongues in wounds (2.3.5-17). The beast with many heads becomes in this play a beast with many mouths; at one point it is even a multiple bosom, digesting (3.1.130). The phallic threat of the crowd, felt in its power to level, is thus mitigated by the insistence on a multiply castrated beast; but the tenuousness of this mitigation is suggested by the insistence on tongues in each mouth (3.1.155).

25. Stoller ("Shakespearean Tragedy: Coriolanus," p. 268) and Wilson ("Coriolanus: The Anxious Bridegroom," p. 230) associate Coriolanus's wounds with castration; for Barron ("*Coriolanus:* Portrait of the Artist As Infant," p. 177) his wounds are a mark of his dependence on his mother. Coriolanus's unwillingness to show his wounds may derive partly from a fear that in standing "naked" (2.2.137) and revealing himself to the people as feminized, he might be inviting a kind of homosexual rape — a fear amply justified by the Third Citizen's remark that, "If he show us his wounds and tell us his deeds, we are to put our tongues into those wounds and speak for them" (2.3.5-8; see also Barron, p. 178). Dr. Anne Hayman has suggested to me that Coriolanus's fear of his unconscious homosexual desires, particularly of a passive feminine kind, is essential to his character; she sees his fear of the wish for passive femininity as part of his identification with his mother, who shares the same fear. I am endebted to Dr. Hayman for her careful reading of this paper and her many helpful comments.

26. Donald A. Stauffer, in *Shakespeare's World of Images* (New York, 1949), points out that Rome is less *patria* than *matria* in this play; he discusses Volumnia as a projection of Rome, particularly in 5.3 (p. 252). Virtually all psychoanalytic critics comment on the identification of Volumnia with Rome; Barron ("*Coriolanus*: Portrait of the Artist as Infant," p. 175) comments specifically that Coriolanus turns the rage of his frustration in nursing toward his own country at the end of the play.

27. Rufus Putney, in "Coriolanus and His Mother," *Psychoanalytic Quarterly* 31 (1962), finds Coriolanus's inability to deal with his matricidal impulses central to his character; whenever Volumnia threatens him with her death, he capitulates at once (pp. 368-69, 372).

28. G. Wilson Knight discusses the hard metallic quality of the language at length; he associates it with the self-containment of the hostile walled cities and distinguishes it from the fusions characteristic of *Antony and Cleopatra* (*The Imperial Theme*, p. 156). In a particularly interesting discussion, Danson associates the rigidity and distinctness of the language with the play's characteristic use of metonymy and synecdoche, which serve to limit and define, in place of metaphor, which serves to fuse diverse worlds (*Tragic Alphabet*, pp. 155-59).

# Shakespeare's Comic Sense As It Strikes Us Today: Falstaff and the Protestant Ethic

by ROBERT G. HUNTER

If there are such things as antibodies (and I am told that there are), then let there be such things as antiembodiments and let Falstaff be one. Let him also be an embodiment (there is plenty of room), for Falstaff embodies a large part of my subject, Shakespeare's comic sense. Simultaneously he antiembodies the Protestant ethic. What he is, it is not. What it is, he is not. Did Shakespeare's comic sense serve the body politic by generating Falstaff in an attempt to immunize comparatively Merrie England against those foreign organisms, the Puritan Saints? If so, the attempt failed, and Shakespeare knew it would. The Henriad, I will maintain but not demonstrate, dramatizes, in the rejection of Falstaff, the victory of the Protestant ethic, presenting that social triumph as a psychological event, the decision of Henry the Fifth to labor in his vocation, to do his duty in that royal station to which it pleased God to call him.

Thus Falstaff came into being, almost four centuries ago, during the first insurgency of the Protestant ethic and, perhaps, in response to it. Today we are celebrating the bicentennial of one of that ethic's more elaborate offspring. And do we not sense today that we are living through the decadence and disappearance of the ethic, that we watch going down the great drain of history what Shakespeare saw coming up it? What will take the ethic's place? That seems to me one of today's more nagging questions, and I haven't the vaguest notion of its answer. But we might explore the question by consulting

125

the comic sense of our particular oracle. Let us have a look first at the ethic and then at Falstaff as antiembodiment of it.

The phenomenon that I claim Falstaff antiembodies is authoritatively described and accounted for by Max Weber in *The Protestant Ethic and the Spirit of Capitalism*. Weber identifies the main characteristic of that ethic as "worldly asceticism . . . a fundamental antagonism to sensuous culture of all kinds." He sees the ethic as the result of two theological causes, one Lutheran and one Calvinist. The Lutheran cause is the "conception of the calling." In reacting against the monastic ideal Luther did not entirely repudiate the worthiness of ascetic self-denial. What he did was to replace the insistence upon withdrawal from the world with a "valuation of fulfilment of duty in worldly affairs as the highest form which the moral activity of the individual could assume." To this exaltation of the importance of laboring in one's vocation was added the Calvinist notion of absolute predestination. If you believe that humanity has been irretrievably divided into the elect and the reprobate, then it becomes a matter of some importance to convince yourself that you are a member of the right group. "In order to attain that confidence intense worldly activity is recommended as the most suitable means. It and it alone disperses religious doubts and gives certainty of grace." As a paradoxical result, Protestantism, which proclaims that works are useless as a means of gaining salvation, ends by finding them "indispensable as a means . . . of getting rid of the fear of damnation." "Getting rid of fear" is a key phrase for an understanding of the psychological power of the Protestant ethic and of Falstaff as a compendious alternative to that ethic. Hope of eternal life gets rid of the fear of death. Faith in our election gets rid of the fear of eternal damnation, and contemplating the success of our worldly activity ratifies our faith in election. Success is evidence of salvation. The Protestant ethic is a superb strategy for getting rid of those fears which are inherent in the human condition, fears of time, of death, and of damnation. It is one of the greatest in what Freud calls "the great series of methods devised by the mind of man for evading the compulsion to suffer."

Falstaff is an anthology of such methods. I count and will try to define five, taking them in the order Shakespeare presents them to us. The first I label "living within appetite," the second "play," the third "success," the fourth "carnival," and the last, "hope." Of these the first, second, and fourth are in direct opposition to the ideals and practices of the Protestant ethic. The third and the last are distorted imitations of Protestant ethic methods and I will call them serious parodies, though it makes me uneasy to claim that anything about Falstaff is serious.

The first of Falstaff's methods is the most effective and also the most difficult to sustain. It is common to all of us, originates in infancy, and antedates the fear of time itself. Our first clock is appetite, and time first presents itself to us as that which intervenes between appetite and its satisfaction, and its rebirth. The time we thus perceive through appetite is circular in nature, a time of eternal return. A day is that which separates breakfast from breakfast. There is nothing to fear in time thus perceived as circular, as the element in which pleasure, the satisfaction of appetite, takes place. And much in the reality we begin to perceive outside our bodies appears to confirm the truth of time's circularity. The sun also ariseth, and the sun goeth down and hasteth to the place where he arose. Spring, summer, autumn, winter—spring. Not much of this appetitive, circular time has passed, however, before its passing forces upon us the knowledge that our understanding of time is incomplete. The bodies whose appetites we have satisfied change permanently. Today is not yesterday despite the similarity in breakfasts. Summer returns but last summer will never return. Time, we find, is rectilinear, the shortest possible distance between birth and death. With that discovery our fear of time is born, and our minds must devise methods for evading the suffering in that fear. The method of the Protestant ethic is to glorify time's rectilinearity, to proclaim time the element not of pleasure, but of duty, of the worldly achievement that ratifies faith in our election. This, however, is not Falstaff's way.

*Henry IV, Part One* opens with the King doing desperate battle against the implacability of rectilinear time. "Find we a time" is his plea. A time for peace, for the establishment of order, for the crusade, the achievement that will expiate Richard's murder and convince the King that his soul is saved after all. The second scene begins when Falstaff first waddles into our consciousness on the line, "Now, Hal, what time of day is it, lad?" a question whose total banality inspires Hal to a rather wonderful tirade on the question: "What a devil hast thou to do with the time of the day?", a question that Hal himself proceeds to answer: "Unless hours were cups of sack, and minutes capons, and clocks the tongues of bawds, and dials the signs of leaping-houses. . . ." Hal's conditional answers his interrogative. Falstaff's clock is Falstaff's paunch and the time it tells is circular, revolving from thirst to sack to thirst to sack. From hunger to capon to hunger to capon. From lust to wench to lust to fair, hot wench. Falstaff copes with the fact of time's linearity by stoutly denying it, by doing his best to live his life within the circular time of appetite. Such a life would be a life without fear of time, but of course no moderately conscious life can be so lived. It's not just that capons, sack, and wenches refuse to arrive on schedule—though that is annoying enough. The rectilinearity of time is constantly being forced upon our unwilling minds. Even our best friends are in the habit of saying things like "gallows," and when we try tactfully to change the subject to something pleasant like "a most sweet wench," they refuse to cooperate and we end up depressed, "as melancholy as a gib cat, or a lugged bear."

When this happens to Falstaff, he moves to his second strategy. He answers the reproaches of his superego with the exhilarating language of play—purely verbal play at first. Falstaff copes with melancholy by playing with Hal at finding similes for it: a gib cat, a lugged bear, an old lion, a lover's lute, the drone of a Lincolnshire bagpipe, a hare, the melancholy of Moor-ditch. Having thus put the forces of his conscience on the defensive, he proceeds to polish them off by employing his favorite play method, role-playing. Falstaff has the ability to make anything appear ridiculous by pretending to be it. Here he represses his own tendencies to contrition by pretending to be contrite: "But Hal, I prithee trouble me no more with vanity . . . thou hast done much harm upon me, Hal, God forgive thee for it: before I knew thee, Hal, I knew nothing, and now am I, if a man should speak truly, little better than one of the wicked." What Poins calls "Monsieur Remorse" is Falstaff's first and in some ways best role. Nowhere does Shakespeare make it clearer how the humorous man copes with the certainty of death and the possibility of damnation. By parodying his own fears, Falstaff answers the challenge Hamlet gives the skull of Yorick: he makes us laugh at that. But of course it is not just himself that Falstaff is mocking here. Monsieur Remorse is pretty clearly a Puritan gentleman. He is one of the Protestant Saints whom the Prince of Wales has so far misled as to make him doubt his own election and fear that his conduct indicts him as little better than one of the reprobate. Not only does Falstaff's role-playing purge him of his own melancholy, it accuses the Protestant ethic of being a role that the Puritan thinks (or pretends to think) he is playing in earnest. But it is not only the specific mockery, the parochial satire that the Protestant ethic would find offensive. Falstaff's roles release him from the depressing confines of reality and that, unless done religiously, will not do. Play in all its forms, from morris-dancing to the great Globe itself, is an inadmissible alternative to laboring soberly in one's vocation. But Falstaff, *homo ludens,* goes on playing. On Gadshill and in the tavern his roles increase and multiply: the young desperado ripping off the fat chuffs who batten on the commonwealth ("They hate us youth"); the battered survivor of a better time who sees a virile world of courage and honor among thieves degenerating, disintegrating around him: "Go thy ways, old Jack, die when thou wilt—if manhood, good manhood, be not forgot upon the face of the earth, then I am a shotten herring . . ."; and Sir John Fairbanks, Sr., driving before him two, four, seven, nine, eleven men in buckram; and finally, of course, the King, the Prince, himself. So Falstaff's Protean mind copes with itself, represses and escapes its fears by becoming not dying Jack Falstaff but anything and everything, turning all things to laughter.

But again this is not enough. On the morning after the night before the body whose appetites have been so assiduously satisfied informs the Protean mind that time is rectilinear and he is but Falstaff and a man: "Do I not bate? Do I not dwindle? Why, my skin hangs about me like an old lady's loose gown. I am withered like an old apple-john." And we get a reprise of Monsieur Remorse, rather more Romanist in his second version, I think. Clearly, sterner measures than play are called for. Living in appetite is the strategy of the infant. Play is the strategy of the child. Falstaff is never such a fool as to put away childish things. He knows he needs all the strategies he can get. While retaining the two I have already identified, he moves to those of the mature man and specifically to an antiversion of the Protestant ethic itself. Having parodied the remorse of the Puritan, he now more seriously parodies its results: the determination to labor in one's vocation.

When, in their first scene, Hal interrupts the finer flights of Monsieur Remorse to ask Jack Falstaff where they should take a purse tomorrow, he gets the reply, " 'Zounds, where thou wilt, lad, I'll make one." Upon which the prince observes, "I see a good amendment of life in thee, from praying to purse-taking." Monsieur Remorse's rejoinder is a model of Christian forbearance: "Why, Hal, 'tis my vocation, Hal, 'tis no sin for a man to labor in his vocation." If one wished to be unfair to the Protestant ethic (and I do), one could say that Weber's description of the shift in Christian morality from the medieval exaltation of the monastic ideal to the seventeenth-century Puritan enshrinement of capitalist worldly asceticism is encapsulated in Hal's phrase "from praying to purse-taking." Falstaff's methods in purse-taking are not commercial and therefore his calling is not lawful. But he is not really a highwayman either. The night's exploits on Gadshill are closer to play than to vocation, an especially exciting game of cops-and-robbers. Ordinarily and whenever possible, Falstaff combines the crafts of the professional soldier and the confidenceman. He combines them very successfully. The £300 that he extorts from reluctant draftees compares favorably with the £250 Shakespeare is estimated to have made in a good year and very favorably indeed with the £20 annual salary of the Stratford schoolmaster. And Falstaff is a success on the battlefield as well. He does his duty by leading or somehow chivvying his soldiers into a position where they can be thoroughly peppered, and then he distinguishes himself by stabbing the corpse of Hotspur in the thigh. Does he expect anyone to believe that he and not Hal has killed Harry Percy? It doesn't matter, for there are distinct orders of success in lying. A liar may succeed because he is believed or because he cannot be contradicted. Falstaff is content with the more modest degree, and thus he achieves one of those reputations, common enough in fields other than the military, for having done something or other at some time or other.

The result of these successful labors is the Sir John Falstaff of *Henry the Fourth, Part Two:* Jack Falstaff with his familiars, John with his brothers and sisters, and Sir John with all Europe. Such are the secular rewards of laboring in one's vocation—self-fulfillment and a sense of one's identity confirmed by the respect of the community. And there is no strategy more successful than success for concealing from us our participation in the common human condition. For the Puritan, of course, the rewards of such laboring also include the conviction of one's election and a consequent faith in one's eternal salvation. Falstaff does not go that far, not by some distance. Indeed, his profession is an extension of his play. He has added a new dimension to his role-playing and has begun to pretend really to be what he is pretending to be. To what extent that makes him different from the rest of us, including the ethical Protestants, I must leave it to the subtler masters of the dramaturgical school of social psychology to decide. My point is that as a technique for dealing with our fears of time and death, becoming Sir John with all Europe works very well. Monsieur Remorse is no longer needed to repress the natterings of the superego. Being Sir John is enough.

Or almost enough, for again the body reminds us of our inevitable predicament. The owner of Sir John's urine may have more diseases than he knows for, but Sir John is aware of a good number of them: "A pox of this gout! or a gout of this pox! for the one or the other plays the rogue with my great toe." That great toe, long invisible to its owner's eye, is transmitting the body's tedious message: you cannot conquer time. Falstaff's fourth method for jamming that communication is related to all of the previous three. Carnival is an attempt to regain occasionally and temporarily the bliss of living within appetitive time. It is that period which society sets aside for sanctioned play, for humor, wit, and role-playing. It is the necessary holiday in which we may rest from doing our duties in that station to which it has pleased God to call us. Except, of course, that the Puritans recognized no such necessity. They were opposed to Carnival, but they were equally opposed to Lent—not because they found its lugubrious self-denials distasteful (though they knew there was no merit in them) but because they thought it should be Lent all the year round. Once more, Sir John embodies a different point of view. After a hard day's labor devoted to evading the Lord Chief Justice, placating Mistress Quickly, devising methods for bilking Master Dommelton the slops-maker, and avoiding the importunities of a dozen sweating captains—after such a day, the warrior deserves his repose. Wine, women, and song, sack and canary, Doll Tearsheet and Sneak's noise—all the components of an ideal saturnalia are present in the great festive scene of *Henry IV, Part Two*. But Shakespeare is here aiming to present us with the real as well as the ideal, and real saturnalia has indecorous results: vomit, urine, syphilis, and violence. Our women enter talking of wine and its effects and when asked how she is doing now, Doll replies, "Better than I was—hem!" That "hem," I suspect, is Shakespeare's suggestion to his boy-actor that he should indicate audibly but nonverbally why Doll is doing better than she was. Sir John enters with song: "When Arthur first in court," and urine: "Empty the jordan." A bout of wit follows between Doll and Falstaff on the subject of who is responsible for whose venereal disease. The episode with Pistol brings us to violence and Sir John's valor inspires Doll to ask her little, tidy, Bartholomew boar-pig when he will leave fighting a-days and foining a-nights and begin to patch up his old body for heaven. *Carpe diem* is a motto of carnival, but one of the things we ask of saturnalia is that it make us forget why it is that we want to seize the day. Doll's comment is malapropos and her most flattering busses cannot make Falstaff forget the consequences of linear time: "I am old. I am old." And finally, in spite of the fun and games with Hal and Poins, it looks as if Shakespeare were going to let Falstaff be frustrated by age and time and by the demands of his vocation, for "The man of action is called on" and must leave the sweetest morsel of the night unplucked. Farewells must be said: "Well, fare thee well. I have known thee these twenty-nine years, come peascod-time, but an honester and truer-hearted man. . . ." I thoroughly agree with the Arden editor's note on peascod-time: "The precision with which Mistress Quickly dates a 29-year-old meeting is entirely touching." Just how entirely that is, however, can be understood only if one apprehends the bawdy of "peascod," and to do that one must reverse the syllables. Doing so emphasizes that the time that finally triumphs here is appetitive and circular. Bardolph reenters with a command: "Bid Mistress Tearsheet come to my master." Poins was wrong: desire has not outlived performance. Codpiece time comes round again and Plump Jack lives!

This is a heartening conclusion to a brilliant scene and yet we suspect Shakespeare of suggesting that Falstaff is coming to the end of his strategies. This suspicion is strengthened by the King's magnificent speeches in the next scene on the book of fate, the revolution of the times, and the necessity of meeting one's necessities. The scene that follows informs us that old Double is dead and John of Gaunt, who loved him well, is dead and death is certain, very sure, all shall die, and that the one way left of coping with that perception seems to be to let one's shallow mind wander quickly to the price of a good yoke of bullocks at Stamford Fair. Yet Falstaff continues to labor cheerfully in his fraudulent vocation, and it is not until act 5, scene 3 that we discover that he has been doing battle with time and the prospect of death by employing one strategy more than the four we have already examined. Pistol interrupts senility's saturnalia in Gloucestershire with news of yet another death: the old king is dead as nail in door. Falstaff, whom Shallow and Silence have kept quietly amused to this point, now explodes with excitement: "I am Fortune's steward . . . I know the young King is sick for me . . . the laws of England are at my commandment . . . woe to my Lord Chief Justice!" This is the revelation of a life illusion. Since the first time we saw him in the second scene of the Henriad, Falstaff has never repeated to Hal or us his speculations on what will happen when the Prince becomes the King. We realize that he much overestimates Hal's devotion to sack and laughter, but we have small reason to know, until we find out, that Falstaff thinks Hal's accession will put the laws of England at Sir John's commandment. What here stands revealed is Falstaff's last strategy, his secular, temporal version of a religious faith in one's election to eternal salvation. Falstaff copes with his condition by living in hope, as which of us does not. We must cling to our faith in that intervening event (the doctorate, tenure, the professorship, retirement) which will with millennial effect transform the quality of our existence. Delusive hope was included in Pandora's box lest we should despair and destroy ourselves. What kills Sir John is the destruction of his delusive hope and the consequent knowledge that his future does not exist.

He would have died anyway. Falstaff, like everybody else, is killed by death. But that death is designed by Shakespeare to show us something. The King kills Falstaff's heart, but what impels the King to do so is the desire to do his royal duty by laboring in his vocation. I lack the time to demonstrate why I think Henry of Monmouth stands for the Protestant ethic but I believe that, consciously or not, Shakespeare has transposed into his early-fifteenth-century action the uncompleted spiritual and political struggles of the 1590s. Hal's psychomachia is a battle between Carnival and Lent, and Falstaff is on the losing side. Hal and the protestant Ethic reject Falstaff, but Shakespeare does not reject Falstaff nor does he reject Hal for rejecting Falstaff.

Falstaff defines the Protestant Ethic by being what it isn't, but also by being a different variety of what it is: a means of coping with the fears engendered by the realities of the human condition. The ethic defeats Falstaff because of the superior strength that derives from the religious faith on which it is based—a faith that enables it to cope with our fears by denying that the realities that inspire them are ultimately real, by asserting that linear time will give way to eternity and that death is a transition to eternal life. Falstaff's being what he is, however, poses a great question to the ethic's answer: may not the ethic's faith be as illusory a strategy as any of Falstaff's, finally a form of delusive hope itself? Hal, in accepting his necessary form, must reject Falstaff because the Protestant ethical form cannot encompass the question Falstaff poses. But Shakespeare's art can and does. It encompasses, as always, question and answer and the questioning of the answer. And the questioning of the questioning, for what is the Falstaff action but a demonstration of the inevitable inadequacy of the strategies of which his character is composed? Shakespeare's sense, whether comical or tragical or tragical-comical-historical-pastoral, seems to me to be always interrogative. For me the great thing about Shakespeare's art is its ability simultaneously to reveal and accept our inadequacies, above all the inadequacy of our answers. The motto carved on the temple of our particular oracle is, "Your answers questioned here."

# Shakespeare and the
# Abstraction of History

by ALVIN B. KERNAN

Much of the difficulty of specifying Shakespeare's conception of history comes from the number of different histories that appear in his plays: G. B. Harrison's type of gossipy chronicle history of the year the Thames froze over, the bright comet appeared, and the glassworks was built; E. M. W. Tillyard's, and Hall's and Holinshed's, moral history of the Tudor Myth, tracing out the punishment of the kingdom for rebellion and usurpation; the romantic popular history of Good Queen Bess, the defeat of the Armada, and Sir Walter's cloak; the stern Marxist history of class warfare in which the Protestant middle class, identified with capitalist economics and democratic politics, seized power from the landed feudal aristocracy and the kings; or, most recently, Jan Kott's "grand staircase of history," the meaningless search for power and the endless death of kings.

The critics who have investigated the Shakespearean view of history have tended to make the playwright a spokesman for one particular view of history or another, which runs against the primary critical predisposition of our time to see the plays as anything but polemical or ideological. They are, of course, intensely concerned with political, social, and historical issues — even the comedies are set within a frame of a political state and raise issues of authority — but Shakespeare always complicates history, as he complicates everything, by elaborating the psychology of the characters, by introducing numerous voices to express a variety of attitudes, by multiplying perspectives, and above all by the use of language that always enriches but at the same time makes ambiguous whatever it handles.

The dominant criticism of our time always shows us a dense dramatic foreground that allows many possible interpretations. If we think at one moment in, say, *Henry IV, Part Two*, that we are watching moral history work itself out in the rejection of Falstaff, we are at the same time uneasily aware that this is also the culmination of Hal's scheme begun long ago in the Boars-head Tavern to build a political image. Shakespeare does not resolve such ambiguities as these, and as a result we get not the abstractions of History, with a capital "H," but a series of complex, many-faceted events, linked to the mysterious motives and morally ambivalent energies of remarkable men and women.

It is noticeable that the plays contain no such full panoramas of past and future as appear in Books 11 and 12 of *Paradise Lost* where the Archangel lays out for Adam the whole dreary course of human history. When history is defined in Shakespeare with great clarity and certainty, as in Ulysses' speech on order, Octavius Caesar's presentation of himself as destiny, or Brutus's ex-planation of why Caesar must bleed, the situation is always thoroughly ironic. Ulysses' view of history has no practical application to the chaos at Troy, the *Pax Romanum* is about to be achieved by destroying all the vitality in the em-pire, and Brutus in his efforts to achieve freedom and liberty is bringing about tyranny. The most characteristic Shakespearean scene of men con-fronting history, trying to frame their understandings of the historical pro-cess, is one in which the future is seen only darkly, seen in the Tolstoyan man-ner, not the serene image of vast emptiness seen by André lying wounded on the field at Austerlitz, but rather of Napoleon dispatching orders that have no effect on the battle's outcome into the powder-smoke covered field. Shakespearean figures face to face with history are usually more aware of their ironic position as they try to puzzle out the direction of the future: Richard II, his old kingdom and old structure of ceremonies and hierarchy in ruins, in his dark dungeon at Pomfret trying to "hammer it out"; Hotspur dy-ing, following out the long mysterious process in which thoughts are subject to life, life to time, and even beyond time, which must have a stop, some unknown emptiness; Henry V, his identity obliterated by darkness and a cloak, trying to reason, not very satisfactorily, with his soldiers about a king's responsibility for death and history, looking at the distant firelight from the French camp on the eve of Agincourt; Hector knowing as surely as we do that Troy must fall, but knowing also that he cannot believe it, even as he argues with Troilus that the moral law of nations and the survival of Troy requires returning Helen to the Greeks; Macbeth trying to make sense of those palter-ing symbols of the future, the armed head, the bloody babe, and the child crowned, trying to unravel the duplicitous and doubled predictions of the witches about fair and foul and won and lost. If the Shakespearean world has a direction, the men and women who give history its substance are usually unable to see it clearly, and when they think they do, they are always mistaken about what they are doing and where they are going.

It is not that Shakespeare is not fascinated with history, only that he never seems to be able to rise to such a grand abstraction as History. And yet the temptation ultimately to find a historical pattern in him is irresistible — the plays are art, after all, not reality—and when one peers long and hard enough—so I tell myself—it is possible to see at least the shadows of a continuing historical procession in which an old order, a world of community, feudal, hierarchical, humanistic, is always passing on. Its kings are always terribly vulnerable like Richard II, Old Hamlet, or Duncan; its knights die like the French chivalry at Agincourt, or like Hotspur, Antony, and Coriolanus, at the hands of more efficient powers; its crucial ceremonies of trial-by-combat, duel, coronation, ritual feast, or procession fail to achieve their social functions in Elsinore and in Rome; its gods do not respond to confident invocations or to agonized prayers in extremity; the bond of identity with a humane nature and the order of the cosmos disappears on Lear's heath; and even a kind of ready good nature and self-indulgent appetite that seem possible only in an older, more easy-going world are obliterated in the Boarshead Tavern and Cleopatra's Egyptian palace. Perhaps the summary image of the passing of this older world comes in *Lear* where the King, the peer, the band of knights, the fool, the honest servant, the feudal lord, the dispossessed beggar, and the legitimate child are driven out of the castle, to face the dreadful forces of a new, indifferent nature on the heath, to disappear at last into despair and death on a great battlefield.

The force that destroys the old order is always, or almost always, of the same nature: as rational and vital as Edmund, as sure of how to get and hold power as Bolingbroke, as efficient as Claudius and Octavius Caesar, as able to shape its face to the moment as Richard III, as ambitious as Lady Macbeth, as relentless as Iago. But the old order destroys itself as well, for it is always reckless, self-indulgent, thoughtless, trustingly vulnerable, often childish, and its passing comes to seem as inevitable as the progress in individual lives from innocence to experience. No doubt the universality of this pattern at the psychological and social level in the plays gives it much of its power, but it represents at the same time a definite historical movement as well, the transformation of Christendom, more specifically the late Middle Ages and the humanistic High Renaissance, into the modern world. Although we tend to separate the Middle Ages from the Renaissance, Shakespeare seems to collapse them in such a way that many of the values of Renaissance humanism blend with those of feudalism and chivalry to form a mythical old kingdom in which a Renaissance price like Hamlet is part of the same historical complex as a feudal king like Lear and a pagan knight like Hector. Shakespeare presents this historical change as both terribly sad and as necessary at once, and always shows it only through an immediate dense foreground of vital men and women and complex actions, which make it possible to see and assess the change in many different ways.

# Myth and Naturalism: Merchant *to* Macbeth

## by NICHOLAS BROOKE

It seems that it is myth and archetype that have replaced religion for the twentieth century, not poetry. Poems and plays are often regarded as little more than media for the transmission of myth; and myth is therefore thought of as more permanent than the forms in which it is transmitted. So the problems of art are sometimes seen as the adjusting of universal myths to contemporary realities. I doubt that; I believe rather that the interaction of myth and realism is mutually modifying, producing a mythology as contemporary, and therefore as temporary, as the realism. But that proposes, at least, the central importance of *both* to any understanding of art.

In Shakespeare's early work, especially the comedies, the potential conflict is glossed over in the fanciful forms of Mannerism in which myth is hardly serious and reality is freely distorted. The last acts of *Love's Labour's Lost* and *A Midsummer Night's Dream* do indeed confront the problem sharply if briefly, but in *The Merchant of Venice* the conflict becomes an essential part of the structure. The play alternates between a freshly realistic presentation of the mercantile world of Venice (with a newly elaborate realism of character in Shylock) and a more conventionally romance (fairy-tale) world of Belmont. They incorporate, of course, opposed value systems, which confront one another in Act 4. The myths of romance and of Christianity are conflated; they do not go unquestioned, and it is the play's salvation that Shylock can protest so disturbingly — there is always an appeal from art to nature. But an over-neat pattern is still worked out in the last act's triumph of Belmont, a moonlight myth not far enough from the moonshine that Gratiano returns to the dawn of common day.

This conflict is patent in *Troilus and Cressida,* though the Greek mythology is not Christian, and only remotely romance. All three recur, however surprisingly, in *All's Well.* Shakespeare changed the heroine's name to Helena, and the Fool, Lavatch, makes the Greek allusion explicit in his bawdy song about the rarity of virginity. Military prowess hardly dominates, it is so muted; but it is there in Bertram's image that excites Diana (another carefully chosen name) and her mother; and a military world is there too in the practical joking that so savagely exposes Parolles. Exposure, in fact, is the play's strongest dramatic mode. The Countess has to force out of Helena, in Act 1, her confession of ambitious love for Bertram; and she does it by trapping her with the steward's eavesdropping. Helena confesses only what she has to as each drop is squeezed out of her, and the last is still kept back, the intent to marry him. Bertram is trapped by Diana into surrendering his ring—no actual whore could do it more neatly, nor be better briefed for the job. And just afterwards Parolles's exposure is complete enough to bring him to the apt comment,

> Who cannot be crush'd with a plot?
> (4.3.314)

The play's brilliant last scene, the trial of Bertram (and Diana) by the King, is entirely a matter of exposure by traps, until Bertram's arrogant blustering is finally penetrated to confession after confession, and so to confrontation with Helena:

> If she, my liege, can make me know this clearly
> I'll love her dearly, ever, ever dearly.
> (5.3.309-10)

The least romantic of romantic affirmations.

It is usually said of *All's Well* that it lacks any consistent language or dramatic mode. I think that is a mistake. Its characteristic mode is exposure by traps; and what is exposed is the reticence with which men and women guard their egotism. Throughout the play there are only two soliloquies that offer any insight into a person: one is Parolles's after his exposure:

> Simply the thing I am
> Shall make me live.
> (4.3.322-23)

The other is Helena's at the end of 1.1:

> I think not on my father . . .
> What was he like?
> I have forgot him. . . .there is no living, none,
> If Bertram be away.
> (1.1.77-83)

The language is distinctive—and to my mind singularly impressive—in its

very bareness. *All's Well* lacks imagery because it eliminates it, except for one
that is sharply definitive, Helena's comment on Parolles's entry:

> these fix'd evils sit so fit in him
> That they take place when virtue's steely bones
> Looks bleak i' th' cold wind. . .
>                    (1.1.100-102)

The clarity is of the same order as Lavatch's "I am driven on by the flesh,"
and it leads through Helena's distrait bawdry with Parolles about virginity, to
her conclusion:

> The court's a learning place, and he is one —
> *Par.* What one, i 'faith?
> *Hel.* That I wish well. 'Tis pity —
> *Par.* What's pity?
> *Hel.* That wishing well had not a body in't
> Which might be felt . . .
>                    (1.1.173-78)

The reticence that struggles to just so much declaration is painful, and it is
striking. It is of a piece with Parolles's "Simply the thing I am [a braggart and
a fool]. / Shall make me live," or with the King's retort to a courtier's flattery:

> I fill a place, I know't.
>                    (1.2.69)

This bare language I have claimed as the play's unique achievement. It is,
strikingly, naturalistic in impulse, and it is of a piece with the private
domestic pitch the play so largely sustains in handling its aristocrats, courts,
armies, and evocative cities (Paris and Florence). It is characteristic that
Helena's cure for the King is possibly her father's drugs; possibly fairytale
magic potion; possibly divine intervention; very possibly her sexual power,
which revives his lust and overcomes his depressive fear of old age and im-
potence. The King is a sick man who has lost confidence in his doctors. The
Countess is a motherly soul, partly sentimental and partly sharp. The Floren-
tine ladies are more calculating than virtuous about Bertram's pursuit of
Diana.

It is a mistake, however, to think the play merely naturalistic, inappropriate to its romance plot, as it is a mistake to think Caravaggio's religious
paintings merely essays in social realism, related to religious myth only by the
need for ecclesiastical patrons. Such critical errors are common about both
painter and dramatist, who were contemporaries. Actors and directors have a
harder task than critics: they cannot be so selective. *All's Well* does have a

romance theme in its romance plot, and it enacts that at length: Helena's cure for the King might indeed be a stranger magic than sex (if such exists); her pursuit of Bertram is all conducted in couplets without a hint of irony, and ends with a pretense of death to trigger its final success. In this naturalistic context the mock death is hard to take in, which is sharply different from *The Winter's Tale*. What is more, Helena *can* be seen with romantic eyes: Coleridge fell in love with her, and he was not alone.

But the couplets that utter this other dimension are themselves unusual: they only rarely assert the full chime of completed form; usually the rhymes are unstressed and the sentence structure set against the verse rhythm; and they never have a sustained rhythmic continuity. They approximate to the broken movement of the blank verse, and they function, not as eloquent affirmation, but rather as reticent mask. After Act 1 what Helena thinks or feels is undeclared: unknown and unknowable. The myth is enacted, but it is not celebrated. Its celebration would violate the naturalism to which it is — so improbably but so brilliantly — related.

In other words, *All's Well* is misunderstood as showing a naturalism constricted by a traditional romance plot. It is an extraordinary experiment in relating naturalism to myth. It is brilliant, but limited by its own brilliance — limited, in fact, by the reticence that forbids any affirmatory eloquence. We know the myth rather by allusion than by exposition. *Measure for Measure* has often been seen in similar terms, though always more doubtfully. It too confronts myth with naturalism and penetrates false masks by confrontation and exposure. But in *Measure for Measure* the striking reticence of *All's Well* is exchanged for a variety of contrasting, indeed clashing, eloquences: Isabella's "man, proud man, / Dress'd in a little brief authority," the Duke's "Be absolute for death," Claudio's

> Ay, but to die, and go we know not where;
> To lie in cold obstruction, and to rot. . .
>
> (2.2.118-19; 3.1.5, 117-18)

in *All's Well* egotisms are exposed; in *Measure for Measure* they are given superb and conflicting utterances. And romance itself has its striking, though very brief, expression in Mariana's first appearance and the boy's song. It is a context in which romance themes — like those of *The Merchant*, related to Christianity — can more plausibly be given a voice, though (such is the achieved realism) with great difficulty, indeed awkwardness. The transition from Claudio and Isabella's confrontation to the Duke's banal plotting is the most awkward in Shakespeare, for it abandons both ends of the equation, myth and naturalism alike. His prose is as much a mask as Helena's couplets, and we can never know how to respond to him. But the equation becomes the dramatic center of the play and emerges in the final procession of couples: the

Duke with Isabella, who has made no response to his declaration of marriage; Mariana with Angelo, who would prefer death to marriage; Lucio with the whore of whom he has said "Marrying a punk, my lord, is pressing to death, / Whipping, and hanging"; and Barnardine as obstinately solitary as ever, brought back on stage only, it would seem, to *be* part of this procession. The mythological conclusion is presented with all the counterforce of realism in a single, extraordinary, visual emblem.

The mode is very different from *All's Well*, but the problem of relating myth to naturalism is evidently the same. The last plays solve it by inverting that presentation. Overtly, they are mythological — indeed, they project their myths where the early plays had glossed over theirs, or *All's Well* had masked its. Their naturalism — and it is pervasive — is in the detail, the local handling. Superficially their achievement seems to be an alien aesthetic; actually, I suggest it springs from the same problems I have discussed in earlier plays, turned upside down. All Shakespeare's comedies — all his plays — are concerned with myth (in this sense, romance and Christianity are equally mythic) and with its relation to realism. His last solution to their cohabitation is to flaunt the myth, and to let that flaunting declare the potency and the irony at once. The continuity is precisely that from Caravaggio's naturalism to Rubens's overt mythic exuberance linked with explicit naturalism of flesh and warts — and Rubens was Caravaggio's greatest admirer (and buyer).

I cannot now develop that suggestion, and would rather end with the play that most fully deploys both ends of the equation, and makes most explicit the necessity, and the problems, of relating them: *Macbeth*. It has been the center of two radically opposed traditions of criticism. On the one hand, Bradley's nineteenth-century realism focused on the exceptionally naturalistic presentation of Macbeth and Lady Macbeth, and especially on their relationship to each other. On the other hand are L. C. Knights, Wilson Knight, and Cleanth Brooks, who understood the play almost exclusively in terms of its imagery. To both traditions the play appeared to be typical. In fact, it appears to me to be not so much typical as in both respects extreme.

The Macbeths are Shakespeare's only extended portrayal of marital intimacy. They know each other's thought when it has barely been hinted; they both echo and complement each other's strengths and weaknesses, and interchange sexual roles to do it. In 3.2 they exchange back again, as Lady Macbeth retreats into regret and Macbeth looks forward to peace by murder:

> *Lady M.* What's to be done?
> *Macb.* Be innocent of the knowledge, dearest chuck,
> Till thou applaud the deed.
> (3.2.44-6)

Despite her resumption of supportive rigor in the banquet, they never regain intimacy.

That is a brilliant demonstration of psychological perception—the ultimate, perhaps, in Shakespeare's concentration on character, and its presence here suggests a function of that concentration: the creation of a stage image of nature, the mirror of ourselves. But it does not, any more than in *All's Well*, exist alone. The play can seem to be explicable in naturalistic terms alone, but it has also that extraordinary display of imagery, no less complete, and only tangentially related to psychological revelation. The most extraordinary of all the play's image sequences, Macbeth's

> And Pity, like a naked new-born babe,
> Striding the blast, or heaven's Cherubins, hors'd
> Upon the sightless couriers of the air . . .
>
> (1.7.21-23)

emerges from an acute psychological speech, but transposes into a mode that cannot be accounted for in psychological terms. Their intimate exchange of thoughts is used to project language and imagery whose likeness is hardly a matter of their thoughts, but a continuity in the play that offers the audience a dimension totally outside naturalism. The actors' problem with these speeches is that they move from personal "thinking aloud" into a level of purely imagistic language that is strictly impersonal, making the speakers rather mediums than individual psyches (through *medium* is far too explicit a word for a phenomenon that is strictly theatrical). The demand is unusually strong for visualizing (of a strange kind); but the visualizing demanded seems to be primarily ours; it is theirs only in the generalized sense of their tending to "see things"—"No more sights."

In that, it mediates between psychological naturalism and the play's other dimension, the supernatural (or mythic). The play shows not only a great many supernatural phenomena, but a remarkable range of them. The weird sisters appear to Banquo, Macbeth, and the audience; the dagger to no one but Macbeth, and even he knows it is an illusion; Banquo's ghost is seen by the audience and by Macbeth, but by nobody else on the stage; Duncan's horses eating each other are words only, but words affirming fact, like Lady Macbeth's "I have given suck"; the horses of heaven's cherubim are words as well, not facts at all. The play is an exploration of the degrees and forms of illusion, and its study of illusion mediates between natural and supernatural, between (in the ill-defined terms I have been using) naturalism and myth. It distinguishes sharply between them—which is why it could be so complete to such alien critical traditions—and entirely interfuses them as well: "Nothing is, but what is not." It is part of the process that illusion is finally dispelled in rationally explicable phenomena: sleep-walking, the movement of Birnam Wood, and Macduff's unnatural birth, which lead to a very actual head bleeding on the end of a pike (a purely theatrical illusion of horrid naturalism). Illusion is systematically dispelled as much here as it is in the end of *The Tempest*, although there the process is carried to its logical conclusion as the actor steps out of his role to deliver the epilogue.

In all these plays the two dimensions of myth and naturalism are sharply opposed and contrasted, but the concern, always, is with their mutual dependence. And that is finally interpreted through an understanding of illusion—a direct calling attention to illusion—which mediates between the rationalism and the imaginative extravagance of the seventeenth century: the aesthetic of baroque art. The fanciful dissolution of the facts of nature that distinguishes mannerism, as it distinguishes much of Shakespeare's early work, is subjected to a discipline of naturalism that obscures but never supersedes imaginative concern with myth; and that in turn yields the problem of how to articulate myth without violating naturalism. The exploration generates, in a remarkably short space of time, the development of an entirely original form of dramatic art through a series of apparently contradictory experiments. They are, I believe, part of a single coherent development, one that closely parallels the exactly contemporary development of baroque art through Caravaggio and Carracci to Rubens and Bernini. Shakespeare was not a belated Renaissance figure—he was the first of the great baroque artists.

# Shakespeare: The Man in the Work—Reflections on a Reflection

## by L. C. KNIGHTS

I have been invited to speak on "Shakespeare: the Man in the Work." I am sure that you will see the limits of what can be usefully said. You will not, for example, expect me to extract from the plays reflections of the kind of biographical fact collected—or of speculations refuted—by Chambers or Schoenbaum. And because Shakespeare's chosen art form was drama it could not, in the nature of things, provide opportunity for the man to speak in the first person: as Dante, for example, in the *Commedia* tells us not only of his theological beliefs and religious values, but of his political ideals, his views of Florence, Italy, and the Empire, his literary tastes and models; even an ancestor, Cacciaguida, appropriately appears in the *Paradiso*. We can of course deduce a good deal about Shakespeare's values—his "view of life"—as we listen to the plays, though we certainly can not reduce it to any sort of system; we know a good deal about the range of his reading and, if only from his various parodies, we can learn something about his taste in contemporary literature. But we know nothing of his "beliefs" in any formal sense, and any attempt to summarize his values is likely to yield only a handful of generalizations.

Where we begin, strange as it may appear, is with Shakespeare's technique—the *how* of his dramatic craft. From the start it shows Shakespeare intent on *making* something, on "concentrating upon a task which is a task in the same sense as the making of an efficient engine or the turning of a jug or a table-leg."[1] In his essay, *Construction in Shakespeare*—an essay that deserves to be more widely known than it is—Hereward T. Price spoke of Shakespeare's "eminently constructive mind."[2] He drew his illustrations

143

mainly from the early plays, but there is hardly one that does not show this strong constructive power—in such things as the effective disposition of episodes and characters, in parallelisms and contrasts, and, when the plays are performed, in grouping and movement. And this dramatic craftsmanship serves, is essentially one with, a virtually inexhaustible poetry that not only *defines* with unparalleled fullness, but has a connective vibrancy such that you never know when some apparently minor phrase or image, in electric connection with some part of the total context, is going to spring to life and enrich that context. Each of the greater plays, in short, is an artifact showing the characteristics of all great works of art—or, for that matter, of great religious teaching: it does not simply convey a preformed "meaning"; in the measure that it is "an energy system" it calls out corresponding energies in the reader or spectator—perceptions, sympathies, recoils, questionings. That is why no work of art is static. Separated from, though not independent of, its author's life and times, its continuing life is necessarily a changing one: since, if we are really responding, it probes and questions us, often in some rather disturbing ways, we can not expect to think and feel—to sense the meaning—in exactly the same way as our ancestors, or as other of our contemporaries.

I have not, as you may imagine, wandered from my subject. The only "personal" poetry we have from Shakespeare is his Sonnets. These are personal in tone and frequently use the form of what has been called "impassioned meditation" or of direct address. (Melchiori has noted that the percentage of first- and second-person pronouns is greater than in any other Elizabethan sonnet sequence.[3]) Here we learn a great deal about the man who wrote them. He clearly felt the beauty of changing natural forms, and delight in nature is matched by an equally keen sense of transience:

> How with this rage shall beauty hold a plea,
> Whose action is no stronger than a flower?

He was aware of many trades, professions, and social relationships. Imagery and allusion alone declare him an *observant* man. Judging by the best of the sonnets, he knew sexual passion, passionate friendship, betrayal, disappointment, and frustration. It is, however, wasted labor to try to extract biographical information from these remarkable and varied poems. For what distinguishes the greater sonnets is that they too are extremely formal artifacts, and it is in subjecting himself to formal exigencies that the poet seeks, not to "unlock his heart," but to explore, and reach the moral—that is to say, the human—essence of a dramatized situation.[4]

So many of the preoccupations of the plays—and I suppose, since these reveal a man totally committed to what he was writing, we may call them personal preoccupations—are present in the Sonnets that selection is unavoidable. I shall choose one strand for brief examination.

*Sincerity, authenticity, integrity,* are words that we often hear today; but the area of concern they point to has been central to human con- sciousness—in religion, philosophy, literature—since mind began to reflect on itself. Sonnet 123 begins

> No! Time, thou shalt not boast that I do change,

and it ends

> This I do vow and this shall ever be,
> I will be true despite thy scythe and thee.

"True," in its double sense of genuineness and commitment, is one of those words—like the word *free*—that was of especial importance to Shakespeare. Lionel Trilling, in his examination of the idea of "sincerity" in the modern world (in *Sincerity and Authenticity*), took his start from the words of Polonius:

> This above all: to thine own self be true,
> And it doth follow, as the night the day,
> Thou canst not then be false to any man.

In context, since Polonius is the speaker, the irony is obvious: but behind the irony something important is being said, linking being true to oneself and be- ing true to others. It is not, however, a simple idea, and there are two son- nets—both as baffling and ambiguous as they are significant—that approach the question of sincerity and directness of living from different angles. The difficulties of Sonnet 94, "They that have pow'r to hurt and will do none," are notorious. As Stephen Booth has said, the very first line "begins a process of creating a state of mind in the reader in which contrary but inseparable reac- tions uneasily coexist." The sonnet tries, and fails, to hold together conflicting feelings. Nevertheless, the main drive is against "the lords and owners of their faces," the rigidly self-contained. Their selves have a protective mask, and in this sense they are not "true": an obvious reference is to Angelo. Sonnet 121 on the other hand seems virtually to define sincerity as an expression, indeed an assertion, of a given self:

> 'Tis better to be vile than vile esteemed,
> When not to be, receives reproach of being,
> And the just pleasure lost, which is so deemed,
> Not by our feeling, but by others' seeing.
> For why should others' false adulterate eyes
> Give salutation to my sportive blood?
> Or on my frailties why are frailer spies,
> Which in their wills count bad what I think good?
> No, I am that I am, and they that level

> At my abuses, reckon up their own,
> I may be straight though they themselves be bevel;
> By their rank thoughts, my deeds must not be shown;
> Unless this general evil they maintain,
> All men are bad and in their badness reign.

At a first reading it seems that one is invited to be on the side of the speaker, who affirms his own individuality against the censorious "others" ("For why should others' false adulterate eyes. / Give salutation to my sportive blood?"). But what is opposed to the conventional moral judgments of the world is simply a "feeling" that the "pleasure" sought by the speaker is "just" or right for him because it suits his "sportive blood"; and the conclusion of the octave,

> Or on my frailties why are frailer spies,
> Which in their wills count bad what I think good?

sounds merely petulant.

The sestet begins with the tremendous assertion "No, I am that I am," which is a direct echo of the words spoken by God to Moses in Exodus 3:14; and it has been argued that Shakespeare is asserting his faith in the divinity of man. "The God of Shakespeare is *the man within*" (Melchiori, p.115). I don't think we can extract any such profession of faith from the sonnet. The line I have quoted is utterly different from, say, Blake's

> Thou art a man; God is no more:
> Thine own humanity learn to adore.

Nor can I get much sense from Wilson Knight's remark that here Shakespeare "asserts a kind of beyond-good-and-evil claim for himself" *(The Mutual Flame,*   p. 14). The pivotal line does not get much support from what precedes it, and what follows reads less like an expression of the self's "inherent strengths" than rather exasperated self-justification.

All the same, something rather interesting has emerged. "No, I am that I am" looks, not toward *Exodus,* but to other parts of the Shakespearean context: to Richard of Gloucester ("I am myself alone") and to Edmund in *King Lear.* Edmund is fully explicit ("Fut! I should have been that I am had the maidenliest star in the firmament twinkled on my bastardizing"), and in speeches too well known to quote he expresses a component in Renaissance free thought that had a considerable history before Diderot put a version of it into the mouth of Rameau's nephew. It is the view that Nature has made us what we are, and if that includes appetites and impulses conventionally disapproved, it is still "natural" to follow them: "All men are bad and in their badness reign." It is that possibility which the poet of Sonnet 121 grudgingly concedes as the only grounds on which "others" may assimilate him to themselves. As soon as it is stated it is clear that it is at least as glib as the speaker's own self-justification. In this imagined dispute neither of the two parties emerges with much credit.

In pursuing into the plays the lines of thought opened up by the beginning and the ending of the sestet of Sonnet 121 we may learn quite a lot, not about "Shakespeare the man," but about Shakespeare the imaginative man; and we may see reason for being content with that. One example must suffice. *Hamlet* clearly comes close to what we know from other sources to have been personal concerns of the author. Hamlet's knowledgeable theater talk might have come straight from the Mermaid Tavern. His catalogue of "the whips and scorns of time" is a direct echo of Sonnet 66, "Tir'd with all these, for restful death I cry." The play's central action has to do with the betrayal of trust, the betrayal of friendship, the failure of fidelity. And from the first line to the last we are aware of the enveloping darkness, that "black night" of Sonnet 73 that follows inevitably on day—"Death's second self that seals up all in rest." Death is an absolute that the modern consciousness tries to ignore. But *Hamlet*, far from ignoring it, perpetually forces it on our consciousness. It is against this insistent awareness of death and the unknown, of the darkness without and within that lies behind all everyday ambitions and complacencies, that men are shown making their self-determining choices. Against that background

> There is no shuffling; there, the action lies
> In his true nature, and we ourselves compell'd
> Even to the teeth and forehead of our faults
> To give in evidence.

We will ignore for the moment that "we ourselves" is not simply spoken by Claudius, someone out there on the stage; it implicates the audience. The central, though not the only, act of choosing is of course Hamlet's. Is he to believe the Ghost and avenge his father? In a matter of such moment—which symbolizes and draws into its orbit *all* acts of retaliation—we may expect Shakespeare the man to be profoundly involved. It would, I think, be proper, in any full consideration of "Shakespeare's thought," to recall that shortly after *Hamlet* he wrote *Measure for Measure,* which is about forgiveness; and that in a late play the central character endorses Montaigne to the effect that "the rarer action is in virtue than in vengeance."

But what does *the play* say to us? The play, because we see Hamlet's task, not in the light of a supposed literary tradition—that of "the revenge play"—and not in relation to Elizabethan theory and practice in such matters, but as the action presents it. Even what Henry James would call the "authority" of the Ghost cannot be determined solely by what we know of Elizabethan ghostlore. What the play shows us, when we consider it directly,

is what happens when a mind as fine as Hamlet's gives itself entirely to a command that issues from a world to which, in essential ways, he does not belong.
And lest this seems like an anachronistic importing of modern prejudice, we
should notice that, apart from Hamlet, the play gives us three instances of
revenge, of getting one's own back, that, to say the least, seem to call for a
critical judgment. There is the long exposition of Denmark's recent history in
1.1 — a story of violence meeting violence in a kind of chain reaction. There is
the speech of the First Player in 2.2, about the way in which "the rugged Pyr-
rhus" — "hellish" a few lines later — deals with Priam: on which our only comment can be to the effect that if this is "aroused vengeance" it is pretty horrible. And there is that other son with a father to avenge — Laertes, whom John
Vyvyan (in *The Shakespearean Ethic*) calls "Hamlet's deadly twin." Part of
the exchange between Laertes and Claudius runs:

> —What would you undertake
> To show yourself your father's son in deed
> More than in words?
>         —To cut his throat i' th' church.
> —No place, indeed, should murder sanctuarize;
> Revenge should have no bounds.

Since the speaker of the last line is King Claudius, we are, to say the least, provoked to some reflection.

None of this, of course, imposes a judgment on what Hamlet should or
should not have done. Indeed, it is of the essence of the case that no solution is
possible. I have merely wished to show that the man who made this play constructed it so as to provide cross-lights and echoes that prevent any simple
answer to one of the central questions that the play forces on us.

There are other echoes that inhabit this unweeded garden. Early in the
play Laertes' and Polonius's coarse *certainty* about the ways of the world is
brought to bear, vigorously and at length, on Ophelia's *un*certainty. Neither
can see in Hamlet's attentions to the girl anything more than an attempted
seduction. Since neither father nor son knows anything about love, the scene
can fairly be described as experience poisoning innocence. In essential ways
Ophelia is as isolated in her world as Hamlet is in his; her only guideline is the
apparently authoritative command to listen to the voice of the past, the
crudely generalizing voice of experience, and to deny life. Perhaps
Shakespeare wants to suggest to us that the voice of experience is not always
an entirely reliable guide.

> Had they deceived us,
> Or deceived themselves, the quiet-voiced elders,
> Bequeathing us merely a receipt for deceit?

He is certainly suggesting something we need to keep in mind, since he himself did. Laertes' last words to his sister are, "remember well / What I have said to you"; and Ophelia, " 'Tis in my memory lock'd, / And you yourself shall keep the key of it." When all this excellent advice has done its work and Ophelia is mad, she distributes flowers, each with some symbolic significance. To Laertes she gives rosemary—"There's rosemary, that's for remembrance; pray you, love, remember." Perhaps all this throws some light on the Ghost's "Remember me," and his demand for vengeance.

But the play is not only about revenge. It is about the near impossibility of deciding in crucial matters, the near impossibility of knowing other people; it is about certainty and uncertainty, about being trapped and being alone; it is about the unending struggle between life and death. And when it *moves* us—engages us fully in the action—it is useless to ask what the playwright thought of any of these matters; often enough "equalities are so weigh'd that curiosity in neither can make choice of either's moiety." Shakespeare has simply made a great work of art which, like all great works of art, reflects—or, better, calls into active life—something momentous in ourselves, something that, as both Herbert and Coleridge said of the Bible, "finds us,"[6] that questions us, and forces us in turn to question it again. We are, then, not dealing with a message from a master mind, however subtly "encoded," that, when received, will tell us something about the experience or the opinion of the sender; we are engaged with something that calls on us to think and imagine, with a sincerity and intensity that supples and strengthens the fibers of our moral being. It is, in short, the artist's fidelity to experience, his fidelity to language and his craft, that makes *us* ask—not in an intellectual way, but with our alerted imagination—what in such circumstances it means to be "true."

We can not, then, say we know *nothing* of Shakespeare the man in his works. We know him *through* the works, as James Baldwin brilliantly described him in his quatercentenary tribute, *Why I Stopped Hating Shakespeare.* "I think [he said] that he walked the streets and saw them, and tried not to lie about what he saw; his public streets and his private streets, which are always so mysteriously and inexorably connected; but he trusted that connection." Which is another way of saying that Shakespeare, in play after play, devoted immense technical resources to the service of an art that, for all its power of giving immediate enjoyment, was primarily an instrument of the imagination as a form of knowledge—not of knowledge as "given" but as living power.

If this is so, at this point, further questions about the man in the work are worse than irrelevant. They come into the category of all those devices of criticism and scholarship that substitute "knowing about" for active, and therefore personal, "knowing." We are all professionals here, and I am sure that as scholars and teachers we all need to keep the distinction I have just made in mind: to recognize that all our activities are ancillary to the great transaction that takes place between *this* play and *this* reader, or *this* audience. All this, to be sure, leaves the professional with plenty of work to do, and we rightly honor the great scholars. To provide information that elucidates, that clears away prejudice and blatant misunderstanding, to suggest criteria of relevance, to call attention—without what Buber called "the gesture of interference"—to this or that in structure or language that may help a single person to follow the play's guiding and to go behind structure and language to the point where the object of contemplation is virtually one with the perceiving subject—this is surely worthy of a lifetime's effort. This, I think, is an especially necessary reminder at the present time, when, as professionals, we all run the risk of a self-regarding professionalism. As Fuseli remarked to John Constable concerning the general level of submissions to the Royal Academy, ". . . as the conveniences and instruments of study increase, so will always the exertions of the students decrease."[7] I need hardly mention the factors I have in mind: "the Ph.D. Octopus," our academic systems of appointment and promotion ("How much have you published this year?"), the proliferation of mechanical aids that can seduce potentially first-rate teachers into the paths of a second-rate scholarship: anything, in short, that does not, directly or indirectly, serve the kind of living knowledge of the plays that we find, sometimes to our surprise, "is but an adjunct of ourselves." Not, however, to the selves we thought we were, but to selves that have grown, through happy or through tragic knowledge, into new selves, still changing, and therefore liable to return to the work of art to find that that too has changed.

On the day when I received your flattering invitation to speak on an impossible subject in an impossibly short time, I happened to read in the *Times Literary Supplement* Walter Kaufmann's essay "Rilke: Nirvana or Creation" (December 5, 1975). In the course of it he quoted a poem by Rilke that impressed me when I read it long ago in J. B. Leishman's collection, *Requiem and other Poems* (1935). The poem is *Archaic Torso of Apollo,* and since it is beautiful (even in translation) and decidedly relevant to my present purposes, I should like to end by reading it in Kaufmann's version.

> We did not know his high unheard-of head
> where his eyes' apples ripened. Yet his torso has
> retained their glowing as
> a candelabrum where his vision, not yet dead,
>
> only turned low, still shines. For else the breast
> could not blind you, nor could we still discern
> the smile that wanders in the loins' faint turn
> to that core which once carried manhood's crest.

> Else would this stone, disfigured and too small,
> stand mute under the shoulders' lucid fall,
> and not gleam like a great cat's skin, and not
>
> burst out of all its contours bright
> as a great star: there is no spot
> that does not see you. You must change your life.[8]

It is, I think, by a legitimate metaphoric leap that we can think of the missing head of the statue as Shakespeare the man, the creating intelligence, and of the torso as what we have left to us — works of art that invite us, not to go behind them, but, with an energy they themselves call out, to submit ourselves to their grave or mocking questioning, and to make of them — which is, to make of ourselves — what we can.

## Notes

1. T. S. Eliot, "Four Elizabethan Dramatists," *Selected Essays* (London, 1932), p. 114.

2. Hereward T. Price, *Construction in Shakespeare,* University of Michigan Contributions in Modern Philology, no. 17 (Ann Arbor, 1951).

3. Giorgio Melchiori, *L'uomo e il potere: Indagine sulle strutture profonde dei "Sonetti" di Shakespeare,* Einaudi Paperbacks (Turin, 1973), 1:2. See the statistical table on p. 14. (The book now appears in English as *Shakespeare's Dramatic Meditations: An Experiment in Criticism,* [Oxford University Press, 1977].)

4. The best attempt I know to relate formal structure to urgencies of meaning is Stephen Booth's *An Essay on Shakespeare's Sonnets.* Another brief but important study is Winifred Nowottny, "Formal Elements in Shakespeare's Sonnets: Sonnets I-VI," *Essays in Criticism* 2 (January 1952), reprinted in the Signet edition of the Sonnets, (New York, 1964).

5. The phrase is Erik Erikson's, *Insight and Responsibility* (New York, 1964), p. 111.

6. Such are thy secrets, which my life makes good,
> And comments on thee: for in ev'ry thing
> Thy words do find me out, & parallels bring,
And in another make me understood.
> George Herbert, *The H. Scriptures, 2.*

7. C. R. Leslie, *Memoirs of the Life of John Constable,* ed. J. Mayne, Phaidon Pocket Series (London, 1951), p.224

8. Reprinted from *Twenty-five German Poets: A Bilingual Collection,* ed., trans., and introduced by Walter Kaufmann (New York: W. W. Norton & Company, Inc., 1975).

# Johnson, Shakespeare, and the Dyer's Hand

## by JAMES BLACK

It is indeed certain that whoever attempts any common topick, will find unexpected coincidences of his thoughts with those of other writers; nor can the nicest judgment always distinguish accidental similitude from artful imitation.

Rambler No. 143[1]

Samuel Johnson's manner of writing has often been artfully imitated, but it is nearly impossible to find one specific writer upon whom he modeled his own style. W.K.Wimsatt, after an intensive exploration of possible antecedents,[2] believes that Johnson's style is a mirror of Johnson's experience; that only the kind of man he was could have written as he did. To have written a more general prose, Wimsatt thinks, Johnson would have needed "a more relaxed habit of imagination, a more ready capacity to collaborate with the variety and frequent incongruity of real experience."[3] It is precisely an intuitive ability to "collaborate with real experience" that Johnson himself identifies in Shakespeare's style: in the preface to the Dictionary he says that the "diction of common life" can be read in Shakespeare's works; and in the preface to his edition of Shakespeare he argues that "the dialogue of this author . . . seems scarcely to claim the merit of fiction, but to have been gleaned by diligent selection out of common conversation, and common occurrences" (7:63). If we knew nothing about Johnson or Shakespeare, and took Wimsatt's and Johnson's observations at face value, we might well surmise that Shakespeare lived in the world while Johnson did not—that here are two stars of English literature that "kept not their motion in one sphere."[4]

But what I hope to show is a certain convergence in the styles of Johnson and Shakespeare, a convergence that by no means makes Shakespeare one of

Johnson's stylistic antecedents, but that is nonetheless surprising in itself. I am going to examine as well the somewhat odd situation whereby Johnson's "professional" connection with Shakespeare—a connection that stretched from 1745 until 1773—was so very rarely reflected in his conversation or his writing.

It goes almost without saying that Johnson recognized in Shakespeare a well of English: there are several thousand quotations from Shakespeare in the *Dictionary,* where he is cited more often than any other writer.[5] It might be reasonable to expect that in his other writings Johnson would often go, consciously or otherwise, to this well. The conscious visitation is readily confirmed. Johnson's professional association with Shakespeare lasted from the "Miscellaneous Observations on the Tragedy of Macbeth" and a proposal for a new edition of Shakespeare (1745) through a renewed proposal in 1756, the issue of the edition in 1765 with a second printing in that year, a third edition in 1768, and on to a fourth edition with Johnson's own revisions in 1773. Shakespeare by no means occupied all of Johnson's time, of course: between 1745 and 1773 he accomplished the *Dictionary* and a massive canon of prose. But Arthur Sherbo suggests that Johnson "never completely forgot the edition he had projected in 1745, and most of what he wrote in the next twenty years was eventually grist to his editorial mill."[6]

Yet, if we look at the products of Johnson's other mills for these years, it does not appear that Shakespeare is very strongly present in Johnson's writing. In the *Rambler,* for instance, which Johnson wrote twice weekly from March 1750 until March 1752, 208 numbers contain only eight citations of Shakespeare. Of these citations two are allusive, five are direct quotations, and one is an indirect quotation. It would seem that Johnson is a little reluctant to frame direct quotations, except for illustrative purposes as with the *Macbeth* passage, "Come, thick night . . . ," which is cited in an essay on "Poetry Debased by Mean Expression" as a cautionary example of admitting "low" words. Perhaps Johnson's reticence about quoting directly in his *Rambler* essays reflects a wish not to have other verse competing with the epigraphs that aptly announce and summarize the theme of each paper. In fact, of the five direct quotations from Shakespeare that appear in the entire *Rambler,* three are in papers supposedly written by correspondents—purported English readers who are on their mettle and citing authority. In the 138 *Adventurer* papers there are two Shakespearean quotations, one by a "correspondent." In 103 *Idlers* Shakespeare is quoted twice (once by a "correspondent") and alluded to once. The *Rambler* and *Adventurer* (1753-54) were carried on by Johnson before 1756, when he formally set himself to edit Shakespeare; the *Idler* (1758-60) was a concurrent project with the edition. But the *Idler* shows no more of a Shakespearean influence than the other journals.

It seems that we may conclude that Shakespeare had no great influence upon Johnson's prose style in these years. If the process of writing be as Johnson himself describes it in *Rambler* 77, one by which the author "tortures his fancy and ransacks his memory" (*Works*, 4:44), then Johnson did not very vigorously ransack his own formidable recollection insofar as his stores of Shakespeare were concerned. Perhaps when he was presenting morality in the persona of the Rambler he had not yet arrived at the conviction he later expressed in the "Preface to Shakespeare," that moral principles are to be derived from Shakespeare's works;[8] perhaps as the Rambler he felt that classical allusions were more impressive and appealing to his readership. The epigraphs to the *Rambler* essays usually are from classical authors, but we shall see Johnson agreeing that Shakespeare is "classical" too.

Curiously, it is not only the few seized opportunities to cite Shakespeare that we notice in Johnson's essays. Also noticeable are what might be regarded as opportunities missed. In *Rambler* 70, for instance, Johnson, in a "survey of the moral world," discusses the three divisions of virtue into which he says all men fall. The largest class of people "are in a kind of equipoise between good and ill, . . . whom a small addition of weight turns either way." No one, he says, can be surprised at lapses into vice, for

> Among the sentiments which almost every man changes as he advances into years, is the expectation of uniformity of character. He that without acquaintance with the power of desire, the urgency of distress, the complications of affairs, or the force of partial influence, has filled his mind with the excellence of virtue, and having never tried his resolution in any encounters with hope or fear, believes it able to stand firm whatever should oppose it, will always be clamorous against the smallest failure, ready to exact the utmost punctualities of right, and to consider every man that fails in any part of his duty, as without conscience and without merit; unworthy of trust, or love, pity, or regard; as an enemy whom all should join to drive out of society, as a pest which all should avoid, or as a weed which all should trample. (*Works*, 4:5)

Setting out from the same ground as *Areopagitica*, Johnson has in this one sentence given a precise and detailed portrait of that magisterial, icy, and implacable character who stands at the center of Shakespeare's own study of fugitive and cloistered virtue — Angelo in *Measure for Measure*. The parallel seems to be unconscious, for after reading this passage in the *Rambler* one quickly turns to the *Measure for Measure* notes in the Shakespeare to see what Johnson has to say on Angelo's self-righteous words, " 'Tis one thing to be tempted, Escalus, Another thing to fall . . ." (2.1. 17-18); but Johnson lets the passage go without comment. Yet, when in the same *Rambler* Johnson goes on, "Since the purest virtue is consistent with some vice, and the virtue of the greatest number with almost an equal proportion of contrary qualities, let none too hastily conclude that all goodness is lost . . . ," there is an almost uncanny parallel with Mariana's defense of Angelo:

> They say best men are moulded out of faults,
> And, for the most, become much more the better
> For being a little bad.
>                        (5.1.437-39)

This speech also goes without comment in the notes on Shakespeare, where Johnson says only of Angelo that his "crimes were such, as must sufficiently justify punishment, . . . and I believe every reader feels some indignation when he finds him spared" (*Works,* 7:213). It is disappointing not to see the Rambler engage more fully with this dramatic representation of his essay. *Measure for Measure* is a representation of the central argument of another *Rambler* as well, No. 81:

> One of the most celebrated cases which have been produced as requiring some skill in the direction of conscience . . . is that of a criminal asking mercy of his judge, who cannot but know that if he was in the state of the supplicant, he should desire what pardon he now denies. *(Works,* 4:62)

Almost as if Shakespeare had versified Johnson or Johnson had prosed Shakespeare, this exact question is put to Angelo first by Escalus and then by Isabella.

> Let but your honour know . . .
> That in the working of your own affections,
> Had time coher'd with place, or place with wishing,
> Or that the resolute acting of your blood
> Could have attain'd the effect of your own purpose,
> Whether you had not sometime in your life
> Err'd in this point, which now you censure him,
> And pull'd the law upon you.
>                        (2.1.8-16)

We can only ask, what does Johnson mean by his reference to "One of the most celebrated cases which have been produced . . ." on this line of argument? Does he mean a case in law? Could he mean in *Measure for Measure?* The parallel between play and essay remains to tease us, and certainly at the very least exemplifies those "unexpected coincidences of . . . thoughts" which Johnson wrote about in *Rambler* 143.

Cautioned by that essay against making too much of unexpected coincidences, we may be wary about assuming that because Johnson uses in *Ramblers* 54 and 196 the analogy of life with a theater he thereby has or should have in his mind Jaques's "All the world's a stage. . . ." The terms of Jaques's speech on the world as a stage and on man's "acts" as being seven ages were firmly in Johnson's mind, however, for a supposed correspondent in *Rambler* 116 refers to boys "creeping like snails unwillingly to school"

(*Works*, 4:253). And it is striking how the more philosophical speeches in *As You Like It* seem just nearly to float to the surface of Johnson's prose from time to time. Compare, for example, the Duke's speech (2.2.5-11) with this from *Rambler* 29:

> Adversity has ever been considered as the state in which a man most easily becomes acquainted with himself, and this effect it must produce by withdrawing flatterers, whose business it is to hide our weaknesses from us . . . ; or at least by cutting off those pleasures which called us away from meditation on our conduct, and repressing that pride which too easily persuades us, that we merit whatever we enjoy. (*Works*, 3:155-56)

But if the *As You Like It* passages are, so to speak, close at hand in the *Rambler* essays, why does Johnson not come closer than a reminiscence or half-echo? I sense an unwillingness to quote, rather than ignorance or forgetfulness of mutual words on a common topic — Boswell was quite rightly dazzled by the enormous store of "originals and correspondent allusions [that Johnson had] floating in his mind" (*Life*, p. 138). We might think that Shakespeare was used sparely in Johnson's essays because he is not a classical author. But this argument is disabled by a conversation between Johnson and John Wilkes (Boswell reporting):

> The subject of quotation being introduced, Mr. Wilkes censured it as pedantry. JOHNSON. "No, Sir, it is a good thing; there is a community of mind in it. Classical quotation is the *parole* of literary men all over the world." WILKES. "Upon the continent they all quote the vulgate Bible. Shakespeare is chiefly quoted here." (*Life*, p. 1143)

Though Johnson aims to contradict, and Wilkes quickly defers (with Shakespeare squeezing in as classical), the pedant of Wilkes's side of the argument is not too far removed from the "literary man" of Johnson's side, especially if the literary man has literature and nothing more. As Boswell shows, Johnson could become defensive at being typecast, even among his friends, as only a literary man. The following exchange took place in 1781:

> In the evening we had a large company in [Mrs. Garrick's] drawing room . . . .Somebody said the life of a mere literary man could not be very entertaining. JOHNSON. "But it certainly may. This is a remark which has been made, and repeated, without justice; why should the life of a literary man be less entertaining than the life of any other man? Are there not as interesting varieties in such a life? As a *literary life* it may be very entertaining." (*Life*, p. 1141)

The carefully maintained persona of the Rambler is not a "literary man," but a man of practical and experienced wisdom, who speaks not just of books but of life. Even the classical epigraphs are chosen not merely as "literary *paroles,*" but to universalize the wisdom. Johnson is much more in agreement with Wilkes's point when, in the "Preface to Shakespeare," he expresses the futility of trying to recommend Shakespeare by selection: "His real power is not shewn in the splendour of particular passages. . . , and he that tries to recommend him by select quotations will succeed like the pedant in Hierocles, who, when he offered his house to sale, carried a brick in his pocket as a specimen" *(Works,* 7:62). Despite the fact that in his time the "Beauties" of various English authors were being anthologized, it is not Johnson's way to dwell upon particular lines or passages, even from Shakespeare. Shakespeare, like the whole libraries that Johnson was "born to grapple with" *(Life,* p. 722), was to be taken by Johnson complete; the quotations in the *Dictionary* are there for the purpose of illustrating words in use, not to recommend Shakespeare. In the notes to his edition of Shakespeare, Johnson very rarely pauses to comment upon the merit of an individual passage. His policy is stated in the preface: "The poetical beauties or defects I have not been very diligent to observe" (*Works,* 7:104). In his *Rambler, Idler,* and *Adventurer* essays Johnson will not be "literary," will not pedantically exhibit the specimen brick, will not number the streaks of the tulip.

This reticence is the more noticeable if we compare it with Boswell's practice in literary quotation, especially in the two works where Boswell is writing about (and speaking with) his hero — the *Life* and the *Journal of a Tour to the Hebrides.* Boswell loves to quote Shakespeare and to dress a scene with an apposite passage; he enjoys showing that he has "originals and correspondent allusions" floating in *his* mind. Johnson, he will say, first displayed his poetical powers "and gave the world assurance of the Man" when he published *London (Life,* p. 86); he recollects that the Hebridean tour was planned about "witching time o' night" (p. 572); that Johnson had an awful "fear of something after death" (p. 579); recalls his own "morn of life" (p. 859); writes to Johnson using the dreadful phrase "in my mind's *ears*" (p. 893); calls Lichfield Cathedral a "solemn temple" (p. 710), friendship "the wine of life" (p. 213). The contemporary laird of Calder is, like Shakespeare's ill-fated thane, "a prosperous gentleman" (*Tour,* p. 234). Life at Armidale is not just boring but "weary, flat, and unprofitable" (*Tour,* p. 259). Boswell marks his written quotations with inverted commas or italics more, one feels, to advertise the fact that he *is* quoting Shakespeare than merely to acknowledge a borrowing. In the *Tour* he quotes, alludes, and recites everywhere. Johnson, in his account of the journey, has not a single quotation from Shakespeare.

In these accounts their minds appear to be moving on characteristic lines: Boswell quotes, alludes, and recites; Johnson tells a round, unvarnished tale (he would not have called it that). Somehow, Boswell seems anxious to impress — showing his credentials, giving the literary *parole.* Most of the time, Johnson tolerated Boswell's literary eruptions, and perhaps even enjoyed

Boswell's elocution practice. But Boswell's playing with quotations could also be a weariness and a bore to Johnson. Debating between themselves, late one night, the point that a man would wish to be virtuous though he had no other motive than to preserve his character, Johnson takes the quite commonsense if unethical view that vice hurts no one's character in this world. He is pressed by Boswell, knows he is arguing against his own principles, and when Boswell will not let the matter drop he becomes increasingly testy, until

> JOHNSON. "Vice does not hurt a man's character so as to obstruct his prosperity . . . ; [Bolingbroke] acquired his fortune by such crimes, that his consciousness of them impelled him to cut his own throat." BOSWELL. "He cut his throat because he was weary of still life, little things not being sufficient to move his great mind. . . . Might [he] not have felt every thing 'weary, stale, flat, and unprofitable,' as Hamlet says?" JOHNSON. "Nay, if you are to bring in gabble, I'll talk no more. I will not, upon my honour." (*Life*, pp. 993-94)

Shakespeare adduced in the service of wrong ideas or misplaced reasoning is "gabble"; Johnson's opinion of the preface to Capell's edition of Shakespeare is that in it Capell "grabbles monstrously" (*Life*, p. 1069). He simply will not tolerate the devil's citing Scripture for his purpose.

And then there was Shakespeare recited for money, perhaps recited so without even being understood by the actor. Johnson, of course, believed acting to be merely recitation (so did Coleridge).[10] Bennett Langton recalled Johnson as saying that "a man must be a poor beast that should read no more in quantity than he could *utter* aloud" (*Life*, p. 1088). This conviction underlines his opinion of Hannah Pritchard, a co-star of Garrick's in *Macbeth:* "Her playing is quite mechanical. It is wonderful how little mind she had. Sir, she had never read the tragedy of Macbeth all through. She no more thought of the play out of which her part was taken, than a shoemaker thinks of the skin, out of which the piece of leather, of which he is making shoes, is cut" (*Life*, p. 616). Acting is "[exhibiting oneself] for a shilling"; or Colley Cibber "[clapping] a hump on his back, and a lump on his leg, and [crying], 'I am Richard the Third' " (*Life*, p. 863).

Boswell complains that Johnson has not mentioned Garrick in the "Preface to Shakespeare," and asks if he does not admire Garrick. Johnson's answers are satirical:

> "Yes, [I admire Garrick] as 'a poor player, who frets and struts his hour upon the stage'; — as a shadow." BOSWELL [who can't quite see that he is being paid in a verbal coin that he, and Garrick, have issued so often as almost to threaten its value]. "But has he not brought Shakespeare into notice?" JOHNSON. "Sir, to allow that, would be to lampoon the age. Many of Shakespeare's plays are the worse for being acted. *Macbeth*, for instance." (*Life*, p. 416)

Macbeth was Garrick's most famous and most overwrought Shakespearean role.

Despite his scorn for players in general,[11] Johnson loved and respected Garrick, who, he said, had treated "his good fortune with deference, [had] advanced the dignity of his profession, [and] made a player a higher character" (*Life*, p. 925). But Garrick had his reward and applause, "had it dashed in his face, sounded in his ears, and went home every night with the plaudits of a thousand in his cranium" (*Life*, p. 925); so Johnson felt quite free to "mortify [him] after the great applause he had received from the audience" (*Life*, p. 1070).

Shakespeare may have been the "god of his idolatry" (*Life*, p. 412), but Garrick was high priest. And he did posture somewhat: "Now I have quitted the theatre," he is reported to have said to Johnson, "I will sit down and read Shakespeare." Johnson's wry rejoinder was " 'Tis time you should" (*Tour*, p. 323 n. 1). To know the lines without quite understanding them — this is what Johnson censured in all actors. Garrick apparently had Shakespeare and other authors in his mouth at all times: his conversation, said Johnson "is a dish of all sorts" (*Life*, p. 708).

I believe that with Boswell on one side of him spouting Shakespeare and with Garrick on the other, Johnson deliberately preserved a reticence about joining in. In their circle, the Club, during the literary chats and debates — Is the description of Dover Cliff in *Lear* the most evocative passage in literature? Is the night of Macbeth's shard-borne beetle dark enough? — the literary paroles are being flourished, instant impressions and easy effects are being made, "the sure returns of still-expected rhymes"[12] are being collected. Johnson will not play these games, or not play them for long. Shakespeare belongs in the heart, not in the drawingroom. It is the boy who ran out of the cellar to reassure himself with daylight while reading *Hamlet,* and the man who could not bear to reread *Lear* because he was so moved at Cordelia's death, who breaks up a cool discussion when *Lear* is brought in: "[Dover Cliff] should be all precipice — all vacuum. The crows impede your fall" (*Life,* p. 413). This may be as much as to say, "Hands off *Lear*; stick to *The Mourning Bride.*" Johnson would have nothing to do with Shakespeare's being used for social games of another kind. Boswell told him of "a club in London, at the Boar's Head in Eastcheap, the same tavern where Falstaff and his joyous companions met; the members of which all assume Shakespeare's characters. One is Falstaff, another Prince Henry, and so on — JOHNSON. 'Don't be of it, sir' " (*Tour*, p. 325).

Johnson could and did occasionally quote Shakespeare in conversation, but not, as I have suggested, at the level of social games. It is probable that he recited on the road from Forres to please Boswell. Writing to Boswell after a difference between them, he reaches unerringly for the idiom that will reassure his reader: "I love you as a kind man, I value you as a worthy man. . . .

I hold you, as Hamlet has it, "in my heart of hearts' " (*Life,* p. 640). To quote in this manner is to use Shakespeare's words for what Johnson says they are (*Works,* 7:64), the language of men.

In contrast to Johnson's use of Shakespeare to reassure Boswell, Arthur Murphy and Boswell recalled that Johnson fed his own terrors with Shakespearean passages. But there is no reflex emotional response to these passages in Johnson's notes on Shakespeare. If, as Murphy and Boswell say, certain of Shakespeare's painful lines about death and dissolution fostered Johnson the man's creepy apprehensions, Johnson the editor is unmoved.

It is to Johnson the editor to whom we should turn to see what "impregnation with the Shakespearean aether"[13] took place. In keeping with his belief about the futility of trying to recommend Shakespeare by select quotations and with the style of other of his essays, there are in all of his "Preface to Shakespeare" only five direct citations. Two are purely academic: ironical illustrations of the point that too much time has been wasted by scholars in searching out classical sources for simple phrases used in the plays. Two other quotations are employed, again ironically, when Johnson writes of the minor critics who attacked Warburton for *his* Shakespeare: "When I think on one, with his confederates, I remember the danger of Coriolanus, who was afraid that 'girls with spits, and boys with stones, should slay him in puny battle'; when the other crosses my imagination, I remember the prodigy in Macbeth,

> A falcon, tow'ring in his pride of place,
> Was by a mousing owl hawk'd at and kill'd."
>                                         (*Works,* 7:100)

All four of these citations are used in dismissive contexts, as sticks to beat the pedants.

Not so the fifth quotation, which is from *Troilus and Cressida* and climaxes the magnificent paragraph in which Johnson writes of Shakespeare's transcending all obstacles:

> Shakespeare . . . came to London a needy adventurer, and lived for a time by very mean employments. Many works of genius and learning have been performed in states of life, that appear very little favourable to thought or to enquiry; so many, that he who considers them is inclined to think that he sees enterprise and perseverance predominating over all external agency, and bidding help and hindrance vanish before them. The genius of Shakespeare was not to be depressed by the weight of poverty, nor limited by the narrow conversation to which men in want are inevitably condemned; the incumbrances of his fortune were shaken from his mind, "as dewdrops from a lion's mane." (*Works,* 7:88-89)

Johnson left no formal autobiography, but nothing could be more self-descriptive, more expressive of his own early struggles and his eventual triumph, than this paragraph of his on Shakespeare. It therefore is little wonder that Johnson, echoing Hamlet, says that Shakespeare is, above all writers, "the poet who holds up to his readers a faithful mirror of manners and of life," or that the Preface returns again and again to this theme of "mirroring," "reflecting," "imaging."[14] For it is Johnson himself who stands reflected in Shakespeare's achievement, who could say to Shakespeare as Hermione says to Leontes, "My life stands in the level of your dreams."[15]

Not only do the careers of these two men fuse for a moment in the Preface; the Preface is also marked in places by a marriage of minds, as Johnson's thought and style take on the coloring of Shakespeare's. As Johnson points his readers to the text, the flavor of his own prose attests that he has been fully engaged there himself. And strangely, the cadences of the Preface's prose are most Shakespearean just when Johnson is being most editorially "detached." Complaining of Shakespeare's addiction to punning, he writes, "[a quibble] has some malignant power over his mind, and its fascinations are irresistible. . . . A quibble is the golden apple for which he will turn aside from his career, or stoop from his elevation. A quibble, poor and barren as it is, gave him such delight, that he was content to purchase it, by the sacrifice of reason, propriety and truth. A quibble was the fatal Cleopatra for which he lost the world, and was content to lose it" (*Works*, 7:74). Johnson first tries Atalanta's golden apple, but this is not forceful enough; only a Shakespearean analogy will suggest the power of words over Shakespeare. And only Shakespeare's Cleopatra will do: "for which he lost the world, and was content to lose it" might be filtered through *All for Love, or, The World Well Lost*, but "the fatal Cleopatra" is not Dryden's Cleopatra but Shakespeare's. (Dryden's Cleopatra is no more fatal in herself than an accident victim.) Indeed, not only is Shakespeare in this part of the Preface an Antony fascinated by the fatal Cleopatra of a quibble, but Johnson himself is touched by the spell of Cleopatra's great dream of Antony. In that dream Antony is magnificent, and careless with his great gifts: "in his livery / Walk'd crowns and crownets: realms and islands were / As plates dropp'd from his pocket";[16] Johnson's Shakespeare-Antony drops "precepts and axioms . . . casually from him; he makes no just distribution of good or evil" (*Works*, 7:71).

I will not be overcome by this charm, Johnson seems to say again and again in the Preface. Yet, when he comes to write the most myth-debunking part of his discussion, the famous criticism of the Unities (*Works*, 7:75-79), Shakespeare seems to take over. "It is false," says Johnson, "that any representation is mistaken for reality; that any dramatick fable was ever credible, or, for a single moment, was ever credited." Advocates of the Unities suppose "that when the play opens the spectator imagines himself at Alexandria, and believes that his walk to the theatre has been a voyage to Egypt, and that he lives in the days of Antony and Cleopatra. Surely . . . he that can take the stage at one time for the palace of the Ptolemies, may take it in half an hour for the promontory of Actium." Again, this is not Dryden's version of *Antony and Cleopatra* (which observes the Unities), but Shakespeare's, and now the strange thing begins to happen to Johnson's prose: "If the spectator can be persuaded that his old acquaintance are Alexander and Caesar . . . he is in a state of elevation above the reach of reason, or of truth." Not many people see "their old acquaintance" perform roles in the professional theater; Shakespeare did, and so did Johnson (Garrick is in the "Preface to Shakespeare" after all). And as Johnson argues at his most forcible on behalf of reason and real life as being distant from fiction and "the heights of empyrean poetry," that distance seems abruptly to narrow:

> The truth is, that the spectators are always in their senses, and know, from the first act to the last, that the stage is only a stage, and that the players are only players.

In Johnson's argument there is the cadence of that argument's antithesis, a passage wherein life and fiction, living and playing, are not separated at all. The beat of Johnson's words responds to the beat of Jaques's, "All the world's a stage, / And all the men and women merely players." Consciously or unconsciously, Johnson has let Shakespeare's idiom come through; Shakespeare, to use a phrase of Virgil's, flits conqueror through Johnson's mouth.[17]

One would like to think that Johnson recognizes the conquest, and consciously surrenders; that the "similitude" is not accidental. I believe, and have tried to show, that he always stood on guard against what he himself might have called "promiscuous quotation," for he was a master of words, not a slave to them, and certainly he refused to be like some of his acquaintances, a slave of Shakespeare's lamp, however bright. But in the Preface, sympathizing and empathizing with Shakespeare, he comes to harmonize with him as well; and, imbued with Shakespeare's plays, he becomes for a short time an example of the phenomenon Shakespeare himself wrote about in Sonnet 111:

My nature is subdu'd
To what it works in, like the dyer's hand.

### Notes

1. All references to Johnson's prose writings cite *The Yale Edition of the Works of Samuel Johnson* (New Haven, 1960). References appear hereafter in my text as *Works*. All references to Boswell's *Life of Johnson* cite the Oxford Standard Authors edition, ed. R. W. Chapman (Oxford, 1960).

2. *The Prose Style of Samuel Johnson* (New Haven and London, 1963). See esp. chap. 8.

3. Ibid., p. vii.

4. Cf. *Henry IV, Part One*, 5.4.64.

5. Arthur Sherbo, *Samuel Johnson, Editor of Shakespeare*. Illinois Studies in Language and Literature, vol. 42 (Urbana, 1956), p. 15.

6. Ibid., p. 8.

7. A *Merchant of Venice* allusion is in *Rambler* No. 183; *Merry Wives* in No. 20; *Troilus and Cressida* in No. 121; *1 Henry IV* is quoted in Nos. 72 and 145; *Romeo* in No. 107; *As You Like It* in No. 116: *Macbeth* in No. 168. *Hamlet* is echoed in *Idler* No. 9; *Macbeth* is quoted in No. 44 and *As You Like It* in No. 50; *Coriolanus* is cited in *Adventurer* No. 99; *2 Henry IV* in No. 137.

8. See *Works*, 7:64-65.

9. Isabella asks Angelo to examine himself in 2.2. 137-42.

10. See the "Preface to Shakespeare": "[Spectators] come [to the theater] to hear a certain number of lines recited with just gesture and elegant modulation" (*Works*, 7:77). See also S. T. Coleridge, *Select Poetry and Prose*, ed. S. Potter (London, 1933), p. 342.

11. See, for example, Johnson's observation on the generosity of Wilks, an actor who helped Richard Savage: "To be humane, generous, and candid, is a very high degree of merit in any case; but those qualities deserve still greater praise, when they are found in that condition which makes almost every other man, for whatever reason, contemptuous, insolent, petulant, selfish, and brutal" ("Life of Savage," in *Lives of the English Poets*, ed. Arthur Waugh [Oxford, 1906], 2:102).

12. Cf. Alexander Pope, *Essay on Criticism*, 1:349.

13. *Life*, p. 297.

14. Cf. *Works*, 7:62, 65, 78, 90.

15. *The Winter's Tale* 3.2.81.

16. *Antony and Cleopatra* 5.2. 90-92.

17. Cf. *Georgics* 3.9: "virûm volitare per ora."

# When Homer Nods:
# Shakespeare's Artistic Lapses

by T. J. B. SPENCER

Matthew Arnold is reported by Furnivall to have said that he refused to write on Shakespeare because the British public would not endure the truth to be told (*Transactions of the New Shakespere Society*, 1887-92, pp.ii, 211), What the British public can endure to be told—or, for that matter, what the American public can endure to be told—may admit of a wide solution.

But we know what Arnold meant. In fact, in spite of his refusal to write about Shakespeare, he was not himself one of those who never "spoke out." He did, on several occasions, give us a piece of his mind on the subject. He permitted himself to say that in the English eulogy of Shakespeare was to be seen "much of provincial infatuation" (Preface to Wordsworth, 1879). This was a harsh saying from one of the vice-presidents of the New Shakspere Society.

In 1876 Stopford Brooke published his little *Primer of English Literature,* once famous, often reprinted, and the source of many of the clichés of English literary historiography—a work whose influence on our ways of thinking about English literature has yet to be assessed. Stopford Brooke naturally gave a good deal of space to Shakespeare, who was "the greatest artist the modern world has known. . . . In the unchangeableness of pure art-power Shakespeare stands entirely alone." This kind of "provincial infatuation" was not to be endured by his reviewer.

> When we call a man emphatically *artist*, a *great artist*, we mean [retorts Arnold] . . . not merely an aim to please, but also, and more, a law of pure and flawless workmanship. As living always under the sway of *this* law, and as, therefore, a perfect artist, we do not conceive of Shakespeare. His workmanship is often far from being pure and flawless.

> Till that Bellona's bridegroom lapp'd in proof,
> Confronted him with self-comparisons —

There is but one name for such writing as that, if Shakespeare had signed it a thousand times, — it is detestable. And it is too frequent in Shakespeare. (Reprinted in *Mixed Essays* [1879], pp. 193-94)

This is congruous with Arnold's many other acerb utterances about Shakespeare. It is curious that, while modern literary criticism owes a generally acknowledged debt to Arnold, his views on Shakespeare should have been largely ignored. Except in this Congress. It is appropriate (and the organizers of the Congress are to be congratulated in this matter) that we delegates can this afternoon, at an early point in the week, divide into two sections: that some should go to hear my honored friend Lionel Knights, and have an opportunity to meditate on Shakespeare's meditations; and that others of us should have an opportunity of coolly assessing Shakespeare's powers and achievements as an artist, his control of his materials, his artistic responsibility and irresponsibility, his care and his negligences. This separation, already on Tuesday, into the geese and the stoats has been made possible because Richard Levin and myself not only have been permitted and encouraged, but have positively been *commissioned,* jointly to play the role of the death's head at the party, the jester amid the solemn incoronation, the diabolical advocate at the sanctimonious canonization. Our purpose is to ensure that the World Congress does not display the sin of *hubris* or overconfidence amid the world praises of the world's darling. We are here to exclaim, not so much that the Emperor has no clothes, as that he has serious rents in them, and that sometimes he is to be caught with his trousers down.

On 19 December 1785 Fanny Burney was sitting in Mrs. Delany's drawing room at Windsor, when King George III came in, and there ensued the immortal conversation that she has herself recorded so vivaciously in her *Diary.* From Voltaire and Rousseau, the conversation passed to a discussion of the theater, and so to Shakespeare. "Was there ever" (cried the king) "such stuff as great part of Shakespeare? only one must not say so! But what think you? — What? — Is there not sad stuff? — What? — what?" (*Dairy and Letters of Madame d'Arblay,* ed. Austin Dobson, 6 vols. [1904], 2:344).

King George III is a British monarch from whom I think one may (in the context of this time and place) venture to differ on a matter of taste. And how wrong he was: not so much for finding sad stuff in Shakespeare, but for supposing that one must not say so. None of the great poets of the world has suffered such persistent disparagement, nor from so many of the greatest minds of Europe. Other great poets, it is true, have come in for occasional dispraise at various times. Homer, Virgil, Dante, Racine have sometimes been thought to be overpraised. But Shakespeare, alongside all the bardolatry, has been pursued by fault-finders of eminence. He has been censured by rival dramatists like Robert Greene and Bernard Shaw; disparaged by philosophers like Hume and by supermen like Napoleon; despised by rough diamonds like William Cobbett and by artificial pearls like Lord Chesterfield. He has been admonished for his limitations even by those who had comparable creative vigor, such as Goethe and Tolstoy. Shakespeare's reputation, like his genius, was a hardy plant, stubborn and resistant in its development.

It is salutary to be reminded how many powerful minds have grappled with Shakespeare, have chosen to wrestle with the angel, rather than be trodden underfoot in a posture of adulation. The anguished censure is as eloquent as the eulogy. Lord Acton admitted that he "was repelled by Shakespeare's flagrant insularity, his leaning for obvious characters, his insensibility to the glories of Greece and the mystery of the Renaissance" (essay on George Eliot). For Walt Whitman, Shakespeare was the representative of "the feudal, ecclesiastical, dynastic world over there. . . . the superbest poetic culmination-expression of feudalism . . . in the attitudes, dialogue, characters, etc. of the princes, lords and gentlemen, the pervading atmosphere, the implied and expressed standard of manners, the high port and proud stomach, the regal embroidery of style, etc." There was, therefore, in Shakespeare nothing "consistent with these United States, or essentially applicable to them as they are and are to be." Is there one of those works, Whitman asks, "whose underlying basis is not a denial and insult to democracy?" (*Democratic Vistas,* 1870). Shakespeare had "a style supremely grand of a sort, but in my opinion stopping short of the grandest sort, at any rate for fulfilling and satisfying modern and scientific and democratic American purposes." And in *November Boughs* he continued the attack: "The comedies, exquisite as they certainly are, bringing in admirably portrayed common characters, have the unmistakable hue of plays, portraits, made for the divertissement only of the élite of the castle, and from its point of view. The comedies are altogether non-acceptable to America and Democracy." Nevertheless, in later years Whitman discovered that it was not convenient to have Shakespeare on the opposing side. In his essay "What Lurks behind Shakespere's Historical Plays," he expounded a theory that Shakespeare was a kind of crypto-democrat who by the very intensity with which he represented the "feudal, ecclesiastical, dynastic world over there" was secretly undermining it. "A future age of criticism," he suggests, may after all discover in Shakespeare's plays the scientific "inauguration of modern Democracy . . . which now holds secure lodgement over the whole civilized world."

You may perhaps think that Walt Whitman's censure of Shakespeare for Americans is not to be taken altogether seriously (or at least not seriously in the way he did). But some of this kind of censure is more affecting than the adulation, and more profitable to us; for there is something to be learned from it, even from its refutation. It is not really possible or profitable to refute the eulogy. Nor would it be fair to quote Whitman's rejection of Shakespeare without also noting the strength of American eloquence in favor of Shakespeare. Here, for example, is the opinion of James Russell Lowell in an admonitory address, "The Poetical and the Practical in America," delivered at Cambridge, Massachusetts, in 1855:

> Were our little mother island sunk beneath the sea, or worse, were she conquered by Scythian barbarians, yet Shakespeare would be immortal England, and would conquer countries, when the bones of her last sailor had kept their ghastly watch for ages in unhallowed ooze!

Wrote the wise Sir Thomas Browne:

> He that endureth no faults in men's writings must only read his own . . . mistakes, inadvertency, expedition, and human lapses, may make not only moles but warts in authors who not withstanding, being judged by the capital matter, admit not of disparagement. (*Christian Morals,* 2.2)

The careful scrutiny of Shakespeare's writings has, for centuries, revealed many aberrations from common sense and abnegations of artistic responsibility, the "inadvertency, expedition, and human lapses" of which Sir Thomas Browne wrote; and it is a state of affairs that has admitted of a good deal of disparagement. Much intellectual effort has, since the eighteenth century, been expended on clearing up this stable of Pegasus, demonstrating that supposed faults are subtle beauties; that, in the world of art, Shakespeare (like his own Julius Caesar) never did wrong but with just cause.

For persons with minds that are both intellectually scrupulous and unnaturally tidy, the surviving texts of the plays of Shakespeare can seem to be rather messy and ragged, crying out for the posthumous care of a literary executor, to make the incompletely polished writings of the deceased fit for submission to the eyes or ears of the censorious world. It has been known for centuries — at least since the time of Ben Jonson — that a careful perusal of the plays reveals discrepancies, characters with inconsistent details and characters abandoned without explanation, "false starts," plot incidents that are introduced and underdeveloped, irrelevant puns, incongruous bawdry, senseless anachronisms, and so on. The instinctive creative energy of Shakespeare was too strong and unrestrained (apparently) to avoid these irritating lapses of taste or good sense or common sense.

King Alfonso the Wise wished, we are told, that it had been possible for him to have been consulted during the Six Days of Creation, for he felt that he could have suggested several improvements. In the seventeenth century Thomas Burnet, looking up at the stars in the sky, fell to wondering at the inexplicable behavior of the Creator in making such a mess of his task of putting them into position:

What a beautiful Hemisphere they would have made, if they had been plac'd in rank and order, if they had been all dispos'd into regular figures, and the little ones set with due regard to the greater; then all finisht and made up into one fair piece or great Composition, according to the rules of Art and Symmetry. (*The Sacred Theory of Earth*, 2:xi)

The Creator seemed, to the tidy-minded Thomas Burnet, to have behaved without full artistic responsibility in the performance of his allotted task. Many honest, and otherwise intelligent, critics have felt the same about Shakespeare.

Generally, the eighteenth century regretted the faults and negligences of Shakespeare. But much energy was spent in the nineteenth century, and still more in the twentieth century, to blind us to their existence, by the intellectual subtlety that has been exercised in order to explain them away. Much of the best Shakespeare criticism, especially of a historical kind, tends, taking its cue from Ben Jonson, to explore the literary and dramatic and intellectual background of the plays, demonstrating how far Shakespeare did our Lyly, Kyd, and Marlowe outshine. But it may be that the important aspects of Shakespeare's literary gifts may be intelligible by comparison with his near-peers, abundantly overflowing creators, rather than with the second-raters whom he succeeded in outshining, that the better-documented literary genius of Dickens or Balzac or Tolstoy may be equally or more helpful and rewarding for our understanding of Shakespeare.

We know that Dickens could hold an enormously complicated "world" in his head during the composition of a novel; that he could readily expand (or subtract) a scene or part of a scene according to the exigencies of publication. The analogy of Dickens rather supports Coleridge's views of Shakespeare's process of character-creation—that Shakespeare was able to hold a whole character in his head, complete (as it were), and to give out appropriate bits of it at various points in the play, so that we must interpret any single character-episode by reference to the complete character (insofar as we can discern it) that Shakespeare held in his mind. This may sound suspiciously metaphysical at first, yet it seems to be a not unfair description of Dickens's usual mode of characterization, and therefore it may well be not unlike Shakespeare's.

Shakespeare does seem to give evidence of holding more in his head about a play than is actually explicit in our texts. The number of "missing scenes" is a little distressing, and should alert us all to the imperfect nature of our texts of these stageplays. We can bear the loss of the scenes relating to the German "cozeners" in *The Merry Wives of Windsor*. But one may reasonably regret the scene (attested by the Bad Quarto) in which Horatio and the Queen come to terms, thus explaining the confidential relationship between them, which would seem unreasonable and inexplicable from the earlier part of the play in the vulgate text.

One of the scenes of which I much regret the loss is the episode of Lancelot Gobbo and the Moorish girl. It would have provided a neatly comic contrast to Lorenzo and his Jessica, the Jewish girl, an artistically contrived sub-subplot. Because it is a "missing scene," I wish that someone would restore the work of art to us; I mean, write it for insertion in the play. Perhaps Mr. John Barton, who has rewritten so much "immature" Shakespeare for performance, should be encouraged to try his experienced hand at some of the missing scenes in Shakespeare's mature plays. Alternatively, the International Shakespeare Association might organize an international competition for the composition of this and other lost scenes in plays which, like the Venus de Milo, have been severely damaged by the loss of important parts, due, not to the disasters of Time, but to theatrical truncation.

Even a comparatively "well-made" play like *Much Ado About Nothing* survives only in a text that shows many signs of being a work of art "in progress." Shakespeare begins by giving Leonatus a wife, Innogen, a mother for Hero. But later he discovers that it will not do at all for Hero to have a mother on stage, and so he abandons Innogen without troubling to delete her. He gives Antonio, Leonatus's brother, a son. But this won't do, because a young male in Hero's family would be the one to avenge her honor and challenge Claudio; so Antonio's son is silently discarded, and Hero is inconsistently regarded as the heiress of the whole family. Worse still, there are vestiges, or rudiments, of an "inset" scene relating to an earlier, broken-off affair between Benedick and Beatrice, a vital episode, one might suppose, for understanding their relationship; but it is only tantalizingly referred to.

In a famous and mature play like *Macbeth*, short and economical though it may seem, there are many details unexplained and superfluous. The bleeding Captain who brings the news of Macbeth's victory is introduced by Malcolm:

> This is the Sergeant,
> Who, like a good and hardy soldier, fought
> 'Gainst my captivity.
>                 (1.2.3-5)

But no such incident of Malcolm's life's being saved by this Sergeant (or Captain) appears in the play. It is a superfluous and irrelevant allusion, especially in an introductory, identifying speech. Furthermore, that a severely wounded man, who is "faint" and whose "gashes cry for help," should be the one sent to bring news of victory to the King is itself irritatingly contrary to common sense.

All the world knows that the night of the murder of King Duncan is one of the great poetical evocations in literature: the deadly silence in which Macbeth and Lady Macbeth are alone and moving—a silence made more palpable by allusion to one or two sounds—a terrible silence broken (as De Quincey and now every high school pupil explains) by the knocking at the gate.

         Now o'er the one half-world
Nature seems dead . . .
               . . . and wither'd Murther,
               . . . with his stealthy pace . . .
Moves like a ghost. — Thou sure and firm-set earth,
Hear not my steps, which way they walk . . .
               the bell invites me. . . .
               Hark! — Peace!
It was the owl that shriek'd, the fatal bellman . . .
               . . . Didst thou not hear a noise?
I heard the owl scream, and the crickets cry.
Did not you speak? . . . When? . . . Now? . . . As I descended?
Ay.
Hark! . . .
               Whence is this knocking? —
How is't with me, when every noise appals me?
               . . . I hear a knocking
At the south entry . . .
                         (2.1.49 ff.; 2.2.,14-18,57,65)

Soon Macduff goes in to awaken the King, and we await the revelation of the murder. In the moments of suspense Macbeth tries to keep up the conversation with Lennox, who tells us about a terrible storm that has visited the night:

         The night has been unruly: where we lay,
         Our chimneys were blown down; and, as they say,
         Lamentings heard i' th' air; strange screams of death,
         And, prophesying with accents terrible
         Of dire combustion, and confus'd events,
         New hatch'd to th' woeful time, the obscure bird
         Clamour'd the livelong night: some say, the earth
         Was feverous, and did shake.
         *Macbeth.*              'Twas a rough night.
         *Lennox.*    My young remembrance cannot parallel
         A fellow to it.
                         (2.3.55-64)

But nothing of this was heard, apparently, during the murder (2.1 and 2). I suppose we can summon up our intellectual courage and stiffen the sinews of our ingenuity and demonstrate that there is no incongruity or inconsistency here; that the storm is a metaphysical or metaphorical one indicating the tumult and disorder in the minds of Macbeth and Lady Macbeth, or in the universe when regicide is rampant. And so on. But though I am capable of doing this sort of thing and can appreciate the skill with which it is done by others, I am not entirely satisfied with my own honesty in the intellectualizing of the two incongruous impressions, both so eloquently given in the play.

First, I note that the absurdity is rarely noticed and rarely commented upon; and some otherwise sensitive readers have admitted to me that they have not noticed anything wrong. This is really a compliment to Shakespeare's artifice, not necessarily a compliment to his art. He can wile the bird from off the tree. His silence in Macbeth's castle during the murder is so brilliantly conveyed, and his unprecedented storm during the same night is so plausibly related, that we give ourselves credulously to the beguiling by the master. Shakespeare's lapses in artistry sometimes give testimonies to his amazing art.

My rough calculation, on a fair sample, is that in each of Shakespeare's extant thirty-seven plays there are at least a couple of dozen instances where he can be reasonably said, on grounds of common sense, to lapse from severe artistic control of his materials — an arithmetic total of around a thousand. In a large body of theatrical material, a thousand is not a large number. Ben Jonson, in the privacy of his notebook, retorted to the claim of Heminges and Condell that Shakespeare wrote easily without correcting, without blotting, "Would he had blotted a thousand!" I find this a surprisingly accurate estimate. But because Shakespeare wrote about 100,000 lines, the desideration that he should have blotted (i.e., corrected) a thousand is numerically a very small percentage (only about 1%), and even if "a thousand" is taken metaphorically, perhaps not so impressive. "Many particulars" (wrote Dr. Johnson in the Preface to his *Dictionary*) "will admit improvement from a mind utterly unequal to the whole performance."

A homogenization of Shakespeare into perfection (so common nowadays in academic books on Shakespeare) has a flattening effect on criticism. It damages the accessibility of Shakespeare, by obscuring from notice all those signs of his being a busy artist and professional, constantly experimenting, without time to repeat his experiments. "One never finishes a book — one abandons it," says Paul Valéry of less-pressured writing than the provision of stage plays for a professional repertory company. We have come to see the artistic fascination of *Timon of Athens* as being an abandoned play. The defects so visible in *Timon of Athens* are discernible on a smaller scale in the rest of the canon. It is no provocative paradox to say that all Shakespeare's plays show signs of being "abandoned" rather than "finished."

Yet we have two important safeguards against the homogenizing of Shakespeare's plays into perfection. One is that, although there has for some time been, among academic critics, a reluctance to accept, without subtle examination, any artistic lapses in Shakespeare, this attitude has never been tolerated in the theater.

The modern theater is a permanent and perennial champion of Shakespeare against bardolatrous postures. *There* the customary attitude must be that "something will have to be done with this old play to make it bearable or enjoyable or acceptable to a modern audience," or to enable it to give adequate expression to the director's preoccupations, personal misery, and artistic originality. Our directors still (in Charles Lamb's phrase) get their hooks into this artistic leviathan. The contradictions of *King Lear* can be smoothed out and the play made artistically acceptable by revising it into a nihilistic experience, by the judicious omission of all those confusing touches of compassion and tenderness among the characters. It can be simplified into a sermon on the value of Christian patience. Even Gregori Kozintsev, in his admirable film of *King Lear,* felt, for all his artistic integrity, that he could not include Gloucester's imaginary leap from Dover Cliff or the ambiguity of his breaking heart; instead, Edgar piously digs his father's grave and Gloucester's soul is received into bliss amid the singing of the heavenly choir on the sound track.

Our second safeguard against credulity in the perfectionism of Shakespeare is (or ought to be) our students, many of whom are coming into contact with certain plays of Shakespeare for the first time. I am impressed by the indignation that is aroused by (for example) *Measure for Measure* and *All's Well that Ends Well.* There is (I am sometimes quite eloquently told) a lack of moral — and therefore artistic — conscience in Shakespeare in his bestowing, approvingly, admirable females on such unpromising males as Bassanio, Bertram, Orsino, and Posthumus. When told that Bassanio is a "drip" (or whatever the transiently current colloquialism may be for a despised young male), I find myself springing to the defense of Shakespeare. The love of Portia (I explain) and the affection of Antonio elevate Bassanio; the devotion of Helena must raise Bertram in our esteem, just as the strong approval of Helena by all the sympathetic characters in the play protects her from any imputations of indecorum. Shakespeare's artistry is perfect in ordering this — and so on.

Yet, in this respect I sometimes think I set a bad example to my students (though not such a bad example as some of my friends and colleagues, whose names I won't mention now) by constantly explaining Shakespeare's artistry, defending his artistic decisions, in resistance to the natural repugnance felt by the open-minded young. Those of our students who are either intelligent or are gifted with mimetic powers, naturally and prudently imitate us as a step on the pathway to academic success. Thus is the torch of Shakespearean perfectionism handed down from one academic generation to another.

> . . . we but teach
> Bloody instructions, which, being taught, return
> To plague th' inventor.

In making these observations before you this afternoon, I feel that I am fighting for a real Shakespeare. However often the skeptic and relativist may say that we shall only see what we can and that we can only see what we must, and however deeply we may be imbedded in the "situation," yet true criticism, like all worthy intellectual feats, is a leaping out of the "situation." The history of Shakespeare criticism is itself a cautionary tale, a warning against an insolent view of criticism as a steadily progressing pursuit of truth. It is easy enough to be amused by the follies and preoccupations of the past, and few of those who write about the history of Shakespeare criticism can resist the temptation to be funny about it, whereas they ought to try to rise to the dignity of the theme. We, too, need a good-humored awareness of the kinds of bias that deflect our minds nowadays.

# The Delapsing of Shakespeare

## by RICHARD LEVIN

It must have taken some courage for our Trustees to arrange this session on Shakespeare's artistic lapses, because a substantial body of Shakespearean commentary is now devoted to proving that there are none. This trend can be seen, for instance, in a recent study of *The Two Gentlemen of Verona,* which begins by announcing that the play "still needs to be saved from its critics," and then quotes as an example H. B. Charlton's verdict, published some 35 years earlier:

> Clearly, Shakespeare's first attempt to make romantic comedy had only succeeded so far that it had unexpectedly and inadvertently made romance comic.[1]

According to the author of this study, the very idea that Shakespeare did something unexpectedly and inadvertently here is "astonishing." And if it now seems astonishing to suggest that Shakespeare lapsed in *The Two Gentlemen of Verona,* one of his earliest and least admired plays, the fate of the rest of the canon may easily be imagined. It stands in imminent danger of becoming lapseless.

This trend can of course be viewed as simply the latest manifestation of our old friend, Bardolatry, which Alfred Harbage has shrewdly anatomized in his essay, "The Myth of Perfection."[2] But more general causes must be involved, since the trend is by no means limited to the Bard. Other writers have been undergoing a similar revaluation in the critical arena and are now also approaching perfection. This is largely the result, I believe, of the dominant form taken by literary interpretation today, the form that has come to be known as "the reading." We are now so familiar with the reading, both as producers and consumers, that we may not always be fully conscious of its implications.

One is that the reading should be new; it should discover the real meaning of the work for the first time. Another is that the reading should be close. Almost all interpretations, no matter how far off or far out they may seem, now claim to be based upon "a close reading of the text," because few critics would care to admit that they were engaged in any other kind of enterprise. Consequently, one cannot tell just what it is supposed to be, but its purpose is clear enough: a close reading is designed to produce a new reading, by proving that the real meaning of the work is different from the apparent or plain-sense meaning yielded by the presumably unclose readings of previous critics. Curiously, we often find that the closer the reading professes to be, the farther is the distance between these real and apparent meanings. Indeed, in one of the most extraordinary performances I have seen, an article published last year which undertakes to show that Falstaff is actually "a covert St. John" with "a heavenly vocation," the author is concerned that we may think his reading is *too* close—that we may, in his words, "object that my interpretations require an unbelievably close reading."

A third implication of the reading, most important for our purpose, is that it should vindicate the work by providing a justification for all of its parts. A. L. French has noted that many critics now "habitually start from the assumption that there must be a way of 'explaining' everything that happens in a play: if there are things we can't explain that is the fault of our incompetent reading and not of Shakespeare."[3] Thus the reading cannot find that any parts of the work are defective, since that would be regarded as a failure of the critic, a confession of his inability to justify them. And the method for justifying them has already been suggested: it is by a close reading that demonstrates that what seemed to be defects to earlier commentators, who judged them in terms of the play's apparent meaning, will turn out to be virtues once we have grasped its real meaning. Of course, this places the critic in something of a dilemma, since he must claim that this real meaning is conveyed by the work with perfect artistry, so that his reading will be a vindication, and at the same time claim that it was never conveyed to anyone before, so that his reading will be new. But more of that later.

The recent proliferation of these new, close, vindicatory readings can be attributed primarily, I think, to two fashionable approaches to interpretation that are admirably suited to this task of creating a distinction between the work's apparent and its real meaning, and thereby transforming its apparent defects into real virtues. One is the thematic approach, which assumes that the real subject of the work must be an abstract idea, usually called the central theme, rather than the particular actions that are only its apparent subject. This thematic abstraction thus provides the strategy for the critic's rescue operation. Portions of the play that previous commentators thought ineffective or inappropriate or disproportionate—the show of the Nine Worthies, for instance, or the Clown scene in *Othello,* or Mercutio's Queen Mab speech—can be saved by subsuming them under the central theme. And since one can always find some theme, such as appearance versus reality, art versus nature, reason versus intuition, or the like, that will encompass any combination of characters or events, no matter how diverse, this strategy cannot fail to justify any part of any play. If through some mix-up in Jaggard's shop a scene from *Coriolanus* had been printed in the middle of *Cymbeline,* a resourceful thematist would have no trouble showing how it contributed to the play's thematic structure. This approach has the power to confer instant perfection upon every play it touches, for there are no artistic lapses so grievous that they cannot be redeemed by the all-forgiving embrace of the central theme.

But I have perhaps said enough about thematism elsewhere,[4] so I would like to concentrate instead upon the second approach that has been responsible for so many of these new, close, vindicating readings—the ironic approach. Whereas the thematic approach creates a new meaning for the play by rejecting the play's apparent subject, the ironic approach achieves this by rejecting the play's apparent values. Typically, it discovers that the presentation of a character or an action that seems to be sympathetic, and that has been understood in that way by virtually everyone up to now, is actually meant to be antipathetic or ridiculous. Thus it too provides an all-purpose rescue strategy, since it enables the critic to claim that any apparent lapses in this presentation are really intentional and therefore virtues. According to this approach, then, Shakespeare can never nod, because whenever previous commentators found him dozing off—in failing to win our acceptance of a character or action—it now turns out that he was wide awake, being deliberately and of course brilliantly ironic.

This is the tactic adopted in the study of *The Two Gentlemen of Verona* cited at the outset. Charlton, you will recall, said that Shakespeare had unexpectedly and inadvertently made the romance comic. The critic who found this charge so astonishing answers it by asserting that Shakespeare *meant* us to see Valentine as comic—in fact as a "nincompoop"—and to see his surrender of Silvia to Proteus at the end as "a gesture of sublime, fatuous egotism [that] one word from Silvia would explode." Unfortunately, he never tells us why Shakespeare does not have her speak that word, and then marries her to this nincompoop. Another critic, similarly, explains away the difficulties in the resolution of *Measure for Measure* as conscious ironies: "There is not a botched-up happy ending, for the mood of the ending is more satirical than happy." And another claims that this ending is unsuccessful because Shakespeare wanted it to be, which therefore makes it successful after all:

> I believe the final effect should be an uneasiness and dissatisfaction, which the spectator never consciously articulates. In addition, if we judge by the radically divided critical response, Shakespeare has succeeded in destroying community within his audience, a destruction that mirrors the lack of community in the weddings at the end of this "comedy."

And the excesses of *Titus Andronicus* — one can scarcely call them lapses since there is so little in this play to lapse from — have been vindicated by another critic as "a huge joke" perpetrated by Shakespeare, who is "disporting himself" and "laughing behind his back" while he is "pulling our leg."

This new gospel of justification by irony is now being spread to other playwrights of the period. Only sixteen years ago Robert Ornstein considered the possibility that the much-criticized ending of *Antonio's Revenge* was sardonic; but he rejected this means of salvaging the ending because the facts of the play were against it.[5] Such heroic self-restraint seems quaintly old-fashioned today. Now the wish is father to the facts, and several new ironic readings of Marston's ending have appeared which discover that it "deliberately travesties the accepted formula" and "beg[s] an ironical interpretation" and "can only be interpreted as consciously outrageous," and so on. As one of them puts it, "much of the so-called clumsiness, nonsense, and bad writing are there for deliberate effect." In the same way, a recent reading of Jonson's *The New Inn* asserts that "much of what is ridiculous in the play is intentionally so." And if the ironic approach can do this for *Antonio's Revenge* and *The New Inn,* it can certainly dispose of any artistic flaws in Shakespeare by making them the products of conscious art. Thus this approach has reversed the biblical scheme: before it arrived we had a fallen Shakespeare capable of lapses — a postlapsarian Shakespeare, but with its coming it has given us a new, innocent, prelapsarian Shakespeare.

The ironic approach has proved very useful in eliminating not only Shakespeare's artistic lapses, but also what might be called his moral lapses. I am not happy with the term, but have adopted it to refer to those attitudes assumed or endorsed in the plays which seem morally defective in our time. Perhaps the most obvious examples are the attitudes underlying *The Taming of the Shrew, The Merchant of Venice,* and *Henry V,* which would now be called, respectively, male chauvinism, antisemitism, and jingoism. It can reasonably be argued that Shakespeare incorporates some qualification of those attitudes in each play; but that is not enough for the new Bardolater. He must prove that Shakespeare is actually attacking them. Of course, the only way to prove this is by an ironic reading of these plays, which discovers that their real values are the opposite of their apparent values. And since a major obstacle to such a reading is the ending of each play, in which the proponents of these unacceptable attitudes achieve complete success, the ironist must insist that the ending cannot mean what it seems to mean, and what it has been taken to mean up to now. I call this maneuver "refuting Shakespeare's endings," since it tries to persuade us not to believe them.

We have all seen how it works. Faced with the need to explain away Kate's final speech on wifely obedience, one critic says, "It would be *simpliste* to regard this statement of total passivity at its face value, and as a prognosis.

The open end of *The Taming of the Shrew* is Katherina's mind, undisclosed in soliloquy." Several critics have recently argued that the conclusion of *The Merchant of Venice* shows the Christians celebrating at Belmont to be at least as guilty as Shylock, if not more so. According to one account:

> Belmont is as flawed as Venice. Most important, because Belmont's inhabi- tants are oblivious to their flaws, their festivity is artificial, ambiguous, and highly ironic. . . . Belmont is equally tainted by suggestions of perversion, guilt, hypocrisy, and unhappiness. . . . The rotten core of undiscovered hy- pocrisy is still present, and will remain undiscovered and unresolved.

And a number of new ironic readings of *Henry V* insist that Henry's final triumph at Agincourt is actually presented as a defeat, because it is immoral or impermanent or is somehow responsible for the Wars of the Roses. (In- cidentally, the earliest use of the term *new reading* that I have found is in an article entitled "A New Reading of *Henry V*," which was published in 1919 — I think the date is significant — and which reveals, in italics, that *"The play is ironic,"* since it "is a satire on monarchical government, on im- perialism, on the baser kinds of 'patriotism,' and on war.")

I have no time to refute these refutations of Shakespeare, although I might ask in passing just how we are supposed to be made aware of the undisclosed contents of Kate's mind, or of the rotten core of hypocrisy at Belmont if it re- mains undiscovered, or of the nature of Henry's defeat when the Chorus and all the characters keep telling us that it was a great victory. It is more impor- tant, I believe, to try to understand the purpose and the consequences of these ironic readings. Their purpose emerges very clearly in the program an- nounced by one of the foremost refuters of Shakespeare, early in his chapter on *Henry V:*

> To think of [Shakespeare] as a jingo is as difficult as to think of him as a Jew- baiter. Our examination of *The Merchant of Venice* demonstrated, I hope, that he was not the latter. The charge that he was the former is equally worthy of examination.

And his ensuing examination discovers, not too surprisingly, that *Henry V* is not a jingoist play at all, but an ironical indictment of jingoism. The point is that this kind of critic feels called upon to clear Shakespeare of "charges," to maintain Shakespeare's infallibility in morals as well as in art. And to ac- complish this he must resort to what Clifford Lyons aptly termed "that philosopher's stone of the critic, irony, [which] so readily transmutes unac- ceptable motifs into golden opinions"[6] by proving that the plays do not really mean what they say. This is the inevitable penalty of idolization. To remain worthy of our worship, the idol's meaning must be changed, like that of our other sacred texts, to conform with current beliefs.

This ironical transmutation of values is not limited to these three plays, but is rapidly spreading throughout the canon. Thanks to this approach, we not only have been given an untamed Kate and a hypocritical Portia and a defeated Henry V, but are now also being told that Romeo is "something close to a mass murderer," that Juliet is "almost gross" in the "ugliness" and "rawness of her sexual hunger" (in which she "comes very close to panting like an animal"), that Hamlet is "a soul lost in damnable error" who becomes "demonic," that Desdemona is "proud" and "self-righteous" and guilty of "moral hypocrisy," that Prospero is a "type of Satan," that Duke Vincentio is as bad as Angelo, and Hector as bad as Achilles, and Malcolm as bad as Macbeth, and so on. Each of these examples comes to us from a different critic, but they all spring from the same motive as the ironic readings previously considered—from the need to prove Shakespeare's moral infallibility. For in each case the critic believes that the apparent meaning of the play embodies false values, and hence cannot be the real meaning. But these new ironizers disagree on what the real meaning is, since they divide roughly into two opposing schools. On the right are the traditionalists who claim that Shakespeare endorsed all the orthodox values of his time, and therefore insist that the apparently sympathetic treatment of any character who falls short of those values must be ironic, so that his plays can qualify as conventional moral exempla. And on the left are the modernists who claim Shakespeare as our contemporary, and therefore insist that his plays must be presenting an ironical challenge to received values, or to all value, so that they can qualify as existential statements. (Indeed, the critics of this second school seem to feel that the absence of pervasive irony in any play would in itself be a serious failing, from which Shakespeare must be saved.) It is highly ironic that these two hostile groups of ironizers should now be allied in this campaign to refute Shakespeare. Yet their diametrically opposite readings have the same basic purpose—the desire to vindicate the plays by purging them of what the critic considers to be moral lapses.

The consequences of such readings may be less obvious. I can imagine that some people might agree with my objections to their methodology, and still maintain that they are, at worst, harmless, and that at best they may indeed achieve their purpose of enhancing our estimate of the plays and of Shakespeare himself. But I do not see how an ironic reading makes these plays better; it simply makes them incoherent, both ethically and aesthetically, by undermining the internal standard of judgment upon which their meaning depends. Nor does it make Shakespeare a better artist. On the contrary, it would make him much worse, since it asks us to believe that he expressed himself so ineffectively that his real meaning was not noticed for almost four centuries. This is the dilemma of the new, vindicating reading that was mentioned earlier: if the reading is new—that is, if it has never been communicated to anyone before—then it cannot also be a vindication of Shakespeare's skill as a communicator.

The attempts of these critics to escape this dilemma expose the basic weakness of their approach, and ultimately, we shall see, contradict its avowed purpose. One explanation they offer is that Shakespeare had to conceal his intention, because of public opinion or the censorship. This might be called the "two-audience" theory: it finds in the play an apparent meaning that Shakespeare was forced to present in order to deceive the mob or the Master of the Revels, and an opposite, real meaning that he wanted to present to the wiser sort. But the theory could only apply to a few plays—those whose alleged real meaning might have antagonized the public or the state, and even for them it cannot show how this meaning could have been simultaneously concealed from and revealed to the two audiences.

A second explanation avoids both of these difficulties by claiming that Shakespeare set out to deceive his entire audience, but only for their own good, since he later undeceived them in order to teach them a lesson. This might be called the "therapeutic deception" theory, which one dedicated refuter of Shakespeare has recently advanced to justify his ironic readings of most of the tragedies:

> Perhaps the art of tragedy consists in this very temptation to confusion—for the sake of our subsequent recognition of our folly. That is, a tragedy's beguiling heroisms serve to prompt mistaken judgments, so that then we can confess and evaluate our proneness to illusion.

The trouble with this theory is that everything depends upon our being undeceived in the ending of the play, which would therefore have to embody an especially clear judgment against those "beguiling heroisms." Yet in each of our examples we saw that the opposite is true—the judgment of the ending is apparently very favorable to the characters whom the refuter disapproves of, which of course is why he must try to refute that ending.

For this reason these critics often fall back upon a third explanation, a modified version of the "therapeutic deception" theory, in which the final enlightenment does not occur at the end of the play but later when we examine the play in our studies. Such an examination must in fact be assumed in all of these refutations, since they could not possibly be worked out by anyone during a performance of the play, or even during an ordinary reading of it. In this view, then, the play is no longer something to be experienced, either on stage or in print, but something that must be laboriously deciphered, through one of those "unbelievably close readings," until it is finally made to yield up its hidden meaning. But that presents a new difficulty, since it is obvious that the overwhelming majority of viewers and readers have never attempted such an operation and never will.

This third explanation, therefore, really implies a fourth: Shakespeare must have aimed each play at two distinct groups, the general public whom he permanently misled with his apparent meaning, and the elect few whom he temporarily misled for their own good, since he counted on their buying a copy of the play (even of those plays not published during his lifetime), and puzzling over it until they discovered the deception. This combines the two earlier theories; but here, it should be noted, unlike the first version of the "therapeutic deception" theory, most of the audience is never undeceived; and, unlike the first version of the "two-audience" theory, there is here no motive for Shakespeare's deception, unless it be sheer snobbery. Now he is not writing *for* his audience but *against* them. It is an ugly picture of moral irresponsibility, but it seems to be the logical conclusion of this sequence of explanations, and therefore the real, although rarely acknowledged,[7] rationale of the refuters of Shakespeare, since it is the only way they can avoid making him a bungling artist who is unable to communicate his meaning. Thus we arrive at the crowning irony of this ironic approach: its avowed purpose is to vindicate Shakespeare's morality; but in order to do this it must bring his artistry into question, and in order to salvage his artistry it must sacrifice his morality.

Furthermore, this campaign to eliminate Shakespeare's moral lapses not only diminishes him, but also diminishes us. For surely one of the primary values of literature lies in the insights it can give us into different ways of perceiving the human experience. But it can never do this if we go to the work determined to find there a mirror of our own minds. And that is exactly what happens when we try to make Shakespeare morally infallible, which can only mean that we make him agree with us. This is the necessary result of both the thematic and the ironic approaches, because of their separation of the play's real from its apparent meaning. As M. H. Abrams has observed, this separation is "used as a handy gadget to replace what an author has said with what a commentator would prefer him to have said."[8] The central theme that each critic finds in the play usually seems to echo his own beliefs — indeed, we all know critics who manage to find their favorite thematic idea in many very different works and authors. Similarly, an ironic reading enables the critic to prove that the real meaning of the work is whatever he himself believes in. The discovery that Shakespeare, or any other author, always agrees with us may be comforting (although it must also be rather boring), but it is a pretty sure sign that we are misreading him, and consequently cutting ourselves off from an enriching experience.

Nor do I think, finally, that even the elimination of Shakespeare's artistic lapses is harmless, for it too diminishes him and us. If we cannot recognize the flaws in his plays, we will not properly appreciate their virtues. And the mental gymnastics required to explain away those flaws will probably affect our sensibility, and certainly our credibility — a point made by Alfred Harbage in the essay cited earlier:

> Evidence of blindness to defects or inconsistencies casts suspicion upon testimony about merits or consistencies. . . . What shall we think of praises of *Hamlet* by one who has raved over *Titus Andronicus?*[9]

Moreover, the elimination of his artistic lapses will prevent us from appreciating Shakespeare's remarkable development as a playwright. And the understanding of that development from *Titus Andronicus* to *Hamlet* surely gives us a much more impressive sense of human achievement than anything we get from the new Bardolaters, who want their god to spring from the brow of Stratford, already epopt and perfect. For all these reasons, then, I urge that we try to close this open season on Shakespeare's lapses — both artistic and moral — before they become extinct, and join forces to conserve what still remains of this endangered species, as a valuable part of our cultural heritage.

## Notes

1. *Shakespearian Comedy* (London: Methuen, 1938), p. 43. Since I am not concerned with the particular "delapsing" readings in themselves, but only as examples of this general trend, it seemed inappropriate to single them out by the usual documentation.

2. *Conceptions of Shakespeare* (Cambridge: Harvard University Press, 1966), pp. 23-38; originally published in *Shakespeare 400*, ed. James McManaway (New York: Holt, Rinehart & Winston, 1964).

3. *Shakespeare and the Critics* (Cambridge: The University Press, 1972), p. 5.

4. "Thematic Unity and the Homogenization of Character," *Modern Language Quarterly* 33 (1972): 23-29; "Some Second Thoughts on Central Themes," *Modern Language Review* 67 (1972): 1-10; "Third Thoughts on Thematics," *MLR*, 70 (1975): 481-96; "My Theme Can Lick Your Theme," *College English* 37 (1975): 307-12.

5. *The Moral Vision of Jacobean Tragedy* (Madison: University of Wisconsin Press, 1960), p. 155.

6. " 'It appears so by the story': Notes on Narrative-Thematic Emphasis in Shakespeare," *Shakespeare Quarterly* 9 (1958): 293.

7. It is acknowledged by the critic who wanted to clear Shakespeare of the "charges" of jingoism and anti-Semitism: "Drama. . . . must make a wide and immediate appeal to a large number of people of ordinary intelligence. . . . The public does not want the truth. It wants confirmation of its prejudices. . . . What the poet is seeking, on the other hand, is the secret of life, and, even if he would, he cannot share [it] with a crowd in a theater. . . . He can share it only with the few, and with them mostly in solitude. . . . And so [Shakespeare's] greater plays are one thing as drama and another as poetry, one thing on the outside, another within."

8. "Five Types of *Lycidas*," *Milton's* Lycidas: *The Tradition and the Poem*, ed. C. A. Patrides (New York: Holt, Rinehart & Winston, 1961), p. 215.

9. Harbage, "The Myth of Perfection," p. 35.

# Truth and Relevance in Shakespeare Production

## by ROBERT SPEAIGHT

A famous English novelist once told me that he wanted to found a Society for the Prevention of Cruelty to Shakespeare, and only the other day Dr. Jonathan Miller, one of our most intelligent and innovative stage directors, declared to me his belief that "one could not let Shakespeare alone." The argument swings between these two poles. Of course people have been interfering with Shakespeare ever since Davenant — who was at least Shakespeare's godson and rumored to be something more — omitted the scenes and characters of low life from *Measure for Measure,* turned Angelo into a respectable prig, and decided that Macbeth, instead of asking the messenger:

> The devil damn thee black, thou cream-fac'd loon!
> Where gott'st thou that goose look?

should more properly have asked him: "Now, friend, what means thy change of countenance?" Nahum Tate conveniently widowed Cordelia, married her off to Edgar, and sent Lear to doze at their fireside. Colley Cibber's "Off with his head — so much for Buckingham!" was a temptation that, for many years, no performer of Richard III was able to resist; and it was not until the end of the last century that, in England at least, Fortinbras was allowed to turn up at the right moment. When a Victorian spectator complained of Cleopatra that she was "so unlike our own dear Queen," the cue was given to Sir Frank Benson to alter the charge against Falstaff of "tearing a poor whore's ruff in a bawdy house" to "tearing a poor girl's ruff in a boarding-house." So there is nothing new about bringing Shakespeare up to date, only you run the risk of making him very quickly look old-fashioned.

I see no reason why a gathering of Shakespeare scholars — the latchet of whose shoes I am unworthy to unloose — should not pat each other on the back instead of hitting each other over the head. So I shall roundly declare the last three-quarters of the century to have been the golden age of Shakespeare scholarship, although it has been the golden age of little else. We know — or conjecture — much more about Shakespeare's stage, and any intelligent production of his plays takes these conjectures into account. If we carry reaction so far as to have a curtain at all, we do not drop it in order to display "another part of the battlements." We subscribe to Dover Wilson's dictum that "a Shakespeare play is like a succession of waves through which the spectator moves like a swimmer." Certainly the thrust or open stage, which has pretty well established its orthodoxy on this side of the Atlantic, is an aid to continuity, although it imposes on the actor a restlessness that I, personally, can find distracting. Speech loses much of its effect when it is combined with movement. There are scenes in Shakespeare that ask for a stillness, and also for a perspective, that a theater in the round, or in three-quarters of a round, forbids. But you cannot have it all ways, and some ways are better than others. The history of the stage teaches us that Shakespeare will stand up to anything, except a radical infidelity — or a multipurpose auditorium.

I well remember the first production of *Hamlet* in modern dress. It brought people to the play who would otherwise have run a mile from it. Hamlet's costume suggested that he was on his way to the golf course, although under the circumstances he would have needed very considerably to increase his handicap. Audiences who would scarcely have noticed if Claudius poured himself out a glass of wine sat up in their seats when he mixed himself a Scotch and soda. It was plausible that Ophelia should be buried on a rainy day — all those umbrellas reinforced the melancholy of the scene — and one was left to suppose that the rain only began to fall when the procession entered, otherwise Hamlet and Horatio would surely have cut short their colloquy with the gravedigger and exchanged the discomfort of the churchyard for the shelter of the church. Polonius — and the actor came from a well-known family — was at least a credible Prime Minister at a time when we took our Prime Ministers from the House of Lords. He looked quite capable of losing the American colonies.

The shock treatment was salutary, as it so often is when the patient is one of the problem plays — and *Hamlet* is nothing if not a problem. In 1938 it brought *Troilus and Cressida* wonderfully alive, with the Trojans all from the best private schools, myself as Ulysses got up like the First Lord of the Admiralty on a visit to the Mediterranean fleet, and a Pandarus who might have stepped out of Noel Coward. At about the same time Orson Welles gave us his memorable *Julius Caesar.* This worked beautifully on that bare stage until the antifascist motivation broke down, and a good deal of camouflage and a good many cuts were necessary to disguise what is apt to happen when high-minded liberals take to regicide. By the time Antony and Octavius have got to work, there is not much sign of civil liberty. Were they even allowed to get to work? I don't remember.

This brings me to the question of fidelity. What kind of play do you think this is? What do you think Shakespeare was trying to say—and never mind if you don't agree with him? If you don't like what he is saying, you had much better not produce the play at all. I have even seen a production of *Romeo and Juliet* inspired by the notion that Romeo and Juliet were not really in love with each other, and that their marriage, for the short time it lasted, was a dismal failure. It's all very well to have a bright idea, but it matters immensely that the idea should be the right one. "All that glisters is not gold" will help you to choose the right method as well as the right casket. Only when you have honestly asked yourself these questions, are you entitled to play about with the options of medieval, Elizabethan, eighteenth-, nineteenth-, or twentieth-century dress; realistic or surrealist decor, or no decor at all; an integral or an abridged text; a proscenium or an open stage. You will also do well to bear in mind the actor's power of making you forget what sort of costume he is wearing and what kind of stage he is acting on—if he speaks the speech set down for him as Shakespeare would have had it spoken. As I look back on fifty years of playgoing, I more often recall what the actor has done with the part than what the director has done with the play. Very often it is the way he spoke a particular line: Olivier's "I *am* the sea" from *Titus Andronicus,* and his "When will this fearful slumber have an end?" Perhaps this was one of the 60 lines in *Titus* that Sir Israel Gollancz magnanimously allowed to Shakespeare.

Nevertheless, we have been living, and are still living, in a director's theater. If there is one production from the past that I should love to recover, it would be Granville-Barker's *Twelfth Night.* But this was in the days when pleasure, rather than relevance, was a theatrical watchword. Barker was defiantly up to date, but it was Shakespeare's date, not ours—although by a combination of invention and fidelity he made it ours as well. And this brings me to Peter Brook, in whom sheer genius is sometimes at odds with mere fidelity. Brook's *King Lear* was dominated by the idea that *Lear* is a tragedy of the absurd; he took his cue from Gloucester:

> As flies to wanton boys, are we to th' Gods;
> They kill us for their sport.

I will not labor my own point of view that *Lear* is a tragedy of redemption, with strong Christian undertones. Shakespeare does not ram his meaning, or his message, down our throats; his "negative capability" sees all round the question. Peter Brook had a perfect right to his pessimism, but he had no right to trim the text to suit it. The blinding of Gloucester is the most painful scene that Shakespeare ever wrote, but just when humanity is shown as almost past redemption he brings in Cornwall's three servants to redeem it. This essential coda was omitted. Similarly, in the last act, Edmund was not allowed his contrition — "Some good I mean to do in spite of mine own nature" — and, instead of being led off the stage as the dramatist instructed, he was left to encumber it until Edgar dragged him away, like a carcass fresh from the *abattoir*. The bodies of Regan and Goneril were not brought back, and we were thus robbed at the end of the picture we had at the beginning. "There was once an old king and he had three daughters" — only now the old king was dying and the three daughters were dead. If Peter Brook wanted an unhappy ending this should have been enough for him, and it had the slight advantage of being what Shakespeare wrote. As a French student remarked to me: "Il a transformé Shakespeare en Brecht."

But with *A Midsummer Night's Dream* the case was altered. Peter Brook does not believe in fairies, and neither do we. Folklore is not our natural habitat. But Peter Brook is a master of theatrical magic, and by combining the virtuosities of the circus with a scrupulous regard for Shakespeare's metrical score, he recreated — there is no other word for it — the play as Shakespeare might have visualized it if he had had the misfortune to be living in the twentieth century. It celebrated more than the wedding of Theseus and Hippolyta, for the marriage between the spectator and the play, between the actors and the audience, was more joyfully consummated than ever before in my experience. Here, too, was the perfect alliance of invention and fidelity. The doubling of Theseus with Oberon, Hippolyta with Titania, and Puck with Philostrate, might well have tempted Shakespeare to exclaim, if he were looking on from Parnassus: "There are more things in heaven and earth, Horatio; I thought I had thought of everything, but I had never thought of *that*." The production was at once contemporary and timeless, for the play itself — though we can make a shrewd guess as to when and where and how it was first performed — had wings that take it out of time.

For Shakespeare this was rather rare. It is much easier for a modern audience to suspend a disbelief in fairies than to achieve an even provisional belief in the value of chastity. Isabella's "More than our brother is our chastity" is the stiffest hurdle that any actress has to face; one watches them approach it like a nervous steeplechaser. The situation — so runs the argument — could be saved by situation ethics. But situation ethics were an escape route from an ethical impasse unknown to Shakespeare or to Shakespeare's audience. That audience was not, I think, easily shocked; but it would have been outraged if Isabella had agreed to Angelo's proposal. Her fault was not in rejecting it, but in letting Claudio know that she had the choice of accepting it, and when he showed — to say the least — a certain disappointment that she had not done so, to round on him in terms not far removed from hysteria. Isabella had courage and integrity; now she must learn compassion. That — as

I see it — is the point of the play, so modern in some respects, so medieval in others.

I recall two memorable productions. When Peter Brook, at Stratford, sent his prisoners circulating round the stage, one expected them at any moment to break out into "Freiheit, freiheit. . . ." Here was a rancid Hogarthian realism. To the difficult last act he brought clarity, if not exactly comfort. Barbara Jefford was made to hold the longest pause on theatrical record before she went down on her knees to plead for Angelo. A more recent production by Jonathan Miller was even more riveting, though in one or two respects more questionable. He set the play in the Vienna of Wittgenstein and Sigmund Freud. Certainly Angelo — and Isabella perhaps — were plausible subjects for the Doctor's consulting room. For the first time in my experience, Isabella replied to Claudio's breakdown with uncontrolled hysteria; her immaturity was suddenly laid bare. But Dr. Miller saw that in the last act Shakespeare had left the options ajar, if not exactly open. The director is faced here with two crucial choices. Does Isabella plead for Angelo because she has genuinely forgiven him — not knowing as yet, remember, that Claudio is alive? Or does she do so out of consideration for Mariana, whom Angelo has just been forced to marry? Dr. Miller chose the second alternative. Isabella positively gabbled her appeal to the Duke, evidently *contre coeur.* That leaves her with the Duke's proposal, or hinted proposal, of marriage — "if you'll a willing ear incline." Isabella is given nothing to indicate whether her ear is willing or not; and clutching at this wisp of straw Dr. Miller made her abruptly turn her back and return to her novitiate — which is probably what she would have done in real life, if real life had brought her into that unlikely situation. The Duke returned, disconsolate but resigned, to the Ministry of Internal Affairs, having done something to restore the rule of justice as distinct from the rule of law, and a little to clean up the red light district of Vienna. I happened to disagree with Dr. Miller's interpretation of Isabella's plea for Angelo and to endorse her refusal of the Duke's proposal. But these are open questions, and the director has the right, and the obligation, to answer them one way or the other.

He must first ask himself: How did Shakespeare envisage a play? Was he thinking of Essex when he wrote *Coriolanus?* Did he see these noble, or not so noble, Romans as we see them in the statuary that meets us in our museums, rather like Victorian bishops or headmasters, and against a background of the forum reminiscent of the dreary prints that used to hang in the classroom?

> their hats are pluck'd about their ears,
> And half their faces buried in their cloaks.

Lucius's description of the conspirators in *Julius Caesar* does not suggest togas that have just come from the laundry. And what about Cleopatra's "Cut my lace, Charmian"? That indicates a Cleopatra as Tiepolo imagined her in his painting of that famous and fateful supper. In the single drawing we possess of what appears to be a performance of *Titus Andronicus,* the characters wear Elizabethan dress with classical accoutrements. Everything tends to show that Shakespeare thought the Roman plays sufficiently relevant to stand up to contemporary costume, and that an audience seated on the banks of the Thames found no difficulty in transporting themselves to the banks of the Tiber.

Many years ago, when I was playing Coriolanus for William Poel, that eccentric pioneer had the idea — an excellent idea as it seemed to me — of dressing the play in the costumes of the French *directoire.* This, he argued, was a military and revolutionary play, and that was a military and revolutionary period. Unfortunately, he had second thoughts, and they were not very happy ones. Apart from anything else, he perversely cut the play to ribbons. But here we need not be pedantic. Any production is at the mercy of public transport — assuming that such transport is available — and of the hour at which people choose to dine. I take leave to doubt whether *Hamlet* was played in its entirety at the Globe. If the performance began at two o'clock in a winter afternoon, the twilight would have obscured Burbage's facial play before the end of the Closet scene, and if the rest was silence the rest was darkness also. We are right to play Shakespeare uncut as far as possible, but if a passage is bound to be incomprehensible to 95% of the audience I see no point in keeping it in. Shakespeare was not afraid to let his pen run away with him, as it did in *Richard III,* and in parts of *Henry V* and *Troilus and Cressida;* but he was a man of the theater, and aware of theatrical necessities. If Burbage had whispered to him that "this was too long," I do not think he would have sent it to the barber's with Burbage's beard. What matters is that the rhythm of the verse, and the sense and structure of the play, should be preserved.

We do wrong, of course, to take the historical tetralogies out of the Middle Ages; and whatever they may have done at the Globe, and whatever Tiepolo may have thought, it is perilous to put the "serpent of old Nile" in a farthingale. Egypt is an important character in the play, and Cleopatra should always remind us of the map. But except for the Histories and the Roman plays, the director is generally safe to keep a play in the period of its composition. Thus he will realize — though he seldom does so — that *Lear* is a Jacobean tragedy — that it has nothing to do with Stonehenge. When the young Gordon Craig was bothered about what to do with Oswald, Henry Irving muttered to him after a magisterial pause: "Hem, hem, m'boy — Malvolio." You do not add a cubit to the gigantic stature of the play by setting it among menhirs and dolmens. You do not make it any more timeless by taking it out of time. It is from the paneled luxury of a Jacobean mansion, and from the rustling of "robes and furred gowns," that Lear is driven out onto the heath. So, too, with *Macbeth,* much of which was expressly designed to flatter the reigning monarch. You may answer, of course, that the flattery of monarchs no longer means very much to us, and that the theater would be a dull place if our directors always played for safety. Certainly with the comedies they have no need to do so. Jonathan Miller, with Olivier's inspired assistance, turned Shylock into a nineteenth-century Rothschild, facing his enemies across the mahogany of a Victorian board-room. This was Forsyte country, accurately mapped, although Belmont fitted into it less easily. Then I take the case of *Much Ado.* Sir John Gielgud, with Peggy Ashcroft evidently born under a dancing star, gave us a delicious and perfectly orthodox Elizabethan production, which was rightly acclaimed on both sides of the Atlantic. Franco Zeffirelli, at the Old Vic, turned the play into a burlesque and lost most of its legitimate laughs in consequence. I confess that I fled before the church scene, not wishing to disturb still further proceedings that were disturbed enough already. At Stratford Douglas Seale translated us to the world of Donizetti, and the play survived the journey without damage. The Bourbons were reigning over Naples and the Two Sicilies, and Don Pedro obviously spoke for them. This was carnival time with the painted carts in procession, and the *elisir d'amore* was not slow to quicken. Last, but by no means least, I delighted in Joseph Papp's recent production of the play on television. The "old South" is rather more remote from us than Shakespeare's Messina—although Shakespeare's Messina, with its "pleached orchard," is some distance from Sicily. Only Dogberry, I thought, resisted Mr. Papp's brilliant transposition. British constables are like certain wines; they don't travel. My point is that three out of these four productions, widely as they differed in method, respected the truth of the play—which is at once a melodrama and a comedy of manners.

So, Ladies and Gentlemen, we shall be wise not to confuse truth with orthodoxy. All too often orthodoxy can petrify the truth it is trying to express. The Shakespearean truth was known only to Shakespeare himself, and if you had asked him what it was, he might have replied, like T. S. Eliot when he was asked the meaning of *The Cocktail Party:* "The play means what you think it does." Shakespeare's plays were the fruit of Shakespeare's experience—the experience, surely, of his imagination no less than of his life. The production of his plays is the fruit of our experience as well, and it is our privilege to interpret them. Whether our interpretation is an enrichment or a deformation is a matter for our aesthetic conscience. But only when we have sat down before Shakespeare like a little child, and diligently searched for his meaning, are we at liberty to take our toys out of the cupboard and play with them.

# Acting Values and Shakespearean Meaning: Some Suggestions

## by MICHAEL GOLDMAN

Most of my work in the past few years has been concerned not with particular performances and productions, nor with how to mount or prepare them, but with the performance values implied by the text. The medium of drama, as I understand it, is not words, or the stage, or even actors; it is acting, and I am trying to learn to read Shakespeare's plays as compositions in the medium of acting. Let me avoid misunderstanding; my bias is neither antipoetic nor antiverbal. There can be no question that Shakespeare's text must be primary for us, but his text is a design for performance; every word is meant as a performed word. I suppose that I am more concerned at this moment with addressing the reader or critic than the director or actor, but what I am trying to say to readers and critics is that the fact of performance by actors is the great governing fact as far as the art of writing plays is concerned. It is, I think, a rather obvious fact, but its implications are largely neglected, because of the influence that purely literary expectations and techniques have had on reading and criticism.

In this essay I would like to outline, in a brief and sketchy way, a few methods and general considerations that I have found helpful, and that I think might reward further study. I shall begin by making one or two theoretical claims, and then offer some suggestions about practical criticism.

First the theory. A play is an event that takes place between actors and an audience. Others, of course, have helped prepare the event. Indeed, great preparation—which as far as I can judge has always required a great text—has always been needed to make the theatrical event great. But the event itself consists of actors speaking and moving before an audience; no one else is involved. Thus the process of acting in any play will be as much a part of the

190

dramatic experience as the play's action or its verbal style. More accurately, action and style will be perceived through acting, just as the action of a poem is perceived through language. This means that any discussion of a Shakespearean play that does not treat the proper acting of it as part of Shakespeare's fundamental design is not a discussion of the play as a work of dramatic art.

Acting is an essential part of any play's imagery. What we perceive in the theater, the accumulation of experience out of which we construct our sense of "the play," is primarily and preponderantly an experience of acting. (The only experience that is not an experience of acting is our experience of the nonhuman spectacle, of the stage as a physical object, of lighting, scenery, music, props — and these in general are articulated by, or carefully suited to, the actor's art.) As a result, there will always be a significant connection between the small figures of acting — the local, repeated patterns of process by which the actor keeps his projection of the character alive and interesting — and the larger action of the play, just as there is a connection between the brushstroke of a painter and the felt significance of his design. This leads to at least one broad principle of critical method: that any analysis of a great play should probably begin with defining the acting problems of its major parts, especially with the precise sense of accomplishment their performance conveys to an audience, for this pleasure irresistibly influences its experience of the play.

Each great Shakespearean part seems to have its defining set of acting problems and rewards, and these bear a suggestive relation to the larger business of the play. It is clear, for example, that the interpretive problems that confront the actor who plays Hamlet are very similar to those which confront the Prince in making sense of life at Elsinore. Our response to the actor who plays Hamlet well — to the particular skills he demonstrates and the kind of difficulty he overcomes — is as much part of that play's meaning as our response, say, to its verbal imagery.

The part of Hamlet confronts the actor not so much with problems of execution as with problems of interpretation, of transition, of expressive coherence — the problem of finding a way to make sense of the innumerable, highly various, separate bits of execution that constitute the role. Variety, as Dr. Johnson points out, is the "particular excellence" that distinguishes *Hamlet,* and Hamlet is the most various of roles. The actor who plays the Prince has to keep shifting styles, masks, aims, modes of attack. Not only Hamlet, but the other characters in the play — and the audience — are constantly trying to make sense out of a remarkable variety of disparate and perplexing doings. The difficulty of making sense out of action, one's own action and other people's, is a central motif in the play, and it is echoed, refined, and kept before us by the accomplishment of any actor who succeeds in finding and expressing an inner coherence adequate to the major role.

When Hamlet reminds the players that they must not get lost in the whirl-wind of histrionic effects of which they are capable as professional actors, but must instead find a principle of control, a tempering smoothness, he is of course talking about his own problems as a character, especially in the stressful scenes he knows lie ahead, where his rapid emotional transitions will perplex the court, his mother, and, at times, the audience. But Hamlet is also reminding us of the difficulties that face the actor who plays Hamlet's part. The kind of poise it takes to hold the mirror up to nature in the role of Hamlet is an emblem of, a kind of histrionic objective correlative for, the kind of dif-ficult spiritual readiness under stress that Hamlet, the character, is struggling to achieve.

My analysis has certainly been too brief to be entirely persuasive, but it is the method, the kind of consideration being raised, that I wish to emphasize. I can make my point clearer by looking at another example. If we consider the title roles of *Antony and Cleopatra,* we find that a very different acting quality is required, and that, again, this quality is tested and commented on by the action. It might be called the quality of raw presence.

The play makes of the actor's presence a kind of metaphor or embodiment of the type of greatness, at once personal, physical, and yet curiously independent of material fact, that is one of its major subjects. *Antony and Cleopatra* is a play about greatness, and the discussion of greatness is the activity to which the play's characters devote most of their time. Speech after speech, indeed scene after scene, shows them commenting on each other's greatness, acknowledging it, praising it, measuring it by various standards, being moved or changed by it, proclaiming their own greatness, considering what greatness means. Love is also a subject of the play, of course. But the claim of the lovers — and even of their enemies — is that they are great lovers, no pair so famous, and their language of love, particularly when quarreling and making up, is the language of fame, nobility, and superhuman comparison. Greatness, as the play conceives it, is primarily a command over other people's imaginations. It depends on what people think of you and what you think of yourself; it is an innate quality rather than a result of one's actions or achievements. On the lowest level it is style, effective self-dramatization; at the highest, a means of overcoming time, death, and the world. It is registered in the behavior of audiences; and a concern for greatness is reflected in a concern for audiences.

The actors who play Antony and Cleopatra have to convince us from the start that they possess this quality. They have to do so not by their ac-tions — much of the time the action they are allowed does not prove greatness but at best asserts it — but by their direct command over our imagination. Without the audience's immediate assent that this man, Antony, looks like someone whom we feel willing on faith to measure by superhuman com-parisons — without this, the play will be tedious, empty at the center, and indeed actionless, for whatever binding sense of movement we get from the play must depend on our constant apprehension of Antony's and Cleopatra's greatness as a genuine issue—our sense that from these two lovers there springs a power that can dominate memory, command extravagant loyalty, and exact the fascinated attention of the entire world.

We might compare other tragedies in which the heroes are considered great according to one definition or another, but in which they are given early opportunities to exhibit that greatness in action. Othello, for example, illustrates his nobility, courage, composure, and authority in the first act through conflict, by moving against and overcoming the hostility or doubt of Iago, Brabantio's men, Brabantio himself, his fellow Senators. But Antony and Cleopatra must establish themselves in an atmosphere that comments constantly upon their greatness yet does not challenge it in action. If anything, what they do early in the play—and throughout most of it—works against their greatness, or against the ordinary measures of greatness in their world. The drama comes from their giving to all things a touch of majesty, making vilest things "become" their greatness.

Consider the problems of an actor who must enter on the lines:

> you shall see in him
> The triple pillar of the world transform'd
> Into a strumpet's fool.

The strumpet's fool might not be that hard to manage, but the triple pillar of the world—who even as a strumpet's fool remains the triple pillar of the world! "Stand up, Mr. Jones, and try to look like the triple pillar of the world." It has the rawness, the unsupported nakedness of the initial awful moment in an actor's audition, which in most cases is the crucial moment—when you step out and the producer, not waiting to see you tapdance or do your James Cagney imitation, says, "He'll do" or, far more likely, "He won't do"—and "doing," in fact, depends not on what you do but what you are, on something in you—that, as they say, you either have or you don't. It is raw presence that is wanted. And the play makes use of, draws its meanings out of that raw appeal, the claim pure presence in an actor makes on an audience's minds and lives.

Shakespeare has written a part that will reward and exhibit this power in the actor who possesses it. When in the third and fourth act Antony pulls back repeatedly from dejection, we respond to the radiance that returns; when he makes his followers weep, we can watch him deliberately using it. The power of presence in an actor is perilously close to glamor, but it can be taken beyond the limits of glamor by art. This is what the actors of Antony and Cleopatra are required to do, and the process works as a metaphor for that greatness Antony and Cleopatra both manifest, a greatness that comes to be

associated with the power of the imagination. Now, this is not the same quality that Hamlet makes paramount; nor is it, for example, the quality
stretched and tested in *King Lear*—the ability to keep reaching new and well-
discriminated levels of response to pain. In each case the quality emphasized
becomes part of the poetry of the play.

I am not simply saying that the actor of King Lear shows us pain in a play
about pain, the actor of Othello jealousy, and so forth. What I mean is that
the very problems posed by the need to achieve the qualities demanded by the
role become part of the meaning of the play. Let me try to make this clearer.
In *Lear,* the need for the leading actor to be outdoing himself in responding
to pain cannot be met by appearing to hold anything back in the opening
scenes. The actor must find a way to seem to reach an extreme from the start
and then break through again and again to worse and worse. How much more
can he take? we ask, and the sense of taking it, and the histrionic poetics of
taking it, become part of our experience of the play. I wrote about this a few
years ago in a book called *Shakespeare and the Energies of Drama*; now it
seems to me that much more can be done to link the poetics of acting Lear
with the poetry of the play. For example, one way an actor has of making an
emotion exact and vivid in a difficult scene, of preventing it from becoming
general or merely indicated, is to concentrate on an image or object. If he
feels in danger of losing an emotion or falsifying it, or of failing to differentiate it sufficiently, he may focus on a button, an eyebrow, or a chair, and
make that the recipient or evoker of his feeling. Now, Shakespeare has built
just such a technique into the role of Lear, made it, in fact, a recurring image—what might be called a histrionic image. The kind of focusing I have
described happens repeatedly, and it is part of the play's subtle and growing
insistence on human feeling as a source of value in the chaos of cruelty and
pain. Repeatedly we come down to those precious squares of sense which
Regan lies about in the opening scene. The button at the throat, the pin and
the pin-prick, the tears whose wetness Lear tests, the handclasp, the Fool's
shivering body, Cordelia's lips—these are all concrete focal points that keep
the actor's feeling fresh. They keep the part alive, they keep the pain coming
and growing and our perception of it fresh—instead of wiping out both the
actor and our ability to respond delicately. Thus they carry the audience further, in spite of the burden of unpleasantness; they give us an artistic achievement that we could not have without the burden. They give us the sensation
of advancing further into pain than we thought we could take, and advancing
not into generalized emotion or monotony, but into greater awareness,
greater sensitivity, which could only be achieved by going this far, by having
these many stages of exact response to increasing pain. And this, I think, is an
important part of the art and vision of *King Lear.*

I would like to turn now to another type of effect, one that comes through
very strongly when a scene is acted, but that is likely to be overlooked in

reading. This is the effect of emotional coloration or mood. It is likely to be quite as important as the words themselves. Indeed, rather than competing with the words or drowning them, the mood works to change the words, to modify their meaning, and thus becomes part of the poetry itself.

One could, for example, undertake a useful study of Prospero's anger in *The Tempest,* a study that would proceed on two levels. The first would deal with the content and imagery of Prospero's anger as expressed in the language of the play. This would explore that regular nagging, buzzing, beating disturbance that Prospero feels from time to time, particularly when contemplating the fallibility or weakness of mankind. It would help to define Prospero's anger as a recurring emotional motif with a precise intellectual content. The second level would complete the picture by tracing the way the emotion of anger colors scenes and speeches in which Prospero appears, altering the manifest  verbal content significantly.

The most striking instance occurs in the famous speech on dreams. The passage is usually played with the emotion suggested by the lines out of context: serene wisdom, grand confidence, advice to the young — a godlike survey of our insubstantial pageant. Yet the immediate context indicates a very different emotion. Prospero is angry, visibly and uncommonly disturbed:

> *Ferdinand:* This is strange! your father's in some passion
> 　　　　　That works him strongly.
> *Miranda:*　　　　　　Never till this day
> 　　　　　Saw I him touch'd with anger, so distemper'd.

His anger presumably is noticeable throughout his speech, for at the end of it he refers to his vexation as persisting. Indeed, after he has concluded, "And our little life is rounded with a sleep," Prospero seems to be apologizing for what he has just said:

> 　　　Sir, I am vex'd;
> Bear with my weakness; my old brain is troubled:
> Be not disturb'd with my infirmity.

His mind, as he goes on to say, is still "beating."

Naturally, I must expect disagreement over details of interpretation here, and again my concern is to note the value of a method rather than insist on a conclusion, but it seems to me that Prospero's speech has a different and rather richer meaning if we imagine it as rising out of and counterpointed by his anger. The Prospero I hear is not instructing us from a great distance on the mutability of earthly things, but working his way toward an acceptance that at this moment has its freight of bitterness. In preparing his revenge and in guarding against Caliban's plot, Prospero has campaigned patiently against the vices and human failings that typically goad him to anger. Now he must accept that the very human weakness that he has labored against is but an instance of the imperfection and instability of earthly things. Returning to Milan has meant much to him; his plans have been carefully laid and triumphantly executed; but now he is forced to recognize that they too are of a baseless fabric. Like the towers, the palaces, the whole world, himself, they are no more than a dream. The realization angers him — and this is itself a weakness, an infirmity, but this too he must acknowledge to be his. My reader may hear the speech somewhat differently, but my point is that by paying attention to the emotional indicators on the page, we can hear the performance in Shakespeare's words. We can hear the voice of an actor, and not that of a reverent reciter conveying one of Bartlett's more familiar quotations.

Closely related to this is the question of Miranda's inattentiveness in 1.2. We all remember that Prospero chides Miranda for not paying attention in that scene, but the critical fact is that he does so only during a very brief portion of his narrative, lines 77-106. This is the passage where he introduces the subject of his brother's treachery. Here his anger swells up, and Miranda cannot listen closely enough to satisfy him. The fact that still has power to shake him is "That a brother should be so perfidious." In the speech on dreams, we can watch Prospero's anger finally turning on himself.

I shall mention but one more broad category of technique worth watching for in Shakespeare — the manipulation of our theatrical expectations. Shakespeare never has trouble being as plain as day — when he wants to be. As early as the *Henry VI* plays he is able to use stage movement, rhythm, and costume to impose a clarifying order on multitudes of people and events. So when we come, in *Cymbeline*, on speeches which, even in the study, present a hopeless confusion of names and circumstances, we can guess that Shakespeare has something special in mind. The audience can scarcely make full sense of a speech (3.3.79-107) in which an entirely new character steps forward, and in the midst of asides about hunting and snatches of remembered dialogue rapidly informs us that he has brought up the two stolen sons of Cymbeline, that he is called Morgan but his real name is Belarius, the son called Polydore is properly Guiderius, while Cadwal, on the other hand, is Arviragus. Why has Shakespeare chosen to tell a complicated story in a more complicated way, simultaneously introducing three new characters, each of whom has two names, any one of which is very easily confused with two of the others? Especially since half the names are unnecessary. Clearly he wants the plot of *Cymbeline* to seem as bewilderingly complex as possible, in order, among other things, to heighten our awareness of the concluding scene as a comic *tour de force*. But my point again is one of method. We must watch our rhythms of expectation — and the way Shakespeare plays with our awareness that we *have* certain expectations.

Sometimes Shakespeare raises, thwarts, or satisfies our expectations surprisingly, as in the statue scene in *The Winter's Tale*, where we *know* Hermione is dead and yet eagerly keep scanning the peculiar hints that maybe she is not and that the story can finally end the way it has made us want it to. Or the scene where Hamlet finds the King at prayer and we are forced to balance our aroused desire for revenge with our knowledge that revenge plays do not end this way, especially in the middle of the third act. This device seems to be especially prominent in plays of mixed genre, the so-called problem plays or romances. Because, in the theater, we are part of a large group of diverse individuals, we are likely to be more aware there than in the study of variations in possible response to a scene—and thus, I would think, of divisions in our own response. Shakespeare seems to like to move us on the pivot of a divided response, as in both the statue scene and the bear scene in *Winter's Tale,* where an expectation gradually dawns that is likely to be felt at different moments in different parts of the theater—or in different parts of one's mind.

Methods and examples might easily be multiplied, but my message in this paper is really a very simple one. It is that we should pay attention to Shakespeare as a writer for actors, pay attention to what he gives his actors and requires of them, and to the ways he uses actors to shape an audience's response. These are not *production values* in the carelessly deprecatory sense the phrase is sometimes given, the sense of grace notes added after the mighty fact of Shakespeare's creation is over. What I am talking about is *part* of Shakespeare's creation. To ignore the presence of the actors, as the text allows them and requires them to be present, is simply to refuse to read all that Shakespeare has written. It is like deliberately skipping every other word. Of course, one-half of *Hamlet* is a lot more than none, and the purely literary Shakespeare can keep us busy and happy and even wise. But it is a mistake to speak as if we have a choice between a literary Shakespeare and a theatrical Shakespeare. The choice is rather between some of Shakespeare and more of him.

# Sight and Space: The Perception of Shakespeare on Stage and Screen

## by J. L. STYAN

I believe that "the play" is what an audience perceives, whether it is on the stage or on the screen. Not only is the printed text merely the score, the roughest of blueprints (to use the current clichés) for the actual experience of the play, but the performance itself is not the experience either. It is rather the occasion for stimulus and reaction, in which the meaning and value of the experience reside finally in what an audience takes away. So in discussing Shakespeare on stage or screen, it is not productive to assert that one medium is better or worse than another. It may be that what is seen on a particular stage and in a particular film is of a wholly different order, and neither may be as Shakespeare intended.

Therefore it is not helpful to argue that Shakespeare's verbal images get lost or go astray when translated into visual images on the screen. The British film director Karel Reisz once told me that he thought film's impact was eighty percent visual and twenty percent verbal; if on the stage it is fifty/fifty, it is a mistake to try to equate what is unequal. We may feel embarrassed when visual and verbal images jar, as when Hamlet's "sea of troubles" becomes Olivier's waves breaking at the foot of the castle of Elsinore, or when Orson Welles as Macbeth speaks his "Tomorrow, and tomorrow, and tomorrow" accompanied by shots of storm clouds that suggest a change in the weather; as one reviewer, Paul Dehn, reported, "There will be a deep depression, and a deep depression, and a deep depression over Scotland." However, incongruity is not unknown in stage productions either. In 1951 Michael Benthall offered a masquelike *Tempest* in which the "wild waters" of the shipwreck were distractingly represented by the backsides of so many undulating sea nymphs, and some will know of Max Reinhardt's *A Midsummer Night's Dream* in which Titania's fairy train was staffed by a number of very substantial fairies.

Unfruitful arguments also surround the degree of realism imposed upon a Shakespearean play. Shakespeare has many striking scenes which are basically realistic in conception, and many moments in which he supports the actor by realistic detail: he knows, after all, that an audience needs reassurance that, even in the most ritualistic of plays, there is a link with its own reality. Nevertheless, most of Shakespeare is unconcerned with such illusion. Now it may be that the film, because of the nature of the photographic medium, tends to fill its visual vacuum with realistic details. But the truth is that, historically, both stage and screen have sinned in decorating Shakespeare's scenes to the point of smothering them. It amuses us now to remember Olivier's sea of troubles and wonder whether we are yet to have a glimpse of the slings and arrows of outrageous fortune; or to see Polanski's Macbeth naked in bed with his Lady and ask again Bradley's realistic question (in his notorious "Note EE"), How many children had Lady Macbeth? But not so long ago great stage actors like Beerbohm Tree had Richard II riding across the stage in Her Majesty's Theatre on horseback, sank a complete ship for *The Tempest,* and polluted the wood near Athens (and part of the theater) with live rabbits.

It is arguable that the strictly visual elements of the play are common to both media. If the spectator sees Hamlet dressed in his "nighted color," with all that this implies for the Prince's initial attitude in the play, the perception will be much the same on stage or screen. If, however, the film is in monochrome black and white, like Olivier's *Hamlet*, there must be some loss of affective meaning when Shakespeare calls for the conflicting color of the gaudy court. But frequently the film can emphasize the intended perception with point and insight, as when Kozintsev stampedes his horses at the appearance of the Ghost, or when Olivier presents Richard Crookback in close-up and direct address to the audience for the opening soliloquy in *Richard III.* When Tyrone Guthrie directed Alec Guiness in *Richard III* at Stratford, Ontario, in 1953, he had Richard open the play by strolling out onto the balcony and, according to Walter Kerr's review on 15 July in the *New York Herald Tribune,* "swinging one leg over its side like a slightly dour monkey" as he slowly surveyed the audience with a grin on his face. Both Olivier's and Guthrie's effects worked well. And sometimes the film can stimulate the intended perception in a unique way, as when in *Hamlet's* gravediggers' scene that magic skull, representing as it does first Ophelia's death, then the memory of poor Yorick, then Gertrude's mortality ("let her paint an inch thick, to this favor she must come. Make her laugh at that"), that universal skull was in Olivier's hands suddenly covered by his shadow, so that the bone seemed to be clothed in his own flesh, and thus finally to represent himself.

Nevertheless, not all the visual effects possible to the play in performance are common to both media. It is possible to distinguish two elements of visual communication, I think, in which each medium speaks differently. The first of these is the element of improvisation, which is characteristic of live performance. Every part in Shakespeare is in some degree an invitation to the player to improvise with his lines, to flesh out the skeleton provided by the code of words. Before a live audience this act of fleshing out is noticeably responsive to the reactions of those watching: a characterization grows richer or poorer according to the quality of immediacy generated by the theater event. An audience's sense of "now" distinguishes live theater from any mechanical substitute, and it is this quality of freshness and spontaneity that colors the whole experience of the play, and must vary from night to night. In Shakespeare there is, however, a great range between those lines which are disciplined by the control of the verse and the sort of action that permits freedom to improvise. When Malvolio plays the "turkey-cock," "practicing behavior to his own shadow," having "the humor of state," and so forth, the lines indicate what the actor must do. But as characterization relaxes, as it does for the clown in frontal address to the audience, Shakespeare gives the actor more and more freedom to respond to the audience and build upon the reaction to the response. At this point the film is at a loss. And some of Shakespeare's greatest scenes are left entirely to the moment, it would seem. For one well-known example, the duel between Viola and Andrew Aguecheek in *Twelfth Night* is marked in the text by the barest of stage directions: *"They draw."* It is as if Shakespeare sets up a pregnant situation, matching an effeminate man with a girl dressed as a man, and then leaves the rest to the actors and their improvisation. There are a hundred ways of fulfilling that simple stage direction with hilarious results.

There is a second and more fundamental visual element in which the grammar of the film and the grammar of the theater are at odds. This is the control of space possible to the camera's eye and to the human eye. In my teaching, I find that silence and space are the two aspects of Shakespeare's art that have been generally neglected. The film appears to have complete freedom in space, and certainly it is very much at home with all the contrasts of mood and tone, place and action, of which the Elizabethan stage was capable, and in which Shakespeare so much delighted when he built one scene upon another. The camera's eye is able to place a precise emphasis when it so wishes, as when it records a smile on Marlon Brando's face so that Antony can convey that the battle in *Julius Caesar* is going well. And crosscutting back and forth between Iago and Othello can convey moment by moment the progress of their intimacy in the temptation scene. But the camera's eye, whether in close-up or in long shot, whether in particular or in general, whether catching the gnarled hands of Orson Welles as Macbeth the murderer or the colorful but unfocused survey of the field of Agincourt in *Henry V*, can see only one thing at a time, Cyclops that it is.

The human eye is a dozen simultaneous cameras, able to zoom in for a close-up and take a general picture simultaneously. The point is clear when you see Chekhov on the screen, since Chekhov deals in the multiple ironies of a large family group with each member responding individually. At best the camera can catch one or two faces at a time as it tracks or cuts back and forth, and the general disintegration of the family in *Uncle Vanya,* when Professor Serebriakov announces that he is going to sell the estate, is lost as an effect on the screen. On the other hand, Ibsen tends to write for pairs of characters, and his duologues at critical moments come across very well. This distinction between these two great realists indicates the degree to which each has conceived his action visually.

In the opening scene of *Romeo and Juliet,* the human eye can watch the main contenders, Tybalt and Benvolio, in their fight and also be sharply aware of the growing melee about them. It can watch Hamlet closely as he considers suicide in the "To be or not to be" soliloquy, while simultaneously taking in the image of a pious Ophelia at her orisons, and of Polonius and the King shaking the arras in the background, the total picture compelling us to modify the Prince's speech as both a religious and a political statement. It can see Macbeth as he invokes the darkness, and simultaneously link "night's black agents" with the murderers of Banquo as they make their fearsome entrance. In all these instances we are faced with a complexity of perception that came naturally to the Elizabethan stage with its multiple acting areas, a stage whose size and neutrality encouraged two or more things to happen at once. And if in a film the thinking is done in the cutting-room, in a rhetorical drama like Shakespeare's the editing, as it were, occurs whenever the form and style of its language change. The harsh and colloquial lines of Lady Macbeth after the murder of Duncan,

> These deeds must not be thought
> After these ways: so, it will make us mad

are set shockingly against Macbeth's incantations as his imagination takes flight:

> Methought, I heard a voice cry, "Sleep no more!
> Macbeth does murther Sleep," the innocent Sleep;
> Sleep, that knits up the ravell'd sleave of care.
> (2.2.32-36)

Macbeth and his Lady are playing on different levels, and as the audience, guided by the poetry, perceives the difference, so it separates the practical concerns of the lady from the urgent demands of the dreamer's mind. As the ear focuses on the longer, rounder speeches of the man, so the eye tries to dismiss the woman and her distracting interjections. The spectator in the theater controls his own spatial relationships as he answers the needs of his perception, while the film director with his one eye tends to thrust himself between the performance and its audience.

Shakespeare's sense of space and spatial meaning are communicated differently on the open stage and on the screen. There are at least five separate spatial effects for which the human eye works in ways other than those of the camera's eye.

1) A character in soliloquy, seen alone on some 1,000 square feet of platform space, is *not* the same as in a film close-up, as is often maintained. The film captures the intimacy, maybe, but not the simultaneous quality of isolation. However, the film can achieve the isolation of a Hamlet or Lear by long shot, relying upon qualities in the actor's voice to maintain an illusion of intimacy.

2) The presence on stage of two characters positioned in depth can exercise a powerful control over an audience's disposition toward them, determining its degree of sympathy or antipathy. So in the first court scene in *Hamlet*, Claudius is to be observed upstage at a distance, and we respond with more warmth to a downstage Hamlet, even when he is silent. Shakespeare helps the responses, of course, by contrasting their ages, their costumes, and so on, and by giving the King the cold, smooth, Latinized, political language of a remote and upstage character. On the three-dimensional open stage, this upstage-downstage, north-to-south differentiation of characters comes easily. The camera, on the other hand, has a problem: to gain the focus on one character, it may easily lose it on the other if there is blocking in depth. The prime example of this difficulty in recent years was the injustice done to Olivier's Othello when his upstage performance, marked by declamatory verse ("Farewell the tranquil mind, farewell content; / Farewell the plumed troop, and the big wars"), was equalized by close-ups of Frank Finlay's Iago speaking intimately in prose. It was said that Iago stole Othello's scenes.

3) Any duologue assumes its dramatic qualities by the space, or lack of it, between the two speakers. When Antony and Cleopatra, or Othello and Desdemona, first greet each other, the implicit directions in their lines indicate that they embrace and kiss ("Here is my space," "The nobleness of life / Is to do thus," "And this and this the greatest discords be," etc.). By contrast, the idealizing balcony scene in *Romeo and Juliet* is managed differently. Shakespeare is careful to place Juliet out of reach of Romeo, and this distance adds to the lyrical and ethereal quality in their words. Remove the balcony, so to speak, as Castellani did by melting away the iron bars that divided the lovers with the zooming lens of the camera, or as Zeffirelli did by having Romeo climb a tree to bring the lovers into close-up, and the "bright angel," the "winged messenger of heaven," and the "dear saint" begins to look a little fleshly.

4) Movement to telescope space between two characters must be observed by the spectator. The sexual tension implicit in the first scene between Angelo and Isabella in *Measure for Measure* is strongly reinforced by the closing of the thirty or forty feet between them when Isabella first begins her plea for her brother's life. At all times in this scene (2.2) Angelo tries to keep his distance, at first appearing haughty and cold, even turning his shoulder on Isabella as she speaks. But Isabella, also cold and pious like the nun she aspires to be, has at her elbow none other than Lucio, of the Devil's party. Time and again he invites her to do a better job of persuasion:

> —Give't not o'er so. — To him again, entreat him. . . .
> To him, I say.
> —You are too cold.
> —Ay, touch him: there's the vein.
> —O, to him, to him, wench! He will relent;
> He's coming: I perceive't.

Lucio's lines are all implicit stage directions designed not only to encourage her eloquence, but also to close the gap between the man and the woman, and at a specific pace, tantalizingly slow. For an audience to watch this progress of Isabella across the stage is to induce that special sexual tension which only we can supply when our senses are "betrayed" like Angelo's. The scene enacts the line he speaks in soliloquy after she has left: "The tempter, or the tempted, who sins most?" The answer in stagecraft is that *we* do, since the audience plays both roles, judge and nun, tempted and tempter, just as we play both Richard Crookback and the Lady Anne in another devilishly contrived scene of seduction.

5) Shakespeare divides a scene by taking a character or characters aside from the main group, especially if the image of the group and what it represents remains important as we focus on those who are separated. The requirement is that of split vision. Cordelia is visually separated from Lear and her sisters by her striking asides in the scene of the division of the kingdom. Ignoring this, Peter Brook's shooting of this moment was an exercise in confusion. The viewer must see as well as hear "What shall Cordelia speak? Love, and be silent" as an aside if the formality of the speech and posture of Goneril and Regan is to be perceived ironically. Cordelia must break the symmetry of the ritualistic stage composition for us to anticipate its hypocrisy. In a similar way we must recognize the isolation of Coriolanus from the citizenry when he makes his appearance in the "gown of humility." We must be aware of both parties when Brutus and Cassius are standing apart from Caesar's procession. Malcolm and Donalbain are of equal importance with the rest at the scene of their father's murder when they separate themselves. Examples are legion, and can be multiplied if Shakespeare's scenes of eavesdropping are added. These are scenes of double focus, in which the meaning of the whole is felt

only if both groups are of equal visual importance and if simultaneity in the action is captured. The impact of Iago's ugly aside,

> O, you are well tun'd now,
> But I'll set down the pegs that make this music,
> As honest as I am.
>                   (2.1.199-201)

is inseparable from the harmonious picture of Othello embracing Desdemona.

The eloquent element of space speaks to the audience in some degree from start to finish of performance, constantly making character distinctions and controlling audience responses, constantly underscoring line and gesture. To test the differences between the stage and the cinematic image, the gains and losses in spatial values, recall the fight between Mercutio, Tybalt, and Romeo in the lively movie by Franco Zeffirelli. Here an uncompromising realist takes every opportunity that offers itself in a highly charged, exuberant scene. It is not just that he succumbs to the temptation to open out the scenes for their pictorial possibilities, with shots of Verona's beautiful courtyards and sun-scorched walls. (We have come to expect this kind of thing when a stage play is adapted for the screen.) It is as if Zeffirelli is bent on sinning happily against the declamatory style and the academic approach. The energy of his street scenes comes of fine cutting-room judgments, a mercurial camera, and a ranging, not to say sprawling, sense of battlefield.

In Zeffirelli's idea, it is Mercutio, not Tybalt, who seems to be looking for trouble, and it is Mercutio whose imaginatively expanded details of characterization steal the scene from Romeo. Nor is Romeo's presence much felt during the subsequent duel. When Mercutio whistles with the sword at his throat, has his rapier pinned to the ground, and pretends cowardice by running up a cart in the piazza; when he humiliates Tybalt with some pretty business with a pitchfork and puts him in a temper—in all this Zeffirelli's focus is wholly on his favorite and we are repeatedly offered Mercutio's point of view.

The scene extraordinarily extends the action of the fighting, where such emphasis is barely suggested in the text. Repeatedly the element of realistic spontaneity is introduced (as when Mercutio chances on a pitchfork, or Romeo grabs a weapon at the last minute). The natural street setting is thoroughly exploited for a deadly arena, the pace of the battle pursued for suspense from square to street and back again. Physically it is exhilarating, and spatially it is wholly convincing, although, clearly, the energetic use of the actors in their work area is not always conceived for the sake of the tragedy. Is all this of a sufficient representation of Shakespeare's careful plan for his own stage: the spaced-out rhythm of the scene, with Romeo's static moments of isolation and evaluation, principally designed to keep the spotlight on Romeo, not Mercutio, and on the play's theme? Shakespeare's scene, the turning point in the play, is planned to show Romeo in the painful process of becoming a tragic hero.

Zeffirelli's kind of film-making disguises the conflict between author and director remarkably well, and maybe we would rather have the zest of this kind of treatment at any price. But what might happen in another kind of crowd scene in which spatial tensions constitute the whole point of the action? Space is not necessarily marked out by movement, and while the eye or the camera may generalize the mood or atmosphere of a scene, a dramatic sense of space most often calls for stillness and focus. In this it is as if the eye of the spectator must be free to travel between himself and the character, as well as between character and character, measuring distance, absorbing reactions, re-creating tensions by his perception, an act of instantaneous mutuality. Thus by perception two characters become a dramatic relationship, the two become one, a third something.

To put this another way: a stage ought not to be seen as a kind of makeshift room. In a realistic play, characters enter, exit, and behave as if they were at home in a kitchen, a living room, a bedroom, or whatever. Space has been subjected to the reductive forces of verisimilitude, and in its turn a film made in the realistic mode will have its camera eye seem, as in life, to glance from one person to another, itself a third person in the room. But only on rare occasions did the Elizabethan stage try to be a room (Capulet's ballroom, Isabella's convent, Macbeth's banquet hall). Most of the time it was an unlocalized, neutral area, available to be split into two, three, or more parts, with clear distinctions made between one character and another, this group and that. Only the spectator is in a position to connect the characters or the groups by making simultaneous perceptions. These perceptions are the basis for interpretation by an audience, and to relate and synthesize what is perceived from moment to moment is to make drama meaningful. We see Viola trying to escape her duel with Andrew Aguecheek as he is simultaneously trying to escape his with her; as a result, we equate the mock man with the effeminate man and find them equally ridiculous. We see Puck casually arrange Helena next to the sleeping Demetrius, and Hermia next to Lysander. In this puzzle perhaps Puck gets the help of the audience, if it can remember who belongs to whom. But certainly he displays his rather amoral fairy precept that "Jack shall have Jill," that is, it doesn't matter much to him who is Jack and who is Jill as long as he gets the sexes roughly right. As a result, we recognize the joke that the pairs of undying lovers are virtually interchangeable.

I have selected a scene as complicated as the play scene in *Hamlet* (3.2) in order to illustrate this kind of spatial interpretation. The film director must choose: either show Hamlet's face watching the King as the King watches the

Players, whereby we lose the King's reactions, or show the King watching the
Players, whereby we lose Hamlet. The camera can select first one and then
the other and then the third, but in so doing the director does our perceiving
and so our thinking for us, and the quality of immediacy and simultaneity
may be lost, the very basis of tension felt in the audience.

There is another difficulty, one of interpretation. In John Dover Wilson's
view, Claudius "must be lured gradually and *unconsciously* into the trap, and
then caught — squealing. In other words, the audience must feel satisfied that
he knows nothing of what awaits him," and he goes on, "We must show either
that the King was not watching the dumb-show . . . , or that he was not unmoved as he watched it" (*What Happens in Hamlet* [Cambridge, 1935], pp.
146,151). And so we very often see the King looking the other way when the
dumb-show begins, too busy drinking or making passes at the Queen. In this
argument Dover Wilson is motivating the actor realistically, and not seeing as
the audience sees. In my view the King must see the dumb show from start to
finish, and we must see him see it, if the spatial tensions in this scene of
unspoken feelings are to be given their proper beginning.

One or two of the scene's visual and spatial elements are of special importance. First, there are at least three centers of visual attraction, each seen by
the audience and seen to be seen by each other: Claudius and Gertrude,
Hamlet and Ophelia, and the Player King and Queen. I believe also that the
on-stage audience of courtiers, with their changing reactions to "the murder
of Gonzago," is important to the outcome of the scene. The full quality of tension in the scene can be felt only if each center is situated so that each can supply the audience with a separate perception. In this way the audience should
see all the groups interacting at the same time. Elizabethan sightlines permitted the spectator to watch the mousetrap play, the response of Claudius and
his Queen to what they saw, and to be aware of the court watching
everything. Above all, the audience should have the sense of watching the
play and its royal spectators *with* Hamlet, aided by the presence of Horatio.
Dramatic tension in the scene arises from watching the watchers being
watched.

Second, Shakespeare's text indicates how the blocking could be arranged,
as if the author were working the visual problems out in his head as he wrote.
Hamlet as the royal entertainer is given the job of stage-manager; but then,
this is appropriate, since he wishes to be sure his contrivance will work.
Hamlet tells Horatio to "get a place," presumably where he can be the
Prince's surrogate eyes. Hamlet has a word with the King, Polonius, and the
Queen as he guides each in turn to the area of the throne, that is, upstage in
the conventional position where King and Queen are visible to everyone,
especially to Hamlet and the audience. He has also already chosen his own
place:

> *Queen:* Come hither, my dear Hamlet, sit by me.
> *Hamlet:* No, good mother, here's metal more attractive.

$$(3.2.108-9)$$

Upon this, he takes the opportunity to seize Ophelia's arm and lead her downstage to the position where he can watch the throne: it is pretty obvious that he is not really concerned whether Ophelia has a good time or not. The wide open spaces of the middle of the platform are thus left free for the performance of the Player King and Queen.

There are signs all through the performance of the play-within-the-play that Hamlet is at least watching the throne, although all his remarks in this respect turn upon Gertrude, not Claudius: "Look you how cheerfully my mother looks," and, upon Ophelia's comment on the brevity of the dumb-show, "As woman's love." It is as if there is nothing unusual to report about the King's behavior. When the Player Queen speaks of widowhood, Hamlet is alarmed lest Gertrude, not Claudius, should stop the show: "If she should break it now!" And it is his mother whom he teases first with "Madam, how like you this play?" All this is at least to suggest that Hamlet is watching as he said he would, and encouraging us to look where he is looking. If from his downstage position we see chiefly the back of his head, we are constantly aware of his mind and attitude if only because he talks so much, and up to a point we feel him to be our representative on the stage at this critical moment.

But it is evident he is getting no reaction from the King, and in the end Hamlet's attention is turned upon Claudius himself, the cause and purpose of the whole device. If the swift performance of the dumb show has served to start a silent contest of wits with Claudius, the long speeches of the Players, growing more particular in their words, serve to draw out the suspense. By the silence of the King, this is a visual suspense, and it is a suspense for Hamlet as it is for us. Certainly it is Hamlet himself who can stand it no longer, and it is he who breaks the tension as his voice rings out across the theater to his uncle: the taunts are heard in the tone of "poison in jest" . . . "mouse-trap" . . . "begin, murderer" . . . " 'a poisons him i' th' garden for's estate," the sibilants full of hate, the words so violent that it is not unlikely that Hamlet has been lifted to his feet in his vehemence. The court audience has an important task at this stage. As it hears Hamlet's pointed comments, and as it grows aware of the play's criticism of the royal house of Denmark, in ones and twos it switches its attention to the throne. We the real audience see the onstage audience begin to understand that the murder of Gonzago is in truth the murder of King Hamlet. To my mind it is this concentration of public notice together with Hamlet's insults that cause the break in tension and bring Claudius to his feet for the climactic cry, "Give me some light—away!"

From this reading of the scene, based upon its spatial elements, it is not possible to determine whether the King has revealed his guilt by stopping the play, or has merely expressed his exasperation at his nephew's insults. But for all Hamlet's self-questioning, was there ever any doubt in the audience's mind that Claudius was guilty? I take it that the real dramatic interest of the scene lies not in the audience's chance to prove the accusations of the Ghost right or wrong, but in our pleasure in observing the tensions, strongly visual and reinforced by carefully placed words, between those who are watching each other as much as they are the play itself. It is a time-honored principle of the drama that an audience appreciates most that knows most — and certainly if it knows more than the characters themselves. The silences between the watching groups, between the King and the Player King, the Queen and the Player Queen, between the King and Hamlet, Hamlet and the Queen, and between the Court and the Throne — the silences do the talking.

It is as if Laurence Olivier knew this when he filmed the scene virtually as dumb-show, allowing the camera to speak for the actors. His 1948 film of *Hamlet*, like Zeffirelli's *Romeo and Juliet*, was based on a stage performance. Tyrone Guthrie had directed Olivier in an energetic, Freudian production at the Old Vic just before the war in 1937. Olivier's decision to make the film in black and white was to enable him to use deep-focus cameras and to match tone to mood. In the event, the black and white added to the monotone of the film's slow pace and the persistent rolling of the camera along the corridors of a labyrinthine palace, the cavernous castle of Elsinore. One critic generously suggested that the camera moved around the set like "a silent observer of great events, eager not to miss any." In effect, the audience was entirely at the mercy of this relentless camera, and what it chose to observe, and for how long. Olivier added to this his deep-focus technique, gratifying a camera with a special penchant for peering into bedrooms. The film was a long one, in spite of many cuts and omissions, and it was decided to make all the points of the play scene with virtually no words at all. Olivier's roving camera, aided by William Walton's brooding score, picking up the expressions on the faces of the opposing forces as the Players mime the poisoning, and ending with a full shot of the panic in the court on "Give me some light!" may give us enough to test the capability of the film medium to handle a scene like this.

Olivier's camera works hard to grant us many points of view. We see Hamlet's keen anticipation as the court makes its formal entrance. We take note of Polonius's taking note of Hamlet at Ophelia's feet, as if his judgment of the Prince's malaise has been proved. With Horatio we see the kiss exchanged between the Player King and Queen, and then are shown the initial inattention of Claudius and Gertrude (a concession to Dover Wilson). When Lucianus the poisoner pours his poison in the ear of the sleeping man, the camera sees that Claudius sees and that he is transfixed. When the aroused Player King points his accusing finger at his murderer, along with Hamlet and Horatio and all the court, the camera looks hard at Claudius as if all the evidence were in. When the Player Queen sheds her tears, the camera is swinging freely behind Hamlet and Ophelia, Claudius and Gertrude, Horatio and Polonius. As Lucianus consoles the Player Queen, the camera passes around the circle again, and then again. Finally it comes to rest on Claudius, who climbs to his feet and cries out for light. At this point the set becomes a swirl of movement as the image dissolves to find Hamlet standing poised on the throne with the torch he had thrust in the King's face, and singing at the top of his voice. Hamlet and Olivier have decided that the Ghost was right.

Olivier's rule for this complex scene seems to have been to create tension and meaning out of camera movement. In lieu of Shakespeare's pattern — of the audience watching Hamlet watching the throne watching the players — Olivier has done what only the film can do: provide a constantly changing point of view, but especially cutting between Hamlet and Claudius until the latter cracks up. However, for all the camera movement throughout the scene, the point of view is finally Hamlet's alone — that is, Hamlet is the winner. Now this reading of the scene is a legitimate one, although it is not necessarily Shakespeare's. The important spatial difference between the scene as it might be staged and what we see on the screen is that on the stage Shakespeare can sustain the mystery and promote its ambivalence, as so often in his tragedies, while on the screen it is harder for the camera to remain neutral — it must forever be pointing and making statements.

There is one other related point. In the general absence of words to do the talking, William Walton's music assumes abnormal importance. His ensemble for this scene — the woodwind cor anglais, oboe, and bassoon, plus two violas, cello, and harpsichord — captures very well the idiom of the Elizabethan period. But it is worth noting that the actual structure of the scene, its progress to a crisis, is less dependent upon the Player King and Queen and the glances exchanged by the Court, that is, the internal source of the tension, than upon the external tension induced by the music. It is cheating a bit when the music finally swells up to full orchestration as if to cry "Eureka!"

To summarize: When Olivier's camera travels on the faces of his actors, we see what we are told to see. This treatment is a kind of simplification, for in effect it replaces Shakespeare's cat's-cradle of interactions by spelling out the mood and atmosphere of the scene at secondhand. In the theater, the act of perception is directly experienced, and the scene's dramatic tension is what an audience receives and enjoys in the act of direct perception, since it is part of our creative and interpretative contribution to the making of the play. If the film camera reduces our function and does too much of the thinking for us, dissolving too much of the space that our eyes must scan and span, we remain passive spectators and, with all its urgent movement, the scene is visually a still-life picture.

# The Visual Arts of
# Shakespeare's Day

## by JOHN DIXON HUNT

When Sir Henry Unton died in 1596, while on a diplomatic mission to France, an anonymous, but probably Flemish, artist recorded various events from his private and public life on a panel that is now in the National Portrait Gallery, London. Its engaging, often spirited, panorama provides a useful focus for my survey of the visual arts in Shakespeare's day.[1] It reminds us that Elizabethan painting was almost entirely portraiture—an emphasis that Shakespeare's references to paintings also confirm, for we think of various crucial portraits: Silvia's in *Two Gentlemen,* Portia's inside the leaden casket, the pair that Hamlet enjoins his mother to compare; and there are others. If Sir Henry Unton's artist *was* Flemish, that is also significant, for there was little conspicuous native talent. His anonymity, too, is eloquent of the role of the artist in England, a craftsman practicing a trade rather than looking for personal renown. The portrait section itself hovers between a shrewd attention to Unton's personality, which was quite a rare concern at the time, as Roy Strong has shown in his various studies of Tudor portraiture,[2] and a commitment, which the panel as a whole proclaims, to Unton's *example.* For his image presides over a pageant of typical events: the trumpeting angel and the skeleton of death announce, together with the detail of Unton's birth, what E. M. Forster once called the "unavoidable termini" of human life.[3] The panel, dominated by death, makes its central character simply another human *exemplum*—perhaps a surviving mediaeval emphasis, though the magnificent piece of tomb sculpture is, as we shall see, typically Elizabethan. But it is also as if the whole chronicle of Unton's life and travels, themselves the type of a dedicated public career, is to be read simply as a *vanitas* subject. Erasmus in his *Preparation to Deathe,* published in London in 1538, had written what this Unton panel also exemplifies:

We be wayfarynge men in this worlde, not inhabytantes, we be as strangers in Innes (or to speke it better) in bouthes or tentes, we lyue not in our country. This holle lyfe is nothing elles but a rennynge to deathe, and that very shorte, but death is the gate of euerlastynge lyfe.[4]

Unton was himself a wayfaring man in the world—the images of him in the Low Countries, the French Court, and in Italy and at Oxford testify to that. But it is also worth remarking how little aware the painter seems to be of, say, the Italian or French Renaissance: the artist's image of Venice, basking immediately below the sun, declares little to nothing of Venice's preeminence in English eyes as a popular center of modern Italian culture.[5] I shall have occasion to notice again how random at best, at worst how nonexistent, were evidences of Italian Renaissances in England. Paradoxically, the masque at Sir Henry's banquet has affinities with Italian and French courtly entertainment as well as with English—the Diana who leads the masquers wears a crescent moon in her headdress and holds a bow and arrow and could have stepped out convincingly in Medici *intermezzi*, Valois *ballets*, or Elizabethan progresses.

It is, then, an exhilarating randomness of styles and artistic tastes that characterizes Elizabethan England. Though an earlier example, there is perhaps no better demonstration of the coexistence of strong, continuing native tradition with new Renaissance ideas from abroad than the placing of the Italian sculptor Torrigiano's bronze effigy of Henry VII, assured in its realistic likeness, under the late Gothic fan tracery of the chapel built by that same king. The later sixteenth and early seventeenth centuries are studied with similar cultural juxtapositions: the strange, dreamlike outlines of Nonsuch, which Henry VIII began in 1538, may be an attempt to rival the Chateau of Chambord in France, but it was erected entirely by English workmen and is really no more than what Sir John Summerson calls "an unusually magniloquent expression of the favorite of all Tudor themes, the mass flanked by octagons."[6] Yet the decoration of Nonsuch was certainly influenced from abroad—Evelyn in 1666 suspected Italian workmanship for the "statues and bass relievos" and we may be fairly certain of an Italian inspiration mediated through the School of Fontainebleau. A similar mixture of native and Italianate characterizes the Jacobean Hatfield House: the wings are substantial Tudor, but the central colonnade has a pedigree that stretches back to the loggias of the Farnesina in Rome and the central arch displays all three classical orders, which John Shute had been the first to illustrate in England, drawing upon Vitruvius and Serlio for *The First and Chief Grounds of Architecture* in 1563.

Architecture generally was susceptible rather to decoration from abroad than to basic structural thinking. A Palladian groundplan may lie behind the form of Hardwick and Serlio's version of Poggio Reale at Naples behind Wollaton;[7] but neither façade—extravagant pastiche at Wollaton, romantic castellar at Hardwick—gives away those classicizing models of Italian formal design. The influence of the decorative programs at Nonsuch under Henry VIII, as well as its romantic styling, was to extend throughout Elizabethan and Jacobean architecture. Kirby Hall in Northamptonshire happily mingles rather simple and rectangular Tudor forms with extravagant and sophisticated exploiting of pilaster and ornamentation. What Sir John Summerson calls the "festive" spirit of Kirby[8] is the mood, too, of other examples of prodigy Elizabethan building: often they were devised precisely for the festivals associated with visits by the Queen, and their splendors were designed as both tributes and monuments of loyalty. Their styles vary from the unique coherence of Longleat, the result doubtless of the twenty years of its construction and revision that produced the restraint and refinement of a rhythmic symmetry, to the rather severe and unadventurous treatment of walls at Wimbledon House; yet here there was also a fine example, obviously derived from Italy, of movement between terraces via a series of dividing stairways. Jacobean buildings also maintained these dramatic manipulations of mass, together with a fascination with silhouette and a relative disregard for the interior disposition of rooms. It may serve as a final illustration of the eclecticism of styles—with which, I suggest, there is some analogy to Shakespeare's mingling of native folklore with classical mythology in *A Midsummer Night's Dream*[9]—to point out how the romantic and mannerist rhythms and ornamentation of Audley End, Hatfield, or Bolsover Castle were barely completed before the new and thoughtful classicism of Inigo Jones's Banqueting House began to rise in Whitehall.

There is a crucial element of dream about much of this architecture. Inigo Jones's work in Whitehall or at Arundel House, the reposeful originality of Longleat, the romanticism of Bolsover Castle—all are dreams of a past made afresh in the present. William Harrison's *Description of England* claims that

> If ever curious building did flourish in England it is in these our years wherein our workmen excel and are in manner comparable in skill with old Vitruvius and Serlo (and Alberti's name is joined to theirs in a later edition).[10]

We may capture something of these architectural dreams by viewing the Gate of Virtue at Caius College, Cambridge, in the light both of its allusion to Roman triumphal arches and to the antiquarian enthusiasms of Francesco Colonna's *Hypnerotomachia;* some of the rather clumsy woodcuts of the English version of this work, published as *The Strife of Love in a Dreame* in 1592, suggest the romantic delight in classical revivals that also informs the gate at Caius.[11]

One interior development of Elizabethan architecture was the long gallery, usually devoted to portraits, the dominant painterly form in England at this time. The range of portraiture was as varied in its own way as that of domestic architecture. A huge bulk of mass-produced images was designed to fill the walls of these fashionable new galleries. But some work distinguishes itself from that routine industry. There were the early examples of relentless, High Renaissance realism by Hans Holbein the Younger, in England from about 1531 until his death in 1543. But this dedication to actual likenesses was also extended by Holbein into the invocation of portraiture as historical testimony, modern images of honor and renown displayed for our emulation in the same fashion as classical *exempla* adorned the courts of Urbino or Ferrara. Holbein's cartoon for a fresco in the Privy Council Chamber (executed 1537) shows both Henry VII and Henry VIII and is obviously an imitation of Mantegna's frescoes of the Gonzaga family in the Camera degli Sposi at Mantua, which Holbein knew and which also evinces a determination to celebrate the illustrious example of contemporary figures.

Holbein's style of portraiture, however, was soon overtaken by taste from the Low Countries, notably a mannerist obsession with lavish accessories in a portrait rather than with the sitter's personality: William Scrots's work is of this order. Such an emphasis suited the use of portraiture as a mode of symbolic language: in the vast majority of representations of Queen Elizabeth it is less her character and likeness than her attributes that are the subject (e.g., the Armada or Ditchley portrait). These mythical endeavors could be treated with tenderness and even a touch of fantasy, as in the "Rainbow" portrait, possibly by Isaac Oliver, or with a stiffer, linear formalism, as in the Ditchley version.

A "hand, or eye / By Hilliard drawne," wrote Donne, "is worth an history / By a worse painter made."[12] Nicholas Hilliard is supremely important, as perhaps his invocation by Donne might suggest, for his emancipation of portraiture from a public, even political, to a private art, an occasion for intimate personal secrets. We have the record of Sir James Melville that the Queen was reluctant to show him the "little picture" of her current favorite, Leicester.[13] Limning, as opposed to painting, was the art of capturing "grace in countenance by which the affections appear," "wittye smilings" or "stolne glances." The phrases are Hilliard's, from his "Art of Limning,"[14] and they are redolent of all the pleasures of intimacy; the exchange of miniatures between Edward II and Gaveston in Marlowe's play suggests no less.

The allegorical and symbolical portraiture of the public domain has affinities with another whole range of art, which, though scarcely practiced in England, was obviously known and popular there. The famous image of Sir John Luttrell welcomed from the ravages of the sea by the figure of Peace (1550) is known to be directly influenced by the Fontainebleau School and perhaps more distantly by such allegories as Bronzino's. These figurings of abstract ideas, however eloquent their visual language, still require our verbal elucidation of their meanings. The Luttrell picture actually contains its own verbal addition:

> Mor [than] the rock amlodys [i.e., admidst] ye raging seas
> The constant hear no danger dreddys nor feyars.

That is not at all the full meaning, but the picture's own words initiate our verbalizing about it. Much of the visual art of Shakespeare's day similarly demanded this collaboration between our eyes and our linguistic formulation of seen images. Indeed, the visual items to which Shakespeare most frequently alludes and that I have not yet mentioned—tapestries, painted cloths, mythological representations in any form, woodcuts, illustrations, emblems, tomb sculpture, or the whole repertoire of public entertainment—all involve visual images that either provide a verbal commentary of their own or provoke the spectator to supply one. Even architecture—Sir Thomas Tresham's triangular lodge at Rushton, for instance—deployed a symbolism to which we are required to contribute our verbal elaborations of trinitarian doctrine.[15]

Mythological scenes, such as those offered to Christopher Sly during the Induction to *The Taming of the Shrew* or known Italian examples of, say, Correggio, invite our participation in their narratives. Just as the Lord and his servants elaborate upon the stories of Io, Daphne, and Apollo (admittedly to titillate Sly's imagination, but I suggest that they would adumbrate thus even in front of the pictures), so Elizabethans and Jacobeans would enter into the adventures of Correggio's Jupiters, drawing (usually) upon their Ovidian reading to "complete" the experience of a picture. The mythologies of Giulio Romano, the religious subjects of Sebastiano del Piombo, or the work of any of the other Italian artists noted in Jonson's *Discoveries*,[16] such as Titian or Tintoretto, were taken as invitations to participate by interpreting—and interpretation meant verbal elucidation.

Writers were surrounded by such visual imagery: in their embroideries, maybe woven at the famous Sheldon *atelier*, established in Warwickshire in the 1560s, or those cheaper versions, painted cloths, to which Shakespeare makes frequent allusion (we know, too, that his maternal grandfather mentioned eleven such cloths in his will). At one end of the social scale the Venetian ambassador could comment specifically upon the rich tapestries at Elizabeth's coronation, noting that one of the Acts of the Apostles was from a design by Raffael d'Urbino.[17] At the other were Mistress Quickly's "fly-bitten Tapestries," and somewhere in the middle Sir Bounteous Progress's bed-curtains "wrought in Venice, with the story of the prodigal child in silk and gold." What is common to all such visual items is their concern either with symbolism—see the emblems from Alciati and Whitney decorating the borders of the Hatfield tapestries of the seasons—or with moral instruction—Costard, it will be recalled, proposed to emend one representation of the Nine Worthies as a result of the curate's thespian inadequacies. Not only pageants of the Worthies, but sequences of the Liberal Arts (in Sir Nicholas Bacon's small banqueting hall at Gorombery Manor), Petrarchan triumphs of Time, Fame or Death (Wolsey's tapestry collection), "portraitures of Sibyls" (Shakerley Marmion's *The Antiquary*) and "shapes . . . wrought by skillful Painters" (Drayton) all required more or less sophisticated interpretation, in which activity the verbal joined the visual experience.[18]

Title pages were a particularly intricate example: as visual gateways (often actually imaged as such) to a wealth of words beyond, they signal that territory by images both available and arcane that we would do well to understand before proceeding. The architectural and sculptural symbolism of title pages should also remind us of the close connections that Kernodle established between buildings and theatrical structures in his book *From Art to Theatre*. I am convinced that we neglect—doubtless for lack of suitable evidence—the extra point given to speeches in the Elizabethan theaters by the presence alongside the actors of images that serve elsewhere—on buildings, in gardens, or on title-page architecture, for instance—to embody ideas. When the Viceroy in *The Spanish Tragedy* discourses on blind Fortune "Whose foot [is] standing on a rolling stone" (1.3.29), when Horatio and Belimperia vie with allusions to Cupid, Mars, and Venus (2.4.29 ff.), the effect is much more precise and sharper if we think, not just of references to visual items elsewhere, but to those very symbolical artifacts upon the stage structure itself.[19]

Emblems, allegorical images, combined with verbal elaborations of meaning, were the basic format of the widely practiced art of tomb sculpture, to which Shakespeare makes frequent allusions: there might be symbolic figures—Patience and Grief, perhaps, on a monument, or more representational forms—Gratiano's grandfather "cut in alabaster," together with the essential, amplifying adjuncts of literary epitaphs. Philip Brockbank has pointed to the intricate involvement of funerary art with the scene of Talbot's death in *Henry VI:* the inscription on Talbot's actual tomb in Rouen retains its "lapidary formality" in Lucy's lines as we gaze (the injunction is to "See") at Talbot with his son "inhearsed" in his arms.[20]

But the most obvious conjunction of image and text is the emblem book. Both its history and its possible influence upon sixteenth- and seventeenth-century writers have been much elaborated[21] and I need not linger upon it now. Whether they be the more learned productions of a Whitney and a Wither or the popular woodcuts of Roxburgh Ballads, the pictures are translated into words—Wither's into his own "Thus all things wheele about" or a Roxburgh woodcut into "Time hath, my lord, a wallet at his back." (Yet I must say I have always thought Ulysses' speech, rather than alluding to such *visual* emblems, was intended skeptically to display its speaker's sententiousness by making him borrow the *language* of these moral handbooks.)

Just as emblem books prospered as a result of the mass production of wood-cuts and, later, of copperplate engravings, so did more general book illustration and the circulation of individual prints. But it is very difficult to judge what emphasis we should lay upon a writer's debts to, say, illustrations in Holinshed or engravings by Dürer,[22] well known as both were. Fluellen's disquisition upon Fortune may start by noting that she is "painted blind," but even as we reach for the visual sources, Fluellen concludes by saying that "the *poet* makes a most excellent description of it" (emphasis added). An essential feature of visual-verbal dialogues in the Renaissance was not the copying in one form of the other's devices, not the transcription, but the translation of ideas and images into the other medium: a rivalry, in short, the *paragone* between poetry and painting, to which *Timon of Athens* contributes.[23] Botticelli painted the *Calumny of Apelles,* based upon a famous literary text of Lucian, which itself described a painting, in order to emulate literature and even to display his painterly superiority — Alberti had specifically recommended the subject to the modern painter in 1436.[24] Accordingly, Botticelli strives to outdo the literary source, notably in his restoration of pagan forms to pagan topics (the figure of naked Truth). Similarly, it seems to me, we may do wrong to search for sources of the Trojan painting in *The Rape of Lucrece* or of Christopher Sly's mythologies, when the poet may simply be seeking our commendation of his literary skill in outclassing the image-makers at their own art.

In *Muiopotmos* Spenser probably had no pictures in mind at all — though Titian's *Jove and Europa* (in the Gardner Museum) is sometimes invoked;[25] a direct debt to Ovid is more probable with no visual mediation except that of Ovid's own imagination. In yet another case, that of Chapman's *Hero and Leander,* we know — thanks to D. J. Gordon[26] — that the poem drew upon Vicenzo Cartari's *Le Imagini de i Dei de gli Antichi* (Lyons, 1581). Cartari's "sourcebook" of classical divinities itself relied upon literary accounts like Ovid's, but was illustrated with images of gods and goddesses that provided instant visual *formulae.* The English version of Cartari, *The Fountain of Ancient Fiction* (1599), did not, however, have pictures — so poets with no Italian would have relied anyway upon a literary text. It is a fact to recall when we would seek too readily for pictorial sources.

Ben Jonson's *aperçu* that painters "aspire to truth so much, as they are rather lovers of likeness than beauty"[27] testifies to his contemporaries' fascination with realism in visual art as much as with Neoplatonism. The bias of art toward lifelikeness — one thinks of Hermione's statue or of Marina's needlework compostions of "Nature's own shape, of bud, bird, branch, or berry, / That even her art sisters the natural roses" — had the important consequence of involving the spectator more thoroughly with its world, like the birds deceived by painted grapes in *Venus and Adonis,* which "Do surfeit by the eye and pine the maw." What Richard Haydocke in his translation of Lomazzo called the "Arte . . . whereby the unskillful eye is so often cozened and deluded, taking counterfeit creatures for the true and natural"[28] was just one aspect of a Renaissance delight in intricate psychological adventures on the boundaries of art and nature. Its roots reach into the early excitements over the discoveries of perspective; some at least of its more luxurious branches blossomed as the masque and the (much neglected) art of garden design both in Italy and in those countries, notably France and England, to which Italian gardenist ideas were carried. It is these manifestations of what is generally called Mannerism to which I must finally and briefly turn.

The intrigues of perspective[29] are announced in two earlier Tudor pictures, the Holbein *Ambassadors,* with its skull that requires us, as with another picture—a head of Edward VI—to shift our ground to get them into proper perspective: "rightly gazed upon," they "Show nothing but confusion, ey'd awry / Distinguish form" is how Bushy explains it in *Richard II.* Perspective pictures needed to be seen from one particular point and even from a fixed distance, especially those which were viewed as reflections in a mirror seen through a hole from behind their own surface! Alberti pointed out what was the evident excitement of such developments in the geometry of optics, that all things became relative and the individual human being alone provided the measure and the meaning of what he contemplated. A simple version is the double head with a different image upside down from rightside up. And there are many literary references to double images on opposite sides of vertical slats, which changed as the spectator moved past them: Hilliard painted one of a woman and a figure of death; Cleopatra thinks Antony "painted one way like a Gorgon, / The other way's a Mars"; and Chapman has some famous lines on

> A picture wrought to optic reason
> That to all passers-by seems, as they move,
> Now woman, now a monster, now a devil,
> And till you stand and in a right line view it,
> You cannot well judge what the main form is.

Yet the radical consequences of these painterly excitements for the drama would seem to be the fashion in which audiences are presented with an exercise in manifold perspectives—the Host and Julia in man's clothes watching Proteus woo Silvia, or Troilus and Ulysses and Thersites watching Diomedes and Cressida. It is a technique upon which the Jacobean drama rings infinite and subtle changes.

The Italian stage had, of course, seized the opportunity of perspective stage designs. Perspective is here just another manifestation of art delighting one with its illusion of reality. But it may have had the additional excitement of serving as the backdrop to artificial representations of life that themselves only serve to remind one of the often unnerving prospect of the actual world as a theater (a *theatrum mundi*) where we may be spectators, or even, perplexingly, actors.[30] These Neoplatonic visions of theater, joined with perspective stage sets from the Italian theater, descended upon England in the early years of the seventeenth century. The masque under Inigo Jones invoked perspective sets and, presumably like Italian court entertainments, seated the royal spectator at the only apt point from which to view them.[31] By comparison, the Teatro Olimpico, designed by Andrea Palladio for a society of equals in Vicenza, offered each spectator in its amphitheater his own perfect perspective.

The masque brings into new arrangements many of the visual traditions I have touched upon: collaboration between words and images, architectural and decorative symbolism, nice confusions of art with nature, elaborate psychological involvements of real spectator with illusionary spectacle. It also capitalizes upon its affinities—rarely remarked—with Italian garden art.[32] Not only did Inigo Jones borrow designs from *intermezzi* that had been, as such events frequently were, performed in gardens or that portrayed gardens in their set, but his own visions of transformation may be paralleled with the metamorphic world of Italian Renaissance gardens: the rocks in *Oberon* open to display the palace, just as the "rocks" of Buontalenti's grotto in the Boboli Gardens "part" to reveal the nymphaeum. In the parks of the Villa Medici at Pratolino or the Villa D'Este at Tivoli the visitor became a mobile spectator of Ovidian dramas and complicated iconographical programs, which caught him into their world of illusion and idea. The Italian Renaissance garden, it may even be argued, began to assume a special place in the Englishman's experience of art. A relatively early traveler like Hoby simply records "pleasant walkes and faire gardens"[33] in his travel journal; but Fynes Moryson, George Sandys, and Thomas Coryat later testify to more intricate responses; Sir Henry Wotton elaborates with skill and insight upon a garden's dramatic and psychological potential:

> I have seene a *Garden* (for the maner perchance incomparable) into which the first *Accesse* was a high walke like a *Tarrace,* from whence might bee taken a generall view of the whole *Plott* below but rather in a delightfull confusion, then with any plaine distinction of the pieces. From this the *Beholder* descending many steps, was afterwards conveyed againe, by severall *mountings* and *valings,* to various entertainements of his *sent,* and *sight:* which I shall not neede to describe (for that were poeticall) let me onely note this, that every one of these diversities, was as if hee had beene *Magically* transported into a new Garden.[34]

We know that such Italian gardens began to be copied in England—the ubiquitous Venetian ambassador reported on Prince Henry's "many gardens and fountains"[35] in 1611. And garden experiences were readily echoed in other events. To explore Pratolino's intricate and mobile waterworks or to read the *Ovidian bas-reliefs* at the Villa D'Este was of a piece with assisting at a Jones masque or at King James's entry into London. On that last occasion an elaborate device — the arch of the New Arabia — actually represented a garden fountain, which, upon the King's approach, came alive and enacted some edifying allegorical entertainment for his majesty.[36] It was yet another visual event that a writer like Shakespeare might have witnessed.

This has been, necessarily, a scramble through visual anthologies. Perhaps its format will have served at least to alert us to the enormously rich and disorderly deposits of art — fine and applied — to which writers had access. We have still much to learn about which art works were known to Elizabethan and Jacobean writers and about what the temper and structures of their visual ideas were; but of this exciting and evidently fruitful interchange between the arts there can be no doubt. As Jonson put it, "Whosoever loves not *Picture,* is indeed injurious to Truth; and all the wisdom of Poetry."[37]

## Notes

1. My brief for the Washington congress was to survey the visual arts in Shakespeare's day, and I have retained the format of that occasion, while revising some of the more awkward moments of a presentation with slides. With some expansion of references this piece now suggests, I think, the sheer range of visual references that literary critics must make their own before any profitable and "interdisciplinary" maneuvers between them can be made. In addition to the specific references in the following notes, I was indebted in composing this paper to M. F. Thorp, "Shakespeare and the Fine Arts," *PMLA* 46 (1931): 672-93; A. H. R. Fairchild, *Shakespeare and the Arts of Design, University of Missouri Studies* 12/1 (1937); and Karl Wörmann, *Shakespeare und die bildenden Künste* (Leipzig, 1930).

2. Especially *The English Icon: Elizabethan and Jacobean Portraiture* (London, 1969).

3. *Two Cheers For Democracy* (London, 1951), p. 85.

4. Quoted from 1543 edition, A4 verso.

5. The prominent place of Venice among Unton's travels does perhaps record the special esteem of English Protestantism for a republic that successfully withstood Papal authority. Frances Yates has shown how this esteem was confirmed by the publication of Paolo Servi's *History of the Council of Trent,* taking place first in England — in Italian in 1619, in English the following year. See "Paolo Servi's *History of the Council of Trent,"Journal of Warburg and Courtauld Institutes* 7 (1944): 123-43. I am grateful to Professor J. Trapp for this reference.

6. *Architecture in Britain 1530-1830* (first paperback edition 1970), p. 34, where Evelyn's remarks are also quoted.

7. *Ibid.,* pp. 71 and 67.

8. *Ibid.,* p. 47.

9. On this theme see David P. Young, *"Something of Great Constancy." The Art of "A Midsummer Night's Dream"* (New Haven, Conn., 1966), especially pp. 12 ff.

10. W. Harrison, *Elizabethan England: From "A Description of England,"* ed. L. Withington (London, 1889), p. 117.

11. See the Scholars' Facsimiles and Reprints edition of the *Hypnerotomachia* in its English

version (Delmar, N.Y., 1973), which contains a useful introduction by Lucy Gent.

12. "The Storm," lines 3-5.

13. See Roy Strong, *Tudor and Jacobean Portraits* (London, 1969), and *The Elizabethan Image,* catalogue for Tate Gallery (1970).

14. *The First Annual Volume of the Walpole Society* (Oxford, 1912), p. 23.

15. See Summerson, *Architecture in Britain,* p. 79.

16. *The Works of Ben Jonson,* ed. Herford and Simpson (Oxford, 1947), 8:612.

17. Frederick Hard, "Spenser's 'Clothes of Arras and of Toure,' " *Studies in Philology* 27 (1930): 162-85.

18. These examples are drawn from the very interesting appendix (on "Knowledge of the Arts") to Samuel C. Chew, *The Pilgrimage of Life* (New Haven, Conn, 1962), pp. 260 ff., and from Hard's article, cited in n. 17, p. 168 (for Wolsey's tapestries).

19. I owe this point to J. P. Brockbank. And in a related field of presentational iconography see John Doebler, *Shakespeare's Speaking Pictures; Studies in Iconic Imagery* (Albuquerque, N.M., 1974).

20. See J. P. Brockbank, "The Frame of Disorder —*Henry VI,*" in *Shakespeare's Histories,* ed. W. A. Armstrong (Penguin Books, 1972), p. 95.

21. See, among many others, Rosemary Freeman, *English Emblem Books* (London, 1948); Mario Praz, *Studi sul concettismo* (Milan, 1934); and *Studies in Seventeenth Century Imagery* (London, 1947); J. Hoyle, "Some Emblems in Shakespeare's *Henry IV* Plays," *ELH* 38 (1971): 512-27; Samuel Schuman, "Emblems and the English Renaissance Drama. A Checklist," *Research Opportunities in Renaissance Drama* 12 (1969): 43-56.

22. See Helen Morris, "Shakespeare and Dürer's Apocalypse, "*Shakespeare Studies* 4 (1968): 252-62. Since delivering this paper I have also been allowed to read an interesting discussion of the background of Christian myth and iconography for another play: F. G. Butler (Rhodes University, S. Africa), "*Macbeth* —The Great Doom's Image."

23. On Shakespeare and the *paragone,* see Anthony Blunt, "An Echo of the Paragone in Shakespeare," *JWCI* 2 (1939): 260-62. Another dramatic presentation of this theme may be found in *Queen Elizabeth's Entertainments,* ed. L. Hotson (London, 1953), pp. 20-22.

24. Alberti, *On Painting,* trans. J. R. Spencer (London, 1956), p. 90.

25. See article cited in n. 17. Significantly, Spenser deserts Ovid in making Minerva win the tapestry-weaving competition by the lifelikeness of her art, not by her guile.

26. See D. J. Gordon on Chapman's debt to Cartari, *Modern Language Review* 39 (1944): 280-85.

27. *Works of Ben Jonson,* 8: 610.

28. *A Tracte Containing The Artes of Curious Paintings, Carvinge and Building* (London, 1598), iii verso.

29. On perspective see, among other works, John White, *The Birth and Rebirth of Pictorial Space* (London, 1957) and the items cited by Inga-Stina Ewbank, "Webster's Realism, or, 'A Cunning Piece Wrought Perspective,' "*John Webster,* ed. Brian Morris (London, 1970), p. 161 n. 4, and Allan Shickman, " 'Turning the Pictures' in *Shakespeare's England,*" *The Art Bulletin* 59 (March 1977): 67-70.

30. On the theme of *theatrum mundi* see Jackson I. Cope, *The Theatre and the Dream* (Baltimore, 1973) and the works cited on p. 268 n. 4.

31. See Stephen Orgel, *The Illusion of Power* (Berkeley, Calif., 1975), pp. 10-11 and the accompanying illustrations.

32. See S. Lang, "The Genesis of the English Landscape Garden," *The Picturesque Garden,* ed. Nikolaus Pevsner (Washington, D.C., 1974), pp. 3-29 and *The Genius of the Place. The English Landscape Garden 1620-1820,* ed. John Dixon Hunt and Peter Willis (London, 1975), pp. 36-37.

33. *The Travels and Life of Sir Thomas Hoby,* ed. E. Powell, in *Camden Miscellany X* (London, 1902), pp. 13, 35, 45. For later and more detailed responses to Italian gardens, see the

material cited in the next note, and George Sandys, *A Relation of a Journey begun An. Dom. 1610,* 3d ed. (London, 1632), p. 272; A. H. S. Yeames, "Rome in 1622," *Papers of the British School at Rome* 6 (1913): passim; Thomas Coryat's *Crudities* (Glasgow, 1905), 2:6-7 and 35; Fynes Moryson, *An Itinerary* (Glasgow, 1907), 1:225, 237, 239, 293, 319. A general survey of the English interest in Italian gardens is offered in my essay, " 'The Garden of the World': The English Experience of the Italian Renaissance Garden," in *Country Life,* 5 September 1977.

34. In *The Genius of the Place* (see n. 32), pp. 48-50; there are other allusions to Italian gardens in this anthology.

35. Quoted by Roy Strong, *The English Icon,* p. 56.

36. Stephen Harrison, *The Archs of Triumph* (London, 1603).

37. *Works of Ben Jonson,* 8: 610.

# Shakespeare's Portrayal
# of Women: A 1970s View

"It is *always* terrible for women"

## by INGA-STINA EWBANK

When the Norwegian Society for Women's Rights in 1898 gave a banquet for Ibsen, the aged playwright disconcerted his hostesses by making a speech in which he disclaimed any connection with women's rights. "Of course," he said, "it is incidentally desirable to solve the problem of women; but that has not been my whole object. My task has been *the portrayal of human beings.*"[1] Insofar as a cat may imitate a king, I too have been tempted to stand up and say that I am here under false pretenses: first, because I have been too busy, academically and domestically, *being* a woman to take account of that vast and important literature *about* being a woman which has come out of various countries, but particularly the United States, in the 1970s; and second, because I believe that Shakespeare, if he had been a Methuselah and attended that banquet, would have said much the same thing as Ibsen. In other words, and with what I believe is commonly called female logic,[2] I have felt that I neither had a subject nor was qualified to speak on that subject.

But it did not take much thinking to overthrow that logic. There is a sense in which every woman who has seen and read Shakespeare's plays becomes, by definition, an authority on his portrayal of women; for, like one's womanhood, the plays have a way of pervading one's life and engaging with one's every act—so that I, for one, have never been able to feed my babies without reappraising Lady Macbeth's readiness to dash out the brains of hers. Also, Ibsen's statement contains a false dichotomy: the problem of women versus the portrayal of human beings. Of course he knew it. He was not betraying the insights of *A Doll's House* and the other twenty-three plays he had written but was teaching his listeners the lesson that the portrayal of women is not a separate issue from the portrayal of human beings generally, and that, if you portray human beings with the sensitivity of a poet, then you are, if not solving, at least exploring the problem of women. This, I think, was Shakespeare's way. I do not think he was either a feminist or an antifeminist—though partisan readers could no doubt read antifeminism into *Macbeth*, the opposite into *Othello*, and (somewhat disturbingly) both into *King Lear*. Nor do I think that he deliberately set out to portray women. He wrote *plays*, in whose infinite variety there is an almost infinite variety of insights into the nature of women—plays about the relationships of human beings, some of whom are male and some female. It is not necessary to quote Cleopatra's horror at the prospect of having "Some squeaking Cleopatra boy [her] greatness / I' the posture of a whore" to remind you that Shakespeare did not write parts for actresses. But he did, for boys, write parts through which, like Tiresias, he seems to be able to tell us what it feels like being "No more but e'en a woman."

At this point, truisms and generalizations must stop, and I must exemplify. My scope forces me to be ruthlessly selective among a variety of possible ways of doing so. I have chosen to look at some of the language spoken by some of Shakespeare's tragic women, and in particular by Ophelia and Desdemona. My "thesis" is that, while they may seem to represent versions of a female stereotype—often silent or inarticulate, submissive to their men, and ultimately unable to control their own destinies—Shakespeare is interested in these human qualities *not* as female characteristics per se but as part of his tragic vision of mankind: of man's proneness to kill the thing he loves. In other words, their words and silences are part of Shakespeare's exploration of the relationship between language and tragic experience.

Both Ophelia and Desdemona are dramatically distinguished from the society they inhabit by characteristics of style. In the court of Elsinore, very much created for us by its mode of speaking—wordy, self-conscious, patterned, formal, sententious, and full of generalizations—Ophelia stands out through speeches of extreme brevity, simplicity, and directness. Until she goes mad, her longest speech is the description of Hamlet's agonized and silent visit to her (2.1.87-100)—a speech that obviously relies on being *acted* out:

> He took me by the wrist, and held me hard;
> Then goes he to the length of all his arm,
> And, with his other hand thus o'er his brow,
> He falls to such perusal of my face
> As 'a would draw it,

and in which the style is obviously subordinated to substance and devoted to handing over bodily the painful experience. The contrast between this and, for example, Gertrude's elaborate and distanced description of Ophelia's drowning ("There is a willow grows aslant the brook" [4.7.167-84]), is telling.

Desdemona is eloquent enough when defending her love in Venice, but in the frenzied climate of suspicion that Othello creates for her in Cyprus, she too becomes practically monosyllabic and vulnerably direct, as against Othello's verbal onslaughts:

> Why is your speech so faint? are you not well?

and

> I am very sorry that you are not well.
>
> (3.3.287, 293)

To appraise these speech modes, we must take a brief detour. Mrs. Dusinberre maintains that Shakespeare's "women characters relate in one form or another to the assumption that eloquence and argument are masculine."[3] No doubt Lady Macbeth's power of verbally brainwashing her husband may be seen in relation to her "unsexing" herself. But Cleopatra—though she is not typical of anyone but herself, "a lass un-parallel'd" and repeatedly contrasted with "other women"—is sufficient proof that being a woman *can* mean being in command of all the resources of language: of a vast vocabulary, of images ranging from the cosmos to the milkmaid, and of a variety of styles and rhetorical approaches that she can adapt to the occasion and to her interlocutor, be he Clown or Emperor. Clearly, for all the many references that characters in various plays make to the comic stereotype of the loquacious shrew, Shakespeare did not subscribe to Launce's (in itself comic) assurance that "To be slow in words is a woman's only virtue" (*Two Gentlemen* 3.1.327). Katherina herself, though she reforms her ideas of "rule, supremacy, and sway," demonstrates her reformation in a superb piece of eloquence (*The Shrew* 5.2.136-79). Even before we see her on stage, we hear of Isabella's

> prone and speechless dialect
> Such as move men; beside, she hath prosperous art
> When she will play with reason and discourse,
> And well she can persuade.
>
> (*Measure for Measure* 1.2.173-76)

The verbal resourcefulness of the comic heroine may, as in *Much Ado*, be the center of energy in the play; or it is the chief therapeutic force, as in *As You Like It*; or, as in *The Merchant of Venice*, it is the pivot on which the play turns. Even those more pathetic heroines—Julia and Viola—forced to woo other women on behalf of the men they themselves love, delight in using language to create fictions through which they unburden their own heavy hearts. The greatest female talker in the Romances is Paulina, who in a most extraordinary way hovers—in Acts 2 and 3 of *The Winter's Tale*—between being a comic shrew and an embodied conscience, and—in Act 5, scene 1—between being Leontes' Guardian figure and driving him stark mad (5.1.119 ff.). But always, and in the last scene of the play miraculously, her words aim at a restorative effect: "words as medicinal as true, / Honest, as either, to purge him of that humour / That presses him from sleep" (2.3.37-39).

The words of Ophelia and Desdemona, too, are "true" and "honest," but they are not capable of purging the hero or the world of their plays. They are not, because, when it matters most, the hero and the heroine are not able to speak the same language.[4] In one form or another the heroine comes to echo Isabella's plea to Angelo:

> I have no tongue but one: gentle my lord,
> Let me intreat you speak the former language.
> (*Measure for Measure* 2.4.138-39)

There are many occasions in Shakespeare's plays when one character's words, however eloquent in themselves, are meaningless to another character, and often the dramatic situation is then a male/female confrontation—from when the newly bereaved Princess in *Love's Labour's Lost* tells the King "I understand you not: my griefs are double" (5.2.742), to the trial scene in *The Winter's Tale,* where Hermione tells Leontes:

> Sir,
> You speak a language that I understand not:
> My life stands in the level of your dreams.
> (3.2.77-79)

Two of the most poignant of these confrontations are the nunnery scene in *Hamlet,* where an actress has to make the most of Ophelia's outcry, "What means your lordship?", and the brothel scene in *Othello,* with Desdemona pleading, on her knees,

> what does your speech import?
> I understand a fury in your words,
> But not the words.
> (4.2.31-33)

The tragic failure of communiction, to use a modern cliché, in these situations is based *not* on the fact that one interlocutor is female, and thus by definition inarticulate, but on the other interlocutor's absorption in a world, a version of reality, that he himself has created—again largely by his language. Hamlet is of course in most ways the most clear-seeing, and by far the most sensitive, character in his play; but in the area of his relations with Ophelia, his sight and sensitivity turn perverse: instead of penetrating to truth, they destroy. Unlike Othello and Desdemona, who are given ample dramatic time and space to demonstrate to us their togetherness, Hamlet and Ophelia are practically unknown to us, as regards the intimacy they have known. We must deduce it from the tenderness of Ophelia's greeting in the nunnery scene: "Good my lord, / How does your honour for this may a day?" And there is the evidence of the love letter, which we surely are meant to take more seriously than Polonius does:

> O dear Ophelia, I am ill at these numbers. I have not art to reckon my groans; but that I love thee best, O most best, believe it. (2.2.119-21)

I think that the inarticulateness and directness of this Hamlet language, from the days before his great shock, are significant. Even before the Ghost's revelation, Hamlet's experience of his mother's "frailty" — which he transfers to all women, Ophelia included — has to him deprived language of its very credibility:

>                     O, such a deed
> As . . .
>                     . . . and sweet religion makes
> A rhapsody of words.
>                     (3.4.45-48)
>
> (2.2.119-21)

When what the Ghost has to tell him teaches Hamlet that "one may smile, and smile, and be a villain," he is not only made suspicious of everyone else's language but he also discovers, for himself, the possibility of using language as a disguise. He becomes superbly adept at speaking, inside or outside his "antic disposition," everybody else's language;[5] but that also means that he becomes adept at bruising Ophelia — as in the nunnery and play scenes — with his words. Meanwhile Ophelia has been subjected to first Laertes' and then Polonius's assumptions that deception, especially of young princes in their "tenders" to young women, is normal (1.3). In this situation, Hamlet can drive her to the ultimate confusion with his words — can, in the end, kill her with his words as much as he kills Polonius with his rapier. The dialogue in the nunnery scene is particularly terrible when he too is apparently speaking the language of truth and directness:

> *Hamlet.* . . . I did love you once,
> *Ophelia.* Indeed, my lord, you made me believe so.
> *Hamlet.* You should not have believed me; for virtue cannot so inoculate our old stock but we shall relish of it. I loved you not.
> *Ophelia.* I was the more deceived.
>                     (3.1.115-20)

What can she say, but "What means your lordship?" Only in madness can she find a language, one where "her speech is nothing, / Yet the unshap'd use of it doth move / The hearers to collection" (4.5.7-9).

Hamlet's vision of the world as "an unweeded garden" ultimately drives Ophelia to death, wearing the "coronet weeds" of her madness. The vision that Iago imposes on Othello makes him kill Desdemona. It is a vision imposed by entirely verbal means (3.3) of extreme ingenuity, and it makes Othello blind and deaf to the simple, direct truth of Desdemona's defense — insofar as she has opportunities to defend herself. Othello lives by Iago's *words* rather than by the directly embodied truth of Desdemona's being and speaking. I think we have a preparation, a forewarning, for this fatal conjunction in the scene (1.3) before the Duke and Senators of Venice where we are told how Desdemona and Othello came to love each other. Othello gives his version before Desdemona comes on stage, and he presents it as a matter of verbal persuasion: she was enthralled by the romantic tale of his life and adventures. When immediately after, she enters and is given a chance to present her version, it is a matter of essences: "I saw Othello's visage in his mind." *He* thinks that "She lov'd me for the dangers I had pass'd, / And I lov'd her that she did pity them"; *she* sees the falling and being in love as a total absorption of identities: "My heart's subdu'd / Even to the very quality of my lord" (F, Q2 reading). We must not take this as the sum of Othello's conception of their mutual love — the rapturous reunion scene in Cyprus, for one thing, where Othello "cannot speak enough of this content" (2.1.196), ought to warn us against such an easy, "Leavisite," dismissal of Othello.[6] But it is, to Othello, a possible way of speaking of his love and his beloved; and — what is more — it works, for the Duke's reaction is: "I think this tale would win my daughter too."

I find it difficult to believe that the articulateness of Shakespeare's women is a matter of education making them "as eloquent and rational as men."[7] What, of course, we see in both Ophelia and Desdemona is an apparent inarticulateness that is in fact dramatically eloquent — like the leaden casket in *The Merchant of Venice,* whose "plainness," Bassanio finds, "moves me more than eloquence" — and that has nothing to do with women's education but everything to do with truth and closeness to experience.[8] It is not that they are not trained in rhetoric (Ophelia's lament over "a noble mind . . . here o'er-thrown," or Desdemona's comic repartee with Iago as she waits for Othello's arrival in Cyprus, suggests that either *can* speak, in situations that make sense to them), but that they apprehend the words they use as tangible realities. After being dragged through the brothel scene, Desdemona cannot say "whore":

> *Desdemona.* Am I that name, Iago?
> *Iago.*　　　　　　　　What name, fair lady?
> *Desdemona.* Such as she says my lord did say I was?
>
> ( 4.2.120-21)

—not for "Victorian" reasons (again, her repartee in the arrival scene suggests that she is not a prude), but because the word has become unspeakable—both too dreadful and meaningless—since Othello used it to her,

> I took you for that cunning whore of Venice,
> That married with Othello,

and all she can say is "I do not think there is any such woman." This is not culpable innocence but a tragic defenselessness in an unreal world created by unreal (male) language.

In Shakespeare's last plays, women speak *and* are listened to and *understood.* Supremely, this is so with Marina, whose words have the power both to convert the brothel clients and to reawaken her father, Pericles, from the inertia of despair. In *The Winter's Tale* Hermione is most eloquent when, in the trial scene, she demonstrates the uselessness of speech and when, in the final scene's miracle, she is simply silent; yet the issue of that play—as I have already said—is also dependent on Paulina's powers of speech. But in the two tragedies we have briefly looked at, women's speech and silence are powerless, with terrible consequences. Is Shakespeare saying that women must be sacrificed in order that men may learn? And do they learn? In the tragedy that was to follow *Othello,* Lear does learn what Cordelia's plain, literal language means; yet even he is left to die staring at her dead face, language itself cracking under the experience: "Look, her lips, / Look there, look there!" But Hamlet's one declaration of his love, on Ophelia's grave, is not so much a recognition of what he has wasted as a claim to be allowed to mourn as eloquently as Laertes. And Othello may see Desdemona, at last, as "a pearl . . . Richer than all his tribe" and "die upon a kiss"; but what we are left to remember is the terrible mutual suffering contained in "cold, cold, my girl."

"I see it's *always* terrible for women," says Maggie; and the Prince replies "Everything is terrible, *cara*—in the heart of man."[9] Whatever we think of the Prince's right to be an authority on the human condition, I take this dialogue—this conjunction of two sentences—to be another way of putting what Ibsen said to his Norwegian ladies. And I take it also to be what Shakespeare is saying in these tragedies: everything is terrible in the heart of man (i.e., of human beings), and we are often taken there via the heart of woman.

## Notes

1. *Henrik Ibsens Samlede Verker,* ed. Francis Bull, Halvdan Koht, Dirik Arup Seip (Oslo, 1928-57), vol. 15 (1930): 417. The translation of Ibsen's *menneske* into "human being" raises the dilemma, which I shall also be suffering under in the conclusion to this paper, of the absence

from the English language of a single, neutral noun for men *and* women. To anyone brought up as a *menneske*, this is a more-than-linguistic handicap. (The relevance of this handicap to feminism is apparently discussed in a paper by Janice Moulton, "The Myth of the Neutral 'Man,' " referred to in the Winter 1975 issue of *Signs*, p.493.)

2. As exemplified in Mrs. Gradgrind's address to her children: "I declare you're enough to make one regret ever having had a family at all. I have a great mind to say I wish I hadn't. *Then* what would you have done, I should like to know" (Charles Dickens, *Hard Times*, Penguin ed. [Harmondsworth, 1969], p.61).

3. Juliet Dusinberre, *Shakespeare and the Nature of Women* (London, 1975), p. 214.

4. Again, one might contrast these couples with Antony and Cleopatra, whose affinity, as critics have pointed out (see particularly Ernest Schanzer, *Shakespeare's Problem Plays* [London, [1960], pp. 133-34) is partly manifested by linguistic and stylistic similarities.

5. After writing this paper, I developed the point further in *"Hamlet* and the Power of Words," a paper at the International Shakespeare Conference, Stratford-upon-Avon, August 1977, and published in *Shakespeare Survey* 30 (1977): 85-102.

6. Cf. F. R. Leavis, "Diabolic Intellect and the Noble Hero," *Scrutiny* 6 (1937); reprinted in *The Common Pursuit* (London, 1952).

7. Dusinberre, *Shakespeare and the Nature of Women*, p. 224.

8. Ophelia's touching literalness and precision when she tells Polonius that Hamlet has confirmed his wooing of her "with *almost* all the holy vows of heaven" (1.3.113-14) contrasts with the easy hyperboles of other speakers in the play, including Hamlet's speech on her grave and its "forty thousand brothers."

9. Henry James, *The Golden Bowl*, Penguin ed. (Harmondsworth, 1966), p. 534.

# The Uses of Shakespeare in America: A Study in Class Domination

by STEPHEN J. BROWN

A little later, after the Civil War, and with the beginning of the great era of industrialism, there swept in a second wave of immigration, vaster in scope, and far more threatening in kind. Factories, mines, railroads, lumber-camps, all phases of American industrial activity, needed laborers. On every ship they came, by millions now, instead of thousands, and not only Germans and Scandinavians, but Italians, Poles, Slavs, Hungarians, Czechs, Greeks, Lithuanians, Rumanians, Armenians — from almost every clime under the sun. They swarmed into the land like the locust in Egypt; and everywhere, in an alarming way, they tended to keep to themselves, in the larger cities, in mining towns, in manufacturing centers, where they maintained their group solidarity. Foreign in their background and alien in their outlook upon life, they exhibited varied racial characteristics, varied ideals, and varied types of civilization. America seemed destined to become a babel of tongues and cultures.

So spoke Joseph Quincy Adams as first Director of Research at the dedication of the Folger Shakespeare Library in 1932. The response of his white Anglo-Saxon Protestant ruling class to the cultural terror he evoked had been English literature and above all Shakespeare, and his address was appropriately entitled "Shakespeare and American Culture." Using Adams's address as a departure I should like today to explore the uses of Shakespeare in America as an instrument of WASP cultural domination, and my exploration will touch upon Shakespeare in his own time as well as his reception by such Americans as Emerson and Whitman before returning to consider the possible uses of Shakespeare in America for the present and the future. Adams continues:

> Fortunately, about the time the forces of immigration became a menace to the preservation of our long-established English civilization, there was initiated throughout the country a system of free and compulsory education for youth. In a spirit of efficiency, that education was made stereotyped in form; and in a spirit of democracy, every child was forced by law to submit to its discipline. . . . As a result, whatever the racial antecedents, out of the portals of the schools emerged, in the second or third generation, a homogeneous people, speaking the same language, inspired by the same ideals, exemplifying the same culture. . . . On the side of the humanities, that schooling concerned itself mainly with the English language and literature . . . . in our fixed plan of elementary schooling, [Shakespeare] was made the cornerstone of cultural discipline . . . Not Homer, nor Dante, nor Goethe, not Chaucer, nor Spenser, nor even Milton, but Shakespeare was made the chief object of their study and veneration.

> This study and veneration did not stop with the grammar and high schools; it was carried into the colleges and universities, and there pursued with still more intensity.[1]

And so on, in a veritable euphoria of self-congratulation.

In our America of black studies and the Jewish novel, of the pizza parlor, the Polish sausage, the sauna bath, the Japanese automobile, and Arab capitalism, it is difficult for even a WASP such as myself to share Adams's euphoria. But the story he tells of Shakespeare's placement at the center of American education is amply borne out by Henry W. Simon's monograph, *The Reading of Shakespeare in American Schools and Colleges, An Historical Survey,* also published in 1932. As Simon tells it, the order of the story is reversed, with English literature and Shakespeare after the Civil War gradually replacing the classics in colleges and universities, and in turn those institutions' entrance examinations shaping the curricula of the schools. This process was finally sealed with the creation of the College Entrance Examination Board in 1901, and in 1932 Simon could say that every CEEB paper between 1901 and 1931 had assumed a knowledge of Shakespeare.[2] Thus the direction of control is clear: it moved from the top down, and from the Eastern colleges and universities to those of the Middle and Far West.

This is the direction of control that we should expect if we accept, as I do, the analysis of American higher education by Alain Touraine, a long-time French observer of our colleges and universities. In his recently published *The Academic System in American Society,* Touraine states that during the period prior to World War I "the main task of the colleges and universities was to shape the culture of a ruling class. . . . The aim of this new training was to convert the new rich into a social elite, to give to money the nobility and patina of a civilization. . . . These Yankees, the conquerors of new frontiers, wanted to display and enforce their domination just when waves of Italian and Slavic immigrants were sweeping into the country."[3] Which takes us back to Adams, and his discussion of the concurrent, and clearly linked, employment of Shakespeare as an instrument of this domination.

But why Shakespeare in the first place? Is there anything about Shakespeare's vision that might seem to make him especially appropriate as the poet of an emerging ruling class? It would be pleasant but probably misleading to assume that he was selected because he was the best poet available — whatever that might mean, in any case. In matters of class control it is wise not to adduce sentimental causes where more functional causes offer themselves. And in the case of Shakespeare the cause may readily be made apparent, as I hope the following analysis will do.

Just over one hundred years ago Edward Dowden published his brilliant and, in our own time, much-maligned, *Shakespeare: His Mind and Art.* In this book, in the course of a discussion of Shakespeare's social and political views, Dowden cited approvingly his contemporary Walter Bagehot — literary critic and political economist — as saying that Shakespeare "is particularly the poet of personal nobility, though throughout his writings there is a sense of freedom; just as Milton is the poet of freedom, though with an underlying reference to personal nobility."[4] Bagehot's distinction seems to me accurate: Shakespeare is indeed the poet of nobility, and the word *noble* is a key word in Shakespearean tragedy, just as its counterpart *gentle* is a key word in Shakespearean comedy.[5] And both words, though extraordinarily complex in their Shakespearean development, have their origin as fundamental terms of social class. In Shakespeare's time *noble* and *gentle* were still almost interchangeable and defined a ruling upper class of about four or five percent of the English people in what the English social historian Peter Laslett has described as a one-class society.[6] Furthermore, the sixteenth century in England witnessed the elaborate development of the ideology of the gentleman, the ideal representative of this class.[7] And that this class made up the larger share of Shakespeare's audience has been argued by Ann Cook.[8]

That Shakespeare was not personally indifferent to his own class position is amply borne out by well-known details of his life. We know that his mother belonged to one of the oldest gentry families in the kingdom, and that his father, though of lower birth, rose to the position of bailiff, or mayor, of Stratford. We know that both these facts were used to obtain a grant of arms for John Shakespeare (and thus also for his son William) in 1596. We know that when that son retired to Stratford in 1612, it was as a landed gentleman occupying the second largest mansion in the town, and that the terms of his will carefully, if fruitlessly, attempted to secure that estate entire to his eldest male heir. Finally, we know that his last lineal descendant died in 1670 as Lady Elizabeth Bernard.[9]

One is tempted to describe this career as a successful rise into an aristocracy. But I would argue instead that the development of the ideology of the gentleman mediated a shift in basic economic relations from a feudal system of organic interrelationship to a more modern system of what Raymond Williams terms *agrarian capitalism*,[10] with enclosure as an early form of agribusiness and rack-renting as evidence that landowners and agricultural laborers were bound only by the ties of money, Marx's "cash nexus." Thus to become a gentleman more and more meant to become a member of a new capitalist ruling class, at first based on the land, but later on industrial capital as well. That this class system was carried over into the American colonies needs no extended demonstration.

That Shakespeare's comedies embody the ideology of the gentleman should be equally clear. Taking *The Merchant of Venice* as instance—it was the first Shakespearean comedy to be staged in America and remained into the twentieth century the most performed and admired of the comedies in this country[11]—I would cite Frank Kermode's statement that " 'Gentleness' in this play means civility in its old full sense, nature improved; but it also means 'Gentile' in the sense of Christian, which amounts, in a way, to the same thing";[12] but I would add moreover that it means "upper class," belonging to a relatively small group of society's rulers. As C. L. Barber, the most sensitive modern critic of Shakespearean comedy, has observed: "The whole play dramatizes the conflict between the mechanisms of wealth and the masterful, social use of it,"[13] but at the same time he confesses to uneasiness over the Portia-Bassanio Belmont set and their seeming "so very very far above money." For my concerns today the key lines in the play are Bassanio's proud confession of Portia:

> Gentle lady
> When I did first impart my love to you,
> I freely told you all the wealth I had
> Ran in my veins, — I was a gentleman, —
>
> (3.2.251-54)

and he has come to Belmont not only because of Portia's beauty and virtue, transcendent as these may be, but also because to live like the gentleman he is requires money: he has come to wive it wealthily in Belmont. As for Antonio, one scholar has recently remarked, "What is particularly interesting is that in this play a representative of the new (economic) enterprise has replaced the traditional figure of the noble and generous knight. The ideal of the virtuous man, Castiglione's courtier, is transferred from the aristocracy to the mercantile bourgeoisie."[14]

Nor, though it has its own special interest in terms of its centrality in our American context, does *The Merchant of Venice* stand alone among Shakespeare's comedies. In all of them what John Russell Brown has called the "wealth of love"[15] is reserved to members of the ruling gentry class, while the commonalty are kept at a psychic distance through transformation into clowns, incapable of that romantic love which redeems and transfigures their betters. While Shakespeare's clownish commonalty have their coarser graces of honesty, humor, and good sense, they are forever shut out from the higher graces of what Kermode is pleased to call "civility in its old full sense."

But *gentle* also means *noble*, and it was the nobility of Shakespeare's tragic heroes that moved his first significant American critic, Ralph Waldo Emerson. Indeed, one could argue that insofar as Emerson's transcendentalism had a literary origin, he found it in Shakespeare. Maynard Mack has remarked that the tragic world of heroic hyperbole "always opens on transcendence,"[16] and Emerson's journals and notebooks, even more than his published essays, bear abundant witness to his deep responses to Shakespeare. A single instance must suffice. On November 9, 1838, after "The American Scholar" of 1837 and "The Divinity School Address" of the previous July, he records reading *Lear* one day and *Hamlet* the next, exclaiming "How real the loftiness! an in-born gentleman; & above that, an exalted intellect. What incessant growth & plenitude of thought . . . I feel the same truth how often in my merely trivial conversation of dealing with my neighbors, that somewhat higher in each of us overlooks this by-play & Jove nods to Jove from behind each of us. Men descend to meet."[17] The loftiness of Shakespeare feeds Emerson's hunger for transcendence, and beyond this moment of exaltation lay the great essay "Self-Reliance" and in 1844 a call for "The Poet" of the new America.

When this poet announced himself in 1855 with the first edition of *Leaves of Grass*, Emerson wrote him upon receipt of a copy from the poet, "I am not blind to the worth of the wonderful gift of *Leaves of Grass*. I find it the most extraordinary piece of wit and wisdom that America has yet contributed. I am very happy in reading it, as great power makes me happy—I greet you at the beginning of a great career, which yet must have had a long foreground somewhere, for such a start."[18]

Central, I believe, to the "long foreground" to *Leaves of Grass* was Whitman's experience of Shakespeare.[19] As a hack printer and journalist for many years, he received free passes to the New York theaters during the 30s, 40s, and 50s, one of the greatest eras of Shakespearean production in America, as Esther Cloudman Dunn tells us in her fine book *Shakespeare in America*.[20] He carried cheap editions of the plays in his hip pocket, and was fond of declaiming great passages from atop Manhattan buses, or crossing Brooklyn ferry, or running the beach at Coney Island. Late in life he confessed that though "Shakespere, who so suffuses current arts and letters (which indeed have in most degrees grown out of him), belongs essentially to the buried past, . . . he holds the proud distinction . . . of being the loftiest of the singers life has yet given rise to." And "if I had not stood before those poems with uncover'd head, fully aware of their colossal grandeur and beauty of form and spirit, I could not have written 'Leaves of Grass.' "[21]

Yet Whitman was acutely aware not only of Shakespeare's pastness, but also of his possible inappropriateness as a poet for a truly democratic society. Unlike his master Emerson in being no gentleman, or even pretending to be, he said that "the comedies are altogether non-acceptable to America and Democracy."[22] "Everything possible is done in the Shakespeare plays to make the common people seem common — very common indeed."[23] This response was based upon a sharp, intuitive sense of Shakespeare as the poet of a ruling class: " 'Gentle' is the epithet often applied to him. At that time was not its signification 'like a gentleman,' 'of high-blooded bearing'?"[24]

As "Song of Myself" alone makes clear, Whitman's own vision was of an America both nobler and more happily vulgar than that of a gentry-dominated class society. His poetry is one great and warm and good-humored embrace — of men, of women as their equals, of blacks, of Indians, of foreigners of every nation; and it is also an embrace of all classes of men-women, of ladies and gentlemen, of the ordinary working man and woman, and of prostitutes, thieves, and convicts. I have not room here to quote at length — and Whitman, of course, was often long-winded — but a reading, say, of the 1860 edition of the *Leaves of Grass* would confirm what I have suggested. Whitman's vision was truly of a free and equal America of the future.

But Whitman's vision was not shared by the American upper class of his day; as one of its modern descendants, the eminent sociologist E. Digby Baltzell, has amply shown in his book *The Protestant Establishment*,[25] this class after the Civil War gradually withdrew from contact with, if not from control of, the ever-growing alien masses — into their summer and winter resorts, into their country clubs and metropolitan clubs, into their Eastern boarding schools, and (of especial concern to us) into their universities such as Harvard, Yale, and Princeton, which they owned (and still own) and operate. As we have seen, through dominating the new College Entrance Examination Board, these Ivy League universities in turn firmly shaped the English curriculum throughout the American educational system, and placed Shakespeare at the center of that curriculum.

This cultural program, the imposition of white Anglo-Saxon Protestant "civility" from above, is startlingly clear in the words of Joseph Quincy Adams with which this paper began. Just five years before, as the first American scholar invited to deliver the annual Shakespeare address to the British Academy, Professor Ashley Thorndike took as his title "Shakespeare in America," the theme of our own meetings this week. After also reviewing the central place of Shakespeare in American education, he said: "The Athenians had Homer. . . . In a mechanical age, for an enormous democracy, we have made the basis of our education English literature — and Shakespeare. How could we have done better?"[26] As a middle-aged man who has spent much of his life reading, loving, and teaching Shakespeare, I am not sure that we could have. But then again, perhaps as Americans, not Englishmen, we could. I have been reviewing history, but it is scarcely ancient history. The white Anglo-Saxon Protestant "civility" of Joseph Quincy Adams has perhaps become increasingly attenuated, especially since the Second World War; yet I sense that it still dominates most of us in this room today. The gentle Shakespeare broods over us. But where is the wide and warm and good-humored embrace of Walt Whitman?

Where, indeed, if not in Shakespeare himself? And Whitman in his Preface of 1855 pointed the way toward the discovery of a radical, egalitarian Shakespeare: "The old red blood and stainless gentility of great poets will be proved by their unconstraint. A heroic person walks at his ease through and out of that custom or precedent or authority that suits him not." And again: "The messages of great poets to each man and woman are, Come to us on equal terms, / Only then can you understand us, / We are no better than you, / What we enclose you enclose, / What we enjoy you may enjoy."[27] And for all his carping, Whitman well knew that Shakespeare was for him the very model of the great poet.

But to reveal this radical, egalitarian Shakespeare in our criticism and in our productions will require a turning upon and discarding of our old liberal humanism, with its rootedness in class distinctions and class rule. And we must face and exorcise this aspect of Shakespeare systematically and unflinchingly. Only so may *gentle* and *noble* be fully freed from their class moorings, a work that liberal humanism began but could not complete. And the Shakespeare that emerges from this exorcism will, I firmly believe, provide the basis for a new and radical humanism of the future, a humanism that is finally beyond high and low, good and evil, and for which not only everything that lives, in the old sense of that, but everything that exists, is holy. So we must come to see, through Titania's eyes and without condescension, a gentle Bottom, and with Bottom through her guidance Masters Peaseblossom, Cobweb, Moth, and Mustardseed. In such a vision Edgar's "Leave gentle wax" will be more than an idle pleasantry and it will be truly Birnam Wood that comes to Dunsinane. But like Lady Macbeth I am transported beyond the ignorant present. . . . Suffice it for now that we free the radically human Shakespeare from the custom or precedent or authority that suited him not, that the unconstraint of his stainless gentility shine through and beyond the class structure he could not avoid. Only so may we meet him on equal terms and see him with equal eye.

> This is the thesis scrivened in delight,
> The reverberating psalm, the right chorale.

## Notes

1. Joseph Quincy Adams, "The Folger Shakespeare Memorial Dedicated, April 23, 1932; Shakespeare and American Culture," *The Spinning Wheel* 12 (1932): 212-15, 220-31, 230.

2. (New York: Simon and Schuster, 1932). See especially chaps. 4 and 5. For the use of the

CEEB, see Michael S. Schudson, "Organizing the 'Meritocracy': A History of the College Entrance Examination Board," *Harvard Education Review* 48, no. 1 (February 1972).

3. Third of a series of essays sponsored by the Carnegie Commission on Higher Education (New York: McGraw Hill Book Company, 1974), p. 39. For an analogous but less scholarly argument, tilted in the direction of vulgar Marxism, see David N. Smith, *Who Rules the Universities? An Essay in Class Analysis* (New York and London: Monthly Review Press, 1974).

4. Edward Dowden, *Shakespere: A Critical Study of His Mind and Art* (London: Routledge and Kegan Paul Ltd., 1875; 25th impression, 1962), p. 328. The Bagehot quotation derives from an essay entitled "Shakespeare — The Individual," which originally appeared in *The Prospective Review* (July 1853), now reprinted in Walter Bagehot, *The Collected Works; The Literary Essays*, ed. Norman St. John-Stevas, 2 vols. (Cambridge, Mass.: Harvard University Press, 1965), 1:173-214.

5. Marvin Spevack, in "Shakespeare's English: The Core Vocabulary," *Review of National Literatures* 3, no. 2 (Fall 1972); *Shakespeare and England*, ed. James G. McManaway (New York: St. John's University Press, 1973), pp. 106-22, lists *noble* (665), *gentle* (366), and *gentleman* (295) as among a core vocabulary of the 335 most frequently used words in Shakespeare. For recent and interesting work along such lines, see Benjamin T. Spencer, "Shakespeare and the Hazards of Nobility," *Centennial Review* 17 (1973): 20-40 and Herbert Howarth, *The Tiger's Heart: Eight Essays on Shakespeare* (New York: Oxford University Press, 1970), "Shakespeare's Gentleness," pp. 1-23.

6. *The World We Have Lost* (London: Methuen, 1965), esp. chap. 2: "A One-Class Society," 22-52. But see also Lawrence Stone, "Social Mobility in England 1500-1700," *Past and Present*, no. 33 (April 1966), pp. 16-73, and the same author's magisterial work *The Crisis of the Aristocracy 1558-1641* (Oxford: Clarendon Press, 1965), passim.

7. Ruth Kelso, *The Doctrine of the English Gentleman in the Sixteenth Century* (Urbana, Ill.: University of Illinois Studies in Language and Literature 14 [February-May 1929]) is still the standard study, though all this material needs a fresh look. See also John E. Mason, *Gentlefolk in the Making* (Philadelphia: University of Pennsylvania Press, 1935), esp. chap. 2, pp. 23-57 and Sir Ernest Barker, *Traditions of Civility: Eight Essays* (Cambridge: Cambridge University Press, 1948), esp. chap. 5, "The Education of the English Gentleman in the Sixteenth Century," pp. 124-58.

8. See Ann Jennalie Cook, "The Audience of Shakespeare's Plays: A Reconsideration," in *Shakespeare Studies* 7 (1974): 283-305. At the end of this article she promises to propose a new group as alternative to Harbage's solid middle-class workingmen, and has very kindly let me know by private letter that her new group is what she calls the "privileged class," which is, however, dominated by the gentry-nobility. I feel sure that her sense of the matter is correct.

9. For all of this see the latest marvel of extravagant Shakespeareana, S. Schoenbaum, *William Shakespeare: A Documentary Life* (New York: Oxford University Press in association with the Scolar Press, 1975). The ordinary reader, without a knowledge of secretary hand, must still consult E. K. Chambers, *William Shakespeare: A Study of Facts and Problems*, 2 vols. (Oxford: Clarendon Press, 1930), 2, for transcripts of the relevant documents.

10. Raymond Williams, *The Country and the City* (New York: Oxford University Press, 1973), passim.

11. It was first staged on September 15, 1752, by the Hallam Company in Williamsburg, Virginia; see Charles H. Shattuck, *Shakespeare on the American Stage* (Washington, D.C.: The Folger Library, 1976). p. 3. For further evidence of the primacy of the comedy in the American experience of Shakespeare, see the further references in Shattuck. Then consult Henry W. Simon, *The Reading of Shakespeare.* One of the earliest readers contained three scenes from *Merchant* "virtually in entirety" (p. 42); the play dominated early college entrance examination questions on the comedies, and in a wide survey of American high school students in 1924 (as far as I know the last such survey) ranked highest among student preferences of all Shakespeare's plays, i.e., number 30 in a list of 76 possible choices (pp. 144-47).

12. Frank Kermode, "The Mature Comedies," in *Early Shakespeare*, Shakespeare Institute Studies (London: Edward Arnold, 1961). p. 221. This essay has since been included in Frank Kermode, *Spenser, Shakespeare, Donne* (London: Routledge & Kegan Paul, 1971), pp. 200-218.

13. C. L. Barber, *Shakespeare's Festive Comedy* (Princeton, N.J.: Princeton University Press, 1959), pp. 170, 189-90.

14. Giorgio Melchiori, "Shakespeare and the New Economics of His Time," in *Review of National Literatures* 3, no. 2 (Fall 1972).

15. *Shakespeare and His Comedies* (London: Methuen, 1957), pp. 45-81.

16. Maynard Mack, "The Jacobean Shakespeare: Some Observations on the Construction of the Tragedies," in *Jacobean Theatre* (London: Edward Arnold, 1960), p. 18.

17. Ralph Waldo Emerson, *The Journals and Miscellaneous Notebooks*, ed. William H. Gilman, Alfred R. Ferguson, et al., 10 vols. to date (Cambridge, Mass: Harvard University Belknap Press, 1960—), 7:140-41. For other similar expressions of admiration, see 1:296; 3:55, 148; 5:12, 124, 233, 296; 6:284, 285; 7:17-18, 111, 130, 142-43. The list could be extended indefinitely, but it testifies to Emerson's continual reading and excitement about Shakespeare during his most creative years.

18. In Walt Whitman, *Leaves of Grass: A Norton Critical Edition*, ed. Scully Bradley and Harold W. Blodgett (New York: W. W. Norton & Company, 1973), "Prefatory Letter to Ralph Waldo Emerson, *Leaves of Grass* 1856: Emerson to Whitman, 1855," pp. 731-32.

19. Floyd Stovall, in *The Foreground to Leaves of Grass* (Charlottesville: The University Press at Virginia, 1973), seems to me to underplay the role of Shakespeare. The bibliography of the Shakespeare-Whitman connection includes Richard Clarence Harrison, "Walt Whitman and Shakespeare," *PMLA* 44 (1929): 1201-38; Clifton Joseph Furness, "Walt Whitman's Estimate of Shakespeare," *Harvard Studies and Notes in Philosophy and Literature* 14 (1932): 1-33; Alwin Thaler, *Shakespeare and Democracy* (Knoxville: University of Tennessee Press, 1941), esp. chap. 2, "Shakespeare and Walt Whitman," pp. 45-61; Robert P. Falk, "Shakespeare's Place in Walt Whitman's America," *Shakespeare Association Bulletin* 17 (1942): 86-96; Floyd Stovall, "Whitman, Shakespeare, and Democracy," *JEGP* 51 (1952): 457-72, and "Whitman's Knowledge of Shakespeare," *Studies in Philology* 49 (1952): 643-69.

20. (New York: The Macmillan Company, 1939). This book is the model of a readable, "unscholarly" book written by a deeply scholarly woman. In terms of the theatrical history of the period to 1870, it has of course been recently and impressively superseded by Shattuck, cited in n. 11.

21. Walt Whitman, *Prose Works 1892*, vol. 2: *Collect and Other Prose*, ed. Floyd Stovall (New York: New York University Press, 1964), "A Backward Glance O'er Travl'd Roads," pp. 720-21. Whitman's remarks originally appeared in an article entitled "My Book and I," *Lippincott's Monthly Magazine*, January 1887, pp. 121-27.

22. Whitman, *Prose Works 1892*, p. 558.

23. Quoted from Furness, "Walt Whitman's Estimate," p. 17.

24. Quoted from Stovall, "Whitman's Knowledge."

25. *The Protestant Establishment: Aristocracy and Caste in America* (New York: Random House, 1964; Vintage paperback, 1965).

26. Ashley H. Thorndike, *Shakespeare in America*, British Academy Lecture, 1927 (Oxford: Oxford University Press, 1927).

27. *Prose Works*, 2:445. The first passage is cited by Esther Cloudman Dunn, *Shakespeare in America*, p. 273, in her defense of Shakespeare against Whitman, and Whitman against his worse self; and I am more than somewhat indebted to her analysis, though I suspect that I push it rather further.

# APPENDIXES

# Appendix A:
# Seminar Reports

1. Toward the Definitive Text

2. The Shakespearean Actress on the American Stage: 1750-1915

3. Structuralist Approaches to Shakespeare

4. Shakespeare's Audience: Its Preconceptions and Expectations

5. Shakespeare's Later Dramatic Contemporaries

6. The Formal Principles of Shakespearean Comedy (no report)

7. Anticipations of Shakespeare's Romances in his Earlier Work

8. Shakespeare's English

9. Shakespeare's Sources as Clues to Meaning

10. Shakespeare as Spokesman for the Orthodoxies of His Time: The Validity of Some Modern Critical Assumptions

11. The First Public Playhouse, The Theatre in Shoreditch

12. The Future of Shakespearean Bibliography

13. Marxist Interpretations of Shakespeare and Society

14. Shakespeare in Translation

15. Christian Interpretations of Shakespeare

# Toward the Definitive Text

## GEORGE WALTON WILLIAMS, Chairman

The seminar "Toward the Definitive Text" convened promptly on Tuesday, 20 April 1976, at 9:00 A.M. in the Massachusetts Room of the Statler-Hilton. After welcoming international participants and noting with regret the absence of various individuals who had hoped to be present, the Chairman, George Walton Williams, asked for reports on major scholarly editions in progress.

1. Professor Robert K. Turner reported by proxy that the *Variorum* has *As You Like It* typeset and updated bibliographies for *Richard II, 1 Henry IV,* and *2 Henry IV* underway. The *Variorum* committee hopes to publish two volumes in 1976-77, and two or more in 1977-78.

2. Professor Harold Jenkins reported on the New Arden edition, noting that thirty-one volumes had been published—including three in the last twelve months—and that eight others are at various stages of preparation. He remarked on several changes in the character of the edition over the course of the years.

3. Professor Fredson Bowers said that according to his information the Oxford old-spelling edition begun by R. B. McKerrow was at a virtually permanent standstill, and Professor T. H. Howard-Hill added that internal conditions made it unlikely that the edition could be revived at this time.

4. Professor Barry Gaines noted that the old-spelling edition of forty volumes begun with the University of South Carolina Press is being revived and may well be published by Burt Franklin.

The Chairman then turned the attention of participants to the question of the possibility, necessity, and desirability of a definitive text of Shakespeare's works. Participants dealt with various aspects of this question: (1) the impossibility of demonstrating the correctness of individual emendations—and therefore of texts, (2) the unlikelihood that texts, especially in regard to their substantives, could ever be definitively established; (3) the possibility that an *edition* could be definitive in terms of its specific apparatus; (4) the need to return to textual criticism in its traditional emphasis on transmission because bibliography cannot solve all problems; (5) the special difficulties of establishing punctuation, which was treated freely during several stages of transmission; (6) the difference between the critical edition for scholars and the practical but reliable edition for actors and directors; (7) the anomalous lack of a critic's edition when so many other kinds are available; (8) the gray area where emendation becomes modernization and the need for more precise information about the written language of Shakespeare's day; (9) the importance of determining the nature of the MSS behind the plays, and of considering other kinds of autograph/scribal copy than foul-papers/prompt-book; and finally (10) the role that analytical bibliography and especially compositor analysis might yet play in studying this problem of manuscript copy.

To summarize the ideas that emerged through discussion: Emendation is by nature conjectural. One can establish the text of a document, but only in rare cases can one establish that of a work. Editions, not texts, may be definitive in a limited sense. Nevertheless, since emendation is essentially an attempt to reverse the errors produced in the process of transmission, an investigation of that transmission can help define the area in which conjectural emendation must operate and thus analytical bibliography may still have some contributions to make in producing a definitive edition with a critical text.

S. W. Reid, Recorder

## Participants

Thomas L. Berger, Saint Lawrence University; Fredson Bowers, University of Virginia; Georgia Peters Burton, Bryn Mawr College; Janet Cavano, Methodist College; W. Craig Ferguson, The Queen's University, Ontario; Hans W. Gabler, The University of Munich; Barry Gaines, University of Tennessee; Johan Gerritsen, Rijksuniversitat, Groningen; Roger Gross, Bowling Green State University; Jay L. Halio, University of Delaware; Myra Hinman, University of Kansas; T. H. Howard-Hill, University of South Carolina; James G. McManaway, Folger Shakespeare Library; John S. O'Connor, George Mason University; S. W. Reid, Kent State University; G. B. Shand, Toronto; Eric Vaughn, Bowling Green State University; Franklin B. Williams, Georgetown University; George Walton Williams, Duke University.

# The Shakespearean Actresses on the American Stage: 1750-1915

## CHARLES H. SHATTUCK, Chairman

The panelists, and the actresses about whom they submitted notes or papers in advance of the meeting:

*Charles H. Shattuck,* University of Illinois, Chairman

*Barbara Millard,* LaSalle College: Margaret Cheer, Nancy Hallam, and others before 1800

*Carol Carlisle,* University of South Carolina: Fanny Kemble and Ellen Tree

*Gary Jay Williams,* Catholic University of America: Charlotte Cushman

*Joseph Price,* Penn State University: female Hamlets and women in men's dress

*Ben Henneke,* University of Tulsa: Laura Keene and Emma Waller

*Suzanne Jeffers,* Lenoir Rhyne College: Ellen Terry

*Dennis Bartholomeusz,* Monash University: Mary Anderson

*Claire McGlinchee,* Hunter College: Julia Marlowe, Helena Modjeska, and Ada Rehan

*Jeanne Newlin,* Harvard Theatre Collection: Maude Adams

*Mr. Shattuck* spoke briefly about theater historians' preoccupation with the past — the pleasures and uses of theater history: of how as Shakespeareans we extend and enrich our present enjoyment of the plays whenever we can recapture what the plays looked like, sounded like, and meant to playgoers in times long gone. He paid brief tribute to the teacher of several persons present and friend to all present, Arthur Colby Sprague, who knows more about these matters than all of us together. He then offered a series of questions for the panelists to respond to.

244

*QUESTION:* Did any of these eighteenth and nineteenth-century actresses possess special executive ability? Did they lead the profession, or merely support starring male actors and do what they were told to do under male-dominated managements?

*Mr. Henneke* presented Laura Keene as the first woman theater manager in America, operating in New York in the 1850s and through the Civil War years. Her career began in England, but she came to the States to escape from a difficult marital situation. She was a handsome woman and her fine legs should have qualified her for Shakespearean breeches roles, but though she opened her New York Theatre with *As You Like It,* in which she played Rosalind, and later played Puck in *The Dream,* she did not as a manager devote much time to Shakespeare. She admired Shakespeare greatly but she was sure that he would not pay. She once wrote Augustin Daly urging him to produce a now unknown bit of topical fluff because it would outdraw whatever Shakespeare play he was about to offer. Her own production of *The Dream* in 1859 was quite a success but it gained far less profit than *Our American Cousin,* which preceded it. By staging less prestigious but more popular stuff she managed to die solvent. *Miss Newlin* mentioned that Maude Adams, though always operating under someone else's management, always had her own company, which she directed with an iron hand. She was a very demanding performer, and in artistic matters was a stickler for detail. *Miss McGlinchee* claimed for Julia Marlowe that she held her own (no mean accomplishment) with E. H. Sothern. She was his co-star, nothing less, and she had a great deal to do with the direction of their many Shakespeare productions. She was responsible for making up minutely detailed promptbooks, and to insure textual accuracy she made constant use of the Furness Variorum. When working with her earlier partner (and husband) Robert Taber, she was his *rival.* With Sothern she was truly a partner. From earlier times she was experienced in management, having a company of her own. She once produced *Uncle Tom's Cabin* and played Tom in it herself. *Mr. Bartholomeusz* emphasized the managerial accomplishments of Mary Anderson ("Our Mary"), who actually took over Henry Irving's Lyceum Theatre in London for two seasons and ran it herself. There she staged *The Winter's Tale* for 166 nights, its longest run in nineteenth-century England. *Mr. Williams* offered the case of Charlotte Cushman, who, if not in fact a manager, was a fiercely independent star. She held out for her own terms, artistic and financial, against such formidable notables as Macready, Forrest, and Edwin Booth. She left an estate of half a million dollars. *Miss Millard* said that management in the eighteenth century was left to the men, and several of the major actresses married (managed?) the managers rather than engage in management themselves. In the eighteenth century, of course, actors and actresses alike were shareholders in their companies, so they were at least indirectly concerned in management.

*QUESTION:* The bane of Shakespeare production in English-speaking theatres from 1660 on was corruption of the texts, and the process of weeding out the additions by Davenant and Tate and Garrick and the rest was a long slow one. Did any of these actresses contribute to the restoration of the originals?

*Mr. Henneke* reported that Laura Keene called in a Harvard professor to help her arrange the text of *The Dream,* but then she mounted it so elaborately that many passages had to be deleted to allow time for the spectacle. As the stage machinery began to operate less sluggishly, *some* of the lines were restored. But if it was all pure Shakespeare, it was still a butchered script, and it took many hours to perform. Here Mr. Henneke paused to remind us that we at this table would not at all like these old players and productions that we are now talking about. He even suggested that the introduction of actresses was the worst thing that ever happened to Shakespeare, who of course wrote his women's parts for boys. This suggestion led to some side-discussion of the National Theatre's recent all-male *As You Like It.* But eventually the chairman renewed the *Question* and recognized *Miss McGlinchee,* who spoke of the authenticity and reasonable completeness of Julia Marlowe's texts — allowing, of course, for the omission of such crude and vulgar language as would have been offensive to audiences during the pre-World War I generation. *Mr. Bartholomeusz's* Mary Anderson cut the text of *The Winter's Tale* and altered it somewhat to provide continuity and to make it possible for her to double in the roles of Hermione and Perdita. *Mr. Williams* explained that Charlotte Cushman both cut and restored texts, depending on what role she would be playing. Her *Henry VIII* ended with the death of Queen Katharine when (as usual) she played Queen Katharine. When on occasion she played Wolsey, the text was arranged to focus on him. Her most famous textual restoration was that of *Romeo and Juliet,* in which she played Romeo to the Juliet of her sister Susan. She cut out the "Garrick flummeries" — namely, the tearful final exchange between the lovers just before they die; she restored the reconciliation of the warring families.

*QUESTION:* The case of Charlotte Cushman reminds us of the popularity of actresses in roles in which women disguise as men (breeches roles: Rosalind, Viola), or even sometimes of actresses playing roles that belong to the men.

*Mr. Price* has discovered that of all the male roles in Shakespeare, Hamlet has had the greatest attraction for actresses. One hundred seventy women have attempted the role, 27 in America. One woman totaled 1,000 performances of *Hamlet* while touring the provinces. America saw its first female Hamlet at the Park Theatre in New York in 1819, and others quickly followed. Oddly enough, when Charlotte Cushman first attempted the role she was thought to be too masculine to fit the nineteenth-century image of Hamlet — brooding, sensitive, romantic. Yet in 1861 the Congress commissioned her to play a farewell performance of *Hamlet* for them. (The Chairman was here reminded of the nineteenth-century study of *Hamlet* by an American named Edward Vining, who argued that Shakespeare first intended Hamlet to be a woman in disguise. Edwin Booth was much taken by this book, which for the first time recognized the "femininity" of Hamlet. In 1920 the Danish actress Asta Nielsen played Hamlet in a film based upon Edward Vining's idea.) *Mr. Price* further developed the recognition that breeches roles were particularly attractive to actresses and audiences in Victorian times because they permitted displays of feminine physique that would not otherwise be seen in the legitimate theater. *Mr. Henneke* added to this recognition that economics and the star system played their part. There were simply not enough strong women's roles in Shakespeare to satisfy the actresses — especially actresses of size and weight, like Cushman. Emma Walker, who played Iago, expressed the desire for more challenging roles than she found in the standard female repertory. *Mr. Williams* noted that in the nineteenth century Oberon was almost always played by a woman, her lighter voice and graceful manner helping to differentiate the Fairy King's nature from human nature. *Miss Millard* recalled that there was at least one "transvestite" performance in America in the eighteenth century, when Henrietta Osborne played Prince Hal in *Henry IV*.

*QUESTION:* Finally, how would you describe the essential quality of the actresses that you have been studying? What has attracted you to them?

*Mrs. Carlisle:* Oddly enough, the gentle Ellen Tree, with her sweet rapport with audiences, the womanly ideal, became well known for her breeches roles. In her, such roles as Ion became "uplifting," not "masculine." Fanny Kemble thought her the only performer to look like Romeo. Tree's dedication to her art may be measured by her desire to play the Garrick ending of *Romeo and Juliet* as he had done it — pick up Juliet and carry her (F. Kemble) downstage. Kemble refused. Fanny Kemble was herself a fiery, dominant creature, often compared to Edmund Kean, and most outspoken in her personal life. Her most popular Shakespearean character was Beatrice. Ellen Tree charmed audiences; Fanny Kemble seized them. *Miss Millard:* Margaret Cheer, in her three-year career with the eighteenth-century Hallam company, was praised universally. She overshadowed all others. Her career dwindled rather swiftly soon after she was supposed to have eloped with a peer of the realm who turned out to have married someone else. All the eighteenth-century actresses that we read of were known for their musical voices and womanly charm. Nancy Hallam, who probably played Juliet before George Washington, was celebrated by poets for every imaginable beauty that an actress could possess.

*Mrs. Jeffers:* Ellen Terry was a most feminine actress, known for her beauty, charm, grace. Her only breeches roles were Viola and Imogen. She projected an image of goodness, in spite of any scandal connected with her personal life. She had never felt any compulsion to act, and had a terrible memory for lines. However, she took care with her stage appearance, favoring heavy robes that gave her the appearance of a Burne-Jones illustration. *Miss Newlin:* Maude Adams was a child-actress. She had always longed for tragic roles, but was advised by her mother that with her nose she was much better suited to comedy. Like other actresses of her time she was noted for some of her breeches roles, especially Peter Pan and L'Aiglon. Miss Adams actually did little Shakespeare except for some short runs. In 1908 Professor Kittredge invited her to Harvard to play Viola in Sanders Hall on an Elizabethan staging modeled on the Swan drawing.

Mary E. Butler, Recorder
(revised by Charles Shattuck)

# Structuralist Approaches to
# Shakespeare

MARJORIE GARBER, Chairman

Acknowledging the difficulty of defining structuralism as a coherent theory, the seminar focused mainly on how mythology can act as a deep structure for the plays. We considered the possibilities of treating groups of plays as *langue*—plays varied in genre and period, but unified by deep structures of family relationships, generational conflict, and passages from youth to maturity. But within this *langue,* we faced the problem of *parole:* of getting beyond mere taxonomy and avoiding the tautology of deriving structures from the plays and then applying the same structures to the plays. We also recognized the necessity of identifying the process through which the myth transforms itself dialectically, working through binary oppositions.

We agreed tentatively on certain basic evidences for the shaping presence of myth in the plays. First, concrete references to mythic personages and motifs, such as Talbot's use of Icarus in *1 Henry VI* and the references to mazes in *The Tempest;* the repetition of images, and situations, such as boxes in *Cymbeline,* which look good but contain evil; and particularly, the undeniable presence of binary oppositions throughout Shakespeare. Turning to actual critical procedure, we agreed that a properly structuralist concern with structures overrides formal distinctions between plot, image, and character, and depends, finally, on the critic's own creativity and judgment in thinking analogically, finding structures that are new and that assume meaning within the *langue.*

Asking whether structuralism can identify a peculiarly dramatic as opposed to a narrative structure, we noted that the submergence of an authorial point of view in characters interacting, so as to make the play a system in itself, made structuralism appropriate for drama. However, a terminology that takes account of the nature of the play as drama must also relate to the mythic deep structure that resides outside the play. Finally, we discussed the viability of structuralism in the classroom as a way of pointing out Shakespeare's concern with universal human drives and as a means of relating the plays to each other in terms of that concern.

Coppélia Kahn, Recorder

## Participants

Leonard Barkan, Northwestern University; Nirmal-Singh Dhesi, California State at Sonoma; Ann Haaker, California State University at Fullerton; Phyllis G. Hetrick, Defiance College; Mathilda Hills, University of Rhode Island; Gloria Johnson, University of Oregon; Coppélia Kahn, Wesleyan University; Lawrence F. McNamee, East Texas State University; Thomas Allen Nelson, San Diego State University; Gerald L. Price, Columbia Union College; David Redman, Princeton University; Nancy Lee Riffe, Eastern Kentucky University; Volker Schulz, Institut für Englische Philologie, West Germany; Meredith Skura, Yale University; Roger J. Stilling, Appalachian State University.

# Shakespeare's Audience: Its Preconceptions and Expectations

## TERENCE HAWKES, Chairman

Professor Terence Hawkes, Cardiff, Chairman of the seminar on Shakespeare's audience, opened the session by stating that the agenda would include five previously proposed topics in the following sequence: (1) the constitution of the audience; (2) its education: levels of literacy and "oracy"; (3) perceptual modes and intellectual presuppositions; (4) specific instances of audience response; and (5) the modern audience for Shakespeare. He then commented briefly on Dr. Ann Jennalie Cook's study in *Shakespeare Studies 7*, which questioned Professor Harbage's estimate of the Shakespearean audience as largely working class.

Professor Wasson in response said that he had found Dr. Cook's conclusions essentially "on the right track" in their revaluation of the term *working class* as understood in Shakespeare's own time. His work with archives in Norfolk and Suffolk pointed to a lower percentage of the working class in the audience and a higher percentage in the previously overlooked category of out-of-town visitors. Journeymen and apprentices, he said, were not "all that free" to attend mid-afternoon performances at the playhouses. Professor Hawkes maintained that the bulk of the audience remained outside of the top 5% who had political power in England. Professor Sternlicht then raised the question, which was to recur several times, of whether a modern term like *working class* was not anachronistic when applied to a preindustrial society. He further pointed out the danger of underestimating what the penny admission meant to the average Londoner. It was his belief that audiences were made up of "regular attendants" whose presence could be counted on to assure a uniform response to the moral and social tone of the plays. Professor Rothwell added that Elizabethan entries in London parish registers showed evidence of extreme poverty, particularly in the neighborhoods surrounding the theaters in Shoreditch and Bankside. Professor Hawkes still felt, however, that people who regularly spent small sums in alehouses could also find their way into the playhouses. The "dependent poor," who included those newly unemployed as a result of the transition from feudalism to capitalism, probably made up only about 27.2% of the population, though it was noted that this was a high figure. Professor Shibita said that he would like to think that the majority of the audience was made up of wage earners, but confessed some perplexity about how they found time to attend. He raised the matter of underemployment as a possible explanation. "Ale," said Professor Sternlicht, "was 1d a quart, and cheese 2d a pound. A skilled worker earned about a shilling a day." If we add all this up, "Where was the money for that groundling to attend the theater?"

Objecting to the statistical and economic approach as misleading, Professor Charney insisted on looking at audience motivation, not pocketbook. He argued that "the nature of the theater and what it represented," as shown, for example, by the popularity of amateur theater, suggested a deep involvement by broad masses of people. Theater to the poor represented a need, just as today fringe professional theater in major cities such as New York draws in persons effectively outside the economy. Professor Hawkes, agreeing with Professor Charney, remarked that theater was indeed one of the activities that perhaps made poverty bearable. As another obstacle to those who saw the plays as upper class, Professor Goldstein cited the mechanick players in *Midsummer-Night's Dream,* as evidence of the grass roots support for plays; Professor Wasson rejoined that to the contrary he had found a dwindling interest in local drama after about 1540, except for the appearances of strolling players from London.

Discussion then turned to audience levels of literacy and oracy. Professor Hilliard noted that Puritan tracts implied a lack of learning among theater audiences, while Mr. Taylor saw large numbers of theatergoers as "sponsored" by various organizations such as guilds and great houses. That is to say, the audience by and large may have been in proximity to the literate if not literate themselves. There was, despite minor differences among the participants, an almost unanimous subscription to the concept of theatergoers who, though functionally illiterate in most cases, still were capable of *listening* to a degree unknown today. As Professor Charney said, nonliteracy in fact increased the sharpness of the listening faculty. To assume that Elizabethans did not understand what was going on would be a major error; their common bond was not so much class as oral-aural intelligence.

Professor Seward opened the third phase of the discussion (perceptual modes and presuppositions) by citing the generally accepted "psycho-moral" assumptions of the Tudors and Stuarts. The rhetoric of faculty psychology contained ethical as well as psychic implications plain to them but lost today, he said. Professor Mroczkowski added that the homilies should also not be forgotten as one of the more important unifying forces for the audience. Professor Wasson supported the general thesis about lost listening habits by commenting on the wordplay at the end of *Antony and Cleopatra* on "worm" as something invariably missed nowadays but doubtless readily apprehended by audiences of Shakespeare's time. Professor Hawkes reminded everyone that nonliterate communities valued the pun in a way and at a level that has been lost to the print-oriented society.

On the question of "specific instances of audience response," there was tentative agreement that jokes at the expense of groundlings ("inexplicable dumb shows," for example), wordplay, and florid speeches were less designed to alienate or to go over people's heads than to get attention. Professor Black, speaking from the floor, warned against attempting to extract information about the audience from examination of class-conscious attitudes in the plays. Professor Mroczkowski commented on the enormous complexity of the question (how can anyone know exactly how each member even of a modern audience responds to the words in a play?) but asked that more attention be paid to the soliloquies, where Shakespeare is most likely to reveal exactly what he is about. Professor Clark raised the issue of how outsiders coming to London could have grasped all the nuances of dialect spoken by the actors in an age when there was such a wide gap between London and provincial dialects. Professor Charney suggested that action may have meant as much as or more than words, that there was "a gestural and contextual language" that permitted understanding even when every word in a speech was not grasped. He urged that *ex post facto* principles not be applied by assuming that people then needed a gloss to John Donne's sermons as we do today. Donne's sermons were in fact enormously popular with a wide range of the populace. Others, Professors Sternlicht and Mellamphy, added that because action meant more than words, the flow of language, even when not understood, could be therapeutic and soothing.

Professor Rothwell commented briefly on his attempts to infer something about the nature of the audience from the social types in the plays. He conceded that Professor Black's point about the perils of such an enterprise was valid enough, but argued that inadequate knowledge about the precise constituency of the audience made it all the more necessary to explore every possible approach. There is, for example, whatever is to be made out of it, a notable gap between the class structure in the plays (profoundly monarchical) and the constituency of the audience (essentially popular). In the context of some prior remarks about sermons and puritan tracts, Professor Heinemann remarked from the floor that too literal a reading of these attacks on playgoers could lead to some basic misconceptions about the intellectual capacity of the audience.

In concluding remarks, Professor Charney introduced the idea of exploring the "onstage audiences" in such plays as *Midsummer-Night's Dream, The Taming of the Shrew, Julius Caesar, Hamlet, Coriolanus,* and *The Knight of the Burning Pestle* as a way of measuring audience apprehension or of constructing a model of the actual audience. At the end of the hour, Professor Hawkes thanked the seminar and remarked that managing to cover four out of the five topics was an achievement. He hoped that further thought would be given to the fifth and undiscussed topic, the modern audience for Shakespeare's plays.

*Summary.* In getting at the nature of the audience in the Shakespearean playhouse, the seminar considered statistical data, analogies with modern theater, and the internal evidence of the plays. There may have been a slight tendency for those who sought to upgrade the audience to cite statistics and for those who clung to the traditional "cross-section" view to argue from analogies with modern theater, though even this generalization will not stand close inspection. Both camps seemed willing enough (again with exceptions) to use internal evidence, though no one argued that the movement from the internal order of the play to the structure of the audience could be made without caution. There was a reasonable amount of agreement behind apparent disagreements, but the format did not lend itself to leisurely explorations of underlying assumptions. Despite attempts at objectivity, it would seem that students of audience, like the students of the plays, tend to remake their subject in their own image. The statistical data often remain insufficient; the analogies may invite other analogies; and the evidence of the plays, especially given Shakespeare's genius for equivocation, furnishes but glimpses of the truth. The major achievements of the seminar were to examine familiar assumptions with a fresh eye, to reaffirm the importance of oracy as opposed to literacy, and to heighten awareness of Shakespeare's work as stage plays intended to be presented live to real people in actual theaters.

Kenneth S. Rothwell, Recorder

## Participants

Barry Bingham, Louisville *Courier-Journal*; Maurice Charney, Rutgers University; George P. Clark, Hanover College; Leonard Goldstein, German Democratic Republic; Terence Hawkes, University College, Cardiff; Stephen Hilliard, University of Nebraska; P. J. Mroczkowski, University of Cracow, Poland; Kenneth S. Rothwell, University of Vermont; James H. Seward, Meadville, Pa.; Toshihiko Shibata, Tokyo, Japan; Sanford Sternlicht, State University of New York, Oswego; R. Thad Taylor, Globe Playhouse, Los Angeles, California; John Wasson, Washington State University; Steven C. Young, Pomona College; and Stephen Black, Simon Fraser University; Reavley Gair, University of New Brunswick; Margot Heinemann, London University; Ninian Mellamphy, University of Western Ontario.

# Shakespeare's Later
# Dramatic Contemporaries

## H. J. OLIVER, Chairman

The Chairman first reported that, after discussion with the Executive Secretary and Committee, the subject had been reworded or defined as "the importance of Shakespeare to his contemporaries." The seminar would discuss the problems that were set for those contemporaries by Shakespeare's very existence as a dramatist, and by his success. Preliminary correspondence had suggested that opinions might fall into three classes: the first, the common opinion that Shakespeare had been a great influence, and a good one (indeed, that Jacobean and even Caroline drama was what it was because he had virtually created it); the second, that Shakespeare's influence was great but bad, in that later playwrights, instead of working out their own themes, keeping their eye on the dramatic subject, and working in terms of psychological truth, too often fell back on Shakespeare (roughly what David Frost said of Massinger, what many critics—rejecting the theory of "parody"—thought of Marston, and what some think of Shirley, as writer of tragedy); the third, that Shakespeare was not an important influence at all (a theory advanced by John Munro early in this century when he wrote that Shakespeare, unlike Marlowe and Beaumont and Fletcher, "invented no new style"—and added the astounding statement that there was no other truly Shakespearean play until after the Restoration).

Professors Cyrus Hoy and Charles Forker had agreed to lead off, and Professors Harold Jenkins, Scott Colley, and Ernst Honigmann had accepted invitations to add their comments before the general discussion began.

Professor Hoy said that although Shakespeare's influence on his successors could be seen "everywhere you look," in language, incident, and treatment of character types, those successors "were never able to conceive a play in the true Shakespearean spirit." In his last plays Shakespeare had penetrated to a vision beyond reality; and those plays, unlike the tragicomedies of Beaumont and Fletcher, were a dead end as far as the history of the theater is concerned. What Beaumont and Fletcher, Webster, Middleton, and Ford lacked in profundity of vision, they made up for in sophistication; but their plays were based as much on other plays as on life; they reproduced details from Shakespeare, not the Shakespearean vision.

Professor Forker took what he called not a contradictory but a "more optimistic" view. There was carryover even from Shakespeare's romances, in Marston, for one; but the emphasis was different, on fallen man, and so in Jacobean drama we have "Shakespearean ideas reordered and put to a non-Shakespearean use." Taking *Hamlet* alone as evidence, we could see this phenomenon in Marston; in Chapman's *Widow's Tears,* where, for dramatic and tonal purposes, Shakespearean material was adapted in a highly disillusioned comedy; and in the graveyard scene in *The Revenger's Tragedy.* Again, the very theme and structure of Ford's *Perkin Warbeck,* the contrast between Henry VII and Perkin, "the king who is not a king," was the Shakespearean paradox of *Richard II;* and there were the various developments of Shakespeare's love-death pattern.

Professor Jenkins asked whether it was not dangerous to think of Shakespeare's influence as necessarily direct. Using the unexpected but fascinating analogy of Japanese drama, he stressed the tendency of dramatists "to draw upon a stock convention in order to introduce variations from it" and in this way to allow for audience expectations without sacrifices of originality. Might not *'Tis Pity,* for example, be reminiscent not so much of *Romeo and Juliet* itself as of the kind of love tragedy of which *Romeo and Juliet* is the best known example?

Professor Colley suggested that Shakespeare was in a sense the *antagonist* of many later plays. Recalling Harold Bloom's analysis of the problems of all artists who follow a genius, and their consequent "desperate manoeuvers to escape the burdens of the past," he suggested that Jacobean drama—Marston again, for instance—often worked by deliberate distortion of their great predecessor. They were unable to accept his beliefs; we should speak not of their inability to copy but of their conscious variations.

Professor Honigmann was concerned lest from some of the earlier discussion a wrong inference should be drawn. Shakespeare was, surely, a highly sophisticated writer, but his sophistication was "of a different formula" and is seen, of course, in his language and also in his dramatic blank verse. The parallel of Milton proved that a great poet could make things very difficult for his contemporaries; Shakespeare made things impossible. Yet—and this is the remarkable paradox—he did not *constrict* his immediate successors as he did constrict the dramatists of the nineteenth century. Jonson, Tourneur, Fletcher, Middleton could not equal his language and verse, but they were certainly influenced by it—and benefited.

In the following general discussion, Professor Alan Dessen, Dr. Elizabeth Brennan, Professor C. J. Gianakaris, and others joined the panelists; a number of caveats were entered, a number of points made. It was argued that Shakespeare was not necessarily seen by his contemporaries as we see him, as the one on whom they *ought* to be modeling themselves. Indeed, Shakespeare's successors had a different kind of moral vision—more satirical, deriving from disillusionment; and the greater involvement of Jacobean drama in social issues meant that in one field the influence of Jonson was bound to be more important (although several speakers spoke of the impact of *Measure for Measure*). It was noted that at least one regular theatergoer of the 1630s thought that Shirley was a better writer of tragedy than Shakespeare; but it was also pointed out that Jonson's very gibes at "those that beget 'Tales', 'Tempests', and such like drolleries" showed that it was impossible to disregard what Shakespeare wrote. The question was raised whether Jacobean tragedians, anxious—with the possible exception of Chapman—not to compete with Shakespeare in the depiction of the tragic hero, did not prefer to develop the tragic heroine and thereby "change the point of view." Other speakers reminded the seminar that it must not oversimplify either by forgetting that Shakespeare himself was subject to a variety of influences (and did not provide one, constant, model) or by overlooking the possibility that what we saw as borrowings from Shakespeare might be borrowings from plays that had not survived.

The Chairman ventured one comment: that to him the parallels in language, construction, and characterization between *'Tis Pity* and *Romeo and Juliet* were so close that, at least here, more than dramatic genre seemed to be involved; the imitation seemed to be direct, and so detailed as to raise the question whether the audience was not *expected* to recognize it.

No summing up was attempted, but it seemed to be generally agreed that various aspects of the problem of Shakespeare's influence had been defined and some important distinctions made.


## Participants

Robert C. Birss, West Virginia University; Elizabeth M. Brennan, University of London; John Scott Colley, Vanderbilt University; Alan C. Dessen, University of North Carolina; Charles R. Forker, Indiana University; C. J. Gianakaris, Western Michigan University; E. A. J. Honigmann, University of Newcastle-upon-Tyne; Clara Howe, Central State University; Cyrus Hoy, University of Rochester; Harold Jenkins, formerly of University of Edinburgh; Elaine Kalmar, University of Northern Iowa; Michael Newman, Capital University; H. J. Oliver, The University of New South Wales; Thomas Pendleton, Iona College; Catherine M. Shaw, University of California, Riverside; Mark Stavig, Colorado College; Lillian Wilds, California State Polytechnic University, Pomona.

# Anticipations of Shakespeare's Romances in His Earlier Work

## F. DAVID HOENIGER, Chairman

Fifteen scholars whose names are listed at the end participated in this seminar. Each contributed either a short essay or a bibliography on "anticipations" in one or two earlier works. These were made available to all members well before the seminar. None of them was read during the seminar, which met only for an hour and fifteen minutes. Rather, the organizer and chairman divided the papers into seven groups (some consisted of three, others merely of a single paper) and for each asked a different member of the seminar to prepare a four-to-five-minute comment. After it, the authors were given an opportunity to reply briefly, and sometimes there was room for further discussion.

It would be meaningless for this report to concentrate on the discussion itself, stimulating as it sometimes was; rather, the reader will wish to get some idea of the content of the papers themselves. Of these, the bibliographies of previous work naturally required least discussion. They were helpful to the members in preparing themselves for the seminar, and because they included brief critical comments on the quality of previous publications, they ensured that each of us could carry away from the seminar something of useful reference for the future. Two of the best of the original essays that did arouse discussion in the seminar likewise need not be done justice to in this report since they have already been accepted for publication elsewhere: George Hibbard's paper in *Shakespeare Survey 31* and Jill Levenson's in a forthcoming volume of *Shakespeare Studies*. Anyone who desires a full record of our debate may wish to know that a tape of it has been deposited at Eastern Kentucky University. There, one may discover between now and future Shakespeare world congresses how acute or foolish the mortals were who participated in this seminar.

The majority of the contributions involved "anticipations" in the comedies, a few in the tragedies, two in Shakespeare's poems (though no one wrote on the Sonnets), and only one briefly alluded to the English Histories. If Falstaff is regarded by anyone as an anticipation of either Stephano or Trinculo, the point was not raised during the seminar. Some of the papers discussed anticipations of the romances as a whole, but the majority confined themselves to those of one or other of the late plays, *The Winter's Tale* proving a favorite. The variety arose quite naturally; there would have been no sense for the chairman to impose a stricter unity. It did mean that some areas of our subject were not even touched upon, but no one minded that. It also meant that there was a real danger of confusion. That danger proved all the greater because not only did the various papers present views on anticipations of different kind — aspects of characterization, structure, style or imagery, detailed passages, etcetera — but they revealed a lack of agreement as to the implications and the very meaning of the term *anticipations.* This danger was partly overcome by having a more general critical paper on the subject, by Sheldon Zitner, discussed last. The overall discussion did develop fairly satisfactorily, and some left the seminar with new thoughts. If any participant hoped to make use of our debate for a book on the subject, he was probably persuaded otherwise. Some who began in a humor for anticipations found themselves half cured after 75 minutes. Yet the most persuasive of the anticipations that were suggested perhaps withstood the test of our combined critical scrutiny.

The discussion began with a commentary by Sheldon Zitner on three papers involving early comedies and the romances, by Richard van Fossen (*The Comedy of Errors*), Reavley Gair (*Two Gentlemen of Verona*), and Irene Dash (*Love's Labor's Lost* and *The Winter's Tale*). Van Fossen's paper dealt comprehensively with the often-cited parallels between *The Comedy of Errors* and both *Pericles* and *The Tempest,* but also noted that in *The Comedy of Errors* and *The Winter's Tale* alone among Shakespeare's plays Shakespeare withholds a vital fact from the audience: that there is an abbess who is Egeon's wife, and that Hermione is still alive. While in most of Shakespeare's other comedies there is a strong sense of cause and effect, accident is emphasized in *The Comedy of Errors* and in the last plays. Applying a quite different approach, Gair argued in his paper that in *Two Gentlemen of Verona* Shakespeare for the first time faced the problem of how to achieve intensity in dramatic romance, of how to endow characters in such a world, and especially in the play's final act, with real feeling; but that Shakespeare failed, for we cannot credit the play's fairy-tale world. In the romances, Shakespeare solved the problem. The make-believe world achieves credibility. Irene Dash, making use of hints from the books by Philip Edwards and Anne Righter, argued that in the last plays the two worlds of theater and life are more successfully combined than in *Love's Labor's Lost,* but her additional suggestion that in all these plays women respond more nobly to vows and honesty than do the men did not evoke discussion.

Next, Arthur Kirsch commented on the papers by George Hibbard (*A Mid-*

*summer Night's Dream* and *The Tempest*) and Mary Smith *(As You Like It and The Tempest)*. Hibbard's paper presented in telling detail and yet concisely several remarkable "anticipations" of *The Tempest* and *A Midsummer Night's Dream*. Kirsch was full of praise. The paper indeed was a model of how a study of "anticipations" can indeed illuminate further both the earlier and the later works involved. Mary Smith had to face the difficult problem of the extent to which apparent anticipations by *As You Like It* of *The Tempest* are hardly more than familiar characteristics of the pastoral tradition. She emphasized the difference in structure of the two plays. The later play, she argued, "subsumes the former."

In her commentary on the next group of papers, Irene Dash could concentrate on the one by Arthur Kirsch (*Much Ado About Nothing, All's Well That Ends Well,* and *Cymbeline*), the two others being bibliographical. Kirsch's paper again differed markedly in approach from the rest: Shakespeare's preoccupation in the three plays with the theme of fashion-mongering associated with intemperate sexuality. While exploring this theme, Shakespeare moreover involved biblical ideas, Kirsch argued. The two middle or "problem" comedies and *Cymbeline* reveal the mixed nature of sexuality and make us comprehend the presence of and the need for grace.

Ernest Schanzer was the commentator on Jill Levenson's long and strikingly original paper devoted to the problem plays and the romances. The complex argument of this paper would be difficult to summarize, and there is no need to, for a shorter version of it will soon be published. After beginning with the observation that the problem plays and romances are both marked by the conspicuous use of folklore narratives well-known to Shakespeare's audience, as a distancing device, a depersonalizing experience, the bulk of the paper attempted to define fundamental differences. Miss Levenson distinguished two types of folklore materials and two basic ways of using them in drama. The first type, employed in the problem plays, most clearly so in *Troilus and Cressida,* she defined as legend, "half-way to history"; the second, employed in the romances, as fairy-tale or Märchen. In the problem plays, Shakespeare revised the familiar tale drastically, and invited the viewer to resolve the discrepancy between what he had anticipated from the story and the drama's actual development and resolution. In the romances, by contrast, he kept more closely to the original folklore fable, so that the audience could predict the outcome and even the basic formulation of episodes. But of course some of the plays mark these differences in materials and method more sharply than others. While Schanzer's response was rather skeptical, others of the group responded positively to the thesis.

Because John Arthos's good paper on *The Phoenix and Turtle* reached us late, Reavley Gair was able to do justice only to Julian Patrick's contribution on *The Rape of Lucrece* and *The Winter's Tale,* an essay that I hope will be published. Patrick dealt with the episode in the poem where Lucrece remembers a painting of Troy's capture by the Greeks; she does not merely remember but becomes a participant in the story by scratching out with her nails the fair-seeming figure of Sinon. He argued that this incident in the poem's story is an early instance of Shakespeare's use of an experience from a far-away world that individual characters yet experience with intimate directness. Later instances include Miranda's response to the storm in the second scene of *The Tempest* and especially the artistic illusion of Hermione's statue in *The Winter's Tale.* In the statue scene, Patrick argued, the ingredients of Lucrece's attack on the painting are exactly reversed by Hermione's "coming to life." This example of anticipation enables the critic to specify a difference between the function of artistic illusion in tragedy and in romance.

Of the three papers that had been prepared on the tragedies, Richard Van Fossen in his comment chose to concentrate chiefly on Ernest Schanzer's essay, which dealt with the late tragedies and *The Winter's Tale.* Only a few months after the seminar, Shakespeareans in many parts of the world were saddened by the news of the sudden death of this great scholar. Some of the chief ideas he presented in his brief paper have fortunately been published elsewhere; see *Shakespeare Jahrbuch* (1969), pp. 103-21. Schanzer developed the thesis that *Coriolanus* and *Timon of Athens* have, like *The Winter's Tale,* a two-part structure, the second part of which both repeats and contrasts with the first. Examples in *Coriolanus* of such "ironic" and "contrasting parallels" are the welcome to Coriolanus in 2.1 and that to Volumnia in 5.5; also Coriolanus's being called a traitor by Sicinius at the end of the play's first part, and by Aufidius close to its conclusion.

The meeting concluded with a response by George Hibbard to a much broader critical paper by Sheldon Zitner, which took issue with some of the basic assumptions of our endeavor. As some readers of these pages will have guessed, the very subject of our seminar, and perhaps also the way it had been organized up to this point, were prone to lead into pitfalls those among us whose enthusiasm had made them confident that the seminar would indeed result in an abundant gathering of anticipations. Do most great artists really tend to anticipate themselves that way? Would we be justified, for instance, in looking in Beethoven's first to seventh symphonies for anticipations of his eighth and ninth? And if we did, would the resulting "discoveries" help illuminate Beethoven's creative imagination or merely reflect our wishful thinking?

Zitner asked these basic questions without employing the analogy given. He distinguished between what he called a coherent and a daemonic canon of an artist's work. One can see his individual works "as links in a coherent evolutionary history, or they are seen as . . . so many discrete results of independent impulses." By implication most of us had clearly favored the former view, but Zitner's preference was for Shakespeare's imagination as "daemonic"—content with achieving coherence among the materials of the single new, unprecedented play or poem on which he was at work. Further, should we not take more account of how much the Romances "differ from one another"? Zitner selected for special attack the widespread tendency among critics to confuse genuine "anticipations" with mere parallels in plot motif, theme, imagery, characterization, or commonplace poetic devices.

The paper obviously urged greater critical caution in the pursuit of our subject and implied that several of the anticipations that had been suggested were nothing more than parallels. But George Hibbard's reply took the form of an impassioned defense of "valid anticipations," heartening those who needed encouragement. This time, he provided illustrations from other plays than *A Midsummer Night's Dream*, whose connections with *The Tempest* he had revealed so persuasively in his paper. It was a fitting conclusion for a seminar that unfortunately had to be rushed at the end so that the Congress, so crammed with offerings, could proceed to yet different approaches to Shakespeare. The wit and insights of some of its members made the seminar a pleasant occasion.

## Participants

John Arthos, University of Michigan; William Baillie, Bloomsburg State College, Pa.; R. E. Burkhart, Eastern Kentucky University; Irene Dash, Hunter College, N.Y.; W. Reavley Gair, University of New Brunswick, Canada; George Hibbard, University of Waterloo, Ontario; F. David Hoeniger, Victoria College, Toronto; Arthur Kirsch, University of Virginia; Jill Levenson, Trinity College, Toronto; Shirley Morgan, Chadron State College, Neb.; Julian Patrick, Victoria College, Toronto; Ernest Schanzer, University of München, West Germany; Mary Smith, University of New Brunswick, St. John, N.B.; Linda Tolman, Lakeland College, Wis.; Richard Van Fossen, Erindale College, Toronto; Sheldon Zitner, Trinity College, Toronto.

# Shakespeare's English

## MARVIN SPEVACK, Chairman

Since the study of Shakespeare's English is not confined to Shakespeareans, the members of the seminar were drawn from the fields of literature, linguistics, and lexicography. Despite the wide range of their specialized interests — "statistical studies of vocabulary, of syntax, and of rhetorical devices" (Burton); "keeping Shakespeare's language accessible to students" (Feynman); "reconciling 'soft' interpretive speculation and 'hard' linguistic and historical data" (Jones); "chains of mutual metaphorical enlivenment as an underlay to the syntax" (King); "Shakespeare's language and American English" (Lehnert); "diachronic, situational, dialectal, and sociolectal variation in Shakespeare's English" (Neuhaus); "the use of language for characterization" (Nicholl); "the value of linguistic terminology in assessing the merits of Renaissance styles on aesthetic principles" (Partridge); "the grammatic-stylistic range that can be regarded as specifically Shakespearean as distinct from (general) Elizabethan" (Quirk); "a systematic method of research into Shakespeare's vocabulary" (Rosinger) — the members were agreed that individual questions and needs could best be dealt with if the Shakespeare corpus itself were treated in a complete and systematic manner and, further, that this treatment might provide a model for the treatment of other corpora and so link up the ever-increasing sources of synchronic and diachronic information about Shakespearean English, Elizabethan English, and indeed modern English itself. Accordingly, the seminar concentrated its attention on the nature and state of data already derived and still to be derived from the Shakespeare corpus.

The discussion began with a comparison of Alexander Schmidt's *Shakespeare-Lexicon* and C. T. Onions's *A Shakespeare Glossary,* in which it was apparent that certain differences are due to the distinctive conceptions of what such a reference work should provide. Thus Onions selects words that are "exceptional" for modern English but omits the diachronic aspect, which might call for the inclusion of a word like *potato,* a new and perhaps "excep-

tional" word in Shakespeare's time. Schmidt ignores the diachronic, prefer-
ring to gloss all words according to the context in which they appear. A comparison of the entries for *nice* in both works reveals further and striking differences in the number of "meanings," the order of the "meanings," and the
selection of contexts to illustrate particular "meanings." A detailed comparison by Professor Rosinger of these glosses with those in a modern
Shakespeare edition (the recent *Riverside Shakespeare*) showed some form of
disagreement in almost thirty percent of the cases. In all works, both synchronic and diachronic variations are insufficiently treated or even ignored.
The existing Shakespeare dictionaries would appear to suffer from the same
deficiencies as most dictionaries: a noticeable subjectivity coupled with an
equally noticeable lack of structural information, due in no small part to a
rather undeveloped or limited semantic conception. The lack of clarity is
especially apparent in the glosses in editions of Shakespeare, where the
vagaries of synonymy are most in evidence because editors often provide
"synonyms" with little regard for situational variation or registers, not merely
in the relationship between the word glossed and the glossing word but also
among the glossing words themselves. It was agreed that a clear and useful
reference work is to be achieved not simply by the optimization of the present
models—that is, by the expansion of the existing data and the refinement of
the means of new models based on more extensive data and resources than
have hitherto been available.

Thus the discussion turned to the necessity of recognizing, as Professor
Quirk pointed out, that author-specific dictionaries are based on principles
different from those governing universal dictionaries since an author's
language admits of a control impossible in English as a whole, especially
(though not exclusively) in the easy accessibility of all contexts and colloca-
tions. This is important, for "the locus of a word cannot be compartmented
without reference to the coexistence and coweight of alternative meanings"
(Professor King). But because "meaning" may essentially rest upon the accumulation, evaluation, and counterpoising of various kinds of information,
it was decided to look at material that an author dictionary might present as
information in itself, as an illustration of the special perspectives of an author
dictionary, and as preparation for a semantic description.

A selection of material drawn from *SHAD* (A Shakespeare Dictionary)
being produced at the University of Münster, Germany, was then analyzed.
Although the material is in no way final or prescriptive in content and form,
it elicited a lively discussion of both the nature of the data that might be made
available and the manner in which it might best be presented.[1]

In the course of the discussion Mr. Burchfield, while emphasizing the need
for some diachronic basis for a presentation of Shakespeare's English, informed the seminar briefly about the difficulties involved when different dictionaries attempt to elucidate a word as complicated as *nice*, difficulties that

## SHAD: A SHAKESPEARE DICTIONARY

lemma:               fondly

word-class:          adverb (as adjective not in Shakespeare)

frequency:           10

chronological
distribution:

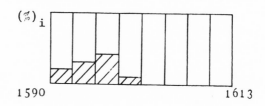

1590                                                    1613

genre
distribution:

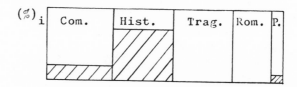

syntactical        only in verb phrases with subjects in the singular
category:          that have a person as referent: pronouns (9x),
                   noun (R2 3.2.9)

    preceding verb: reason (ERR 4.2.57), flatter'd
    (SHR 4.2.31), pass (JN 2.1.253), spur (R2 4.1.
    72), brought (2H4 4.2.119), gave away (3H6
    2.2.38), impose on (R3 3.7.147), dote (LUC 207)

    following verb: plays (R2 3.2.9), speak (R2 3.3.
    185)

semantically       ... like a frantic man (R2 3.3.185); shallowly ...
pertinent          Fondly ... foolishly (2H4); careless father ...
contexts:          (3H6); how fondly ... (ERR, R2 4.1.72, LUC)

morphology/        the Shakespearian semantics is close to the ety-
etymology:         mological base: _fon_, noun (fool); _fon_, adjective
                   (foolish)

    the morphology implies an underlying semantic
    comparison (like a fool)

status:            this sense is obsolete (-1648)

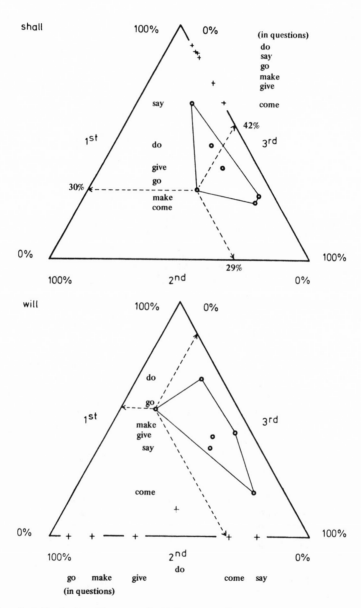

Trinominal distribution (first, second, third person) of 390 *shall* and 576 *will* constructions with six high frequency verbs (circled: ○). 22.05% of the *shall* constructions and 16.66% of the *will* constructions appearing in questions are also given separately (crossed: +) to show the radical drop in second person constructions for *shall* (0%), and in first person constructions for *will* (0%, except for two cases of *do*). The broken lines illustrate how the figure is to be read, using *go* as an example.

HORSE: Morphological Family

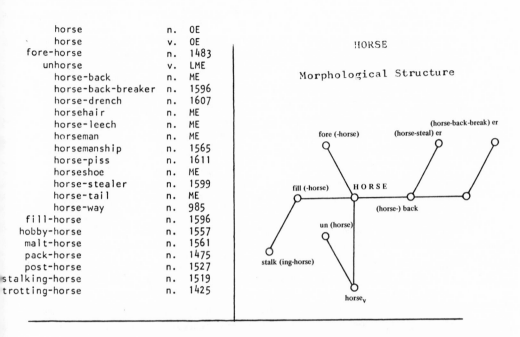

| | | |
|---|---|---|
| horse | n. | OE |
| horse | v. | OE |
| fore-horse | n. | 1483 |
| unhorse | v. | LME |
| horse-back | n. | ME |
| horse-back-breaker | n. | 1596 |
| horse-drench | n. | 1607 |
| horsehair | n. | ME |
| horse-leech | n. | ME |
| horseman | n. | ME |
| horsemanship | n. | 1565 |
| horse-piss | n. | 1611 |
| horseshoe | n. | ME |
| horse-stealer | n. | 1599 |
| horse-tail | n. | ME |
| horse-way | n. | 985 |
| fill-horse | n. | 1596 |
| hobby-horse | n. | 1557 |
| malt-horse | n. | 1561 |
| pack-horse | n. | 1475 |
| post-horse | n. | 1527 |
| stalking-horse | n. | 1519 |
| trotting-horse | n. | 1425 |

HORSE

Morphological Structure

Chronological distribution in Shakespeare's plays of the ratio (in percent) between *-eth* and *-es* suffixes used as third person singular inflectional morpheme with 69 verbs (342 tokens) whose stems end in sibilants (e.g., *loseth*).

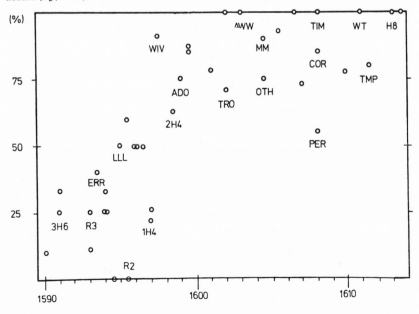

also make the revision of existing universal dictionaries so problematic, with the result that a work like the *OED* cannot be readily revised but has to be supplemented. He then gave a brief report on the state of the *OED* supplements and the *SOED*. Professor Bailey followed with a description of the work being done at the University of Michigan on the Dictionary of Early Modern English (1475-1700) and produced additional diachronic information on *nice* and on the suffix *-ish*, as well as on the morphological family of *horse*, drawn from the Michigan Early Modern English materials. Professor Spevack then described the progress of SHAD, indicating that when the special requirements of an author dictionary, the variegated nature of the material, and the potential of the computer are taken into consideration, it becomes clear that a multivolume work is necessary. He pointed out that the first volume of SHAD would present, at the level of the lemma, morphology, relevant distributional information, and a taxonomic classification of the Shakespeare corpus. Following volumes, addressing individual problems individually, are to deal with syntax, phonology, and the like. The treatment of the Shakespeare data in smaller but homogeneous units of a compatible nature might be one way of approaching the complex problem of semantics, the seminar agreed.

Professor Quirk thought it advisable to extend the efforts to cover Shakespeare's contemporaries, a suggestion perhaps more realizable now than before, given the number of projects underway and the advances in technology. The members of the committee were unanimous in the belief that a grasp of Shakespeare's English is not identical with the glossing of single words, and that the glossing of single words does not necessarily deal with "meaning." They were of the opinion that there is a need for a systematic control of all aspects of the entire corpus and not just of isolated aspects. And they held that only a clear and effective analytical organization of the material can satisfy the wide variety of interests and needs that attract literary, linguistic, lexicographic scholars, and a host of others to Shakespeare.

## Participants

Richard W. Bailey, University of Michigan; R. W. Burchfield, University of Oxford; Dolores M. Burton, Boston University; Alberta E. Feynman, Skidmore College; James L. Jackson, George Mason University; G. P. Jones, Memorial University of Newfoundland; Joo-Hyon Kim, Seoul; Arthur Henry King, Brigham Young University; Martin Lehnert, Humbolt University of Berlin; H. J. Neuhaus, University of Münster; James R. Nicholl, Western Carolina University; A. C. Partridge, University of the Witwatersrand, Johannesburg; Randolph Quirk, University of London; Lawrence Rosinger, Henry Ford Community College; Jürgen Schäfer, University of Augsburg; Marvin Spevack, University of Münster; Joy P. Wells, Washington, D.C.

## Notes

1. For a more extensive description of the nature and aims of SHAD, as well as explanations of the diagrams, see M. Spevack, H. J. Neuhaus, T. Finkenstaedt, "SHAD: A Shakespeare Dictionary," in *Computers in the Humanities,* ed. J. L. Mitchell (Edinburgh, 1974), pp. 111-23; H. Joachim Neuhaus and Marvin Spevack, "A Shakespeare Dictionary (SHAD): Some Preliminaries for a Semantic Description," *Computers and the Humanities* 9, no. 6 (November 1975): 263-70; Marvin Spevack and H. Joachim Neuhaus, "SHAD (A Shakespeare Dictionary): Toward Volume One," *Bulletin of the Association for Literary and Linguistic Computing* 5, no. 1 (1977): 15-22.

# Shakespeare's Sources as Clues to Meaning

## VIRGIL K. WHITAKER, Chairman

Professor Virgil K. Whitaker, Chairman, opened the seminar by emphasizing that the most important function of Shakespeare scholarship is to contribute to the clarification and interpretation of the themes and meanings of Shakespeare's texts, and that source studies have an important role to play in this task in furnishing addditional clues where meanings are doubtful. He requested the participants to confine their remarks as far as possible to the general methodology of using source data in interpreting the meanings of the plays.

Professors Madeline Doran and Kenneth Muir were welcomed as honored guests to the session.

Eschewing the thorny path of methodology, a number of participants gave extracts of papers (doubtless to appear in due time) identifying possible sources of various fragments of various plays. More interesting than this technique, said one speaker, is Shakespeare's "total response" to a source; that is, how he sees it, what he does with it as shown by the changes of detail and perspective he makes. A good underpinning for this and a number of related observations was furnished by the remarks of another speaker, who on the basis of a study of *Troilus and Cressida* found that in treating a given feature of characterization, Shakespeare (1) follows the source as closely as possible, (2) otherwise, follows any popular traditions about the character, but (3) makes any changes dictated by dramatic necessity. A number of speakers cited these *changes* as furnishing the most valuable type of clues.

In a related series of remarks and exchanges, the question of the relative importance of the source materials to the final product came up: one speaker (who doubtless had wandered into the wrong seminar) indicated that the essence of Shakespeare is his *poetry,* and that sources had little to contribute to *that,* while another countered that even the poetry (no definition) is strongly affected by the way a character is presented in the source. Several participants were struck by the fact that important features of the plays were developed from the slightest of hints in the sources, leading to the observation by Professor Whitaker that Shakespeare's "wonderful" imagination seemed to operate best under some slight stimulus. Along the lines of changes dictated by dramatic necessity Calpurnia's dream (*Julius Caesar*) was cited, which one participant saw as altered from the source by Shakespeare to correspond with the concerns of his audience. Another type of response of Shakespeare to a source, that of irritation or boredom, leading to a humorous or parodying treatment of source element, was cited in connection with Brooke's *Tragicall History of Romeus and Juliet*.

The final general theme to surface, introduced from a dissertation in progress, was that of Shakespeare and women, "Male chauvinist or not?"—the speaker concluding that, compared with source characterization, some of Shakespeare's women show a deliberate effort at rehabilitation of feminine roles. Another participant defended Shakespeare against a charge of having Desdemona "flirt and banter inappropriately" with Iago (*Othello* 2.1) by saying that Desdemona is interfering here in order to protect Emilia from Iago's verbal persecutions.

The final speaker recommended traditional ballads as an insufficiently exploited source, and cited examples from the Henry VI plays.

Arthur P. Stabler, Recorder

## Participants

Robert B. Bennett, University of Delaware; Norman A. Brittin, Auburn University; May E. Campbell, Texas A and I University; A. U. Chapman, Western Reserve Academy; Earl John Clark, Northeastern Illinois University; Joan Coldwell, McMaster University; Carol Elizabeth Dixon, Fredericksburg, Virginia; Robert F. Fleissner, Central State University, Ohio; Charles Frey, University of Washington; Robert C. Fulton, University of Tennessee, Chattanooga; Sister Mary Hoover, Notre Dame College; John Mahon, Iona College; Peter Pauls, University of Winnipeg; Thomas A. Perry, East Texas State University; John Shaw, Hiram College; Kezia Vanmeter Sproat, Columbus, Ohio; Arthur P. Stabler, Washington State University; Zelda Teplitz, M. D., Washington, D. C.; Virgil K. Whitaker, Stanford University.

# Shakespeare as Spokesman for the Orthodoxies of his Time: The Validity of Some Modern Critical Assumptions

THELMA N. GREENFIELD, Chairman

This seminar was devised under the stimulus of recent reactions against certain important critics and critical methods that have dominated much of Shakespeare criticism and teaching of the middle twentieth century. The attack has largely aimed at Shakespeare as orthodox moralist, at what J. W. Lever has called the "neo-pietism" of our time. Shakespeare as orthodox thinker is a view characteristically American, although its sources certainly have in part been located abroad, and thus the topic seemed relevant to the American focus as well as to the international nature of the Congress.

For clarification, the prospectus for the seminar began with a series of quotations indicative of the temper of some reactions against the "orthodox Shakespeare":

> It has become increasingly fashionable in academic criticism to extrapolate from Elizabethan drama a moral order, or a moral vision, which is thought to have been the playwright's main concern in his honorary capacity as Christian humanist. (J. W. Lever, *The Tragedy of State,* p. 39)

> Our conception of the Elizabethans has been codified for us into an "orthodoxy," a world-picture which, if it has not yet induced complete apathy about these dull, conformist people, has only failed to do so because generation after generation of readers and playgoers has known that the literature itself offers much more. (Wilbur Sanders, *The Dramatist and the Received Idea,* pp. 1-2)

All too frequently the moralistic school of criticism tends to reject the old fashioned tragic responses, admiration, pity, and terror, in favor of analytical castigation. Simultaneously, it occasionally prefers its own moral idealism to dramatic consistency and truth to human experience. (Harriet Hawkins, *Likenesses of Truth in Elizabethan and Restoration Drama*, p. 14)

Insisting on the primacy of Shakespeare's didactic intention, scholarship would have us believe that the interpretation of the History Plays does not depend on sensitivity to nuances of language and characterization or awareness of Shakespeare's poetic and dramatic methods; it depends instead on the appropriate annotation of the doctrine of the plays. (Robert Ornstein, *A Kingdom for a Stage*, p. 8)

There followed for examination five assumptions that seem to attach to the view that Shakespeare was spokesman for contemporary orthodoxies: Shakespeare's orthodoxies are *the* predominant aspect of his thought. Orthodoxies of Renaissance thinking are fairly clearly defined and we can make assumptions about the unanimity of minds in Shakespeare's audience. Shakespeare centers his plays upon contemporary positions, especially moral. A morally aimed historical view of Shakespeare's art places ideas above action and presentation as dramatic bases; sententious dialogue and biblical allusions are likely to be figural in the plays rather than enrichments. Examination of character must be heavily weighted; tragedy becomes punitive with the tragic flaw or defective will the key to human suffering; comedy is corrective in intent.

The question was also raised as to the validity and usefulness of alternatives of method and orientation offered by critics who lead the attacks. The prospectus concluded with a short list of recommended readings: Dame Helen Gardner, *Religion and Literature* (London, 1971); Harriet Hawkins, *Likenesses of Truth in Elizabethan and Restoration Drama* (Oxford, 1972); Robert Ornstein, *A Kingdom for a Stage: The Achievement of Shakespeare's History Plays* (Cambridge, Mass., 1972); Leo Salingar, *Shakespeare and the Traditions of Comedy* (Cambridge, 1974); Wilbur Sanders, *The Dramatist and the Received Idea* (Cambridge, 1968).

Papers were invited for circulation but not required. Participants responded with the following submissions:

Harriet Hawkins, " 'The Devil's Party': Critical Problems in Elizabethan Drama." Indicative that the question of moralistic criticism goes far beyond Shakespeare, Hawkins's paper attacked the tendency in much modern criticism of Renaissance drama to assume the presence of solutions to all problems presented or to label characters, plays, and playwrights as moral or immoral, orthodox or heterodox. She attacked likewise the assumption that thinking Elizabethans were orthodox, and concluded that great poets of the time often confront us with injustice, inequality, and the harsh truths of unsolved evil.

Robert Grudin, "Shakespeare and Ethical Tradition: Hazard and Justice in *The Merchant of Venice.*" Grudin found *The Merchant* to be a document of sixteenth-century thought but even within that context he finds intentional iconoclasm, moral ambiguity, and skepticism. His Portia is an "enlightened trickster."

Robert Merrix, "Creative Orthodoxy: A Response to Some Shakespearean Liberators." Shakespeare seems orthodox at times and modernly ambivalent at others. Actually, however, he reflects the ambivalence of his own age.

Carolyn Ruth Swift Lenz, "The New Feminist Criticism of Shakespeare." Our own orthodoxies have biased our responses to Shakespeare's portrayals of characters and relationships. Feminist criticism is surveyed to find possible correctives. The paper argues for the need to distinguish between dramatic device and dramatic sanction and between one orthodoxy and many orthodoxies.

Virginia Carr, " 'Book' and 'Counterbook' in Shakespeare's Histories." Henry V is himself an ambiguous figure and elicits ambiguous responses from the audience because he must manipulate his countrymen and also love and be loved by them.

Suheyla Artemel, "The Commitment of Shakespeare to Man." Shakespeare is not a spokesman for a particular group or creed but neither is he the "uninvolved bystander." His universal appeal comes from his drawing upon popular wisdom, Christian thought, and Renaissance humanism.

Waldo McNeir, "A Distinction without a Difference?" To debate Shakespeare's historical, philosophical, or theological orthodoxy is likely to force his plays into the area of verbal constructs at the expense of the theatrical dimension.

At the convening of the seminar, by prearrangement several members commented upon the papers. C. L. Barber addressed himself to Harriet Hawkins's essay. He enlarged upon Hawkins's argument to add greater complexity to the question. In *King Lear*, Barber pointed out, Shakespeare affirms the values of love, mercy, and justice, but those values emerge directly from the human action of the play and are not imposed by the demands of ideology. Barber also praised Lenz's paper as offering a very helpful approach to the problem of what it is Shakespeare sanctions.

Lowell Johnson disagreed with Grudin's focus on the failures in *The Merchant* and argued that the successful characters defend a "larger orthodoxy of the Elizabethan ideal of justice." Although he was willing to see a line leading from *The Merchant* to *Measure,* Johnson did not wish to sacrifice the play's place in the romantic comedies. Ronald Meldrum tied Waldo McNeir's paper to Salingar's *Shakespeare and the Traditions of Comedy* and agreed to the value of emphasizing the theatrical aspect and its tradition.

Those whose papers had no formal assessment by another participant were asked to comment on their own papers, and (except for Virginia Carr) did so, mainly to reiterate their major points. Participants whose papers had received formal responses were called upon to answer if they chose. The meeting was then thrown open to further discussion. Louise Clubb asserted the need for broader studies in Continental backgrounds. Louis Schuster found early sixteenth-century humanistic Bible studies traceable in many places in Shakespeare's language.

Most participants seemed to agree that we must beware of oversimplifying the notion of an Elizabethan orthodoxy and of assuming too readily that we know what Shakespeare's audience was like. For example, the Christian beliefs of the Elizabethans are always referred to in any attempt to describe their "world picture," but sixteenth-century Christianity took many different forms, and sixteenth-century Christians could disagree radically on almost every subject from theology to politics to manners and morals. Consequently, attempts to understand Shakespeare's plays by reference to the views of his contemporaries must proceed very cautiously. Some members of the seminar argued that while Shakespeare was no doubt aware of the major currents of thought in his day, his plays are too complex to be explained in terms of any single system of ideas. He shows the influence of popular culture, Christian thought, and Renaissance humanism, but he espouses none of these uncritically and presents instead an undogmatic vision of the truth about man.

Shakespeare was essentially skeptical of systems and forces us to see what is problematic in human existence rather than what can be easily categorized; even plays that have often been seen as relatively simple are filled with deep ambiguities. Some participants stressed that Shakespeare's plays are neither philosophical treatises nor homilies but dramas designed for production on the stage, and as such are inevitably open to the different interpretations of different directors living in different times and places; to treat Shakespeare as a spokesman for a reconstructed Elizabethan orthodoxy simply ignores the richness to which the dramatic tradition of over three centuries attests. On the other hand, many members of the seminar contended that it is still possible to make use of the idea of an Elizabethan orthodoxy, provided it is introduced with an awareness of the difficulties involved; some of the plays reflect patterns of Christian worship, and certain of the dominant ideas of the time can be felt to have a great power in Shakespeare's work even when they are not affirmed in an unqualified manner. The plays necessarily reflect the pressures of the environment in which they were conceived. In the end, no consensus was achieved, but none was expected. It was notable that the topic called forth discussion, either in the papers or in the meeting, of every type of Shakespearean play.

The subject in itself seemed to generate considerable interest. There was much urging that the problem be further pursued in other forums. Among the very large group of auditors were several persons kind enough to send along offprints and other papers and mention of papers relevant to the subject. Thanks are especially due to Professors Roy Battenhouse, Richard Levin, and Gordon Ross Smith. After the hour, auditors joined the discussion.

Dain Trafton, Recorder (revised by T. Greenfield)

## Participants

S. Artemel, Bogazici University, Istanbul; Virginia M. Carr, Allegheny College; Louise Clubb, University of California, Berkeley; Thelma N. Greenfield, University of Oregon; Robert Grudin, University of Oregon; Harriet Hawkins, Vassar College; Soji Iwasaki, Nagoya University, Japan; Hobart Jarrett, CUNY; Lowell E. Johnson, Saint Olaf College; Carolyn Lenz, Rhode Island College; Waldo F. McNeir (Emeritus), University of Oregon; Ronald M. Meldrum, Washington State University; Robert Merrix, University of Akron; Louis A. Schuster, Saint Mary's University of San Antonio; Dain Trafton, Rockford College; C. L. Barber, University of California, Santa Cruz.

# The First Public Playhouse:
# The Theatre in Shoreditch

## HERBERT BERRY, Chairman

To open the discussion, Professor Berry spoke briefly of his own seminar paper, an up-dated handlist with current call numbers for all extant documents related to the Theatre. He spoke briefly of the work of C. W. Wallace and C. C. Stopes, noting that although transcriptions of the bulk of the documents had been in print since 1913, the material had been little used by theater historians. He then asked Professor Wickham to continue the discussion.

Professor Wickham spoke at some length about the rather "surprising" results of his examination of the plays produced at all playhouses before 1590; there is no textual evidence for the existence of a heavens or of machinery above the stage in any of the early playhouses.

Professor Hosley, picking up on this point, raised the question of the relationship between the physical structure of the Theatre, and that of the First Globe, built from the timbers of the demolished Theatre. On balance, Professor Hosley felt that the Theatre and the First Globe were probably of the same size; this would not preclude changes in the superstructure, which would have provided a "heavens."

Professor Hosley in his formal paper had argued for the relevance of a banqueting house in Calais, raised by English workmen for Henry VIII, to similar "theatrical" structures built in England some sixty years later. Professor Brownstein, while granting Professor Hosley's major point of a continuum of building practice and custom, challenged the conventional assumption that public playhouses, specifically the Theatre, were modeled on the bull- and bear-baiting yards. Professor Brownstein based his argument on the fact that, although elaborate baiting yards on the Bankside were available at the time, Burbage went ahead with the construction of an expensive playhouse in Shoreditch. That he did so suggests that such structures were not suitable for use as playhouses. Although baiting rings and playhouses share some common general features, a roughly circular ground plan on which a number of galleries are stacked, the fundamental function of the baiting ring is to keep the performers and the spectators apart, while the fundamental function of the playhouse is to unite the performers and the spectators. While both seek to promote visibility of the performers, the need to protect the spectators at the baiting ring dictates a structure that is fundamentally unsuitable for use as a playhouse.

Professor Ingram generally agreed with the arguments advanced by Professor Brownstein, and wondered why, indeed, Burbage did not lease rather than build. Professor Ingram's formal paper dealt with precisely the same kind of question: What lay behind the curious arrangement that obtained between the proprietors of the Theatre and the Curtain? What did Laneman really mean when he reported that Burbage and Brayne took "the Curten as an Esore to their playe housse"? Professor Ingram suggested, with due caution, that perhaps it was an arrangement that enabled Laneman to retire from the active management of the Curtain, and one that allowed Burbage to buy the Curtain, as it were, on "time."

The formal participants of the seminar had gone to work with such a will that the allotted time soon passed, and Professor Berry closed the seminar regretting that there had been no time for comments from the many-headed multitude. General applause! A summary of the formal papers presented to the seminar concludes this report.


WILLIAM INGRAM. The paper concerns the arrangement that the owners of the Theatre (James Burbage and John Brayne) and the owner of the neighboring Curtain (Henry Laneman) made in 1585, according to which for seven years Burbage and Brayne took half the profits of the Curtain and Laneman took half the profits of the Theatre. It is a curious arrangement made even more curious by one of Laneman's remarks about it: "the said Burbage and Brayne" took "the Curten as an Esore to their playe housse." Professor Ingram suggests that the purpose of the arrangement was to allow Laneman to give up active participation in the Curtain and Burbage to take control of it, perhaps even to buy it.

OSCAR BROWNSTEIN. The paper challenges the conventional idea that the public playhouses, and specifically the Theatre, were modeled on the bull- and bear-baiting yards. In 1575, when presumably James Burbage was planning the Theater, both the relatively elaborate baiting yards on Bankside were available. Why did Burbage not save himself much money and trouble by simply leasing or buying one of them rather than undertaking the expensive scheme in Shoreditch? Professor Brownstein argues that the traditional design of baiting yards rendered them unsuitable for plays, and that eventually, when the playhouse model was thoroughly established, Philip Henslowe abandoned both his beargarden and his playhouse, the Rose, to construct the Hope, as a house that could accommodate both plays and baitings. The design of baiting yards, therefore, came to follow that of the playhouse rather than vice versa.

GLYNNE WICKHAM. The paper argues that not only at the Theatre, but at all playhouses before about 1590, there were no heavens, no machinery above the stage, no chair of state that could be let down, not even stage pillars holding up a roof over the stage. Of the 29 surviving plays performed in the public playhouses between 1576 and the early 1590s, Greene's *Alphonsus King of Aragon* is the first to mention a flying chair of state, and Greene clearly supposed that a playhouse might not have one, for one of his stage direction reads, *"Exit Venus. Or if you can conveniently, let a chaire come downe from the top of the stage, and draw her up."* Professor Wickham suggests that Henslowe's expenditures at the Rose in 1591/92 and 1595 were to build or rebuild the roof over the stage and to install machinery and a throne in it, that the Swan of 1594 would have had this equipment from the start, and that one of the motives for dismantling and moving the Theatre in 1598 was to rebuild it so as to include such equipment in it.

RICHARD HOSLEY. The paper argues that if the later public playhouses were large, "round" (i.e., polygonal), timber buildings of three stories, then when James Burbage built the Theatre in 1576 such structures were hardly new to Englishmen. Professor Hosley describes the construction, the shape, and the dimensions of one such structure, put up in Calais in 1520, in which Henry VIII thought to entertain Charles V with "pageants and other devices" at the time of the Field of Cloth of Gold. Professor Hosley suggests that the building was about 122' in diameter and 32' high at the outside edge, and that the polygon comprised 16 sections, each of which was 24' wide at its outside edge.

HERBERT BERRY. The paper is a handlist of the documents about the Theatre. It gives the current call numbers for the documents transcribed by C. W. Wallace and C. C. Stopes and printed in their rival books of 1913; a few new documents; and a brief summary of each document. It enables one to read quickly through the history of the four legal quarrels that the documents record. Professor Berry finds Wallace's work much more rigorous and systematic than Mrs. Stopes's, though Wallace was capable, occasionally, of a run of minor mistakes and very occasionally of as many as 7 such mistakes in 13 lines as printed.

D. F. Rowan, Recorder

## Participants

Herbert Berry, University of Saskatchewan;   Oscar Brownstein, University of Iowa; Glynne Wickham, University of Bristol; Richard Hosley, University of Arizona; William Ingram, University of Michigan; Richard Kohler, San Diego State University; D. F. Rowan, University of New Brunswick.

# The Future of Shakespearean Bibliography

JOHN ANDREWS, Chairman

Mr. Andrews opened the meeting by observing that the subject of the seminar was to be enumerative bibliography, as opposed to textual bibliography. He then said a few words about the reason he had suggested a seminar on the future of Shakespearean bibliography. He pointed out that the World Shakespeare Bibliography, published annually in *Shakespeare Quarterly,* was in a period of transition, having had its administrative offices transferred from Simon Fraser University (where it had been edited for a number of years by Rudolph E. Habenicht and Bruce Nesbitt) to the Pennsylvania State University (where it was now being edited by Harrison T. Meserole). He went on to note that the transition involved considerably more than a transfer of administrative headquarters and personnel, inasmuch as Professor Meserole was instituting some important changes in the bibliography: (1) introducing a new system of organization and classsification for bibliographical entries and annotations; (2) computerizing the entry process for the first time in the history of the Bibliography; and (3) beginning the initial phases of a new cumulation, to produce a successor volume to Gordon Ross Smith's *A Classified Shakespeare Bibliography, 1936-1958* (University Park: Pennsylvania State University Press, 1963). Mr. Andrews said that he and Professor Meserole had discussed various means of implementing these objectives, and that they had concluded that the best way to begin the project would be to convene an international gathering of Shakespeareans for the purpose of discussing a specific set of proposals and questions related to Shakespearean bibliography. Mr. Andrews expressed pleasure at the large attendance for the seminar and gave particular mention to the diversity of interests and institutions represented by the members and auditors enrolled in the seminar.

Mr. Andrews next referred seminar participants to materials that had been distributed prior to the meeting: (1) a set of questions under the heading

"Guidelines for Participants"; (2) Professor Meserole's preliminary draft of "Principles, Procedures, and Guidelines" for members of the Committee of Correspondents for the World Shakespeare Bibliography; (3) Robert W. Dent's article "Reflections of a Shakespeare Bibliographer," in *Pacific Coast Studies in Shakespeare,* ed. Waldo F. McNeir and Thelma N. Greenfield (Eugene: University of Oregon Books, 1966), pp. 303-15; and (4) papers and comments prepared specifically for the seminar by Russell Fraser, William A. Gibson, Rudolph E. Habenicht (who was unable to attend), Joan Holmer, Jayne K. Kribbs, Shirley Marchalonis, Kenneth Muir, Tauno F. Mustanoja, and Chester Wolford. Mr. Andrews then asked Professor Meserole to speak for a few minutes about the current status of his planning for the new World Shakespeare Bibliography.

Mr. Meserole noted that the Bibliography to be published in the Autumn 1976 issue of *Shakespeare Quarterly* would feature a "new look." (1) Its classification would be revised in such a way as to make indexing and cross-referencing more efficient. (2) Its annotations would be increased, so as to abstract books as well as article-length studies. (3) Its coverage of theater history and current performance would be considerably broader than in past bibliographies. (4) And, most important, it would represent the first step toward full computerization, to be realized in time for the compilation of the Autumn 1977 Bibliography. On this latter point, Mr. Meserole observed that part of his long-range plan was to employ "retrospective encoding" to build a complete data-bank of Shakespearean bibliographical material, cumulating all entries in the bibliographical file since 1958 (the cut-off date for the last cumulative bibliography) as a first project, and then proceeding to cumulate all earlier entries in all previous bibliographies as a second project. Mr. Meserole pointed out that one of the advantages of computerization was that, once the file was built and properly encoded, it would be possible to provide a scholar with almost instant access to every item related to a particular subject-area. Yet another advantage of computerization, he said, was that it would now be possible to compile a data-bank richer than any printed bibliography, as a consequence of the fact that the computer could be programmed to store more information than would be printed at a given time.

Following Mr. Meserole's report, Mr. Andrews invited participants in the seminar to repond with questions and comments. Mr. Marder expressed a desire to have the new Bibliography organized in such a way as to provide a larger number of categories for classification and listing. Mr. Meserole responded by noting that he and his Committee of Correspondents had felt a need to strike a mean between too many and too few categories; accordingly, they had arrived at a tentative solution providing for a limited number of major categories in the listing of entries while at the same time providing for a much larger number of topical headings under which individual listings might be indexed and cross-referenced (there would be, he said, as many as

100 "access points" in the computerized index whereby the bibliographical file could be searched for scholarly purposes).

Mr. Fraser argued that many scholars and critics would prefer to have a less comprehensive, more selective bibliography than the one traditionally associated with the World Shakespeare Bibliography and the one proposed by Mr. Meserole. Mr. Meserole replied that he would instruct members of his international Committee of Correspondents to exercise discretion in deciding what items to include and exclude, but at the same time he cautioned against the dangers of being too selective; after all, he said, "one man's junk is another man's gold." Mr. Marder spoke in favor of a principle involving little or no selectivity; "exhaustiveness is the best service," he said, "and nothing is inconsequential." Mr. Andrews, noting that one participant in the seminar was the Editor of *Shakespeare Survey,* a journal that had long served Shakespeareans with its selective review articles on the year's scholarship and criticism, asked Mr. Muir for his opinions on the question of selectivity versus exhaustiveness. "The more comprehensive the better," was Mr. Muir's reply; scholars such as Mr. Fraser who desired a selective survey of a given field could continue to turn to such bibliographical essays as those in *Shakespeare Survey,* while scholars in need of a comprehensive listing could make use of the World Shakespeare Bibliography. Mr. Muir added that he would like to see more attention given in the World Shakespeare Bibliography to somewhat peripheral areas of investigation, including comparative studies involving Shakespeare, Shakespearean influences on later work, adaptations and parodies of Shakespeare, and Shakespearean themes and motifs in arts such as music and painting. Mr. Linton, speaking from the point of view of a bibliographer for the Modern Humanities Research Association, seconded Mr. Muir's comments about the need to have more than one kind of bibliography: selective surveys such as those provided by *Shakespeare Survey* and the MHRA, and comprehensive listings such as that provided by the World Shakespeare Bibliography.

Other comments and questions raised for discussion dealt with relatively specific concerns: just how a particular kind of scholarship, such as work on a nineteenth-century editior's proposed emendations, would be classified under the new system proposed by Mr. Meserole; approximately how much it would cost in time and money for a scholar in the 1980s to obtain a list of everything in the file on, say, one Shakespearean play; how soon the various stages of the long-range plan would be implemented.

As the time for the seminar expired, one participant, Mr. Rosenberg, said that he wanted to express the gratitude all Shakespeareans feel for the labors of love performed, often without thanks, by professional bibliographers such as Mr. Meserole and his team of correspondents and compilers. Mr. Meserole, in reply, requested participants in the seminar to feel free to write to him and to other members of the Committee of Correspondents with all manner of suggestions, queries, and information. "I hope to be deluged with mail," he said.

Mr. Andrews thanked Mr. Meserole and the other participants in the seminar for a valuable session and called the meeting to a close at approximately 10:00 A.M.


## Participants

John Andrews, Folger Shakespeare Library; Hoyt Bowen, Western Kentucky University; Russell Fraser, University of Michigan; William A. Gibson, Idaho State University; Tetsuo Kishi, Kyoto University; Jayne K. Kribbs, Temple University; Calvin Linton, George Washington University; Shirley Marchalonis, Pennsylvania State University, Wilkes-Barre; Louis Marder, University of Illinois, Chicago Circle; Harrison T. Meserole, Pennsylvania State University; Tauno F. Mustanoja, University of Helsinki; and Chester Wolford, Behrend College, Pennsylvania State University. The auditors were: David Bevington, University of Chicago; Irene Dash, Hunter College, City University of New York; Barry Gaines, University of Tennessee; Peter Garrison, University of Kansas; Johan Gerritsen, University of Groningen; Werner Habicht, University of Bonn; Joan Holmer, Georgetown University; Harold Jenkins, University of Edinburgh; Raoul Kulberg, Federal City College; Priscilla Letterman, Pennsylvania State University; Charles B. Lower, University of Georgia; Janie McCanley, affiliation unknown; James McManaway, University of Maryland; Donald F. Mehus, New York Institute of Technology; Kenneth Muir, University of Liverpool; Jiro Ozu, Tokyo University; A.C. Partridge, University of the Witwatersrand; Margaret Ranald, Queens College, City University of New York; Marvin Rosenberg, University of California, Berkeley; Joni S. Shumche, University of South Carolina; Charles S. Shattuck, University of Illinois; Walter B. Smally, affiliation unknown; Dorothy Sternlicht, State University of New York, Oswego; Richard W. Van Fossen, University of Toronto; Eric Vaughan, Bowling Green State University; John W. Velz, University of Texas; and Franklin B. Williams, Georgetown University;

# Marxist Interpretations of Shakespeare and Society

## ROBERT WEIMANN, Chairman

The chairman of the seminar, Professor Robert Weimann of the Academy of Sciences of the DDR, suggested three main topics which, although inter-related, may be considered separately for methodological purposes. These were: (1) Shakespeare's work as reflecting and emerging out of the social process of his time, (2) Shakespeare's theater as a productive and educating agent in his society, and (3) the interaction between Shakespeare's past significance and his present meaning as a factor and an agent in society today. Professor Weimann went on to say:

"All the papers . . . for all their diversity and the disagreements they contain, share an approach to history as a comprehensive process in which art and culture, the poetry and the theater, are related to the most basic civilizing and socializing activities of man; that is, his never-ending endeavor to appropriate the natural and physical means of his existence and the struggle among classes and individuals in the process of producing, distributing, and consuming the results of this endeavor. Perhaps it can be said that most of the papers are concerned with the greatness and the specific nature of the contribution which Shakespeare has made to these civilizing endeavors of man in society. . . .

"I think it is along these lines that the Marxist approach can make a distinctive contribution to our criticism and understanding of Shakespeare, especially in the present state of scholarly study. Today both the purely formal and the image-symbol-myth approaches have failed, profoundly and irretrievably, to convey a sense of the unity and vitality of Shakespeare's work as a socially meaningful cultural force in the present world. The recent scholarly interest in Shakespeare as a theater poet constitutes a welcome advance beyond the limitations of the purely verbal and the purely psychological approaches to the plays. Some of the historical revisions in the understanding of the Elizabethan stage seem significant not only in their possible contribution to better modern productions, but also in their new awareness of the interactions between plays and audiences which, at least potentially, helps to emphasize the function of the theater in society. In Shakespeare's time the function of the theater was, as Terence Hawkes once put it, certainly not that of preservation of great literary works. Nor should the theater — whose task is not merely to preserve, but also to revitalize — be confined to that function today.

"But despite the potential critical significance of recent interest in the Elizabethan stage, it has as yet produced few clarifications of any theoretical or methodological consequence. In particular, it has not presented us with any viable alternative to the literary and structural modes of analysis. It has not really come to terms with the process of interaction between the theatrical and the poetic dimensions in Shakespeare's work, and although there is a growing literature on the subject the results are not such that they have established the extent to which, for instance, the quality of dramatic speech or the changing mode of acting can be seen as agents in, the reflections of, the social mode of the theater. Thus while the nontheatrical and ahistorical modes of Shakespeare criticism are now distrusted, a new synthesis has not yet replaced them. . . .

"What is needed is a dialectical sense of the unity of history and criticism by which both the past significance and the present meaning of Shakespeare's theater can be defined through the structural quality and social function of his dramatic art, while that art is similarly defined through his theater. It is only when Elizabethan society, theater, and language are viewed as interrelated that the structure of his dramatic art can be seen as fully functional, that is, as part of a larger, not merely literary, whole, one that is a factor of the civilizing potential in history — then and now.

"To achieve an understanding of the verbal artistry as an element in the total function of, and response to, Shakespearean drama calls for an approach by which, ultimately, dramatic speech can be comprehended as both a process and a vision of society. In the last resort dramatic language must be viewed as part of the history of the society that the Shakespearean theater both reflected and helped to constitute. Finally, increased awareness of the social and theatrical functions of Shakespeare's plays need not preclude, but should rather stimulate, a more theoretically profound insight into, and a more practical criticism of, the verbal arts of drama as part of an achievement larger than language."

General problems of method and approach were dealt with in two papers: Professor Bates discussed the subject of "Marxist Criticism as an Integrative Force" and suggested that "dialectical criticism" offers methodology that can integrate the best contributions of the diversified present-day approaches to Shakespeare, and Professor Siegel contributed notes entitled "Marxism and Shakespearean Criticism" showing that Marxists who seek to analyze the living process of the interaction of literature with the other elements of the cultural superstructure and with the economic base upon which the superstructure is ultimately dependent, have the possibility of attaining a fuller and more unified understanding of the dramatist.

Contributions falling roughly under the first topic mentioned by the chairman included a paper by Margot Heinemann, "Shakespearean Contradictions and Social Change," indicating that the multitude of viewpoints to be found in Shakespeare could not be identified with any single consistent view or ideology and that therefore a Marxist view of the plays must be " 'Two-eyed,' many-sided, stereoscopic." The paper went on to show how this ambivalence in the plays may be said to reflect and influence contradiction not only *between* the social classes, but also within classes and within particular men. A. L. Morton, unable to participate personally, sent a paper, "Shakespeare and History," that examined the idea of history implicit in the English history plays as well as in many other dramas of the canon and noted the changes in Shakespeare's artistic outlook in relation to the political shifts during his lifetime; and Professor Rubinstein in "Bourgeois Equality in Shakespeare" discussed the way this basic tenet of the bourgeois revolution is expressed in the plays and characters of the dramatist.

Papers emphasizing Shakespeare's theater as an activating force in his time included a study by Professor Ehrlich, "Shakespeare's Colonial Metaphor: On the Social Function of Theater in *The Tempest*," suggesting that the poet was seeking, in the colonial adventure, a unity that was disintegrating at home, and had posited values of colonial thinking that were subsequently adopted by bourgeois-capitalist ideology and that have been implicit in all readers and critics of the play hitherto. Professor Goldstein, in his paper "An Outline of the Historical-Materialist Basis of Shakespearean Tragedy," investigated relations between the historical perspectives of the contending social classes on the one hand and the tragic and optimistic elements in the plays on the other; and Professor Weimann, in a paper entitled "Metaphor and Society — Suggestions for a Reconsideration of Shakespeare's Imagery," viewed Shakespeare's imagery as both a process and a vision of society, considering the metaphoric quality of dramatic speech as itself an agent in the social mode of the theater.

The Shakespearean theater "then and now" was the underlying theme of many papers, for instance of the comments by Clive Barker on the subject of "Marxist Analysis and the Contemporary Production of Shakespeare's Plays," which draws on his own experience as a theater director, and the inquiry by Michael P. Hamburger entitled "Gestus and the Popular Theater" suggesting that the corporeal qualities of Shakespeare's dramatic speech, the springs for the attitudes and actions of the players on the stage, are deeply rooted in the plebeian influence and environment of his theater. Correlative to these two was a paper by Professor Dean, "Contention in a Lingering Act: Elizabethan Music and Acting," investigating connections between Anglican Church

Music and Elizabethan acting, which enabled him to make revealing inferences about the acting profession and the quality of acting in Shakespeare's time. Ruth Freifrau von Ledebur, in her "Notes on Marxist Criticism of Shakespeare's Minor Characters," commented on a tendency to overrate plebeian minor characters and their actions in the attempt, justified in itself, to redress the Romantic overemphasis on major characters. Professor Kott circulated a letter he had received from Georg Lukács questioning Kott's interpretation of Shakespeare's sense of history as an absolute power mechanism independent of the concrete historical movements of his time. Professor Metscher, in "Shakespeare in the Context of Renaissance Europe," traced the ideas arising out of social movements in numerous European countries that are transmuted in Shakespeare's dramas, lending them an international or "transnational" significance as an expression of the revolutionary upheavals of feudal society. Professor Southall submitted notes on "Shakespeare — History as Ideology" urging the need to recognize and explore the ideological nature of Shakespeare's works and illustrating his point with an assessment of the ideological roots of the various views of Honor propounded in *Henry IV, Parts I and II*.

The debate on the basis of these papers was extremely lively, intense, and concentrated (albeit far exceeding the official time limit). A long statement by Professor Kott reiterating his position on Shakespeare's rejection of movement in history was contested by most delegates, the most eloquent spokesmen being Margot Heinemann and Professor Siegel; there were also clashes of opinion between Professor Southall and other delegates (again with Margot Heinemann in the lead) as to the degree that Shakespeare's ideology (or false consciousness) in fact limited his much-extolled universality; and between Clive Barker and M. P. Hamburger on the one side and several critics on the other as to the merits of theatrical practice as an indispensable instrument for fathoming Shakespeare's meaning.

With such multitude of themes and opinions, a general consensus was scarcely to be expected. However, a number of points did emerge as acceptable to the majority of the participants. There was, for instance, agreement regarding the historical quality of social relations in Shakespeare's time as a transitional period of relative quiet between the Reformation and the English revolution; there was a consensus on the role of the theater as a mimetic *and* a functional force in his day; on the popular character of Shakespeare's theater as a synthesis of popular tradition, humanism, and the position of the Elizabethan settlement; on the absence of any single or dominant ideology in Shakespeare; on the necessity of dialectical mediation between "past significance and present meaning"; and on the relevance of the Marxist approach as an integrative force in Shakespearean criticism. It was universally felt that this first international seminar of Marxist Shakespeare scholars had proved extremely fruitful and should be followed up by further meetings to consolidate and extend the results attained.

Michael P. Hamburger, Recorder

## Participants

Clive Barker, Warwick University; Paul A. Bates, Colorado State University; James S. Dean, University of Wisconsin; Bruce Ehrlich, University of Nebraska; Leonard Goldstein, Hochschule Potsdam (GDR); Michael P. Hamburger, Deutsches Theater, Berlin (GDR); Margot Heinemann, University of London; Jan Kott, State University of New York at Stony Brook; Ruth Freifrau von Ledebur, Bonn-Bad Godesberg; Allan Lewis, University of Bridgeport; Thomas Metscher, Universität Bremen; A. L. Morton, the Old Chapel, Suffolk; Annette T. Rubinstein, New York; Raymond Southall, University of Wollongong; Dickie Spurgeon, Southern Illinois University — Edwardsville; Paul S. Siegel, Long Island University; Robert Weimann, Akademie der Wissenschaften der DDR.

# Shakespeare in Translation

## WERNER HABICHT, Chairman

In his report on the Investigative Committee on Shakespeare Translation at the Vancouver World Shakespeare Congress in 1971, Professor Toshikazu Oyama drew attention to the impact that Shakespeare criticism, including its modern developments and turbulences, is bound to have on Shakespeare's translators. (See *Shakespeare 71: Proceedings of the World Shakespeare Congress*, ed. Clifford Leech and J. M. R. Margeson [Toronto, 1972], p. 275.) There can be no doubt as to the desirability of further enquiries into the extent to which critical and scholarly achievements have preconditioned the translations and retranslations of each period. But it may also prove useful to reverse the approach and to consider the ways in which the activity of translating and the appreciation of translations in turn generate fresh critical insights into the fabric of Shakespeare's original plays and into the conditions of their reception. As a translator has to cope with every single detail of the text and is not allowed the privilege of skipping over its cruxes or leaving them undecided, his work constitutes the most complete account of a critical response. For this reason it may legitimately be expected that the translators' activities, though primarily directed at non-English audiences, may also prove to be of interest to those devoted to the original Shakespeare, provided that the translators' insights are systematically channeled back into the mainstream of the critical discussion (and into the English language). The annual publication *Shakespeare Translation*, founded by Professor Toshikazu Oyama as a result of the Vancouver Investigative Committee, has already begun to perform valuable services in this respect. Contrastive studies of Shakespeare, using various translations in various target languages as foils, might indeed be envisaged; for this purpose the compilation of bibliographical checklists and the provision of multilingual collections of Shakespeare translations by at least some central libraries should be encouraged.

With such perspectives in mind the seminar proceeded from an attempt to define and illustrate the kind of critical data that can be derived from the process of translation, from the very challenges with which the system of the target language presents the translator, and from comparative translation analysis. Professor Toshiko Oyama, who paid tribute to Richard Flatter's discovery (made in the course of his translations into German) of "Shakespeare's producing hand" in rhythmical details and apparently insignificant words, suggested that facets of meaning can be revealed when key concepts are transferred into a Japanese (or any Oriental) frame of reference — when, for example, *mercy* in Portia's speech is interpreted by the Buddhist term "jihi" and thus linked with the "gentle rain" image translated by "jiu" (which in turn fuses a Buddhist concept with the folk belief in the God of rain, symbolizing fertility); or when "to be or not to be" is rendered by "aru-ka, aranu-ka," which, though evoking philosophical associations different from those of Elizabethan spectators, helps unfold the complexity of Shakespeare's text and reveals points normally hidden to the English reader. Professor Susumu Kawanishi added, on the basis of his paper on Sonnet 73, that Japanese translations can expose a latent emotion in the couplet, even if it is at the expense of Shakespeare's seemingly tight logic. In other words, translating Shakespeare means rendering explicit features that are implicit in the original.

The question of overtones that could or ought to be clarified by the translator also provoked a discussion of such perennial translation cruxes as personification and wordplay. The functional importance of the visual and iconographic associations of personified concepts and prosopopoeic devices was stressed by Dr. Heinz Zimmermann, who in his paper reviewed some of the German translators' solutions. As to puns, Avraham Oz distinguished between those with a mere "local" effect and those whose significance transcends their immediate "location." In the latter case, a rendering of the radiating force of the original ambiguity seems vital and requires the translator's poetic courage. Mr. Oz adduced the evidence of French, Italian, and German examples as well as his own experience with translations into Hebrew, referring especially to the "gentil-gentile" homonymy in *The Merchant of Venice*. Where the natural resources of the target language permit a rendering of only the surface meaning, the implied meanings of the pun might be added by way of commentary — but only as long as the reader is addressed. For the theater it is essential that the exact tone of a scene should be re-created, rather than the individual word rendered, since this may have different associations in different linguistic and cultural contexts. Moreover, punning in some languages would seem to belong to lower sociolinguistic levels than it does in Shakespeare's English; hence, the actual reduction of puns may be a way of being faithful to the original stylistic quality. Dr. Jürgen Wertheimer indeed emphasized the prime importance of preserving the very heterogeneity of stylistic levels; neither more nor less communicative force than is contained in the original should be transmitted.

From problems of style the discussion naturally moved on to more general considerations of the translator's medium. Dr. Jagannath Chakravorty argued, from the Indian point of view, emphatically in favor of prose translations, since only these are compatible with the current conventions of drama and with the expectations of modern audiences, and since the translator's interpretation of Shakespeare cannot escape its local and temporal frame of reference. This contention predictably met with some opposition. The objection that Shakespeare's dramatic verse obviously continues to be popular in English-speaking parts of the world may be somewhat facile, since this proves neither that verse is necessarily congenial to modern theater language nor that it is the automatically preferable medium in Shakespeare translation. But it is also true that, as others pointed out, most modern German or Hebrew translations, for example, are naturally in verse, and that in Korea a prose translation would seem to be unacceptable. The possibilities of systematically imitating in prose the effects of Shakespeare's verse, though admitting of further exploration, will probably prove limited. Nor is the verse element the only factor that tends to interfere with the translator's task of making Shakespeare palatable to modern audiences; attention was drawn to the importance of Elizabethan rhetorical principles and figures, some of which are alien to modern concepts of style and must therefore be reproduced and elucidated in contemporary terms. Similarly, the translator must draw on theater conventions familiar to his audience in order to "translate" Shakespeare's stagecraft; it was indeed suggested that production notes derived from the dramaturgic signals implied in Shakespeare's texts might usefully complement a translation.

But the translator's work also forms an integral part of a tradition of Shakespeare translation in his own language area, whatever his individual reaction to the achievements of his predecessors may be. This tradition may be relatively young, as in Korea, where, as professor Jae-nam Kim reported, serious work of translating Shakespeare from the original (instead of via Japanese or Chinese) did not begin until after World War II; but even so no translator functions in isolation. Where there is, on the other hand, a long-standing tradition, the impossibility of arriving at a definitive translation becomes all the more obvious. Even the classic Schegel/Tieck translation into German has at various times been felt to be dated, though for differing reasons. Each translator's decision as to which aspects of a Shakespeare play are to be emphasized and which to be relegated to the background is tied up with changing cultural, social, and even political issues. As Jerzy S. Sito pointed out, the introduction of Shakespeare into Polish literature in the late eighteenth and early nineteenth centuries was lent weight by the Romantic movement; in postwar Poland Shakespeare's plays had to be freed from this connection, and in being shifted from the context of traditional reception into the present age they revealed a universality that was felt to be capable of imposing order upon the prevailing chaos. By contrast, the idea of translating

Shakespeare "historically" — in the style of sixteenth-century Polish literature, for instance — would seem pointless. It is the translator aware of the potential of his own time who, by shaping his medium in his striving to approximate the nuances of the original, can sometimes exert a creative influence on the target language itself.

## Participants

Jagannath Chakravorty, Jadavpur University, Calcutta; Werner Habicht, University of Bonn; Susumu Kawanishi, Zushi (Japan); Jae-nam Kim, Dongguk University, Seoul; Toshiko Oyama, Tsuda College, Tokyo; Avraham Oz, Tel Aviv; Jerzy S. Sito, Warsaw: Jürgen Wertheimer, University of Munich; Heinz Zimmermann, University of Heidelberg; Muriel Bradbrook, University of Cambridge; Mark Hamburger, Berlin (GDR); Arthur H. King, Brigham Young University, Provo; Louis Marder, University of Illinois, Chicago.

# Christian Interpretations of
# Shakespeare

## BARBARA K. LEWALSKI, Chairman

The chairman, Professor Barbara K. Lewalski, began by thanking the participants for the stimulating papers they had prepared and exchanged prior to the session on some aspect of the seminar topic as she had reformulated it, "Christian Approaches to Shakespeare—Where do we go from here?" She observed that the first approximation of an answer to that question emerging from the diverse papers might seem to be, "We go in all directions at once." She suggested, however, that despite their great diversity, the papers did group themselves around two central concerns. Several addressed, pro or con, the fundamental theoretical controversy as to whether Shakespeare's plays do in fact render a controlling Christian vision of man, of human values, and of the world, and whether criticism that has undertaken Christian interpretations of various Shakespeare plays has been fruitful. Others, without necessarily claiming a pervasive or dominant Christian ethos in the plays as a whole, sought to test the usefulness of particular critical methods for exploring Christian materials and patterns in specific Shakespearean works. The Chairman directed the seminar's attention to the latter issue first, to provide a basis for moving from more specific to more general arguments.

In the papers and the ensuing discussion of them, several participants explored by a variety of methods certain structural and conceptual patterns in some Shakespearean tragedies and romances:

1. Offering the suggestion that the Fall of Man, not the Crucifixion, is the archetype of Christian tragedy, Susan Snyder employed a method of mutual illumination of texts whereby the literary theory of tragedy was used to shed light upon the Genesis account of the Fall, and a paradigm derived from Genesis was used to interpret *Hamlet, Macbeth, and Othello*.

2. Nicholas Knight discussed several allusions and analogies that might seem to define a parallel between the betrayal of Caesar in *Julius Caesar* and

the betrayal of Christ, raising thereby the methodological questions of when, and how, and how much allusions and analogies signify.

3. Invoking Kermode's term, Duncan Harris proposed an analysis of *King Lear* with reference to the several "senses of an ending," that is, the several patterns of resolution that play off against each other: (1) a sense of poetic justice; (2) a perception of tragedy in the failure of justice; (3) a return to precarious balance for the survivors; and (4) a catharsis of understanding for the audience, intimating that full clarity will come at the end of all things. In highly complex and tentative terms this final perspective locates us in a Christian cosmos.

4. In somewhat similar terms, René Fortin discussed *King Lear* as an open form that accommodates both Christian and secular perspectives, and that demythologizes Christianity by disrupting our customary expectations of poetic justice and divine intervention; it asks thereby to be completed by our own meanings and experiences.

5. Making specific use of theological ideas abroad in the land in Shakespeare's time, Dwight Cathcart offered a contrast between the moral world of Shakespeare's tragedies and comedies where *choice* is everything, and the "Puritan" moral world of the romances, concerned with overwhelming guilt and the need for forgiveness — "Pardon's the word to all."

The seminar gave some consideration to the promise and the problems inherent in these methods, as also to approaches involving the use of wider contexts for interpretation:

1. R. H. Butman proposed using theatrical performance as a testing ground for the legitimacy of a Christian emphasis, to see whether highlighting such elements in production enhances or violates the basic spirit of the work.

2. A Christian iconographical context for some plays was offered by F. Whitney Jones. Specifically, several scenes in *Richard III* were discussed as ironic reversals of the traditional iconography of the works of mercy, and of the convert Paul's experience of *agape*.

3. Chris Hassel, Jr., suggested the use of festival liturgy and ceremony as a context for the several Shakespearean comedies presented on or associated with festival days, arguing that several plays seem to have been shaped in some fundamental way by the festival occasion, while others take an affective coloring from it.

The chairman then proposed turning to the larger theoretical issue that several of the papers had addressed — how far the plays present a controlling Christian vision, and how adequately our critical methods explore such Christian elements as are present. Several participants asserted and argued forcefully that the plays are pervasively Christian in some fundamental understanding of that term, and that critics should get on with the business of showing how, and in what ways.

1. Roy Battenhouse urged critics to take the opportunities offered by the challenge to Christian interpretation to get on with defining Shakespeare's sense of Christian tragedy or comedy, exploring the comparative influence of Catholic and Protestant religious traditions upon him, and examining more fully his way of using biblical allusion and analogy.

2. In a somewhat similar vein, Peter Milward urged that primary attention be given to the contemporary religious controversies—Catholic, Anglican, and Puritan—since many controverted issues and concerns must surely be reflected in the plays; he also encouraged the effort to arrive through the plays at Shakespeare's own religious stance.

3. Asserting that the values of Shakespeare's plays are shaped by his medieval heritage, mediated through the miracle/morality play tradition but significantly modified by Renaissance humanist attitudes, Paul Siegel suggested examination of the plays in terms of contemporary social and intellectual conflicts over Christian values, such as, for example, the usury controversy.

4. Accepting as a truism the proposition that Christian culture produces Christian habits of thought, Ben R. Schneider argued that Shakespeare's Christian values were related to pre-Calvinist, "medieval" attitudes of risk, generosity, liberality, and unconditional commitment to love and friendship, rather than to the "Calvinist" ethos of individual righteousness and justification; he urged exploration of the plays in terms of pre-Reformation Christianity.

5. Nan Morrison also assumed the shaping effect of a Christian culture and values upon Shakespeare, and argued that the depth and complexity of Shakespeare's characters owe much to the Christian insistence upon maintaining the difficult balance between body and spirit, finite and infinite: she instanced the treatment of suicide in several plays as a case in point.

Other participants, with different emphases and from different perspectives, challenged the pervasiveness or dominance of Christian elements or of a Christian vision in Shakespeare, commenting especially upon faults in critical method attending much so-called Christian criticism.

1. Coming at this issue by means of a specific argument, W. D. Stewart pointed to the fact that references to Fortune in *The Merchant of Venice* and *Hamlet* balance or outweigh Christian references; he concluded that in these works (and in others) Christian ideas enjoy no special privilege but are placed within an entire constellation of metaphysical concepts regarding the life of man that Shakespeare at various times evokes.

2. Supporting this position implicitly though not directly, Tetsumaro Hayashi proposed a study of *King Lear* from a Zen perspective, indicating that the tragedy's key term *Nothing*, or *Nothingness*, can be illuminated by Zen significations of that term. If the play is thus patient of Zen meanings, it can hardly be exclusively or even predominantly Christian.

3. More comprehensively, William Elton proposed a schema of critical errors — "Seven Types of Misconception" — often perpetrated by Christian critics: (1) oversimplification of Shakespeare's "medieval" cosmos; (2) subjective wresting of texts to prove anything; (3) finding Christ-figures throughout; (4) judging various characters to hell or heaven; (5) turning all the tragedies into Divine Comedies; (6) assuming in Shakespeare a homiletic purpose; (7) excessive allegorizing.

4. Drawing similar criticism to more constructive ends, Richard Knowles analyzed reviews of recent books concerned with Christian interpretation to identify the charges most often levied against its practitioners: (1) that Christian interpretations are often reductive of Shakespeare's characters and his variousness; (2) that they are inappropriate to his concerns; and (3) that treatments of biblical allusion or analogy in the plays often violate dramatic action and lack critical tact. Noting that these charges are not always justified, he suggested that they nevertheless indicate the areas in which greater critical rigor is needed.

Lively exchanges among the panelists and with members of the audience produced no overall consensus, except perhaps on the principle that Christian approaches to Shakespeare should be characterized by very careful historical and critical method, and by a comprehensive rather than narrowly doctrinal understanding of Christianity. A concluding testimony to the catholicity of Shakespeare's vision of life was offered by a member of the audience uniquely qualified to speak a last word on the topic of Christian approaches to Shakespeare, G. Wilson Knight.

## Participants

Roy Battenhouse, Indiana University; R. H. Butman, Haverford College; Dwight Cathcart, University of Maine; William Elton, City University of New York; René Fortin, Providence College; Duncan S. Harris, University of Wyoming; R, Chris Hassel, Jr., Vanderbilt University; Tetsumaro Hayashi, Ball State University; F. Whitney Jones, St. Andrews College; W. Nicholas Knight, University of Missouri — Rolla; Richard Knowles, University of Wisconsin; Barbara K. Lewalski, Brown University; Peter J. Milward, S.J., Sophia University, Tokyo; Nan D. Morrison, College of Charleston; Ben Ross Schneider, Jr., Lawrence University; Paul N. Siegel, Long Island University; Susan Snyder, Swarthmore College; William Stewart, University of Tampa.

# Appendix B:
# A Complete List
# of Formal Topics and Addresses
# from
# the Program
# of the
# Congress

Shakespeare in America

THE INTERNATIONAL SHAKESPEARE
ASSOCIATION CONGRESS

19-25 April 1976  Washington, D.C.  Statler Hilton Hotel

*MONDAY, 19 APRIL*
**SHAKESPEARE IN AMERICA**

7:30 P.M.
**Opening Ceremonies of the International Shakespeare Association Congress**

**Opening Address: "Shakespeare in America," Alistair Cooke**

*TUESDAY, 20 APRIL*

**SHAKESPEARE AND OUR TIME**

9:00 A.M.

## I. Topic: "Shakespeare's Tragic Sense as It Strikes Us Today"

| | |
|---|---|
| *Moderator:* | Derek Traversi, Swarthmore College |
| *Speakers:* | Dame Helen Gardner, University of Oxford |
| | G. K. Hunter, Yale University |

## II. Topic: "Shakespeare's Comic Sense as It Strikes Us Today"

| | |
|---|---|
| *Moderator:* | Moody Prior, Northwestern University |
| *Speakers:* | Nigel Alexander, University of London |
| | R. G. Hunter, Vanderbilt University |

11:00 A.M.

## I. Topic: "Shakespeare's Use and Grasp of History: A 1970s View"

| | |
|---|---|
| *Moderator:* | David Bergeron, University of Kansas |
| *Panelists:* | A. R. Humphreys, University of Leicester |
| | Alvin B. Kernan, Princeton University |
| | Robert Ornstein, Case Western Reserve University |

## II. Topic: "Shakespeare's Portrayal of Women: A 1970s View"

| | |
|---|---|
| *Moderator:* | Louis B. Wright, Director Emeritus of the Folger Shakespeare Library |
| *Panelists:* | Martha Andresen-Thom, Pomona College |
| | Inga-Stina Ewbank, University of London |
| | Catharine Stimpson, Barnard College |

1:30 P.M.

## I. Topic: "When Homer Nods: Shakespeare's Artistic Lapses"

| | |
|---|---|
| *Moderator:* | Arthur Eastman, Carnegie-Mellon University |
| *Speakers:* | Richard L. Levin, State University of New York at Stony Brook |
| | T. J. B. Spencer, University of Birmingham |

## II. Topic: "The Man in the Work: Reflections on a Reflection"

| | |
|---|---|
| *Moderator:* | S. Schoenbaum. University of Maryland |
| *Speaker:* | L. C. Knights, University of Cambridge |
| *Respondents:* | Michel Grivelet, University of Dijon |
| | Ruth Nevo, The Hebrew University of Jerusalem |

3:30 P.M.

**Plenary Meeting of the International Shakespeare Association Congress**

*Lecture:*              "The Search for the Good Society in Shakespeare's Day
                        and Our Own," Joel Hurstfield

*WEDNESDAY, 21 APRIL*

## CONTEMPORARY APPROACHES TO SHAKESPEARE

9:00 A.M.

**I. Topic: "Through Psychology"**

*Moderator:*            C. L. Barber, University of California, Santa Cruz
*Speakers:*             Janet Adelman, University of California, Berkeley
                        Murray Schwartz, State University of New York at
                        Buffalo

**II. Topic: "Through Myth, Archetype, and Emblem"**

*Moderator:*            Joan Hartwig, University of Kentucky
*Speakers:*             Nicholas Brooke, University of East Anglia
                        Douglas Cole, Northwestern University

11:00 A.M.

**I. Topic: "Through Analysis of Performance and Production"**

*Moderator:*            Max Bluestone, University of Massachusetts, Boston
*Speakers:*             Michael Goldman, Princeton University
                        Robert Speaight

**II. Topic: "Through Theatrical Techniques in the Classroom"**

*Moderator:*            Homer Swander, University of California,
                        Santa Barbara
*Panelists:*            Miriam Gilbert, University of Iowa
                        Sherman Hawkins, Wesleyan University
                        Mark Rose, University of Illinois

1:30 P.M.

**I. Topic: "Through the Visual Arts"**

*Moderator:*            Muriel Bradbrook, University of Cambridge

*Speaker:*  John Dixon Hunt, University of London
*Respondents:*  Roland Frye, University of Pennsylvania
Louis Martz, Yale University

## II. Topic: "Through Image, Language, and Rhetoric"

*Moderator:*  Thomas P. Roche, Jr., Princeton University
*Speakers:*  Stephen Booth, University of California, Berkeley
Winifred Nowottny, University of London

3:30 P.M.
## Plenary Meeting of the International Shakespeare Association Congress

*Lecture:*  "Will and Testament: Shakespeare as Culture Hero in an Anti-Heroic Age," Anthony Burgess

*THURSDAY, 22 APRIL*

12:00 noon

## SHAKESPEARE ON FILM

**A Seminar at the American Film Institute, Kennedy Center**
Luncheon

### I. Topic: "Shakespeare on Film: An Introduction"
*Speaker:*  Jack Jorgens, The American University

### II. Topic: "Shakespeare and Film Theory"
*Speaker:*  John Fuegi, University of Wisconsin – Milwaukee

### III. Topic: "Shakespeare on Film: Media Counterpoint"
*Speaker:*  Jonathan Price, University of Bridgeport

### IV. Topic: "The Shakespeare Film as Stage History"
*Speaker:*  Marvin Rosenberg, University of California, Berkeley

### V. Topic: "Sight and Space: The Perception of Shakespeare on Stage and Screen"
*Speaker:*  J. L. Styan, Northwestern University

### VI: Topic: "Shakespeare on Film: A Reprise"
*Speakers:*  Barbara Hodgdon, Drake University

Michael Mullin, University of Illinois
Michael Roemer, Yale University

*FRIDAY, 23 APRIL*

## SHAKESPEARE ON THE STAGE

9:00 A.M.
### I. Topic: "Scenes from Shakespeare: Variations in Interpretation"

*Moderator:*          Roger L. Stevens, Director of the Kennedy Center
*Participants:*       Michael Kahn, Artistic Director of the American
                        Shakespeare Theatre
                      Alan Carlsen, American Shakespeare Theatre
                      Charlotte Jones, American Shakespeare Theatre
                      Carole Shelley, American Shakespeare Theatre
                      Marcia Tucci, American Shakespeare Theatre

11:00 A.M.
### I. Topic: "Creating the Play and the Role"

*Moderator:*          Richard Coe, *Washington Post*
*Speakers:*           Terry Hands, Director of the Royal Shakespeare
                        Company
                      Ian Richardson, Royal Shakespeare Company

12:30 P.M.
### Shakespeare Association of America Luncheon

*Address:*            "Criticizing Shakespeare," Clive Barnes,
                        *New York Times*

2:00 P.M.
### I. Topic: "Shakespeare in the American Theater"

*Moderator:*          Lydia Brontë, Rockefeller Foundation
*Panelists:*          Angus Bowmer, Founder of the Oregon Shakespeare
                        Festival
                      Robert Brustein, Dean of the School of Drama, Yale
                        University
                      Joseph Papp, Producer of the New York Shakespeare
                        Festival

4:00 P.M.

**The Annual Shakespeare Birthday Lecture of the Folger Shakespeare Library**

*Lecture:* "The Riddle of Shakespeare," Jorge Luis Borges

8:30 P.M.
**The English-Speaking Union Lecture** [Presidential Ballroom]

*Lecture:* "America's Heritage of English Common Law," The Right Honorable Lord Hailsham of St. Marylebone, Former Lord Chancellor of England

*SATURDAY, 24 APRIL*

**SHAKESPEARE AS AN INTERNATIONAL PRESENCE**

9:00 A.M.
**I. Topic: "Insights on Lear"**

*Moderator:* Rolf Soellner, The Ohio State University
*Papers:* "The Development of the Myth of the Birth of the Hero in the Role of Edgar," Barbara A. Kathe, r.s.m., Saint Joseph College
"Quarto and Folio *King Lear* and the Interpretation of Albany and Edgar," Michael J. Warren, University of California, Santa Cruz

**II. Topic: "Clues to History in the Drama"**

*Moderator:* Robert H. West, University of Georgia
*Papers:* "Johnson, Shakespeare, and the Dyer's Hand," James Black, University of Calgary
"Meaning Beyond Words: An Example in *The Merry Wives of Windsor*," Alice-Lyle Scoufos, California State University, Fullerton

11:00 A.M.
**I. Topic: "The Joseph Crosby Letters: A New Quarry for Shakespeare Scholars"**

*Moderator:*          Norman Sanders, University of Tennessee

*Papers:*             "Joseph Crosby and the Shakespeare Scholarship of the Nineteenth Century," John W. Velz, University of Texas

                      "Shakespeare on the Stage and in the Parlor," Frances Teague, University of Texas

                      "The Joseph Crosby Letters from a Curator's Perspective," Laetitia Yeandle, Folger Shakespeare Library

## II. Topic: "Fresh Interpretations of Shakespeare's Plays and their Significance"

*Moderator:*          Anne Paolucci, St. John's University

*Papers:*             "His Hour Upon the Stage: Role-playing and Suffering in *Macbeth*," Robert Egan, Columbia University

                      "The Uses of Shakespeare in America: A Study in Class Domination," Stephen J. Brown, George Mason University

1:30 P.M.
## I. Topic: "Shakespeare's Presence in Other Cultures"

*Moderator:*          Harry Levin, Harvard University

*Panelists:*          Eldred D. Jones, The University College of Sierra Leone

                      V. Y. Kantak, Central Institute of English and Foreign Languages, Hyderabad

                      Nico Kiasashvili, Tbilisi State University, U.S.S.R.

                      Jiro Ozu, Tokyo University

3:30 P.M.
## Final Meeting of the International Shakespeare Association Congress

*Lecture:*            "The Singularity of Shakespeare," Kenneth Muir